AF249097

Business Games for Management and Economics
Learning by Playing

Business Games for Management and Economics

Learning by Playing

LEON BAZIL

Stevens Institute of Technology, USA

NEW JERSEY · LONDON · SINGAPORE · BEIJING · SHANGHAI · HONG KONG · TAIPEI · CHENNAI

Published by

World Scientific Publishing Co. Pte. Ltd.

5 Toh Tuck Link, Singapore 596224

USA office: 27 Warren Street, Suite 401-402, Hackensack, NJ 07601

UK office: 57 Shelton Street, Covent Garden, London WC2H 9HE

British Library Cataloguing-in-Publication Data
A catalogue record for this book is available from the British Library.

BUSINESS GAMES FOR MANAGEMENT AND ECONOMICS
Learning by Playing

Copyright © 2012 by World Scientific Publishing Co. Pte. Ltd.

All rights reserved. This book, or parts thereof, may not be reproduced in any form or by any means, electronic or mechanical, including photocopying, recording or any information storage and retrieval system now known or to be invented, without written permission from the Publisher.

For photocopying of material in this volume, please pay a copying fee through the Copyright Clearance Center, Inc., 222 Rosewood Drive, Danvers, MA 01923, USA. In this case permission to photocopy is not required from the publisher.

ISBN-13 978-981-4355-57-5
ISBN-10 981-4355-57-7

In-house Editors: Ms. Juliet Lee and Ms. Sandhya Venkatesh

Typeset by Stallion Press
Email: enquiries@stallionpress.com

Printed in Singapore by B & Jo Enterprise Pte Ltd

Contents

A Synopsis

This book surveys business games and management simulations (their titles are printed in italics and both are referred to as *Business Games*). In the first part we present games and simulations available for education and research from the patents, publications and websites. The second part presents tools for systems engineering design of your own game supported by the platforms **Holarchy** and **SimSoS**. The proposed games are based on 40 years of our experience in designing and using business games for economic research and management education. We tested games for different education levels — from teenagers, students of colleges and Universities, up to the executive MBA level. We describe the mission and organization of different games, required hardware and software, wetware (procedure and rules of the game), evaluation of participation and analysis of results. We also use electronic games as the components of business games. It involves teenagers who are addicted to videogames in educational simulations and games.

Eventually, we introduced many games for courses in Modeling and Simulation, Microeconomics, Logistics and Supply Chain Management as well as in other classes and industrial training courses. We use 2- or 3-dimensional displays of subsystems, their components and phases of design. It allows developing games customized to different educational and experimental purposes. The range of games designed and applied to economics and management courses spreads from the game *"Obla-di, Obla-da"* for two kids up to the *CyberMarket* game for several teams of corporate executives.

Information and documentation on business games that we designed, you may get from our website www.business=games.com.

Acknowledgements

I would like to express my regards to the great Russian teachers professors Leonid Kantorovich and Victor Novozhilov who showed examples of devotion to the science at the cost of their own life. Then I was fortunate to meet British mentors, Professors Steven Vajda and Brian Haley at the University of Birmingham. In America, I am obliged to Professors Don Merino, Fred Jensen from Stevens Institute of Technology and John Farr from West Point Military Academy for the support of my search of better ways of educating engineers and managers.

This book was impossible without the interest and patience of my students who tolerated my experimenting on them with business games. I realize how essential it was having in my classes American students with their *critical* thinking together with representatives of the *creative* European education and *holistic* thinking of Oriental cultures.

I thank for her strong support my wife Nina whom I met first in a business game, and for the help of my son Andrew who made my life pleasant and work productive.

About the Author

Dr. Sc. Leon Bazil retired as Industry Professor from the School of Systems and Enterprises in Stevens Institute of Technology (USA). He specializes in Simulation Models of organizational development in Production, Service and Supply Chain Networks. Prior to working at Stevens, he was a professor at US International University (London, UK), professor and Chair of Cybernetics in Leningrad (now St.Petersburg, Russia) University of Finance and Economics, and the Estonian Business School (Tallinn).

List of Tables

Chapter 4.

Chapter 5.

Chapter 6.

Chapter 7.

Chapter 8.

Chapter 9.

Chapter 10.

Conclusion

List of Figures

Chapter 2.

Chapter 3.

Chapter 4.

Chapter 5.

Chapter 6.

Chapter 7.

Chapter 8.

Chapter 9.

Chapter 10.

Introduction

The Torch Bearers was presented to Stevens Institute of Technology by the American sculptor, Anna Hyatt Huntington. It is the largest cast in aluminum statue 16 feet high.

Introduction

Human life begins with games, starting with a parents' courtship. Kids learn most of their social skills through active games at home, in the backyard, or in kindergarten. In the school, such activities are substituted by didactic teaching methods where the child becomes a passive recipient. This is one of the reasons for many problems in school. That is why kids and teenagers escape to the virtual world of videogames.

Colleges are killing the desire for active learning even further by mandating thick textbooks, boring lectures and artificial exercises. These educational tools are not sufficient even for mathematics[1] and engineering, and certainly not efficient for the teaching of social sciences, especially management and economics. Some colleges refer to exercises as games, but actually teach students in the old didactic fashion. Case studies and video clips somewhat help to fill this gap. Today we may also use videogames with the economic contents such as *Sim City* or *Capitalism.*

History shows examples of leaders employing games for working out successful strategies. Generals played war games as for back as Alexander the Great of Macedonia. Playing *Chess* is useful for training strategic thinking. Sportsmen that are successful in team games are likely to become leaders in industry and government. War games and management simulations in the defense industry and in the intelligence community are providing **SI4C** (**S**ystems **I**ntegration for **C**ompetence, **C**onnectivity, **C**ooperation and **C**ommunication) qualities [Shorrock, 2008]. For business games we are adding two more **C**s: **C**reativity and **C**ompetition extending these capabilities to **SixC**. Games are the most natural and easy ways of learning, that is why they are so popular. Business game converts teaching from *talking about* everything through the *knowing of something* into learning to *make responsible decisions.*

Universities, corporate training centers and business schools started using games for the education of professionals and executives. An airline never places pilots into the cockpit without first training them and then

---

[1]Mathnasiums which recently opened in New Jersey are using "games to help keep the younger ones engaged": www.Mathnasium.com.

regularly testing them on a *Flight Simulator*. Many corporate training centers are building their own "firing ranges" for training professional skill through teamwork. Most advanced business schools supplement case studies by integrated management simulation games like *Capstone*. Business games are the most adequate tools for management training and economics education. Otherwise studying is like learning swimming without the water. The main advantage of business games is integration of separate courses of study in complex and dynamic simulations of the real world.

The Mission of Games

Games perform an essential role in the physical, mental and social development of human personality, family, community and the nation. Sports games promote fitness and enhance the general spirit of life. Videogames provide *edutainment* (*edu*cation + enter*tainment*) for young generations. Business games encourage entrepreneurship by developing the SixCs capabilities of Competence, Creativity, Competitiveness, Connectivity, Cooperation and Communication. Their integration is complemented by management simulations which train players to learn self-control and leadership. For example, outward-bound games by The Leadership Trust in Ross-on-Wye (England) train executives physically as well as professionally. The term ***game*** is attractive and therefore very often abused. Sometimes it is applied to computational exercises and accounting procedures split between "players". Role-playing improvisations in case discussion are especially likely to be called "games". We use them as constructive modules of business games.

The process of ***playing*** is not always based on a game, but every game assumes playing and much more. So playing with Barbie and Ken dolls becomes a game when two or more kids build a model of a home and assign roles to each other. Many videogames are business games in our definition even if they are played alone. The individual plays against the model representing strategy of a virtual computer "partner" opposing to the player. For example, the videogame *Capitalism* simulates changes in resources and product markets in response to a player's decisions.

The following definition of a game as a human activity was offered by Wittgenstein: "A game consists of a set of players, a set of moves (or strategies) available to those players, and the specification of payoffs for each combination of strategies" [Wittgenstein, 1953]. The contemporary theoretical definition of a game as a mathematical model of conflict also consists of lists of strategies and payoffs for imaginary players. Mathematical Game Theory was originated in 1713 by J. Waldegrave with an algebraic description of a two-person card game *"le Her"*. It was later formalized by James Madison for his justification of a two-party political system in the United States [Madison, 1787]. Later this model became the classic *Prisoner's Dilemma* game. An introduction of game theory to the scientific community was successfully done by John Nash [Nash, 1950]. In 1994, Professors Nash, Selte and Harsanyi were recognized by Nobel Prizes for the game theory achievements. John Nash became famous after publishing the book "A Beautiful Mind" [Nasar, 1998] and the movie of the same title in 2001.

Different games are influencing personalities, businesses and communities. Kids play games with dolls and toys to understand their family and social responsibilities. Sports games always prevailed among teenagers, however frequently being substituted by physically passive videogames of the same name. Business games are eventually becoming more used for college and executive education. Social games entertain everybody and especially retirees.

The first business games were designed in the end of 19th century for the emerging trucking industry. But for a long time a practice of business games existed independently from mathematical Game Theory. This theory was applied mainly to military and gambling problems. The further separate development of business games and Game Theory is no longer acceptable. This book includes the initial connections for building this bridge by bringing into business games strict theoretical terminology and models. From the other end, Game Theory may also benefit by using business games for experimental verification of its theoretical assumptions. The other quickly developing entertaining industry of videogames is still has a few business applications. We also try to find connections between them and business games.

So what are essential features of a ***business game***?

The first two of the SixC's capabilities of a business game are ***Competition*** and ***Cooperation*** between individuals and/or teams. It may be simulated on different levels and in different proportions between them. For example, in the *CyberMarket* game [Bazil, 2002] teams of the same structure compete in the markets for the support of the dynamic equilibrium in an economic system. The players within each team are cooperating in playing principal roles presenting the development of a closed economy. The game may be extended internationally when teams are allowed to buy resources and products from each other. The essential capabilities of business games are ***Communications*** and ***Connectivity.*** They represent decisions and argumentations in discussions between the participants of a game. The analysis of results in a final report requires professional ***Competence*** and ***Creativity*** in multimedia presentations.

The central component of a business game is a ***model*** of a technological, environmental, economic or social system. In most cases models are visualized as production and organizational diagrams, material or information processing flowcharts. They may be based on formal mathematical or graphical modules; on spreadsheet computations or decision algorithms. The essential property of a model is the demonstration of a relationship between the decisions of the players and business results. They cannot be connected analytically without considering the conditions of uncertainty. The core of the model should be the integration of economic theory with management experience. Every game, like a real life, entails some elements of risk or luck. In entertainment games uncertainty is a random result of rolling a die, or the picking of a card, or rotating a wheel of fortune. The uncertainty in business games should be generated by the behavior of players: their decisions, conflicts, cooperation and even mistakes.

What are the results of business games?

The contribution of business games and management simulations to education and especially to research in economics and management science is still very modest. It is partly due to the superficial attitude to the term "game" as if it is something that is not serious. But mostly, it is explained by the academic traditions of the separation walls between scientific departments. High schools, colleges and universities are built on the medieval model of written and oral mentoring. Besides overcoming these barriers and traditions, let us consider the amount of effort required for the design and control of a game. It is much easier for a teacher to prepare a lecture, outline the reading assignment from a textbook, conduct exercises and tests. Besides, proper playing of a business game combines mental and physical efforts with emotional tension. But the rewards of this are the satisfaction for participation to both players and instructors.

The present industrialization of education has a negative influence on the graduates of American schools and Universities. They are getting the low ranks in international contests and require retraining if hired by businesses. Business, management and engineering education follows industrial research pattern. Standardization proved to be successful for research and development (R&D) supported by Computer Aided Design (CAD). Now the standardization of the education industry is also supported by glossy textbooks and spectacular websites, by prefabricated instructors' materials and tests. Most universities are now offering courses on-line. They are cheap and efficient in conveying professional information to students. But they may alienate students from professors and from each other and are easily abused by the temptation of cheating and plagiarism. A well designed WebCT course minimizes these possibilities, but still is not able to reflect the human content of economics and management. Teleconferencing cannot substitute participation in a face-to-face creative discussion around the table. There are many advantages of board games in the class: direct control and consultancy by instructor, socializing between students, visualization of results and fairness in grading.

Natural rebellion from that situation arises on both ends of the educational industry population. High schools need reforms because teenagers are bored by traditional mentoring and become addicted to entertaining videogames. Most spectacular videogames for teenager "coach players" are destroying the socializing process, especially because the majority of them are stimulating violence and adventures in the fantastic worlds. On the other end, MBA students and corporate executives have limited time for reading textbooks and lose patience when listening to academics. The largest progress in using business games happens in corporate training centers as they feel the advantages of new approaches and have the resources for developing and equipping games.

Business games should also become an essential tool for research in Behavioral Economics and Scientific Management. The testing of these theories in real life by the academics-turned-officials like Larry Summers and Ben Bernanke costs us (the US) billions of dollars. As real economics does not allow natural experiments, the most reliable testing of a theoretical model could be done by simulations with human factors explicitly presented by players. Some academics who already realize the limitations of a "black box" statistical analysis started testing their research hypotheses on students, others on mice and monkeys. But business games present cheaper, faster and more accurate forecasts of human behavior. [Huizinga, 1955] Huizinga noticed that human behavior is better defined as *Homo Ludens* (Man the Player) than the classic *Homo Sapiens* (The Reasonable Man). We assume that *Homo Economicus* (The Profiteering Man) is the most accurate definition of participants in businesses and enterprises. A business game demonstrates human behavior as a combination of reasoning and emotions.

The highest achievements in game development are historically in military applications. They are based on contemporary "System of Systems" concept as integration of high technology with intelligent human activity. The simulation of military logistics is the example of a business game. The advanced models for business games are developed up to now by the System Dynamics and System Engineering. A system approach to development of business games requires the integration of subsystems concurrent with their individual design and testing by human participation. Even clear rules and detailed descriptions are often misinterpreted or avoided by players. The instructions might be clarified only during the test of a game by professionals. These results may be achieved with tools available only to games: **Vi**rtualization of reality, **Vi**sualization of information and **Va**riation in **T**ime (**ViVaT**). In a well designed and executed game we may also achieve creative competition and the deep emotional involvement of participants.

Examples of business games for different levels of education are presented in Table 1.

Table 1 presents examples of educational applications of business games. They have a large potential spectrum from teaching kids to family finances, up to government officials exploring national economic strategies. In our practice we used business games for simulating technological, environmental, economic and social systems of different sizes and complexity. On one end of this spectrum is our game *"Obla-di, Obla-da"*. It demonstrates the famous Beatles song basic ideas of a market economy to the kids playing roles of Desmond, Molly, their parents and children. On the opposite end of this spectrum is the *Strategem* game designed by Dennis Meadows. It shows national leaders the consequences of their economic and environmental policy.

Table 1.   Application levels of business games.

Level of Education	Mission of a Game	Organization of Game	Schedule of Playing	Examples and Sources
Kindergarten	Entertainment	2–4 kids around the table	5-8 minutes rounds	*Cashflow for kids* [Kiyosaki, 2002] *Pyramid of Nature* [Bazil, 2007] *Aquarium* [Bazil, 2003]
High School	Edutainement	4–8 students in several teams	1-hr class	*Obla-di, Obla-da* [Bazil, 2007] *Monopoly* [Darrow, 1935] *Capitalism* [Kosnik, 1996] *Island* [Kavtaradze, 2006]
Undergraduate college	Introduction to economics	teams of 4–5 students	2-hr class	*Beer game* [Sterman, 1992] *CyberMarket* [Bazilevich, 1979] *MarketSim* [Ruffer, 2005]
Graduate MBA	Advanced management science	teams of 3–4 students	3-hr class	*Career* [Bazilevich, 1984] *Capstone* [Keys, 1990] *ReActOr* [Bazilevich, 1969]
Corporate executives	Organization governance	Individual executive roles	Weekly sessions	*Leadership in Management* [Edwards, 2002] *TranSport* [Bazil, 2007] *Apprentice* [Burnett, 2004] *HELLO* [Bazilevich, 1992]
Professional	Project development	Teams representing subsystems	Tele-conferences	*Rules of Play* [Claypool, 2005] *FinanceSoS* [Bazil, 2010] *NewProDev* [Bazilevich, 1984]
Government	Political regulation	Leaders of departments	Extraordinary Meetings	*Strategem* [Meadows, 1985] *Glo-Bus* [Thompson, 1987] *CyberShockWave* [CNN, 2010]

Most people are familiar with videogames which are based on some story from a popular book or movie. These games include advanced animation techniques sometimes at the expense of the contents or exploiting violence and sex even for business development. The *Lula* series of videogames allows individual players to build an erotica business through personal sex experience with a virtual stunning busty blonde.

Business games cannot exist on paper or in software. To keep a business game alive and up-to-date, a competent game designer or user should play it regularly with appropriate groups of people. Like a stage play director, an instructor needs to orchestrate the game. The instructor should be prepared for possible twists and turns of the game as the behavior of players is often unpredictable and the game environment may change drastically. This implicit knowledge and ability to react to unexpected situations now called a "wetware". Players are supposed to be creative, but within the the limits of the rules of the game. Quite a few business games are described in the textbooks, presented in conferences and workshops, and available from websites. The author participated in different types of games himself and tested his own games as much as possible. The most successful runs of our games (no surprise!) happened in military schools. They have fixed class sizes, good discipline and respect for games due to war games experience and reputation.

Business games also train participants in the presentation of ideas, proposals and in the analytical reporting of results. Every moment of the game requires from the player the ability to act and defend choices or react to the actions of the other players. Unlike all other types of lessons, the players cannot abstain from participation in the game. And with each round of a game this involvement increases. The games also mobilize all of the human senses: the attention to instructions and a changing situation, anticipation of another player's actions, a good recall of the game environment, personal responsibility, imagination and a sense of humor.

The French sociologist Roger Caillois, in his book *"Les jeux et les hommes"* (Games and Men) defined a game as an activity that must have the following characteristics:

- *fun*: the activity is chosen for its light-hearted character
- *separate*: it is circumscribed in time and place
- *uncertain*: the outcome of the activity is unforeseeable

- *non-productive*: participation is not productive
- *governed by rules*: the activity has rules that are different from everyday life
- *fictitious*: it is accompanied by the awareness of a different reality.

[Callois,1957]

The best known business games are able to satisfy these requirements. The *fun* of the game must not depend only on the personality of the instructor, but should be installed in the materials and game procedures. The **ViVaT** (**Vi**rtualization, **Vi**sualization and **Va**riation in **T**ime) approach ensures these properties of the business games. The **Vi**rtualization ability of a game is supported by *separation* in time and place, ensured by roles allocation and the schedule of the game. The players of the same team should share information and computational resources. Competing teams should be better isolated in separate rooms or by the screens inside of a large game hall. The **Vi**sualization of the evolving situation provides everybody with information, so everyone should be ready to present one's decisions and analysis spectacularly. **Va**riation in **T**ime is scheduled either by the compression of time when hours of game simulate years of life or by the magnification of time when a dynamic process is slowly analyzed by its stages. Most business games are using compression of time by simulating weeks, months and years of business activities in hours and days of play. Some games are stretching fast physical or chemical processes from milliseconds into hours of study. For example, the biological process of finding a new proteins configuration by disecting and folding molecules is simulated by the *Foldit* game [McGonigal, 2011].

Games are the best educational tools for teenagers as they actively oppose adult values for the following reasons:

"1. Experiences are judged as to whether they are fun. As young people get older, the degree to which experiences are felt to be fun may depend on the presence of the opposite sex.

2. Glamour, excitement, and an avoidance of "boring" routines are desirable, and wasting time successfully is considered virtuous.

3. The common human elements among associates matter. It is important to share with and not to exploit or use one's friends. There is at least a rhetorical resistance to hierarchy or ranking in social relations.

4. People of superior moral status (for children these were parents, preachers, presidents) who can act as exemplars or proponents of the moral code are not clearly defined or readily recognized.
5. Adult-sponsored interests and activities are rejected, especially when there are parallel activities sponsored by the young themselves or by agencies other than the family or the school.
6. Differentials in power based on formal institutions or adult-based grounds are avoided. Leaders are successful in youth terms, not in adult terms."

[Gagnon & Greenblat, 1978].

Emotional involvement in a business game is essential, but to a certain limit. Games have a positive influence on the performance of an individual and especially of a successful team (Wins facilitate further winning). Sports games are elevating, but sometimes traumatic if defeat is taken too seriously. But negative results of a simulation should not adversely affect the attitude to training in a game. The opinion of one of the most respectable system designers is: "You can learn more from failure than success. In failure you're forced to find out what part did not work" [Brooks, 2010]. Business games should be cautiously used for professional appraisals and organizational promotions. Like in the Olympic Games, active participation, rather than the results of a game should be valued. It is especially essential in games where uncertainty is imposed externally or generated as random uncontrollable events.

Participation in games not only facilitates learning, but demonstrates personal traits and talents. For example, the *perestroika* policy introduced in USSR by Gorbachev at the end of the 1980s allowed us to play field games at industrial enterprises. In the *NewProDev* game on new product development at Saratov Aviation Plant, one of the departmental accountants demonstrated extraordinary creativity and leadership of his team. If the executive jury did not observe it, he would probably have had a slow professional career under the departmental glass ceiling. During the game this junior accountant had been so successful that he was immediately promoted to the executive ranks. In a few years he became the youngest CEO of one of the largest Russian corporations.

The TV business game *Apprentice* in US demonstrates the same mission of the search of young talented managers. Some of them became corporate executives without being offspring of a tycoon. Sports and especially social games facilitate in discovering and enchancing leadership traits. Bill Bradley was a member of the Boy Scouts and all-state basketball player in high school, and was offered 75 college scholarships. He spent his entire ten-year professional basketball career playing for the Knicks, winning two championship titles. Retiring in 1977, he was elected to the United States Senate and was reelected in 1984 and 1990 to leave the Senate in 1997 to run for the US presidency.

Dallas O'Brien won the Stawell Gift, Australia's oldest and richest handicap sprint in 1983. After completing training in the Leadership Trust he was appointed as the chief executive of Athletics Australia. He says: "Athletics is a sport I have a huge passion for teaching me in leadership". O'Brien has spent 18 years working for the international sports management company IMG.

But a business game as a sharp tool may sometimes have a negative influence on individual or team performance. In competitive games there are inevitably winners and losers. It should not be directly used for actual professional or organizational conclusions. That is why the Leadership Trust (Ross-on-Wye, UK) notifies executives before admitting them to the training course that results of their participation in game will not be shared with their bosses. We also base a grading of students' participation in a game not just on absolute results, but by their analysis of results, especially if they are negative. The most valuable learning experience is obtained first from mistakes which players need to correct without fear of shame and punishment. Public arguments and presentations with professionally written reports are showing the success of learning. Students are encouraged to explore as many options of business activity as possible within the allotted for the game time. Well equipped training Centers may use video for replay of the game moments to show participants their points of success or failure.

There are three descending levels of game knowledge: (1) designer or developer, (2) instructor or participant, (3) spectator or reader. The participants are getting the best experience, and you may see it from the report in the Attachment. Reading about business games is not so exciting as for sports fans watching their team. In Part 1 of this book we will try to show you how to use business games. Then, in Part 2 we will share with you our experience in designing business games.

Part 1

CHOOSING A BUSINESS GAME

Education as a process should be complete: lectures and reading should be supported by exercises and verified by tests; business games should be concluded by presentations and by submitting analytical reports. During business games we need to keep records describing the development of the whole story. It generates interesting comments, lively interactions, improvisations and jokes which should not be forgotten. Short sketches and drawings will become the pinnacles for presentations and for the final report of the game.

LEARNING BY PLAYING

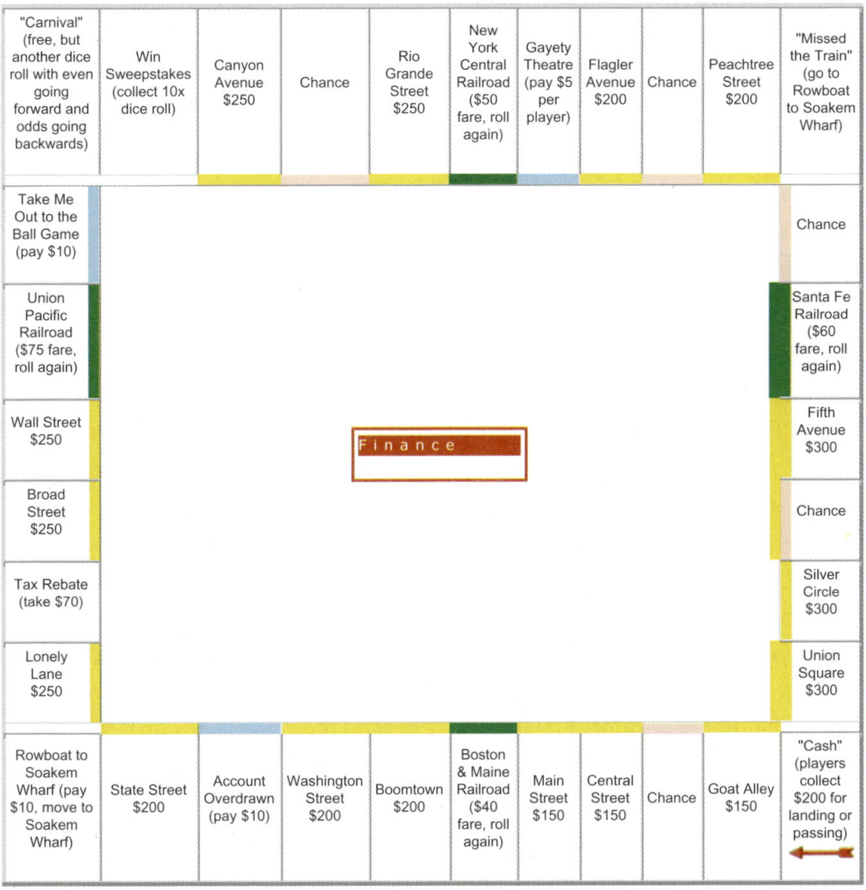

The board business game *Finance* (1932)

1.1. HISTORY OF BUSINESS GAMES

Business games are historically the earliest of all documented games: archeological findings in Ancient Egypt have found boards of the game *Mancala* dating 1,400 years before the birth of Christ. This is a game simulating agricultural business on the wooden board model of peasants' fields:

> "Unfortunately, because so little evidence has survived ... there are a few theories. One is that mancala started as part of a spring planting ritual. The outcome of the game was interpreted as a message from the gods regarding the harvest. Evidence to support this theory is that in many African societies a farming association is made with mancala. The cups on the gameboard represent fields. The playing pieces, usually seeds themselves, are the seeds that are sown into the fields. The circular motion of sowing represents the seasons of planting and harvesting. The capturing of pieces represents crops brought in a harvest time."
>
> [Hanson, 2003].

Jenga and *Chess* are also ancient **board games** that have survived for millenia. They simulate the construction and military enterprises [Scott, 1995]. Board game *The New Moral and Entertaining Game of The Mansion of Happiness* was published in the 1800s in London. This game was based on the Italian *Game of the Goose*, registered in Stationers' Hall in London in 1597 [Pflieger, 2008]. The first American games *Travellers' Tour of the United States* and *Travellers' Tour of Europe* were published in New York in 1822. *The Game of Life* which was designed in 1860 and *Landlords' Game* of the 1900's were the first contemporary **business games** [Magie, 1904]. The last game and the *Finance* game (1932) were predecessors to the first *Monopoly* (1936). Players used the "Chance" cards and cards representing properties that can be purchased for construction of houses. Unlike *Monopoly*, there were no "monopolies" on the board and players built houses only once traveling around the board. The game already had railroads, however these may not be purchased.

The first popular business games were released in the late 1880s by McLoughlin Brothers and Parker Brothers. They were *District Messenger Boy,*[1] *Game of the Telegraph Boy*, and *The Office Boy*. These games

---

[1] http://en.wikipedia.org/wiki/Game_of_the_District_Messenger_Boy

encouraged players to simulate career building based on merit rewards. The board game *Finance* which was originally released in 1932 by Knapp Electric and later reissued by Parker Brothers may be considered the first ***educational business game***. The game, similar to *Monopoly*, is based on the movement of tokens representing players according to the dice throws around the board describing real estate properties. The old game *Finance* like *The Landlord's Game* reflected antimonopolistic sentiments of the beginning of the twentieth century [KNAPP, 1932]. The board of the present *Monopoly* game looks very much like the old *Finance* game now renamed to *The Fascinating Game of Finance* (see Fig. 1.1).

The earliest published reference of the industrial application of business game can be dated to 1933 [Gagnon, 1987]. It was a ***field game*** played with management personnel of the Soviet textile factory "Red

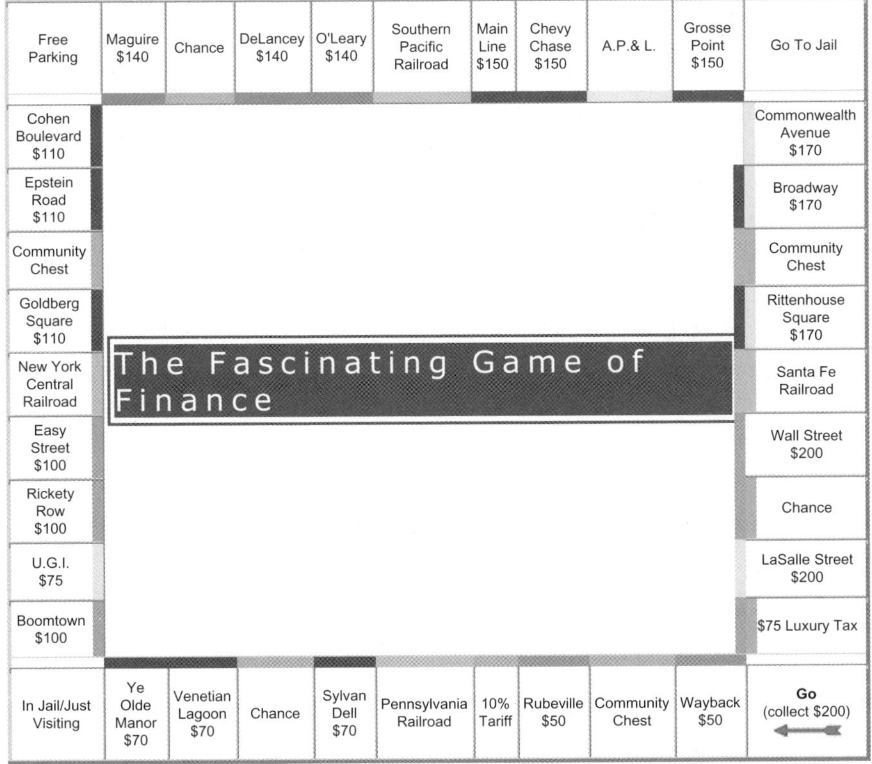

Fig. 1.1.   Board of the *Finance* business game (1970).

Weaver" on weekends when manufacturing shops were closed. Factory executives were playing at their work places when production was simulated by teams of managers. Shop supervisors bombarded executives with management problems of converting the production process from civilian to military products in anticipation of war with Hitler's Germany. So the prototype for the *Red Weaver* game was naturally a war game played in situation rooms. Since then field business games are practiced in corporate training centers that can display physical or virtual models of production processes and charged in training and testing managers. Such games are also used for executive education in industrial and academic business schools. These games are usually played as a competition between small teams of professionals. The oldest game used as a management simulation is the *Capstone* game where teams represent several competing manufacturers of electronic products [Keys, 1974].

The most widely used game for economic education in colleges became the *Beer Game* designed in MIT on a System Dynamics model [Sterman, 1992]. It is organized around a board representing a supply chain with Factory, Distributor, Wholesaler and Retailer sectors. Players make decisions on placing orders for a product (cases of beer). Situations in the system are represented on the game board by the coins or chips that stay in boxes either as inventories or as the goods moving in transit along the supply chain. The uncertainty for players is generated by the limited information about orders placed by the other players. Fluctuations in customer demand are ignited by the delays in filling orders. Teams are competing for the minimization of the sum of inventory costs and penalties for backorders. The game starts for each team with the same resources represented on the board by stacks of chips or coins. All teams, whether they consist of undergraduate students or of experienced executives, behave similarly. They demonstrate the "Bull-whip effect" of the oscillation of orders and inventories with accelerating amplitudes upstream in the supply chain.

The most socially and commercially successful board game *Monopoly* was patented by Charles Darrow in 1935. Since then, it was translated into many languages and became the most popular for family pastime all over the world. It originated as a field game reproducing the real estate market of Atlantic City on the table board. Individual players start with equal amounts of money and develop strategies of buying land and utilities, building houses and hotels. Players are opposing each other and face opportunity of success or failure mainly due to proper strategy and negotiation force. Their success partly depends on random events generated by the "Chance" and "Community Chest" cards and by rolling of two dice. The *Monopoly* enriched the *Landlord's Game* by adding monopolization criteria as the logical conclusion of the game for the winning player. Now there are many versions of the *Monopoly* including videogames in all world languages. This game itself demonstrates profitability in business monopolization of Hasbro corporation by keeping the patent of the game (see Fig. 1.2).

We will use the history of the *Monopoly* game to illustrate three models of business dynamics. The history of this game represents three different types of economic models that we recommend to use for the design of business games in the second part of this book. Figure 1.2 illustrates the ***long-term development model*** as the succession of several consecutive versions of this game for the last 75 years. It is a chain of business cycles with the periodicity of 10–20 years unless interrupted by war. The first cycle (1935–1970) is based on the original interest to this board game for American families dreaming of prosperity during the depression and war. The second wave (1970–1985) may be explained by the rising global

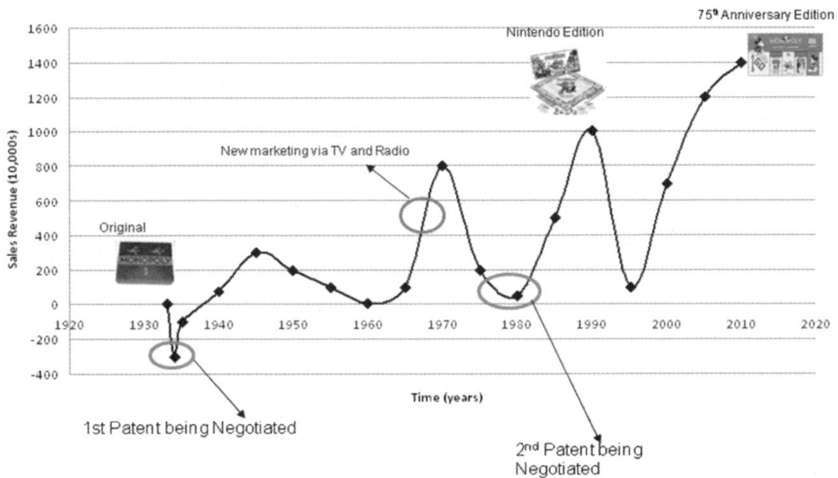

Fig. 1.2. *Monopoly* game development cycles in annual sales revenues.

Fig. 1.3.   Medium-term dynamics of Hasbro stock prices (1985–2010).

demand for this game in other countries. The third cycle (1985–1999) was ignited by the aggressive marketing of the game after the acquisition of this game by the corporation Hasbro. The recent wave (1999–2010) started with the introduction of the digital version of the game. The present cycle starts with *Monopoly Revolution*, the newest version of this game. People in times of crisis like to withdraw from the real life to the game world. It is clearly presented as a medium-term model of modest growth of Hasbro shares prices on the stock market in 1985–2010 period. The ***medium-term model of growth*** within the last business cycles of the game starting in 1985, 1991 and in 2000 is presented in Fig. 1.3.

The cycle that started in 1985 is reflected by the climb of Hasbro's stock price after acquiring the *Monopoly* game patent. Both recent life cycles have a typical medium-term model dynamic of quick growth followed by decelerating into the saturation level before the next life cycle starts. The new cycle of short exponential growth started in February 2010 after the 75th anniversary *Monopoly Revolution* edition was released, followed by the slow but steady climb to the saturation. This represents the ***short-term operations model*** which we use as the most adequate for business games. Figure 1.4 illustrates such detailed dynamics of Hasbro stock price during 2010.

These charts reflect three distinct types of business models that we are supposed to identify before designing a new game. Appropriate models of the game were associated with the current economic situation. The original

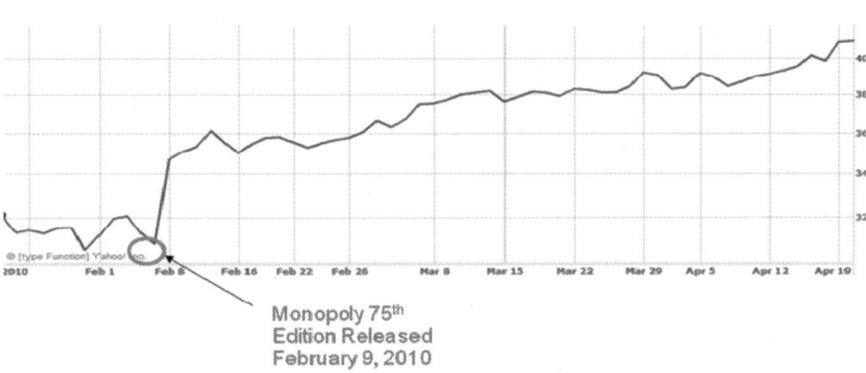

Fig. 1.4.   Short-term *Monopoly* game influence on Hasbro stock price.

version of 1936 was inspiring players to recover from the crisis, but the following versions just changed the appearance, not the contents of the game. In 2010 Hasbro released the new, substansially updated *Monopoly Revolution* version of the game. It changed cash transaction for electronic credit and mini-ATM, while upgrading property prices to realistic scale in millions of dollars. The *Monopoly Revolution* has a circular board justifying the new name, but procedure of the game stays the same as during all passed years. It is still a 1D flibbix (snake-like) structure (Fig. 1.5). More essential are the other features of the new edition: updating prices and introduction of electronic money transactions.

Competitive game producers regularly upgrade their products to be suited to the present economic realities. *The Game of Life* in the middle of the 19th century had strong moralistic contents against gambling. *Finance* and *Landlord* games in the beginning of the 20th century were opposing property monopolization, but in the 1930s became proponents of the opposite. Now games go as far as *Billionaire Tycoon* that allows players to get financial success not only by building up and acquiring businesses, but even by stealing, borrowing and outfoxing opponents by military coups. Our *Career* game unlike the moralization of *The Game of Life* includes such realities of modern life-like tax evasion or keeping a mistress in a foreign country.

So the history of *Monopoly* represents typical integration of the life cycles of games into the business cycles of the industry. It demonstrates

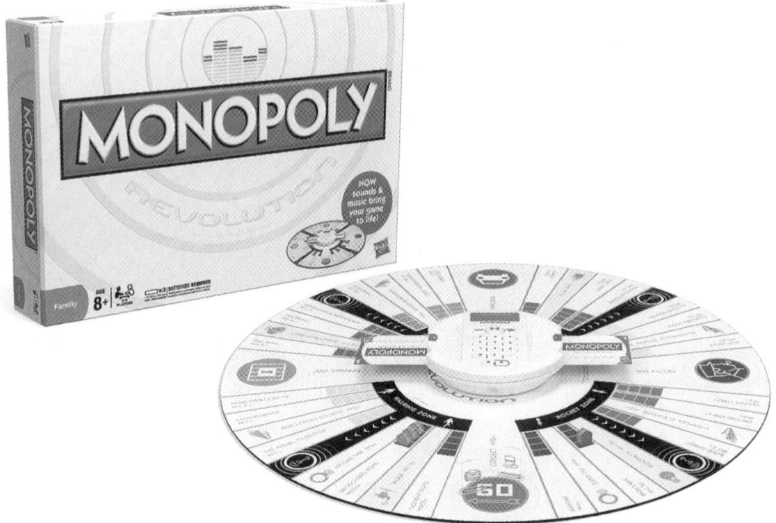

Fig. 1.5.   The new face of the *Monopoly Revolution game*.

three types of models which we will use for business games analysis and design:

- ***short-term processes of operations*** within the separate stage of a life cycle of a game modifications. These processes will be presented by transition matrices for technological and ecological systems and by decision trees for economic and social systems.
- ***medium-term processes of growth*** will be represented by statistical extrapolation within a life cycle or by the analytical model for the whole life cycle of the system.
- ***long-term process of development*** will be represented by System Dynamics and System of Systems models.

The choice of the model prototype for the game from the existing games will be offered in Part 1, and the design of new games will be described in Part 2 of this book.

Other popular games for family budget simulations were designed by Robert Kiyosaki, also for different horizons of personal finance situations. He metaphorically call the short-term financial struggle "rat race" and the long-term investment policy "fast track". Kiyosaki developed a whole school of financial education based on business games using as models balance sheets and income statements. His "Rich Dad, Poor Dad" ideology is supported by *CASHFLOW* board games of different levels: *CASHFLOW 101, CASHFLOW 202* [Kiyosaki, 1990]. Later he adapted the *CASHFLOW Game for Kids* [Kiyosaki, 2002].

But the most popular from ancient to present times happen to be ***entertainment games***, especially gambling. The extent of popularity of card (salon) games we may estimate only by the huge number of clubs and competitions of their devotees. The games entertainment industry is now a multibillion collection of interconnected businesses of videogames designers and distributors that is exceeding the casino industry. The first ***electronic games*** were simulating different kinds of sports starting with *Pong* for table tennis. The most successful for business applications became the *SimCity* game [Wilson, 1989]. It was followed by dozens of modifications (*SimCity 2000, SimCity 3000, SimCity 4, SimCity Societies, SimCity Creator, SimCity DS 2*). The model of *SimCity* inspired a myriad of games with similar prefixes: *SimEarth, Sim Farm, SimTown, SimCopter, SimAnt, SimLife, SimIsle, SimTower, SimPark, SimSafari*, etc. Most of them have elements of economics and management. *The Sims* game [Wright, 2008] which integrated most of this sequel was originally titled just as *SimEverything* and went on to be the best selling computer game of all time [Walker, 2002]. All *Sims* are games against nature sometimes classified as electronic toys. Many other videogames are also advertised as "strategic thinking" developers, but most of their contents are about crime, war, sports, races or space exploration.

Videogames became an exploding multibillion competitive industry due to commercial success among teenagers. These games are modeled after popular novels or movies as part of a promotion for the associated toys and movies. As soon as a game itself becomes popular, designers start offering plenty of extensions and modifications. One of the games with economic content, *Gazillionaire,* is the cash cow of the whole family of games "*LavaMind*" (see Fig. 1.6).

The new game's life cycle begins as a "question mark", and if it has success among fans or early adopters, it becomes a "star"; if it is not so attractive, it falls into the "dogs" category. Then, if it attracts attention of the

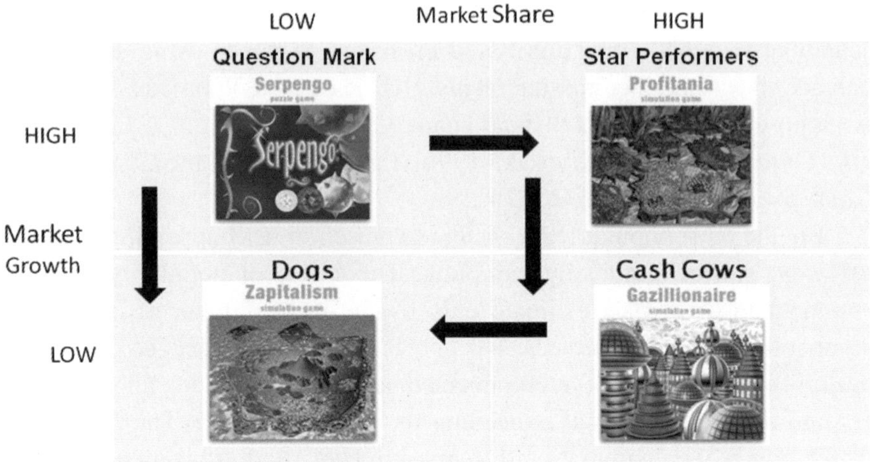

Fig. 1.6.   Portfolio matrix of *LavaMind* family of videogames.

second wave of late adopters, the game brings commercial success becoming a "cash cow" for the designers. They support popularity of such games by publishing the next series of a game using new technologies. The life of the game finishes in the "dogs" cell. Successful card and board games also have digital or video versions. Such versions of board games *Monopoly, Beer* and *Cashflow* are also acceptable for economic and management studies. But too few videogames are specially designed for business education until now. Among them are the games *Capitalism* and *Cartel*. In 1996 Harvard and Stanford Universities began using *Capitalism* for educational purposes:

> "*Capitalism* is a world-class, hands-on learning experience I've used at Stanford School of Engineering and Harvard Business School. Gamers not only learn the subtleties of growing an entrepreneurial business but also learn about leadership and team building necessary in any business situation."
>
> [Kosnik, 1996]

These games are especially valuable for a network of interacting players at colleges or on workstations of system designers. The internet allows playing global simultaneous or asynchronous competitive games between individual players or teams. Teleconferencing networks of virtual project teams may also use games for the simulation of human behavior in the designing of systems as will be shown in Chapter 10.

Role-playing is the less formalized improvisation of behavior by players in an environment described by text, graphics or video clips. It is close in detail and in nature to business case studies and is conducted like a stage play or historical reenactment. It often becomes a part for the game story based on a model of the particular organizational structure. It works well in professional competitions between players or teams. It is based on the chain of periodical introductions of external cases to support dynamics of a developing situation. The example of such an exercise called *Cyber-ShockWave* was demonstrated on CNN in February 2010 as an industrial crisis simulation in the studio's Situation Room. Among the players were the former Secretary of Homeland Security Michael Chertoff and several other ex- and acting government officials. They discussed the national crisis scenarios presented by video introductions of cases of national energy and telecommunication grid shutdowns. Players were required to offer decisions to the US President. This is an example of playing roles of governance in a System of Systems simulation which we will discuss in Part 2.

The introduction of case studies into business games opens a wide class of role-playing exercises for the professional and executive training. The experienced people are able to improvise decision making in complex situations. Changing amateur behavior into professional patterns may be achieved by combinations of case studies and management simulations like *The Flight Simulator.* Combination of a business game and management simulation provides opportunities for education of functional specialists in intelligent departmental decisions. Integration of all these components represents most advanced business games for multidisciplinary education and research.

1.2. TYPES OF BUSINESS GAMES

As we have seen, business games usually represent complex structures and integrated processes. Therefore it is difficult to classify them unequivocally. Game features might be represented in several dimensions: structurally, or as processes and rules for different areas of application.

For the beginning we offer the following classes of business games based first on procedural and then on their structural properties. Some games like *Monopoly* and the *Beer Game* have several formats. They are illustrated by examples of games which were originated or later included in business simulations:

Field Games:
    Physical (*Red Weaver, Leadership Trust, Apprentice*)
    Virtual (*Career, MacMulti, CyberShockWave, SIEMENS Supply Chain*)
    Simulation (*Sim City, Capstone, HELLO*)

Board Games:
    Structural (*Words-in-Sentences, Beer Game, upTick*)
    Procedural (*Island, Monopoly, TranSport, Glo-Bus*)
    System Integrating (*Sims, CyberMarket, CASHFLOW*)

Digital Games:
    Console TV simulations (*Gran Turismo, Gazillionaire, Foldit!*)
    Computer Games Against Nature (*Cartel, Capitalism, EverQuest, Marketplace*)
    Interactive Simulation Network (*MarketSim, Simunomics*)

The most valuable for us is the definition of the purpose of the game. We will explore opportunities of business games for technological, environmental, economic and social studies. Some of the games listed above are originally designed only for entertainment, but we use them for business education by extending them with elements of economics and management. For example, we added to *Gran Tourismo* game quality control charts, learning curves and cost analysis. Rules and procedures of the *SimCity* game are very convenient for a study of urban economics, management and ecology. The *EverQuest* game community of players generated thousands of real eBay transactions added up to the sum close to the Gross National Product of a real country. There are also many "secondary" games, networks or competitions based on games originated for individuals or small teams. For example, the very popular multiplayer competitive online game *Virtonomics* (Virtual economics) based on the structure of *Capitalism*, involves the building of virtual businesses, has more than 550,000 users mainly in Europe [VIRTONOMICA, 2010]. The *IndustryMasters* competition which is run annually by the Indian Institute of Management involves 1,800 students in

600 teams of 3 people each [Hill, 2010]. The *Global Management Challenge* competition started in Portugal in 1980 now attracts 20,000 players from 33 countries. The number and variety of national networks of interactive business games and management competitions in Japan, South Korea, Singapore, China and Russia is impossible to count.

The "serious" large-scale business games, such as the *Capstone*, were initiated in the 1970s for MBA schools and since then they were evolving mainly in increasing computer support while contents were staying the same. They are registered by the Association for Business Simulation and Experiential Learning (ABSEL) founded by Bernard Keys in 1974. It became the largest organization in this field of economic education [Keys, 1990]. Now it includes several hundred academics representing most U.S. business schools. ABSEL organizes annual conferences and regular regional and industrial meetings presenting papers and demonstrating management simulations. ABSEL supports CABSEL, the Center for the Advancement of Business Simulation and Experiential Learning at Georgia Southern College.

Business games registered by ABSEL belong to two types: (1) presenting a model of the whole business, and (2) presenting one of the management functions (marketing, operations, finance, accounting). The first type of simulation is really the business game, while the second may be considered as exercises and cases supplementing corresponding courses. Most of their contents are essentially accounting calculations. "Currently, games are designed around an accounting cycle" [Teach, 1990]. The other significant components of these games are intermediate Cases interfering these accounting cycles. But they are external "happenings", often not generated by the model of a game, "While not particularly realistic, most business simulations do not have major events triggered by stochastic processes" [Teach, 1990].

Among other primarily US organizations are the North American Simulation and Gaming Association (NASAGA), the Organizational Behavior Teaching Society (OBTS) and Eastern Academy of Management Experiential Learning Group. The International Simulation and Gaming Association (ISAGA) has active US and many UK participants. The Society for the Advancement of Games and Simulations in Education and Training (SAGET) is mainly British.

The portfolio of business games may be also stratified according to their scope and complexity. The bottom of the business games pyramid are short simplified simulations of technological or ecological processes like *Shell Game* and *Island*. The top of the business games pyramid is represented by large-scale simulations of global competition like *Glo-Bus* and *Capstone*. The middle levels include games and simulations of such management functions as forecasting, organization and control, then adding marketing and sales, planning and leadership. Most advanced electronic games that were originally designed by the information industry giants for their personnel training often became available free or as a commercial product. The Intel corporation, for example, distributes free game *IT Manager 3: Unseen Forces* which it used for simulating management of its own corporate IT department.

Business games may represent three levels of decision making: control, management and governance:

Control function belongs to the primary business levels, such as equipment operations and maintenance, material processes regulation on the shop floor.
Management function is responsible for the system of production and services by personnel supervision supported by information system.
Governance is the regulatory function in Systems of Systems (SoS) directing businesses and enterprises by the legal rules, indirect regulations and agreements by negotiations.

The build up of the contemporary SoS hierarchy of systems like the New York Metropolitan Transportation SoS is illustrated in Fig. 1.7.

The **Control** of technological systems, subsystems and assemblies is presented in business games by the behavior of players obeying the strict rules regulating production processes and services. The training of operators to control technological systems is provided by videogames and training on the *Flight Simulators* [Bray, 2006]. Pilots, medical doctors and operators of high tech equipment are trained and tested this way to be certified for professional practice. There are many business enterprises which require regular training of their personnel by such simulation exercises.

Typical example of a game for the simulation of a technological system is the *Highway Construction* board game [Whitney, 1995]. It represents

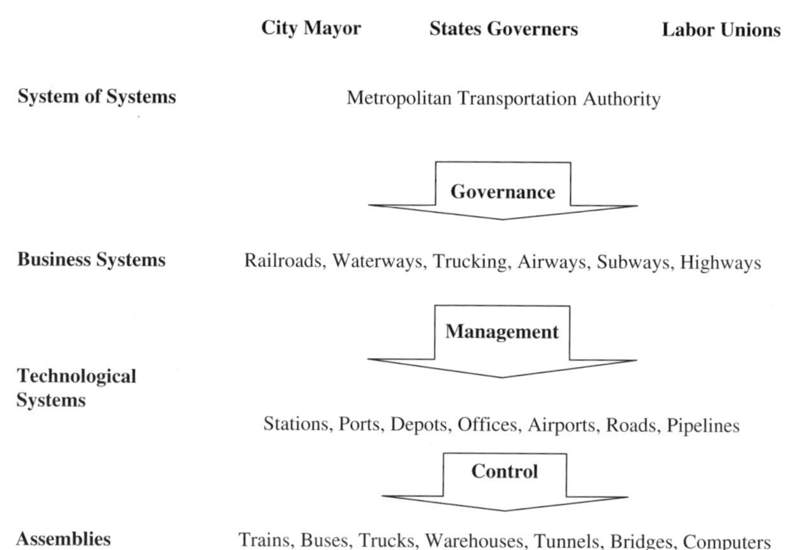

Fig. 1.7. Structure of the New York metropolitan transportation system of systems.

engineering equipment and materials on the assembly level required for construction of highways. The next level of the board represents subsystems, and the top level represents management of the whole system. All resources and activities are presented on cards for display on the board. The most convenient for a board game are technological and ecological systems. The structure of such a board for technological system representation in the business game *Highway Construction* is illustrated in Fig. 1.8.

Business games represent control of technological systems by short-term management decisions. There are three levels of such systems: assemblies, systems, SoS [Shenhar, 2002]. This detailed diamond model of projects measures profile of systems by complexity, technology, novelty and pace. Several assemblies included in one business may be classified as a subsystem of medium size and complexity. The size of a system is defined by the number of subsystems in it. The complexity of a system is measured by the structural diversity and dynamic properties of subsystems.

Management of technological systems is simulated by different board and digital games. A business game simulates the dynamics, creativity and professionalism of players' behavior. The participants in the beginning of the game have the same resources for comparison and demonstration of

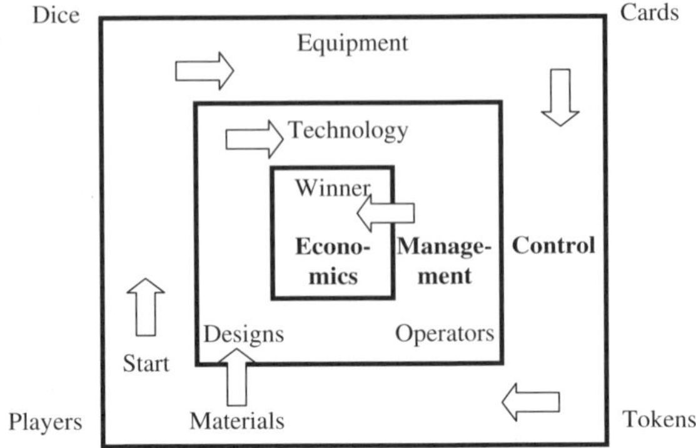

Fig. 1.8.   The board structure for the *Highway Construction* game.

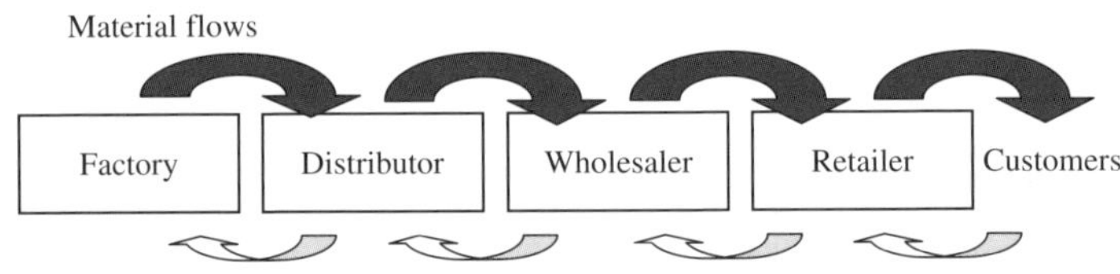

Fig. 1.9.   Structure of supply chain system representation in *Beer Game*.

fundamental properties of a system. They are supposed to make forecasting and optimization decisions. During the game, players and teams interact by presenting their decisions for balancing the interests of several technological systems. The *Beer Game*, for example, represents the supply chain on the board. Each team includes roles of managers in Factory, Distributor, Wholesaler and Retailer (Fig. 1.9).

The *Beer game* was developed on the base of System Dynamics model representing delays in material and informational flows of the supply chain. The rules of the *Beer Game* are very simple:

"Each stage is identical and managed by a different person. The managers strive to minimize their costs by controlling inventories as they seek to meet incoming demand. The simulation shows the response of the factory order rate to a one-time change in customer orders. The decision rule used by each agent in the simulation was estimated from the behavior of actual players. In response to the shock in demand, factory orders exhibit a damped oscillation which returns the system to equilibrium after about 70 weeks. Here the negative loop is the process by which each stage in the supply chain manages it's inventory: ordering more when inventories are inadequate and less when they are high. The delays arise from the time required to process orders and produce and deliver the beer."

[Sterman, 2000]

System of Systems (SoS) such as industrial logistics, transportation networks, financial markets and other SoS are regulated by a ***Governance***. Businesses which participate in SoS are subject to rules established by a mutual agreement or by the decree of a higher authority. For example, independent taxi and limousine companies are regulated by the rules established by the city mayor's departments. They generally cannot optimize their decisions because of their interdependence with other public and private passenger transportation systems. Therefore SoS in a best case achieves for most of the players *satisficing* results supporting existence of SoS as a whole [Simon, 1956]. These SoS may be simulated by field games or Situation Rooms. It allows the integration of autonomous technological and economic systems into environmental and social Systems of Systems. SoS as a network of Systems is defined by the following properties:

"**Belonging**, justifying existing separate Systems to fulfill the purpose of SoS;
Independence, exercising autonomy in System's behavior;
Decentralization, providing Systems with own resources and management;
Diversity, allowing Systems exercising independent entrepreneurial decisions;
Emergence, as ability of Systems for developing new properties."

[Boardman and Sauser, 2009]

Later we will introduce the ***Holarchy*** structure as the platform for business games which integrate hierarchies within systems with horizontal communications between them into SoS. We use the *Holarchy* platform for simulation of existing SoS. The SoS for the transportation industry is illustrated in Fig. 1.7 as integration of vertical hierarchies inside transportation systems with horizontal coordination at each level.

We proposed the ***SimSoS*** platform for business games that simulates new system designs. It adds to the holarchy the dynamics of consecutive stages of SoS development. Holarchy and SimSys platforms will be presented in the second part of the book as the tools for the design of business games.

1.3.   GAMES AS EDUCATIONAL TOOLS

It is difficult to estimate a place that business games occupy in education. The definitions themselves are fuzzy, statistics are approximate. By any estimate business games still do not occupy an appropriate share in the educational toolbox. Some schools and colleges name simple exercises and team projects as games or simulations. The largest obstacle for games implementation is associated with their main strength: interdisciplinary integration. Schools are structured by departments and teachers are presenting their traditional courses topic by topic in lectures and exercises. Schedules are providing classes with small chunks of time. But games require more time for the accumulation of knowledge and dynamics for analysis. The spirit of the game is difficult to preserve with interruptions for days or weeks. Students may be late or absent and therefore lose valuable information. Teams vary in size and players may become wary of risk. Classic amphitheater-shaped classrooms and standard schedules are not convenient for teamwork — that needs modular furniture and appropriate equipment. Preparation and conducting of games requires considerable time and materials. That is why many professors are reluctant to use games, or students have a pessimistic attitude to "home-made" games compared to flashy commercial videogames. The designers of digital games demonstrate caution in balancing educational contents with the entertaining properties of a game:

> "In selecting the subject for a game, we had always to keep in mind our target market and avoid becoming too didactic. Appealing to an interest in a topic or fueling curiosity in one was okay; lecturing was not. Any hint that a game might be "educational" at the expense of its being challenging and enjoyable spelled the kiss of death for the game. Yet, equally important, having selected particular themes in order to attract interest beyond the usual market for games, we couldn't then disappoint by failing to impart some nuggets of information about that subject. It was a fine line to trade, and I'm not sure we always succeeded in keeping balance just right."
>
> [Scott, 2010]

The educational mission might be accomplished if the game combines valid professional content with clearly formulated rules. We should first realize that all students are different, so we need to rely on their individual motivation for learning. Some are skeptical, passive or even obstructive at the beginning of a business game; others are too playful, behaving randomly or wildly. A player's behavior is quickly corrected through teamwork by complementing each other with their individual strengths and attitudes.

Many high schools offer new learning approaches for raising national educational standards in Mathematics, Science, Languages, Arts and Technology. These resources have inspired many teachers to incorporate games into classes in creative ways. Business Education, Economics and Social Studies do not have much of new tools such as games and simulations.

Competition is a powerful factor in a business game motivation unless individual grading scores suppress team results. High school and undergraduate college students are required to keep their attention to game rules and models. They will be able to demonstrate their creativity in the presentation of the game results. The build up of professional knowledge and social skills during the game encourages improvements in the whole educational system. The best results are achieved when sessions of the game are synchronized with topics of theoretical lessons and exercises.

Business games with graduate students and executives need a different attitude. ABSEL is specialized in large games and specifies the following learning objectives of business simulations: basic knowledge, comprehension, application, analysis, objective synthesis, objective evaluation [Burns *et al.*, 1990]. These games need qualified technical support thus allowing participants to concentrate on strategic factors. We achieved the best results in games between teams that included creative undergraduates and mature graduate students.

We recognize the six capabilities (Six Cs) of players ignited by a game: the Competence, Creativity, Connectivity, Communications, Cooperation, Competitiveness. The appropriate tools for developing these capabilities are supposed to be included in a program of a complete educational process (Table 1.1).

Competence is supported by a study of introductory material and by professional answers on the questions generated within a game. Information is digested by the players much faster and kept longer when requested by

Table 1.1.   Capabilities that should be developed by the business education.

Capability	Tools of development	Technical support	Results
Competence	Lectures and exercises	Textbooks and computers	Professional decisions
Creativity	Brainstorming	Lateral thinking and TRIZ	Strategic thinking
Connectivity	Integration of subjects and problems	Game boards, LAN and Intranet	System thinking
Communications	Discussions and presentations	Multimedia equipment	Reporting skills
Cooperation	Networking and trust development	Internet	Efficient teambuilding
Competitiveness	Evaluation of results and motivation	Questionnaires and jury evaluations	Motivation for success and critical thinking

players themselves for making decisions. Professionalism is the underlying base of any business game which provides essential details of reality to the model of a game. It is supported by the search in professional data bases. "Games of strategy are impossibly difficult to get into the market in the United States because the major toy buyers believe that Americans prefer games of chance" [Scott, 2010].

The development of the strategic decisions requires **Creativity**. The enthusiasm of players may not always be ignited at the very beginning of a game, but it eventually builds up during a good game. That capability mainly depends on the personal traits of players, but usually grows during team exercises. It might be enhanced by training methods like lateral thinking [DeBono, 1970], system dynamics [Senge *et al.*, 1994] or with the "Theory of Inventive Problem Solving" abbreviated in the Russian alphabet as TRIZ and well accepted by the US designers [Altshuller, 1988].

Connectivity is the ability of players to combine all relevant knowledge for the complete identification of the problem for properly formulated decisions. Game designers and directors should support a level playing field by informing competing teams simultaneously. Otherwise game organizers may provide information for professionally specialized teams on their request. It is necessary to combine complementary results which primarily apply to system development games.

Communications are the central part of any game. Different games require a variety of provisions or restrictions on communications between players within a team and between the teams. Games ignite the necessity for communications naturally, but sometimes restrictions on communications are essential for the representation of reality. For example, in board games players can face each other around the table while in a real business people may be separated organizationally or geographically.

Cooperation between individuals within a team is the main condition of a team success in the game. Individually oriented games like *Capitalism* do not encourage cooperation, but do not prevent the formation of coalitions either. System development games are intended to encourage cooperation between teams representing different systems (will be discussed later in Chapter 10).

Competition is the strong driving force of a business game. The motivation for success may be supported by material or moral rewards for the winners. Business games are provided by the clear measurement of economic results. Competition is natural between teams, but it may also be useful within a team if it does not grow into rivalry. It may happen when role assignments within a team are random or result of an uneven allocation of resources between the players. Such a situation requires the application of more complex behavioral evaluations by game organizers. That evaluation may be an instructor's conclusion, decision by the jury of executives or mutual appraisals of players. But sensitive personal gradings are not recommended to become public.

A full involvement of a person in the learning process is the main achievement of the educational system. It is difficult to expect such a result when studying becomes a boring repetition of facts and figures. But in order to build the relevant professional knowledge at the introductory stages of a game, players need an understanding of basic scientific principles. A well developed game should eventually go from the first learning stage of ***memorizing*** of game rules and situation to the second stage of ***analysis*** of the appropriate problems. Thus we overcome the boredom of repeating

Table 1.2.   Learning process tools and its results.

Process Results	Repetition	Analysis	Creativity
Memorizing of facts and figures	Textbooks and lectures		
Knowledge of properties	Professional websites and publications	Exercises and tests	Educational games and simulations
Changing paradigms		Case studies and internships	Business games and projects

something "just in case" or even proposing to students as being "useful in the future". The accumulation of critical information increases involvement into subject matter and leads to the professional knowledge as the ability to analyze situations and modify standard decisions. At this moment we stand on the fork of the study road: either learning more into depth of a matter, or to widen the area of study by ***changing paradigms***. Business games are the best tools to offer new solutions for handling management problems in a different way. The correspondence between educational processes and their results is presented in Table 1.2.

Professional education relies primarily on memorizing basic principles through repetition of their applications to different situations:

> "As to *learning* in science and engineering, there is a great deal to be learned, with more asking to be added to the content every day. You are kept so everlastingly busy at learning that there is little time to be creative. Knowledge, of course, is essential to the creative process; but knowledge is not creation. Solving assigned problems does call for some creativity. But if there is no time for practicing creativity "on your own", it won't be practiced. Every faculty feels that a certain large content *must* be crammed in. Every faculty member is under pressure to see that his course covers the ground."
>
> [Moore, 1969]

Management and economic education are more case-oriented than sciences and engineering. Social studies prefer learning by comparison of specific cases. But both ways are not the best to prepare students for creative thinking by changing paradigms. The American educational philosophy of "critical thinking" is supported by volumes of reading, discussing case studies and multiple-choice testing:

> "The [American] system wants the teachers to move the kids along to some kind of mass production schedule. The school system is a factory that moves by the factory's production schedule, not the child's learning schedule. Many teachers have tried to change the system, but as I said, the system of education is like an alligator, a creature designed to survive and not to change."
>
> [Kiyosaki, 1990]

Such educational models are first of all oriented for developing social skills [Lemov, 2010]. That is why America has the best lawyers, while Germany has the best engineers and Japan has the best managers [Howard, 1986]. The European educational system is less illustrative, but more oriented on basic principles of science and engineering. The oriental school of thinking is more holistic and environmental. The greatest progress in the facilitation of creative thinking has been achieved in Japan where kids are involved in playing and the construction of 3D artifacts beginning from kindergarten. The Japanese mentality is a team oriented on community and corporate values.

There are two types of tools for developing creativity by changing paradigm: improvisational and systematic. Improvisational methods are represented by different variations of brainstorming (Delphi, Executive Jury, Focus Groups, etc.). They are applied to collective exploration of new economic possibilities and management approaches. Among the systematic methods are Lateral Thinking [DeBono, 1978], System Thinking [Sage, 1994; Boardman and Sauser, 2009] and TRIZ [Altshuller, 1989]. They are the most efficient tools for finding new decisions of professional problems. The ways of igniting creativity at work were offered long ago:

> "A type of creativity we might call the adaptation game can be played by anyone, almost any time, anywhere. This involves picking up an object, made for a definite purpose, and seeing how many other uses you can think of for it. Consider the Eastman Kodak Company, where a great many creative minds are needed. They have a ten-week course for technicians and executives, and in it, there is a two-week home assignment. Each man gets a "creativity kit" (called a "junk box") having string, pieces of cardboard, sticks, buttons, safety pins, and whatnot. The objective is to

make something. A prime purpose is to jar a man loose from his mental blocks, free his mind, get him out of ruts and dead-end traps: Turn him into a flexible thinker. A mind thus shaken loose and made free-wheeling may, on the job, consider and devise new ways of doing things around the plant."

[Moore, 1969]

We also use such manual exercises in our business games and recommend to include them in the game design. They are especially valuable in childrens' games. Psychological research has established that motor exercises facilitate the child's mental progress [Siegler, 2006]. Our model of communications that support constructive teamwork is presented in the following Fig. 1.10.

Different types of communications are supporting teamwork in corresponding phases of a business game. One stage of the game may require quick and accurate actions, for example, producing or delivering a standard product. It requires conveying experience from the most efficient individual to the other team members. The other stage of the game may require search for decision prototype and adjusting it to the situation of statistical uncertainty. And in the most complicated situation of strategic uncertainty, teams should be creative in generating new paradigms. We used the classical model of a team life cycle illustrated in Fig. 1.11.

The activation of different levels of knowledge also depends on the stage of the team life cycle. During the forming stage of a cooperative

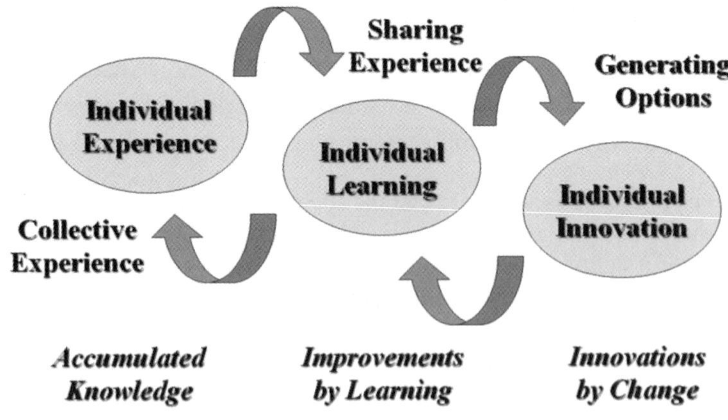

Fig. 1.10.   Communications between team members.

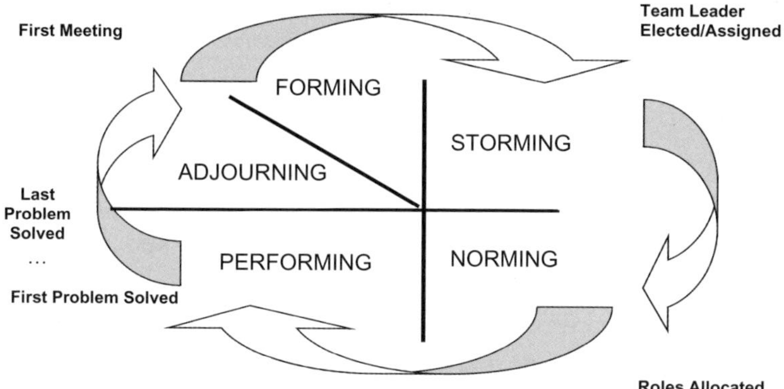

Fig. 1.11.   Team life cycle stages during a business game.

game, information exchange prevails. Storming stage needs creative generating options for the alternative decisions. The norming stage formulates standard, routine actions. During the norming stage the collective experience builds up through the feedback information. Performing stage ignites cooperation process. When individualistic motivation prevails, all communications are restricted. We used statistical analysis on several runs of the *Career* game with different teams of graduate students in the International Business course. It was based on questionnaires that provided us with data for correlation and regression analysis of the following structural and dynamic parameters of teams:

Structure:

- Size of a team defined by the *number of members*,
- *Diversity* measured by the number of different professions represented,
- Number of organizational *subgroups* in a team,
- *Forming* stage of a life cycle measured by the time from the announcement of a team formation till the meeting when a leader is elected or the manager is appointed.

Dynamics:

- *Storming* — time spent for the decision of the first problem, until the roles are clarified,
- *Norming* as time between the first problem formulated and a decision made collectively,

- *Performing* — average time spent on making a decision in a standard situation.

There are different ways of team structure development in a business game: from the requirement of a permanent structure by the instructor's assignments to the free movement between teams by the player's choice. Most business games require stability of teams to allow the accumulation of experience in fixed roles. But the choice of a role should be free, allowing players to try their performance in different functions. So the best arrangement will be for players to rotate between roles and sometimes, between teams, like labor mobility in real life. Teams formed during the play of a business game in a college may become a permanent attachment for many other study and extracurricular activities. It is especially likely for international students who have limited communications and socializing opportunities. We collected and analyzed statistics of teams' structural and dynamic properties during the different games using the classic model of team development.

Statistical analysis of teams' development is possible during the game *Career* because of its flexible structure. The class size of the International Business Management course in this study was between 6 and 22 students. If less than six students were registered, the class was cancelled. When over 20 students registered, the class was usually split into two sections. The number of self-organized teams happen to be between two and six. We found significant dependences between structural and dynamic parameters of teams' development observed during long enough business games. The correlation coefficients between structural and dynamic properties of teams demonstrated by graduate classes in the *Career* game are presented in Table 1.3.

Now we can visualize the correlations between structural and dynamic properties of team development during the business game. The relationship chart below also represents our assumptions about the direction of influence based on either causal dependence or temporal precedence of some parameters over the others (see Fig. 1.12).

Some correlations between structural and dynamic properties look weak because they are actually nonlinear. This assumption is supported by the frequency analysis of data for the relevant variables. We found out

Table 1.3. Correlation between structural and dynamic properties of a team.

	Diversity	Number of subgroups	Number of members	Forming	Storming	Norming	Performing
Diversity	1	0.608**	0.5638**	0.6184**	0.0377	−0.1175	0.159
Number of Subgroups	0.608	1	0.5805**	0.6278**	0.1878	0.0438	0.3389*
Number of Members	0.5638	0.5805	1	0.4263*	0.1542	−0.1786	0.1216
Forming	0.6184	0.6278	0.4263	1	0.3035*	0.3312*	0.4509*
Storming	0.0377	0.1878	0.1542	0.3035	1	0.7033**	0.5976**
Norming	−0.1175	0.0438	−0.1786	0.3312	0.7033	1	0.6802**
Performing	0.159	0.3389	0.1216	0.4509	0.5976	0.6802	1

Note: Significance levels marked by (**) at $p < 0.001$ and (*) at $p < 0.01$.

 Business Games

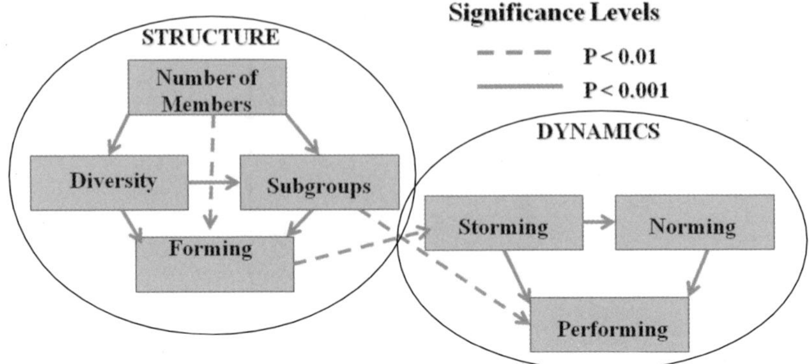

Fig. 1.12.   Relations between structural and dynamic parameters of teams.

that some of them are structured close to the LogNormal distribution. That is why we used logarithmic transformation of such variables (team size in this case). It was justified by the increased statistical significance of correlation coefficients.

The reason for the transformation of some variables is supported by the analysis of their frequency distributions. In other applications we explored binomial, natural and decimal logarithmic transformations for variables of different managerial variety. Binary **control** function of accepting or rejecting results naturally follows binomial distribution. The probabilities of different numbers of rejected items from a supply or production batch are supposed to follow Poisson distribution. Middle **management** deals with larger variations related to LogNormal distribution on the bases starting from Natural logarithms for the choice between three to seven alternatives. It is the standard differentiation base of eight when information quantity is measured in bytes. Executives deal with much higher uncertainty levels equal or exceeding dozens. There the base for the decimal logarithms is justified. The **Governance** function in SoSs is dealing with a large number of participants and unlimited number of possible strategies. It may be analyzed by the Game and Chaos theories.

We found that size as a number of members and diversity of the class as number of subgroups did not exceed six in these classes. Therefore we chose Natural (e) base for LogNormal transformation (Fig. 1.13).

The reasons for the change from linear approximation to a nonlinear model is also clear from the scatterplot illustration (see Fig. 1.14). The

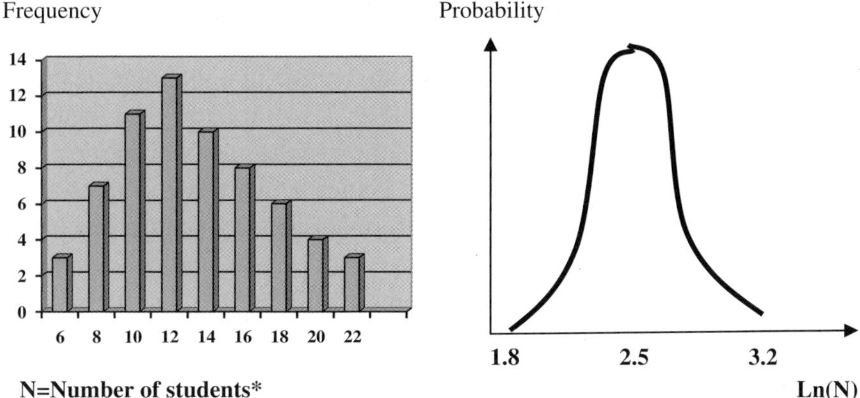

***Rounded upto even numbers because some differences
in numbers happen between beginning and end of game**

Fig. 1.13.   Effect of logarithmic transformation on the team size distribution.

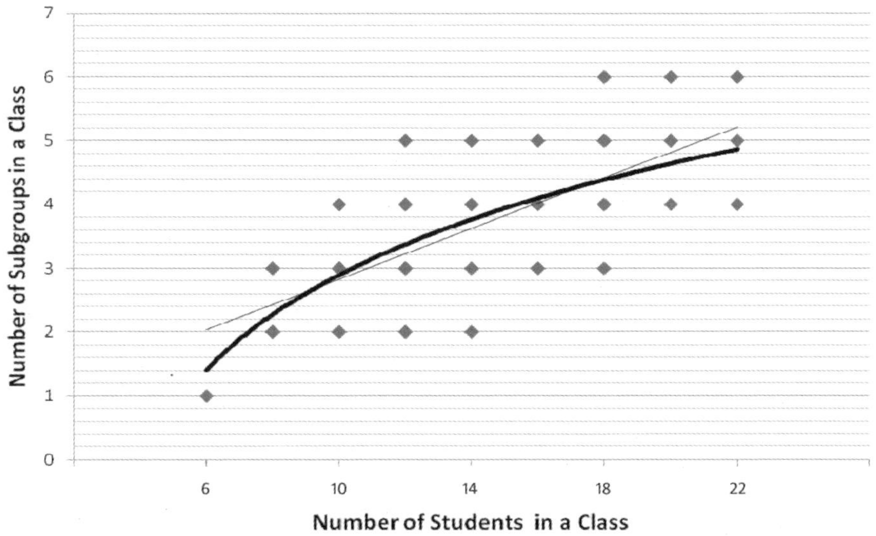

Fig. 1.14.   Nonlinear regression between size of the class and number of groups.

choice of a logarithmic curve is justified by the higher statistical significance
over the linear function. It has clear management interpretation when each
point of curve illustrates dynamics of team development. A nuclear class of
six starts to structure when the small groups of two or three members begin

to form. In a larger classes of over 20 students, the maximum number of these subgroups still seldom exceeds five.

There is a correspondence between the model of continuous learning process (Fig. 1.11) and team dynamics (Fig. 1.13). It allows the measurement of synergy development during a game by informational entropy. The uncertainty of the control function as the choice between two or three alternatives is measured by the quantity of information in bits, or nits. The larger variety of information handled by management is measured either in bytes or in dits. An axiomatic model of learning is difficult to quantify because parameters of discrete structural model are not instrumentally measurable. Time is the most natural unit of measure for these purposes.

1.4. GAME AS A RESEARCH AND DEVELOPMENT (R&D) TOOL

Historically, the earliest games were intended for the research of finding the optimal business and organizational decisions: *Mancala* for seeding the field, *Jenga* for construction, *Chess* for the best military strategy. The games of the 1930s in Soviet industry may be considered as experiments of conversion from civilian to military production. A similar approach was used in the 1950s by the Rand corporation for the reverse: change of American industrial logistics from war to peacetime. It was noted before that business games may be used for the research in behavioral economics. They are providing the explicit presentation of influence of the Human Factor on management decisions. A simulation is the only possible way of testing of business system and organizational structures before their implementation. The main requirement of such testing is the representation by the players of actual human behavior in the proposed system. The entertainment games industry accumulated rich experience of testing their products before offering them to the customers. The manufacturing and service industries have an analogous approach through the study of the market. For example, a business game may be used as the model for a focus group procedure.

"It is apparent that simulation games may be employed for investigating a wide variety of management related topics and that games may, indeed, provide not only a ready and useful research platform, but also a platform that may not otherwise be possible. Basic researchers may use this inventory as a consideration in designing their own studies."

[Dickinson, 2004]

Business games are the best tools for the forecasting of human behavior in technological, environmental, economic and social systems. In research applications of business games, the highest effect of the game may be achieved when decisions of experienced executives are supported by an advice of professional engineers. The executives expose players to the realistic situations within a virtual world. During a childrens' game, parents can clearly notice distinct traits of a kid to choose the best educational path for their child. But as people become older, they change their natural behavior by adjusting it to the cultural, social and professional norms. Teenagers are likely to follow "crowd synergy" by imitating the actions of the strongest in a pack. Meanwhile in most of day-to-day life adults are demonstrating standard, "politically correct" behavior. Only in extraordinary situations does a person reveal the genuine *alter ego* or try to change it. A business game creates stressful situations without real life reprecussions. A game gives realistic stress ratings of economic events (bankruptcy, unemployment, low income, relocation, retraining, etc.). Sociologists obtain these rankings by asking respondents about their decisions in imaginary situations and usually get biased answers [Holmes and Rahe, 1967]. During a business game, players feel these situations naturally, almost like in the real life, because they "vote with their own feet" for different options.

Sooner or later a business game reveals the genuine behavior of players. It may be instrumentally measured by their success in economic terms. But the other variables also need to be used for the estimates of performance in a game. One of them is the time that participants require to make decisions as information delays in System Dynamics model. We can record a number of mistakes, reworks, returns and requests for help; count the frequency of interactions for cooperation and conflicts; evaluate the quality of decisions and responses and encourage creativity in reports and presentations. In some cases, the judgement of performance belongs to the instructor, or to a jury of specialists. But the most accurate is the mutual assessment of players themselves. The motivation of players to achieve individual or collective success in a game is the best by recognition of the peers who can correct deviant behavior faster than the interference of the instructor. Business games are the safest tools for finding out the results of the "law of unintended consequences" [Levitt and Dubner, 2009]. Every run of the game, even with clearly defined rules may present surprises of their unusual interpretation. Students are very innovative in finding loopholes and short-cuts; sometimes they are puzzled or confused in unusual situations and demonstrate obstructive or weird behavior.

The process of generating learning synergy in a game should be cyclical as a spiral of "repetition-analyzing-creation" loops that are rising to the higher level of complexity with each round of a game. This is the way of generating positive synergy of a game. It may be accumulated by teams in competitive games and facilitate the integration between teams in cooperative games.

There are several possible measures of information exchange between members of a team. The simplest is the number of positions in documents supporting teams' decisions. The measurement of performance of different functions of control, management or governance in a game needs specialized variables. First, we reflect the leadership function which is measured by the parameter α (Greek alpha) of instructing. The opposite vertical flow of information γ (gamma) represents proposals to a leader and the reporting on performing of their decisions and explanations α. The intensity of those processes can be measured by the time.

Horizontal communications between members of the team are less formal. They are partly supported by documentation, but mainly consist of informal discussions. We denote it as β (beta) function. The structure of communications in terms α (leadership), β (cooperation and coordination) and γ (following and reporting) is illustrated in Fig. 1.15.

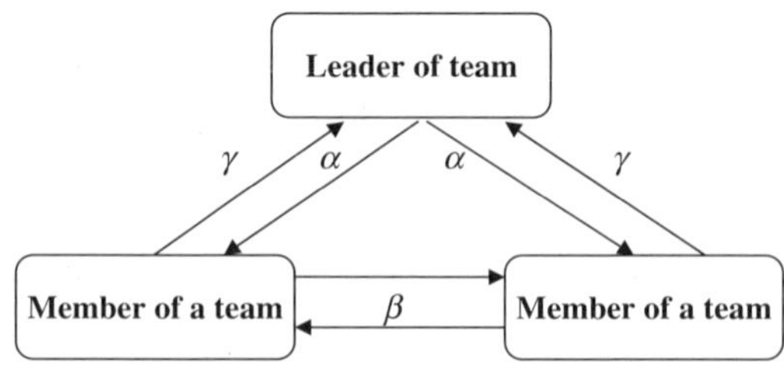

Fig. 1.15.   The structure of communications within a team.

Table 1.4. The matrix of vertical communications between members of a team.

To \ From	Player 1(Leader)	...	Player j	...	Player M	Total sent
Player 1 (Leader)	τ_1	...	$\alpha_{1j}\cdots$		α_{1M}	0 / $\sum_j \alpha_{1j}$
...	...	...	...	...	...	...
Player i	γ_{i1}	...	α_{ij} / γ_{ij}	...	α_{iM}	$\sum_j \alpha_{ij}$ / $\sum_j \gamma_{ij}$
...	...	...	...	...	...	...
Player M	γ_{M1}	...	γ_{Mj}	...	τ_M	0 / $\sum_j \gamma_{Mj}$
Total received	0 / $\sum_i \gamma_{i1}$	...	$\sum_i \alpha_{ij}$ / $\sum_i \gamma_{ij}$	...	$\sum_i \alpha_{iM}$ / 0	$\sum_i\sum_j \alpha_{ij}$ / $\sum_i\sum_j \gamma_{ij}$

Graphical visualization of communications in larger and more complex teams may become messy and may only be complementing the more comprehensive matrix models. Matrices of communications between team members reflect besides the direction of information flows also their intensity. Measuring and recording of information exchange in dynamics of game is difficult, but possible. Time is the best available measure for recording communications between players. The description of vertical communications α and γ within a team is provided by the matrix of communications between all players $(i, j = 1, \ldots, M)$. The matrix is square and has the following structure (Table 1.4).

Matrix $[\alpha, \gamma]$ represents the actual organizational structure of a team. The sequence of rows and columns reflects the activity of players. It goes from the most active in leadership player number one down to most passive in conveying information α member number M. The total quantity of command information which the leader of the team communicates to the other members is $\sum_j \alpha_{1j}$. The leader receives back $\sum_i \gamma_{i1}$ of reporting information from the rest of the team. Player M is an absolute follower with 0 (zero) leading activity. The total quantity of reporting information which he is sending to all other players is $\sum_j \gamma_{Mj}$. All players are numbered and placed in rows and columns of the matrix according to the proportions between sums of α and γ that they have. The totals of rows estimate how active is player in the leadership while totals of columns estimate how much information player is getting from the other players. The difference between the sums of α and γ for each player reflects the relative roles in team decisions making. The larger active communications $i\Sigma\alpha ij$ from player j than its reporting communications $i\Sigma\gamma ij$, the higher the player's place in a team hierarchy.

Main diagonal of this matrix is filled with variable τi representing the time for the individual's education process either by accumulating knowledge, analyzing it, or transforming information. It is not included in the summation of α and γ, but used to check the balance of time recorded by the player. The upper right triangle of the matrix records the intensity of sharing information with other players, lower left triangle — receiving it from the others. The easiest way of measuring quantity of information is by the amount of management documentation exchange. But not all contacts, especially in a dynamic business game, may be documented, so communications should be measured through other metrics. The most accurate record of visible contacts is the amount of time players share with each other.

Horizontal communications may be recorded in separate matrices $[\beta]$ for each round of the game. Their intensity may be measured by the actual time spent in one-to-one meetings between players as well as for general meetings of a team. Matrix $[\beta]$ registers in the main diagonal cells individual efforts of players. The cells around the diagonal are tracking players mutual communications as equal members of a team. The amount of effort which two players put into such communications is supposed to be equal: $\beta ij = \beta ji$, that makes the matrix symmetric over the main diagonal.

The integration of all types of communications between players reflects the proportions between routine, innovation and the creative activities of a team, and between solving problems individually, interactively or collectively. It is presented in the structures of matrices $[\alpha]$, $[\beta]$ and $[\gamma]$. The macrostructure of these matrices is presented in Fig. 1.16.

The leader of a team is supposed to find the right balance between the three components of knowledge formation and assign team members' activities according to their roles and abilities. It will be also used in Chapter 7 to define a leader's responsibilities in game designers' team (Table 7.2). The leader should support a "scanner" in standard situations, a "game

Routine ⟹ Innovation ⟹ Creativity		
Experience Accumulation	**Learning Process**	**Changing Paradigm**
Sharing Facts *Own experience* Acquiring Experience	Teaching Others *Self-Learning* Learning From others	Persuasion Other Players *Own Creativity* Influence By other players

Fig. 1.16.   Macro-structure of matrices of team knowledge development.

champion" if a modified decision is expected, and an "innovator" if a strategic uncertainty prevails.

The units of measurements used for each of the matrices $[\alpha]$, $[\beta]$ and $[\gamma]$ may be different. Matrix $[\alpha]$ is better expressed in number of the instructive documents, matrix $[\gamma]$ — in the volume of reports, matrix $[\beta]$ in the amount of time that each pair of players spent together. These measurements are accurate enough because these numbers are used not for the absolute calculations, but for the estimates of a relative proportion within each type of communications. They will be necessary for the evaluation of personal activity of every player in repeating routine actions, for proposing innovative decisions and in offering radically new approaches.

The measuring of parameters α, β and γ requires recording of all communications between players. It is possible either by players themselves from their personal records, or with the help of external observers. In a case when keeping records is complicated, approximate estimates may be obtained from the questionnaires filled out by players after the game. The estimates of amount of time they are spending for communicating to each other should be regularly verified by their time budgets. This data is subjective and usually biased, so it needs cross-checking or sample verification.

The most accurate is the theoretical scale of measurement of team synergy by ***informational entropy***. Entropy may be evaluated on the base of axiomatic probabilities of a game model and compared with a result of collecting data from one session of game to the next. We propose such calculations to be based on the transitional matrix of Markov chain of states. The approximation of these probabilities is possible by analyzing frequencies of different events registered during the game. We have already demonstrated the calculation of the correlation between structural and dynamic parameters of team behavior based on the team building cycle: Forming-Storming-Norming-Performing-Adjourning. The results of distribution, correlation and regression analysis of our experiments with teams' development in the game *Career* were visualized by arrows connecting structural and dynamic parameters of a game (as was shown in Fig. 1.12).

A measurement of informational entropy needs validation of theoretical hypotheses and the verification of data of the game dynamics. Entropy can be calculated either statistically by probabilities of transitions between states, or dynamically through information flows. The estimate of information flow gives a volume of accumulated experience. The speed of learning is the first derivative of the flow, and the likelihood of changing paradigm is the second derivative of the flow.

Information flow of intensity J in units of information per unit of time available to player i generates all three components of his knowledge:

- *the experience* accumulation is estimated in dynamics by the entropy $H_{(Ni)} = J/Ni$, where Ni is the player's informational capacity per unit of time. Statistical measurement of information entropy is based on the classic formula [Shannon, 1951]: $H_{(Ni)} = -\Sigma pk * \log(pk)$ where pk represents probability of choice from the routine decisions ($k = 1, \ldots, K$). The base of logarithms should be changed from binary to decimal for the different types of communications,
- *the learning* process in dynamics is measured by entropy $H_{(Li)} = Li * dJ/dt$ where Li represents player's i learning ability. It is related to the time required to generate a new decision of the same type. Statistically, it may be measured by $H_{(Li)} = -\Sigma pl * \log(pl)$ where pl is the probability of offering a new decision ($l = 1, \ldots, L$),
- *the creativity* component of proposing new strategies might be measured by the entropy $H_{(Ci)} = Ci * d^2J/dt^2$ where Ci is a parameter of a player's rigidity to the changes. Statistical measure of this entropy is not applicable because new paradigms by definition have no predecessors. We cannot estimate their probabilities either as approximation of frequences,

Low Resistance					High Resistance
R&D	Marketing	Production	Personnel	Finance and Accounting	Legal Department

Fig. 1.17.   Hypothetical ordering of management functional areas on a continuum of resistance to technical innovations.

but only by theoretical hypotheses. The measurement of relative rate of innovation is becoming possible with using indirect estimates like those offered for organization modeling [Morabito *et al.*, 1999]. One polar end on the scale of minimum rigidity they assign to the R&D laboratories and the other end of maximum rigidity to the legal department (Fig. 1.17).

The interrelations between different components of knowledge is noticed by the other behavioral scientist:

"Repetition and practice build competence, but can also impede exploration of untried and possibly better options through habit, inertia, and paradoxically, through improvement itself. As experience with a particular set of routines and behaviors improve performance, the (opportunity) cost of trying other options rises, closing the door to experimentation with other, potentially superior methods."

[Rahmandad, 2003]

An interaction between players during the game may sometimes have unintended consequences. The power struggle for leadership may destroy trust and split the team into fighting coalitions. Some players may be alienated or withdrawn from the team work. Competing for acceptance of different ideas may ignite long unproductive arguments. It was demonstrated by the *Everest* game used for MBA classes in Harvard Business School [Edery, 2009]. Students were expected to climb a virtual mountain performing different roles (instructor, doctor, photographer, enthusiast). The team faced various challenges like oxygen shortage, bad weather and sudden illness. Each member of the team needed to share one's professional information and life experience with the others in order to achieve the team goal: reaching the summit. The game clearly shows how negligence of role playing and rivalry between the players destroys the team effort.

Therefore the main ways of business games progress are in the strengthening of their theoretical base and in the accumulating and analysis of games practice. The theoretical models for business games will be presented in Chapter 2. The possibilities of using much further technologically advanced computer games for the improvement of business games will be estimated in Chapter 4.

MODELS FOR BUSINESS GAMES

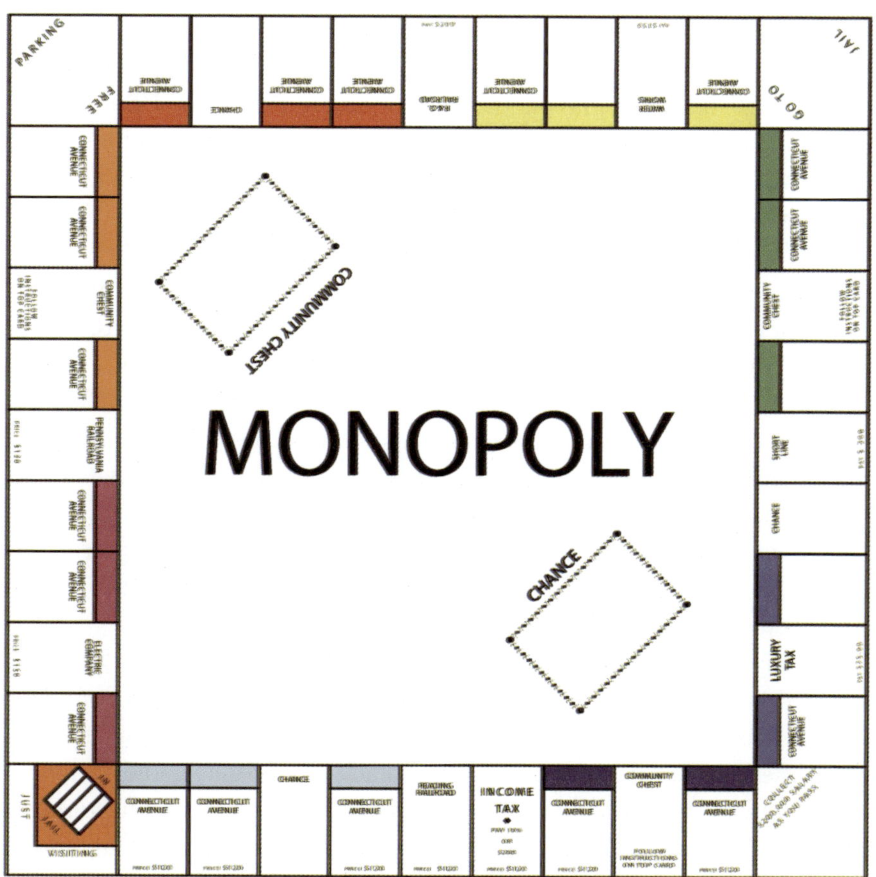

Classic *Monopoly* Game Board (1970)

2.1. THE STRUCTURE OF THE GAME

Every Business Game should have an underlying model of some kind: conceptual for role playing, physical such as a stadium for field game, schematic for a board game or mathematical for electronic games. The model of a game represents the principal aspects of a business enterprise. A conceptual model is the least formal mental image like a story or a description of a business in simplified charts. For example, the interactions between governmental agencies were demonstrated by presentations of officials for the *CyberShockWave* in a CNN situation room simulation. They were playing the roles of consultants to the US President in the virtual fields of energy and transportation. The introduction to the game was presented verbally and with videoclips. Every participant had their own conceptual model of this System of Systems. Similarly, Donald Trump gives verbal introductions to the situation in the TV game *Apprentice.* On the other extreme of a modeling scale is a real physical model of a chemical business which the Leadership Trust has build in the Ross-on-Wye (UK) training center. The network of pipes connecting tanks, barrels of water and bottles of pigments, warehouses and offices is built there for the field game *Leadership in Management.* Yet even such a "stadium", as any model, is the simplification of reality. The HESS Corporation learning centers have scaled models of production lines used for introduction and emergency training of new employees. Most of the games are representing models as schematic images of the businesses on the table board, on the walls and on computer screens.

Today the most commercially successful games are digital management simulations and video games. They hide their models behind a computer screen. It is possible to find these models in either the game manual or by experimenting with the game as with a "black box". Many game designers open software for the players who can make "mods" — modifications to the original models. This software is also used for creating virtual worlds which will be discussed in Chapter 4.

A business game needs to combine several different components of the game model. The initial idea or mission of the game is usually expressed conceptually. Schematic models are helpful to begin designing the architecture of the game. Then the board for the table is needed as an organizing tool representing the roles and procedures of the game. The game board appropriates roles for players in organizational structures and allocates resources within and in between teams. Computer models provide calculations and represent connections between the players' decisions and business results. Information exchange models provide players with connections to the instructor(s) and with communication with the other players. Introductory information and dynamics of the game may be displayed with wall posters or on magnetic boards. Description of roles and rules may be in written handouts, charts, slide presentations and videoclips. Players and/or teams should be equipped with LAN-, WAN- or Internet-connected work stations (desktops or laptops). This way, players and teams may input their decisions and if required, present the reasoning of their choice. These presentations may take place using virtual media or by assembling all players in a multimedia room for the discussion of the intermediate results and for the final analysis of the game.

For business games which are concentrated in one location, we recommend the placement of participants around tables with game boards as virtual playing fields. Game boards are the visual models representing a real structure of business with varying degrees of detail. Boards are useful even if all game information and communications are available on computers. Players in production management games such as *Words-in-Sentences* and *Shell Game* sit along a chart emulating the production line of a factory. The *Beer Game* and the *SIEMENS Supply Chain Management Simulation* display on the table structures of supply chain networks. The players are placed around the table in front of indicated roles. Business games *CyberMarket* and *HELLO* (*Help to Economics of Labor and Logistics Organization*) represent balancing production and services between a network of economic agents. Roles and resources are represented on the board with flowcharts, statistical charts and accounting tables. The *Glo-Bus, GloBiz* and other regional simulations are naturally illustrated by networks and geographical maps. Players of these games are not supposed to sit all the time at the same place. They may move around either to change roles or to make some changes on the playing field, or to meet other players.

System integration games like *Career* and *NewProDev* require the players to move between the teams or around the game board. Game models are visualized in paths of professional and social developments on tables, wall posters or on computer screens. Behind each of them are mathematical models or information processes reflecting the connections between a player's decisions and business results. For the *Words-in-Sentences* game it is the processing of raw materials (letters) into components (words) and then into assemblies (sentences). Supply chain simulations also represent the assembly of components on the larger industrial or regional scale. The *TranSport* and *FinanceSoS* game boards are reflecting networks of horizontal communications and cooperation. Markets simulations such as *MarketSim* and *CyberMarket* use charts and tables of classic Supply and Demand functions, Cost and Learning curves, Production and Utility functions and Production Possibilities Frontier diagrams. Most of these functions are formalized and tabulated in Excel for accounting calculations. System integration games use Markov chain models and decision trees as the description of a person's transitions through life, stages of business development or project subsystems integration.

A business game reproduces a typical or a specific structure of an economic system by the assignment of roles to players and by the allocation of resources between them. Most business games are structured as a competition between teams of a similar organizational structure. The management of a team may be assigned by the instructor, may be established during the Forming stage as struggle for leadership or may change by rotation. The best possible results may be achieved if structure is flexible and it naturally emerges in the process of the game according to the changing situation. The changes are especially dynamic in field games which require positioning of members of a team into leading, supporting and followers roles. Every member of a team bears professional or functional responsibilities. It may combine controlling and managerial functions with operational activities. For example, in the *Leadership in Management* game physically stronger players are delivering heavy materials and equipment while others may keep production lines running and perform quality control. If the instructor has limited information about the abilities of different players before the game, the game starts with the random assignment of roles and equal allocation of resources between teams.

Board games usually assign roles randomly according to the places around the table initially occupied by the players. It may include the movements of some players between the teams as well as reassignments inside the team to different roles. Therefore, some readjustment may be necessary later by playing some kind of a "musical chairs" game. We also highly recommend, especially in high schools and colleges, using hats, T-shirts, labels and other symbols to represent roles of the players. Visualizing names, roles and the color-coding of structures and processes is very helpful for a quick and enthralling start to a game. The experience of videogames also shows that sound effects and music are useful not only as entertainment. It may also be used for the attracting of players attention or before the introduction of a new situation. We use appropriate songs and melodies in *Aquarium* and *Obla-di, Obla-da* games for kids.

In a medium-term executive business game *Capstone* permanent assignments to the certain roles enhance professionalism and support a feeling of responsibility for players. For undergraduate classes we recommend the rotation of roles. This gives participants a chance to experiment and recognize personal strengths and demonstrate one's preferences. It helps to avoid frustration and conflict at the start, the most vulnerable stage of a business game. Role assignments may ignite tension and even destructive conflicts within a team, so the instructor should recognize and prevent them from escalating into a problem. Sometimes, simple rotation will create feeling of equality, but role assignments according to personal traits, experience or ambitions are preferable.

A roles assignment can be supported by exercises and tests from the courses of industrial psychology and organizational behavior with reference to the game process. It integrates different components of the learning experience and provides the substance matters for class experimentation for liberal arts and psychology courses. The coordination of a business game with other engineering and economics courses also enriches the professional contents of the study.

Structure of a "serious" business game follows standard organizational charts with players or teams representing management or executive positions. It arranges players to functional, product, or geographical responsibilities. Players in teams of the classic *Capstone* game which represents competing businesses are functionally specialized. Some players in the *Glo-Bus* game represent management functions, while in *GloBiz* they are playing for regional subsidiaries.

Many business games such as *CyberMarket* and *MarketSim* are based on microeconomic models structured for the roles of principal players in an economic system. These games include the roles of businesses, households, bank and government. Some games such as the *Beer Game* and *Words-in-Sentences* are based on the basic industrial structures. The other games like *Capstone and Glo-Bus* are presenting typical economic systems. And the *HELLO* game was tailored according to the specifics of the St. Petersburg Free Enterprise Zone in Russia [Bazilevich, 1992]. For this game we used the Supply Chain Simulation (SCSIM) model [Ballou, 1992] to generate the flows of the materials, components, products and services through supply channels represented by six teams from factory to customers, as illustrated in Fig. 2.1.

The team of players in the field game *HELLO* represent specialized participants of the Free Enterprise Zone. Each team includes as a minimum three roles of Manager, Accountant and Liason Officer. The Manager is the leader of a team representing it at general meetings, the Accountant keeps records and the Liaison Officer coordinates decisions with the other teams. Their allocation in the situation room is presented by Fig. 2.2.

The Supply Chain Simulation (CSIM) model supports the calculation of results of each round of the game considering statistical uncertainty:

"The product flows are replicated with a Monte Carlo-type simulation. A single, or aggregate, product is used and a single facility, or aggregation of facilities, is assumed at each echelon. The objective is to simulate supply channel performance and costs when various forecasting methods,

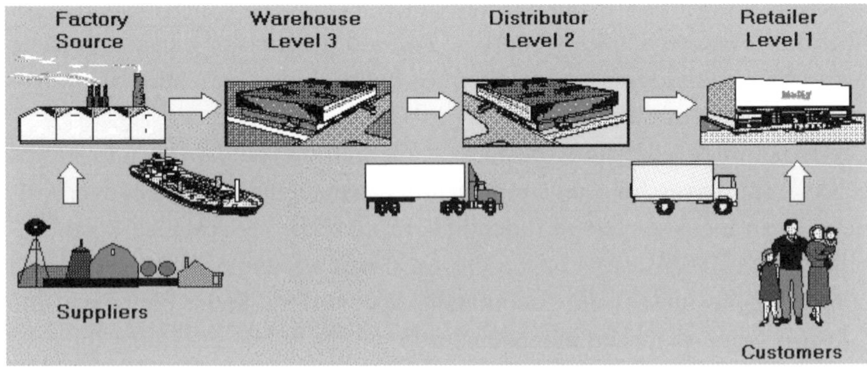

Fig. 2.1.   The structure of general supply channel model for *HELLO* game.

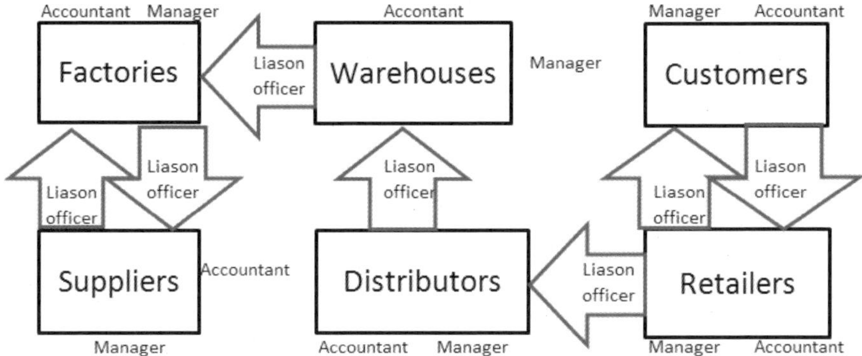

Fig. 2.2.   Teams allocation in the situation room for *HELLO* game.

inventory policies, transportation services, production lot sizes, order-processing costs, and the like are used throughout the supply channel. Reports and graphs are used to portray supply chain performance for different simulation runs."

[Ballou, 1992]

A competitive business game should have an equal number of players and competence levels at the start of a game. The assignment of players for different team roles within each of the competing teams may be changing from one run of the game to the next. For example, every member of a team in *Words-in-Sentences* game has different operational, controlling or managerial responsibilities. The production process is represented by stickers moving along arrows representing an assembly line. The structure of this game with the roles of Manager, Quality controllers, Word producers and Sentences assemblers, is presented in Fig. 2.3.

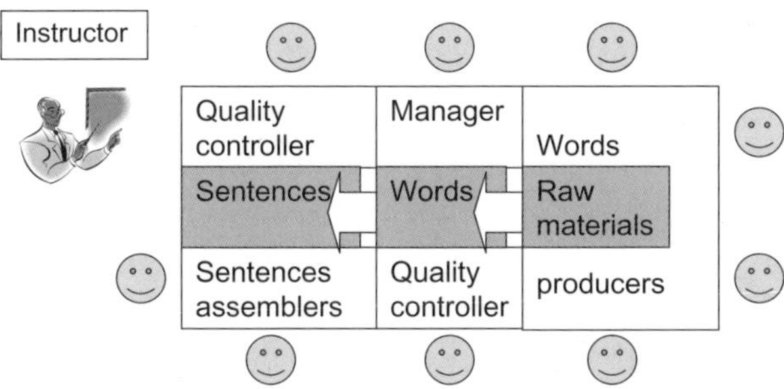

Fig. 2.3.   Allocation of players around the board in a team of *Words-in-Sentences* game.

The introduction to a large business game may be organized as a preliminary team-building exercises. For example, the Leadership Trust uses cave exploration, biking and rafting trips before assigning executives for roles in the professional part of the outward bound game. The Leadership Trust even puts players in a stressful situation such as throwing them from a parachute tower before making immediate business decisions.

2.2. GAME THEORY AND MATHEMATICAL MODELS

Game theory is a branch of applied mathematics that is developing as an academic subject with a small connection to business games practice. This is especially strange because the first applications of game theory were to economics. The founding book on game theory was "Theory of Games and Economic Behavior" by John von Neumann and Oskar Morgenstern [Neumann and Morgenstern, 1944]. They defined the universal basics of game theory that were later developed for the conceptualization of different economic phenomena. On a macroeconomic level they describe strategies and system equilibria, monopolies, duopolies and oligopolies. On a microeconomic level they introduced the payoffs and utilities of business decisions. Some applications of the theory were successfully implemented in business and government practice in bargaining and auctions, negotiations and voting systems.

Business games need the support of game theory to become accurate models of entrepreneurship. Yet few business game designers are using models of game theory and tools explicitly. Instead they are presented as simple economic illustrations in fundamental textbooks such as "Economics" [Samuelson, 1999] and in the more specialized monograph "Games for Business and Economics" [Gardner, 2003].

Basic concepts of game theory like *equilibrium* and *pure strategies* are really abstract and in a sense alien to business practices where dynamics, instability and uncertainty prevail. Reaching equilibrium is a "dead end" for the business game. The enlisting of all possible strategies is practically impossible and counter-creative for the business game. So up to now the main use of game theory for business games is in the intelligent use of definitions like *mixed strategies* and *payoff matrices*. Game theory is also useful for the proper classifications of business games and the analysis of their results. But the main mathematical tools of game theory like matrices and graphs are not yet serving business games to the full extent of their potential. The game ideology has good prospects for the optimization of decisions by the players equipped with computers [Vajda, 1992].

Mathematical accuracy of game theory when it applied to business games is useful for the clarification of the properties necessary for game design. Game theory gives some rigorous and many descriptive definitions and classifications. They are used for the modeling of conflicts between participants; levels of uncertainty they are handling; mathematical models of forecasting and optimization; the motivation of players; structure, schedule and the procedure of the game.

There are two possible types of economic **conflict** between players and teams:

- *Antagonistic* — when competition between players enables the losses through bankruptcy, mergers and acquisitions. *Monopoly*, for example, finishes with the elimination of all players except the winner. These games are usually called "Zero-Sum" games meaning that the gains of one player are achieved at the expense of losses for the others;
- *Cooperative* — when coalitions between players and teams are allowed, for example, the games *MarketSim* and *CyberMarket* where individual players or different teams may trade resources with mutual benefit ("Win-Win" games).

The levels of **uncertainty** for players to make decisions are as follows:

- *Strategic* — when players may not even know all of the strategies available to the other players or teams;
- *Statistical* — when players have information, or theoretical (hypothetical) assumptions about the probabilities of opponents' strategies;
- *Perfect or complete information*, theoretically admissible, but practically unlikely. In this situation players definitely know the consequences of their decisions and actions. Then it becomes just a computational exercise, which may be a part of the game.

The motivation ***criteria*** of game participants are as follows:

- *Maximizing payoff* — trying to get absolute physical or monetary gain of beneficial variable (profit, earnings, property) from the available amount of resources;
- *Minimizing inputs* — save resources such as time, cost or materials to achieve a desirable goal, or to support chosen strategy;
- *Satisficing* — getting acceptable combination of inputs and payoffs.

The process of ***moves*** by players might be different:

- *Sequential* — when players or teams make moves (announce decisions) in turn after the other team — as in most of card games;
- *Simultaneous*, when players prepare decisions independently and announce them at the same moment.

The variety of different game ***structures*** depends on the size of the class and on the complexity of the simulated system:

- *One-player* — or a game against Nature is typical for videogames. The "Nature" is a personification of all opposing to the player forces: natural climate, physical environment and many unspecified factors including invisible competitors;
- *Two-players* — the fundamental concept of the most of game theory applications, otherwise known as matrix games;
- *Multi-players* — more difficult to formalize, but if players may form *coalitions*, then size of the game decreases. It is useful for getting simpler models for a smaller number of strategies and a fewer players.

The ***strategies*** available to the players are as follows:

- *Pure* — chain of distinct decisions which cannot be split into simpler moves;
- *Mixed* — combinations of pure strategies in different proportions;
- *Conditional* — changing decisions in relation to the moves of the opponent.

The ***schedules*** of the game might be different:

- *Finite* — games that represent a predefined number of moves that are usually periods of time;
- *Discrete* — games that are based on a limited number of participants who can use few pure or mixed strategies;
- *Continuous* — games may be played for indefinitely long.

A variety of ***mathematical models*** are available for business games:

- *Algebraic or computational* models are useful for the description of some relations between economic variables, for example the production function can be given as a formula or entry in MS Excel spreadsheet cell;
- *Tabulated*, prefabricated tables which may be used for interpolation of results in relation to the inputs;
- *Matrices*, explicit structural models connecting inputs with outputs, structuring mathematical programs optimization, connecting transitions between different states of elements of an system as a whole;
- *Graphic*, visual interpretation of one of the listed above models: line for algebraic, chart for tabulated, network for matrix. It is the most useful tool for a game.

Game theory as the youngest branch of mathematics accumulated all necessary tools of the sciences. Mathematical models are the most accurate contemporary tools for the theoretical support of the business game concept. The computerization of a game is impossible without mathematical formalization. Models may be explicitly presented to players in graphs, equations, algorithms or spreadsheets; or can remain concealed. Then a model of the game is supposed to be developed in the player's mind by trial and error experience. The extended version of a game may include systematic experimentation and thorough statistical input-output analysis. In most games players need an explanation of the proportions between deterministic models and random event generators. The learning process then goes with accumulation of knowledge through repetition for eventual building up of conceptual models in the heads of players or databases for statistical approximations. This way the process of converting strategic uncertainty into statistical uncertainty becomes a part of the game's learning experience. Well-defined sources of strategic and statistical uncertainty are the

Table 2.1.	Relationship between types of game models and uncertainty levels.

Mathematical properties	Components of business game		
	Economic theory	Random events	Players' behavior
Type of game model	Deterministic decision models	Stochastic models, utility theory	Game theory, Chaos theory
Level of uncertainty	No uncertainty	Statistical uncertainty	Strategic uncertainty
Examples	Production and cost functions, accounting	Variation of quality, customer demand, utility functions	Fashions of consumption

essential features of a business game. The sources of uncertainty include economic theory, random events and players' behavior. The correspondence between levels of uncertainty and various game models is presented in Table 2.1.

Real life demonstrates many instances when elegant economic theory fails miserably against a reality check. The famous Chicago University nest of Nobel laureates failed to predict several economic bubble bursts. Their macroeconomic models are reliable only for short-term forecasting in stable conditions with simple criteria of "rational" business decisions. In real economy evolutionary accumulations are sooner or later alternate with a revolutionary bursts.

There are the following models are typical for the different time horizons:

- ***Short-term operations*** may be presented by models of Markov chains of transitions between the states of a system, by flowcharts or decision trees;
- ***Evolutionary medium-term growth*** may be represented in System Dynamics models as Lower-Expected-Upper bound trends;
- ***Revolutionary long-term development*** changes may be presented as Optimistic, Most Likely and Pessimistic scenarios of a game or explained by the "Chaos Theory" models.

Table 2.2. Model of production process functioning as a transitions matrix.

Following state Original state	B	$\cdots$	M	$\cdots$	W	Total sum of probabilities
B The Best Outcome	$p(B, B)$	$\cdots$	$p(B, M)$	$\cdots$	$p(B, W)$	**1.00**
$\cdots$	$\cdots$	$\cdots$	$\cdots$	$\cdots$	$\cdots$	$\cdots$
M Medium Outcome	$p(M, B)$	$\cdots$	$p(M, M)$	$\cdots$	$p(M, W)$	**1.00**
$\cdots$	$\cdots$	$\cdots$	$\cdots$	$\cdots$	$\cdots$	$\cdots$
W The Worst Outcome	$p(W, B)$	$\cdots$	$p(W, M)$	$\cdots$	$p(W, W)$	**1.00**
Stable state probabilities	$\pi(B)$	$\cdots$	$\pi(M)$	$\cdots$	$\pi(W)$	**1.00**

A ***model of short-term operations*** is the best for presentation of repetitive processes such as production runs and routine management decisions. These models support the process control and supervising management. For example, the fluctuations of product output from one production cycle to the other may be reflected in a square matrix of transitional probabilities from the original states (rows) to the following states (columns). Row and columns are ordered from the best to the worst in Table 2.2.

Transitions between states may be visualized (the ViVaT approach to games) by the Markov chain graph. It complements the matrix if the number of states is not so large and the connections between them are not very dense. Otherwise the graph will be either too large or too messy. Therefore, we illustrate this model by a small 3×3 example of the production process results represented in the matrix of Table 2.3. Corresponding to this matrix graph is presented in Fig. 2.4.

Table 2.3. Example of production process model as transition probabilities of results.

To j From i	Good	Repairable	Broken	Total sum of probabilities
Good product	0.85	0.10	0.05	1.00
Repairable	0.65	0.15	0.20	1.00
Broken product	0.50	0.05	0.45	1.00

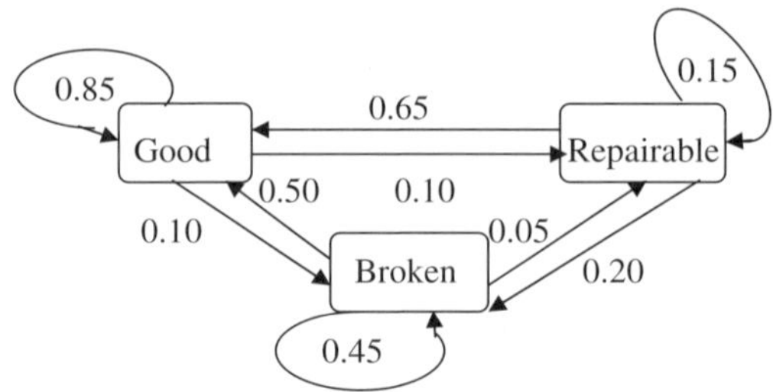

Fig. 2.4.   States change diagram of a production system.

The state changes diagram of the change in this system will reflect all possible states as nodes and all possible transitions as arrows on the graph. The system may change states or stay in the present state according to the transition probabilities. In the business games discrete changes may be presented as soon as they happen (events model). Continuous processes are registered at regular moments of time (periodic model). Figure 2.4 presents transitions between the consecutive events of different product quality according to Table 2.3.

Notice that this diagram represents transitions between different states of production system when every next production cycle brings a better, an identical or a worse result. It has no absorbing states that are possible in the simulation for the particular units of product which may be broken and becomes unrepairable, or when an individual customer will never come to this service facility again.

The visualization of complex systems and processes is useful, but has its limits before the drawing becomes messy. The structure of the transition matrix for an experienced eye reflects a prevailing trend of system trajectory. The concentration of probabilities around the main diagonal of the matrix reflects the stability of the process; concentration of probabilities below the main diagonal in the bottom-left corner reflects the upward trend of improvement; concentration above the main diagonal in the upper-right triangle — declining. Otherwise process demonstrates just a random variation. These "pure" types of matrix structures are illustrated in Fig. 2.5.

In our illustration we see concentration of probabilities along and below the main diagonal of matrix that indicates the trend of improvement.

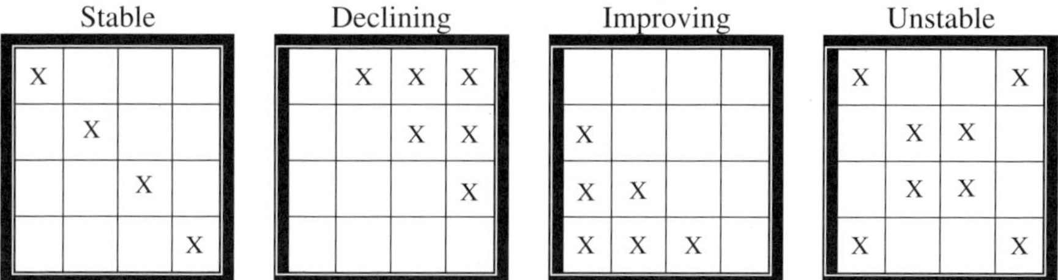

Fig. 2.5.   Structures of matrices for different types of system *operations* model.

The actual structures of these matrices combine several types of operation dynamics. In the *Monopoly* game the matrix of transitions for landing on a state cell "Go to jail" from the other states is represented by the first column and last columns of the transition matrix in Table 2.4. Fortunately the escape from the jail is possible according to the probabilities representing available progress (upper-right triangle of the matrix).

Visualization of possible transitions by a state change diagrams is useful in addition to matrices. It is helpful for the explanations and illustrations of decision opportunities. The appearance of these diagrams as a part of the *Career* game model is demonstrated in Fig. 2.6.

These diagrams show possible paths, obstacles and factors of available transitions for a person between the states of one's life:

"The Model of the *Career* Game is based on Markov chains-transition probabilities matrices and decision trees. Data for the mathematical model of the game should be specific for the student's future profession. It might be collected from admissions and alumni office statistics as well as by questionaires from professionals. The model is visualized by the boards and wall posters which serve as the playing fields and by graphs and matrices presenting probabilities. The playing field represents possible options of advance in general and professional education, in corporate job or in private entrepreneurship, physical and spiritual recreation, and in the comfort of life (housing and personal relations). Flowcharts of available opportunities in each area of life are based on the states of business, person's position, available transitions and conditions of changes. Each step is described by the appropriate management documentation: resumes, job descriptions, time schedules, budgets, etc."

[Bazilevich, 1979]

Table 2.4.   Probabilities for landing on a short term jail stay (as percentages).

Square	Go to jail	Medit. ave	Comm. chest	Baltic avenue	Income tax	Reading railroad	Oriental avenue	Chance	Vermont avenue	Connec venue	Visiting jail
Go to jail	1.212		2.384	5.556	9.322	12.153	13.836	6.250	13.836	11.111	8.28
Medit. Ave	0.863			2.695	6.418	9.113	11.111	5.177	16.667	13.806	11.111
Comm.Chest	0.694				3.423	6.250	8.284	4.167	13.84	16.667	13.84
Baltic Ave	0.516				0.516	3.214	5.556	3.095	11.111	13.809	16.667
Income Tax	0.347				0.347	0.347	2.720	2.083	8.275	11.111	13.831
Reading Railroad	0.338				0.169	0.169		1.014	5.556	8.261	11.111
Oriental Avenue	0.347								2.721	5.556	8.277
Chance card	0.516									2.703	5.556
Vermont Avenue	0.694										2.723
Connec Avenue	0.864										
Visiting Jail	1.211										

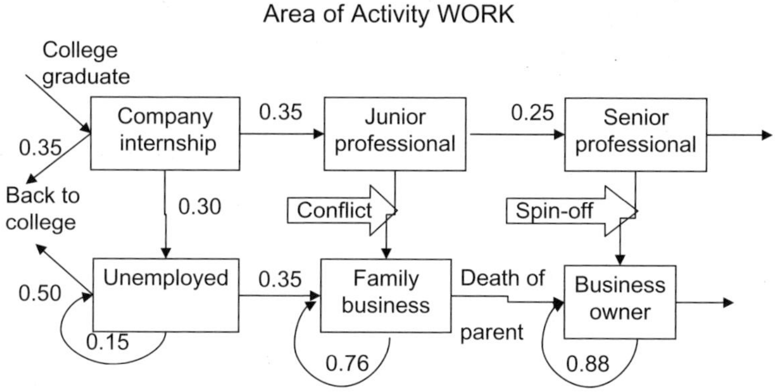

Area of Activity WORK

Fig. 2.6.   Fragment of WORK area diagram for *Career* game.

Short-term business games for undergraduate classes may include limited or simplified management models. These models should be provided via charts, tables and computational templates. For example, *The Shell Game* [Ward & Schwarz, 1995] provides players with information of deterministic times for the processing of jobs with varying amounts of resources. Table 2.5 shows the Gantt chart of a production schedule which should be

Table 2.5.   The *Shell Game* schedule template.

Day _ _ _   **Priority Rule** _ _ _ _ _

Job #	1st hour				2nd hour				3rd hour				4th hour				5th hour			
	1	2	3	4	1	2	3	4	1	2	3	4	1	2	3	4	1	2	3	4
1																				
2																				
3																				
4	R	G	Y	B																
5		R	W	Y	G	B														
6																				
...																				
24	G	B	R	W	Y															

Work stations are represented by initial letters for colors Red, Green, Blue and Yellow.
The symbol W represents the Waiting time when the necessary work station is occupied.

filled in by the player before the simulation of scheduled jobs for processing through the four coloring workstations.

We enlarged the *Shell Game* by adding elements of statistical uncertainty of the quality fluctuations as well as with strategic uncertainty of a player's choice of the priority rule. At the first stage of the game students are simulating technology of craft, then batch and finally assembly line mass production with an analysis of the learning progress of individuals and teams. Then the game is organized for the team around the board shown later in Fig. 3.10 representing the interaction of four coloring work stations.

Evolutionary medium-term growth of a system may be represented by the models reflecting levels of growth with Lower-Expected-Upper bound trends. They should be specified conceptually in the game design as result of modeling or an external case. The concept may be assumed theoretically or deduced from the data collected by registration of the real production or service. The theory represents microeconomic functions and collecting data allows statistical approximation. During a game these hypotheses may be verified as was shown in Sec. 1.3. A theoretical conceptual model for the team leadership style will be demonstrated in Chapter 7. We use Cobb-Douglas production function for resources estimation and the Bass logistic function for S-curve of business growth. The examples of using verification of theoretical models in a business games with statistical analysis were demonstrated in Chapter 1 for building statistical models of team structure and dynamics (Figs. 1.11 to 1.13).

Most evolutionary models represent growth of variable P (population, production, consumption etc.,) at period t by the universal logistical S-curve.

$$P(t) = \frac{C}{1 + \exp\left[-g^*(t - h)\right]},$$

where C is the saturation capacity of the process (limit of growth), $g^*(t-h)$ is the maximum possible rate of growth before it reaches half of capacity at period h which is called half-life time.

The appearance of the logistic model shows its universal shape and relative flexibility in accordance with parameters C, g^* and h (see Fig. 2.7).

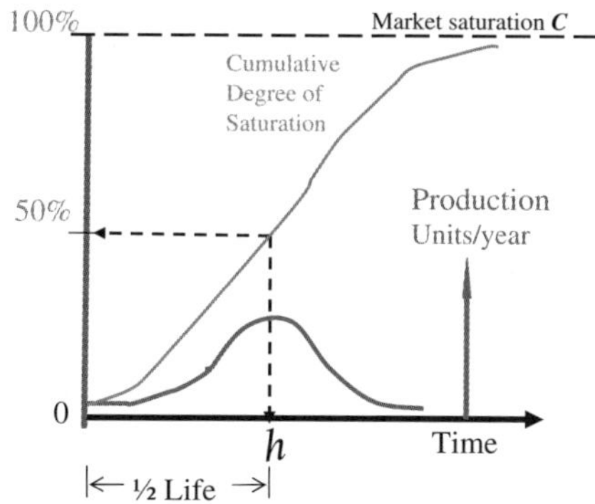

Fig. 2.7.   Logistic curve of a market saturation model.

Medium-term models of economic behavior represent typical processes of evolutionary growth in technological or economic systems. We use them in the *CyberMarket* game for forecasting the size of the economic system. Gradual growth at the beginning is usual for the demand for a new product or service with a current utilization of resources and productivity. This S-shaped model represents the slow introductory stage, then exponential growth and then eventual saturation of a mature technology. The time from introduction to the 50% saturation of the market measures the first half of the life of the current technology. Few exceptionally successful products and technologies are living through the full life cycle. Most of them are substituted by the next generation of better or cheaper products. But technological inventions are more seldom than product modifications. Technologies have longer life incorporating several life cycles based on them several generations of products and services.

The structure of each stage of technology development is reflected in our *NewProDev* game by the S-curve as a sequence of consecutive stages illustrated by Fig. 2.8.

This process of the changing generations of products within current technological possibilities is typical for most industries. For a long-run these models of growth are elements of development or "scenarios" in terms of Game Theory. When plotted, scenarios look like a succession of medium-term S-curves enveloping them into a long-term trend of linear or exponential development (Fig. 2.9).

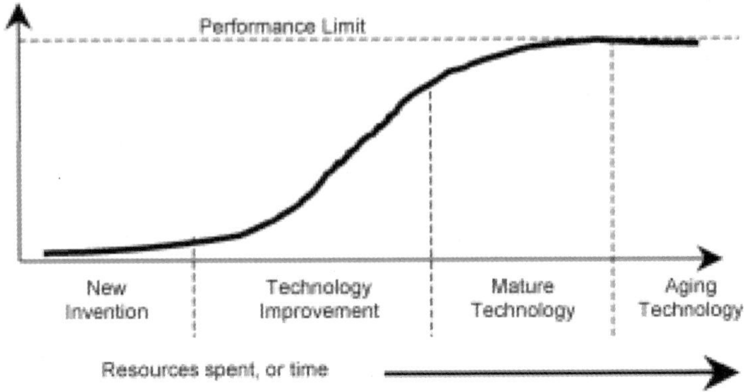

Fig. 2.8.   Technology development stages.

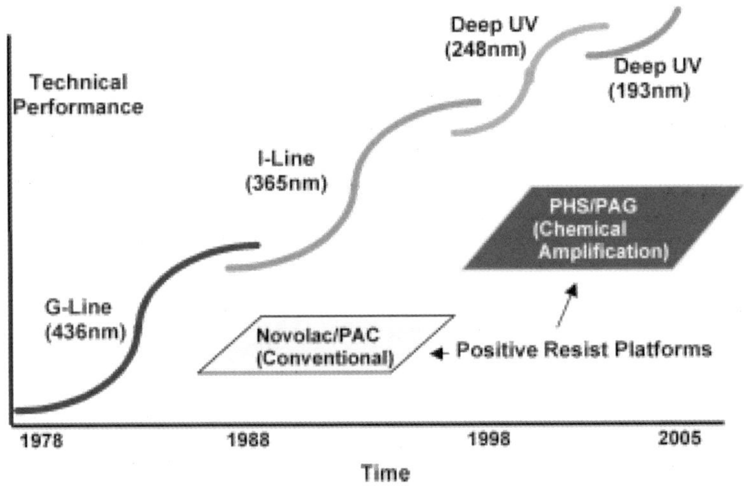

Fig. 2.9.   Development model of generations of exposure tools.

Some technologies follow this model with amazing precision. The regularity of repeating life cycles for the consecutive generations of electronic products was named Moore's Law after Intel corporation co-founder, Gordon Moore [Stokes, 2003]. Moore predicted 40 years ago that the computer processing power could be doubled every two years if it is measured by the transistor counts in a microprocessor. Moore's Law for the capacity of electronic components shows substitution of one generation

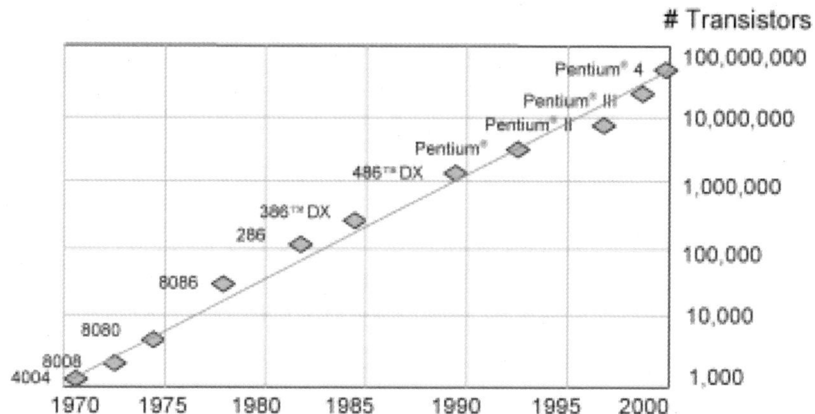

Fig. 2.10.   Moore's law of long-term trend in electronic components development.

of product with the next by increasing the saturation limit 10 times every 1.5–2 years [Bowden, 2006]. This is what we call a ***long-term model of development*** (Fig. 2.10).

Revolutionary changes in the last decade limit extrapolation of this model as current technologies are reaching saturation level for silicon-based materials. Now the density of electronic components is close to the silicon atom size. So components need to change to the new, most likely carbon-based materials or discovery of new information storage and processing principles. In a business game it requires substituting technology forecasting from statistical extrapolation applicable for growth to the scenarios of development. The chaotic situation in the latest generations of transistors is clearly indicated by the large amount of competing products in the market today. The long-term trend is actually the exponential curve because the vertical scale of product density is logarithmic. So the simulation of further developments in computer technologies in the nearest future requires application of business games based on different scenarios.

The business development process also follows a universal S-shaped model, yet unlike more predictable technology, it combines stages of evolutionary growth with periods of drastic irregular turmoil changes in between. Typically, this stage happens on reaching saturation of efficiency and does not take a long time. However, it may decrease the size of a business before a new cycle of growth begins. The integration of short-term models of repetitive operations into medium-term growth models is illustrated by Fig. 2.11.

The short-term model of operations reflects a gradual move of the business up from small to the larger states until size reaches saturation level for this type of business. The size of the business may be limited by technology, by market size or by legislation. For example, the initial "garage" stage started by a couple of entrepreneurs eventually becomes a small business. Then after reaching a size of 50 employees, small business should be incorporated. These processes often happen with some losses of productivity and resources. Conflicts between pioneering entrepreneurs are the highlights of businesses' history. The development of a business as the alternating evolutionary growth stages and shorter but more dramatic radical changes is presented in Fig. 2.12.

Some companies may experience several generations of such developments, especially if they use an organizational strategy of spin-offs for new businesses, mergers and acquisitions.

2.3. SYSTEM DYNAMICS MODELS

Businesses as self-regulating systems are controlled and managed with feedback information. The feedback in the system is defined as two or more variables connected in a closed loop when one variable depends on the other and vice versa. The behavior of the variables in each feedback loop can affect variables in other loops within the feedback system. These variables may be of material, economic, informational or social nature. The simulation of such systems was initiated as Industrial Dynamics by Jay Forrester [Forrester, 1961]. All applications of this approach to the other systems (urban, environmental, political, etc.) were concentrated later under the umbrella of System Dynamics (SD). The most valuable for our research are models presented by John Sterman in the fundamental textbook "Business Dynamics: Systems Thinking and Modeling for a Complex World" [Sterman, 2000]. He designed the most popular *Beer Game* based on an SD model of feedback in a Supply Chain. Games based on SD models are the best tools for the simulation of business ***growth***.

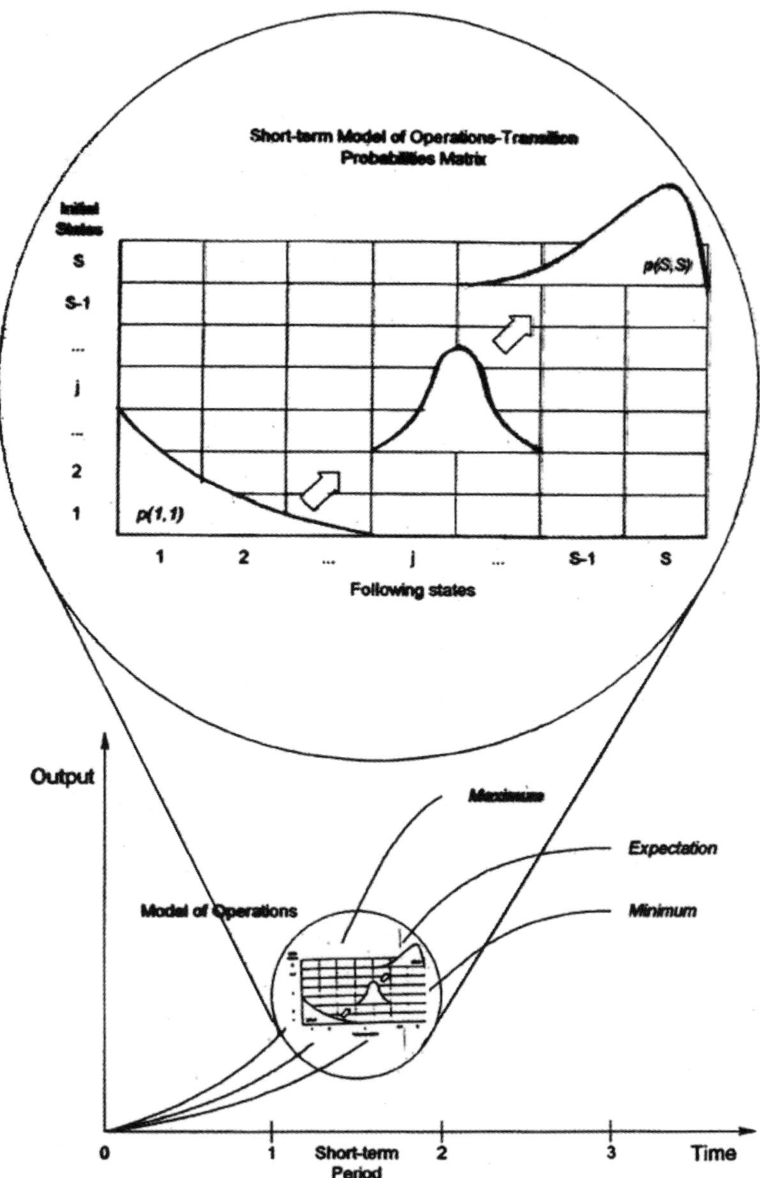

Fig. 2.11.   Integration of short-term operations in a medium-term growth.

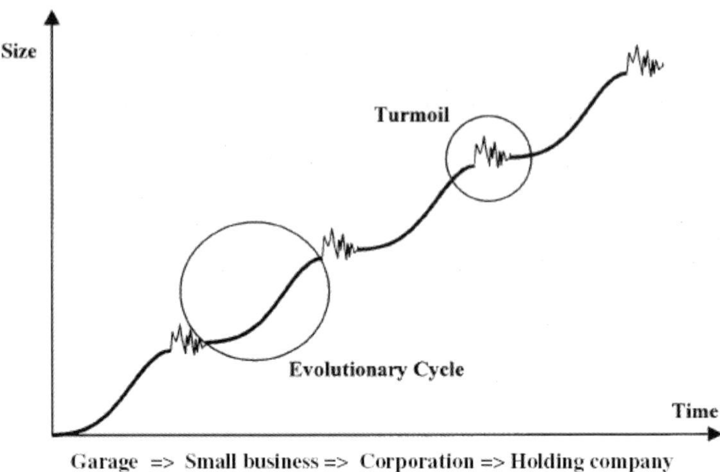

Fig. 2.12.   Business organization development process.

System Dynamics opens two major opportunities for business games development: conceptual and computational. The first was demonstrated by *Beer Game* designer John Sterman [Sterman, 1992]. It realized the idea of a game architecture that reflects an actual organizational structure of a supply chain. We used SD flow charts as the architecture for the *Career* game [Bazilevich, 1979] and *NewProDev* game [Bazilevich, 1984]. The models of different areas of activity in these games are represented by flowcharts that include delays in the interactions between different actions of players. The second capability of SD is the introduction of computer simulations as a part of game process. It was used for generating of revenue dynamics as a result of the interaction between production and sales in a *ReActOr* game [Bazilevich, 1979]. It will be detailed in the second part of this book as a tool for business game design.

The conceptual capacity of the SD model allows the demonstration of business behavior in a complex network of feedback loops. This was shown for the supply chain in thousands of runs of the *Beer Game* in different communities [Sterman, 2001]. The SD model in that game describes how materials and information are moving between stocks. SD allows integration of technological, environmental, economic or social systems. At the same time SD can trace the consequences of the decisions and interactions of the players during a game. Their influence on one another over time is reproduced by a model with flows, stocks, feedback and delays. System Dynamics is effective for the demonstration of control and management functions in technological and environmental systems. It is also able to support the governance of economic and social Systems-of-Systems which are much more complex. Such a computer simulation forecasts system behavior which is usually called counterintuitive.

SD is a powerful tool for presenting concepts of system thinking approach to players. It was first introduced in "The Fifth Discipline Fieldbook" [Senge *et al.*, 1994]. SD ideology relates mainly to medium-term growth processes (demographic, biological, technological, etc.). These evolutionary processes are the substance of the majority of management simulations. Yet typical business games for large-scale businesses like *Capstone* [Keys, 1990], are still used as simple extrapolation models. The most constructive use of SD was demonstrated by Dennis Meadows in the environmental interactive business game *Strategem* [Meadows and Toth, 1985].

SD is also able to model revolutionary events like the "Tragedy of the Commons" when evolutionary dynamics builds up accumulation until breaking threshold of the process. Models for long-term development processes require considering strategic decisions. Strategies of mergers and acquisitions; organizational structure changes and introduction of new technologies can be adequately represented by SD models. Many business games introduce them externally using input from the chance cards. A SD model of the "Limits to Growth" archetype may generate the collapse internally as a result of growth up to the certain limit. Evolutionary accumulation of growth brings the system to revolutionary change through one of three scenarios of development: (1) pessimistic of collapse, (2) optimistic of opening new cycle of growth and (3) stagnation on the limit. The change of the dynamics of growth to possible scenarios of development is illustrated by Fig. 2.13.

Peter Senge recommends the following strategies for the improvement in a "limits to growth" situation:

- Beware of doing more of what worked in the past.
- Try to find interrelationships between your success strategies and potential limits.

- Shorten the delay in the balancing loop to push the system beyond its capacity before it is heeded.
- Anticipate upcoming limiting forces, which are small now, but which will increase as time goes on.
- Look for other potential engines of growth, strengthen the resources which are driving your own growth.

There are several other "archetypes" of growth-to-development dynamics and more of their modifications require different game strategies. "The Fifth Discipline" fieldbook illustrates the possible long-term scenarios of system dynamics in typical cases:

"*'Picking the low-hanging fruit'*: At the beginning of a quality improvement campaign, the first efforts (such as training in the statistical process control tools) lead to significant gains in the quality of products, services, and processes. This lends cachet, support, and impetus to the quality efforts. But as the easy changes (known as 'low-hanging fruit' among quality veterans) are completed, the level of improvement plateaus, much to everyone's disappointment. The next wave of improvements are more complex and tougher to manage; they involve coordinating several different parts of the organization. The lack of organization-wide support, and the attitudes of senior management, now become limits. Unless the company makes more widespread changes at higher levels, its quality gains will be limited.

'*The software artists*': Computer hardware continues getting 'faster, cheaper and better,' at an astonishing rate, virtually without limits. However, the production of software for these increasingly complex machines

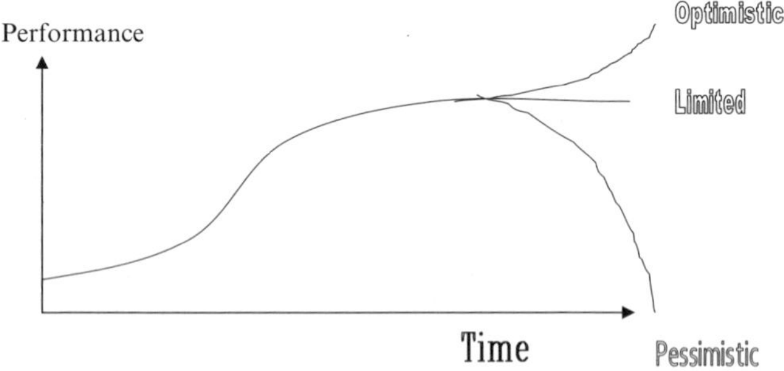

Fig. 2.13.   Dynamics of change from growth to development.

lags behind, often years behind. Without sufficiently sophisticated software, there are limits to the usefulness and popularity of computers. Faced with this limit, hardware producers push to make even faster, better, and cheaper machines.

'Reformers creating distance': School administrators and teachers in a community develop an innovative 'restructuring' education reform effort. However, as the number of restructured schools goes up, the increased community awareness generates a backlash from parents and other community members who don't want innovation and reform. This is aggravated by the fact that the community perceives it had little to say in the reforms. The educators begin to fight harder to get their point across …"

[Senge, 1994]

Such revolutionary long-term ***development processes*** are especially interesting for simulation via business games because they include strategic uncertainty of technological or behavioral changes. Long before one technology reaches its limits, a new generation of technology is usually discovered starting the next S-cycle all over again. Some technologies proved to follow this model with amazing conformity. The business games development trend is also cyclical. Big changes are inevitable, but not so regular as we have seen in the life of the game *Monopoly*. Businesses also show the substitution of one of their generations with the other, new organizational structure. The changes in consumer behavior typically follow long-term model of development. A model of long-term development as integration of several consecutive life cycles was presented in Fig. 1.2 for the *Monopoly* game. It includes business cycles as a result of the interaction between different resources (inventory, production and labor) explained by the SD model:

"The persistence of business cycles despite the complete transformation of every aspect of the global economy testifies to the enduring and fundamental character of the structure underlying the cycle. Though many of the products and technologies used today would be unrecognizable to Adam Smith, manufacturing firms still maintain inventories and still require labor. It still takes time to alter production, acquire materials, and buy new equipment. It still takes time to hire and train workers. An unanticipated increase in demand still causes a drop in inventory, and the only way to rebuild it is to boost production above shipments. Boosting production still require more resources, including labor. Most of the changes in

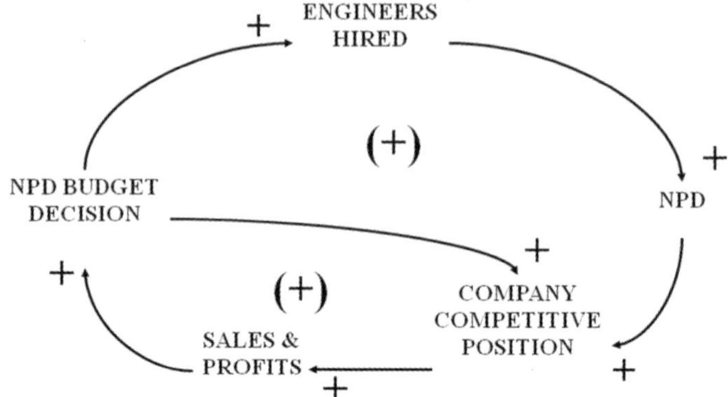

Fig. 2.14.   Feedback system loops for the *NewProDev* game.

technology, market structure, products, and so on over the past 200 years, despite their undoubtful impact on our lives, can be well represented in the model by modest changes in parameters."

[Sterman, 2000]

These models explain the behavior of an economic system by its structure including many feedback loops and in using different material and informational delays between variables. The use of these models for business game design will be presented in the second part of this book.

The basic element of SD is the feedback loop. Two feedback loops we are using in the *NewProDev* game are presented in Fig. 2.14.

The direction of the arrow in a loop indicates which variable exercises influence over the other. It may be a precedence in time or an essential cause of changing one as a result of changing the other variable. The (+) sign near the arrow head tells you that the variable at the tail changes in the same direction as the variable at the head of the arrow. The (−) sign near the arrow head tells us that the variable at the tail of the arrow changes in the opposite direction to the variable at the head. Some variables are interdependent, this is indicated by two opposite arrows.

The feedback loops show interdependent variables: budget increases with increasing profits which depends itself on an increasing company position. This type of a puzzle as "chicken and egg relationship" may be resolved by an SD simulation. The described loop may represent accelerating spiral growth if all its variables are positively connected (virtuous cycle).

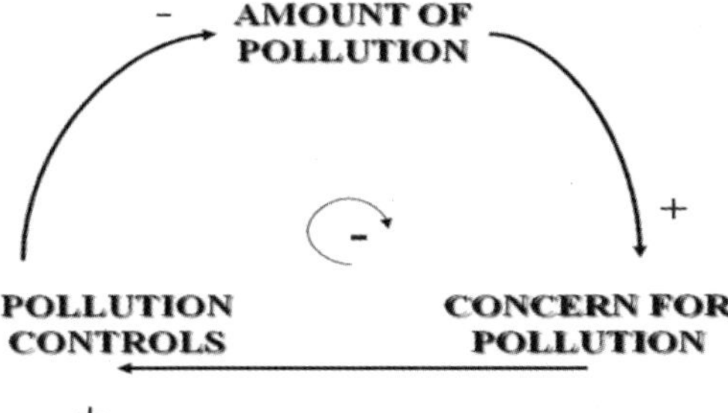

Fig. 2.15.   Balancing feedback loop of an environmental system.

Alternatively, a downward spiral if there is an even number of negative connections (vicious cycle). These processes are representing the reinforcing loop marked in the middle by $(+)$. If a loop contains an odd number of negative arrows, it is the balanced loop, denoted by $(-)$. Such a system will eventually comes to the equilibrium or to the limit. Both loops in Fig. 2.14 are positive, reinforcing process of new products development. An example of a balanced loop is presented in Fig. 2.15.

The causal loop diagram of this type explains the interaction of a physical variable (amount of pollution) with managerial interference (pollution controls) and psychological perception (concern for pollution). This is a balanced loop defined by the result of multiplication along the chain of arrows: $(+)^*(-)^*(+) = (-)$. The resulting dynamics of two basic types of system loops are presented in Fig. 2.16.

Larger and more complex feedback loops represent ever more complicated dynamics. In the real technological, environmental and economic systems it is difficult to introduce hardly predictable human behavior. This behavior can be only effectively demonstrated in a business game by players' decisions. The tool of such representation is called Decision Trees (DT). We will review the possibilities of the introduction of both SD and DT to the business game simulation in the next Secs. 2.3 and 2.4.

The other essential capability of SD is the ability to handle delays in time in the reaction of one variable on the change of the other. System Dynamics defines different types of delays: material and informational. Time for transportation is an example of material delays in technological systems. Delays in fulfilment decisions are typical for information processes in economic and social systems.

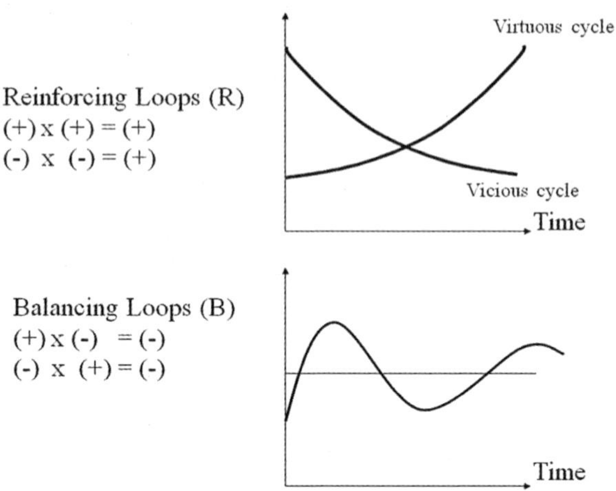

Fig. 2.16.   The behavior over time of two basic system dynamics loops.

Different types of delays are introduced in SD by the order of delay and its average. The delays are classified from the first order or "exponential", which is typical for decision implementation, to the delay of infinite order called "pipeline", which we meet in the purely technical processes. The closest to the management information processing are delays of third to sixth orders which may be called "normal" by their appearance like the Normal statistical distribution. The exponential delay of the first order is demonstrated in Fig. 2.17 representing the immediate reaction of output on input signal with decelerating speed as output comes closer to the limit.

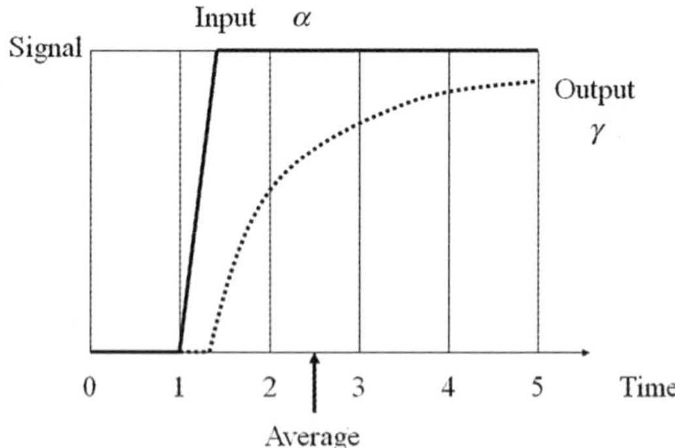

Fig. 2.17.   First order (exponential) delay.

The chart shows a typical example of reaction of a subordinate on instruction given by the boss. The input is the instruction time α (solid line rising from 0 at the moment 1 to the full signal 0.5 hours later). The output γ (dotted line) is the activity of subordinate who starts acting immediately as soon as the input signal is received. The meeting takes about 0.5 hours during which the boss explains his decision. The average time for this job is two hours, and in the first half an hour output reaches 50% of the required level. But then speed of output experiences exponential slowdown, asymptotically narrowing the gap with the result. This reflects the usual immediate jump to the work that eventually is changed to the relaxation after seeing positive results of the first effort. In the *NewProDev* business game we make a distinction between the relatively uncertain time of delaying the preliminary product/project/system designing and predetermined schedules of management and executive decisions.

Third order delay as a "normal" represents slow start of the job, then accelerating performing pace. The 50% of the target is achieved in the first hour and still keeps growing fast, unlike the exponential case. So the whole job is completed within a reasonable time of little more than the expected two hours (Fig. 2.18).

The ultimate type of a delay called "pipeline" of infinitely large order works as a fast jump to the output level after exactly predictable time of two hours. But it consists of 1.5 hours of preparation plus 0.5 hours of the job itself. This type of delay is typical for technological processes where we can know the exact time required for completion of some process. For

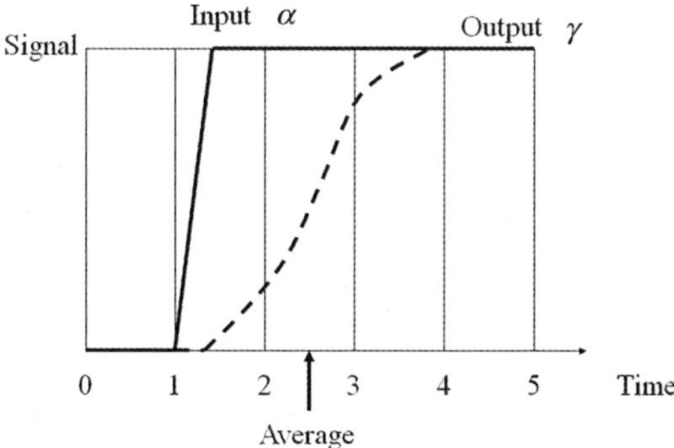

Fig. 2.18.   Third order delay in output.

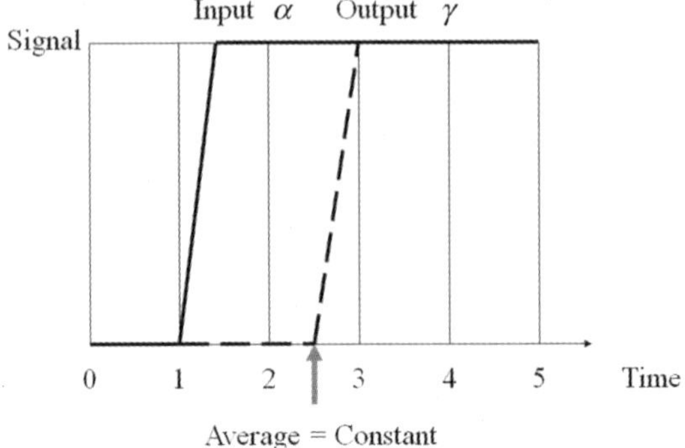

Fig. 2.19.   Pipeline delay of output.

example, transportation of some component from a warehouse to the repair shop takes 1.5 hours and installation of it on the machine takes another 0.5 hour. Illustration of this case for the same average delay is presented in Fig. 2.19.

The three types of delays presented above are essential features of the systems defined earlier. The control of technological systems usually deals with high order (pipeline) delays. For example, automatic processing time is predictable and assumed constant. Management in economic systems is likely to deal with third to sixth order (normal) delays like a reaction of an operator to the order to change of the production line for the other product. And governance in social System of Systems usually meets quick response on their bosses' decisions by the majority of subordinates, but with the much longer extended reaction of smaller groups of laggards. This is reflected by the exponential delay of the first order.

2.4.   DECISION TREES

Decision trees are the basic models quantifying and visualizing processes and the results of management reasoning. A tree consists of branches connecting **decision** nodes (squares), their possible consequences represented by the **event** nodes (circles) and final results by the **terminal** nodes (triangles). The sequence of decisions is conditional on the events, as shown in Fig. 2.20.

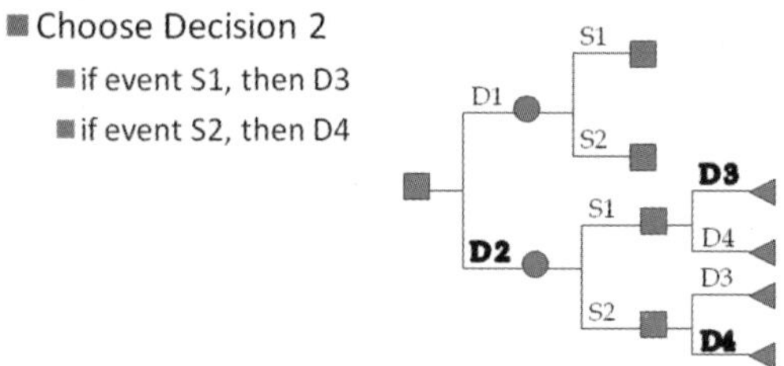

Fig. 2.20.   Main elements of a decision tree.

Decision nodes are quantified by their costs and event nodes are accompanied by their probabilities. Terminal nodes represent final payoffs of the full chains of decisions and events.

> "The decision tree "grows" from left to the right by alternating decisions and events. This model may be just structural representing business or management logic in the case of strategic uncertainty. Then this model is similar to the graph in the theory of games used for presenting steps in strategies exploration. In the case if we may estimate probabilities of different events, players deal with statistical uncertainty."
>
> [Evans, 2003]

The example in Fig. 2.20 represents a multistage decision process when each decision node gives a choice between two options. Number of events may be one or more within reasonable quantity. In the case when a decision may have several consequences (different events), the probability of each should be evaluated. These probabilities drop from one for unavoidable event down to fractions for each of several events, summing up to one for all of them. After estimating probabilities of different events, we can calculate expected payoffs as criteria of decision. Calculations of expected values go from the top of the tree, from the terminal payoffs multiplied by their probabilities. Then we keep calculation of expected payoffs going to the left considering the previous levels of the tree down to the root. The largest of expected payoffs defines the chosen decision at each decision point.

A prototype of the decision tree we used from the textbook example [Evans, 2003] for the *NewProDev* game is presented by Fig. 2.21.

Building of a tree begins from the left from the first decision node, in this case as a choice between preparing a proposal for the new product design

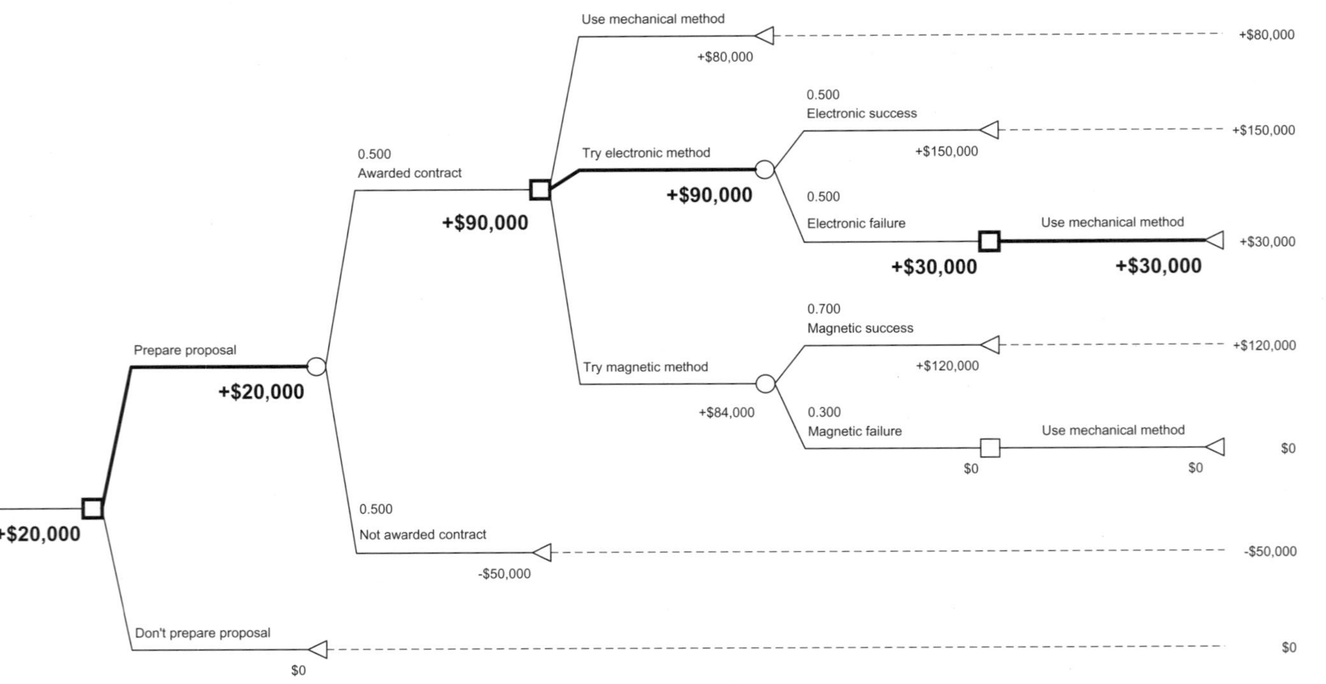

Fig. 2.21.   Decision tree model for *NewProDev* game.

or not preparing it. Every decision node has at least two branches, one of them may be a decision of "doing nothing" with a zero terminal payoff. (In a real business doing nothing usually has negative consequences measured by an opportunity cost.) Number of possible events may be from one for unavoidable consequence, and two or more in the situation of uncertainty. Preparing the contract is followed by two possible events: contract either awarded or not awarded. The uncertainty of this situation is the highest possible: 50:50 chances of each event. In this case we have no prior experience in competing proposals. The outcome of this decision may be modeled by flipping a coin representing equal probabilities of both events. If we are lucky in the awarding of the contract, we are getting $250,000 grant, but in the case of failing we are left with the loss of $50,000 which we had spent on proposal preparation. Then the terminal payoff becomes negative ($-$50,000 loss).

After getting the contract we should decide which technology (mechanical, electronic or magnetic) we choose. That is represented by three branches from the next decision node. Mechanical method is well known, but expensive, and definitely will be successful. It is visualized by the upper branch of the tree terminating in payoff of $80,000, that equals to:

$$\{\$250,000 \text{ (grant)} - \$50,000 \text{ (proposal)}$$

$$- \$120,000 \text{ (cost of mechanical project)} = \$80,000\}.$$

The second, electronic method is presented in the next two branches of the tree. It is new, cheap ($50,000), but with uncertain (50:50) outcome of success. And the third, magnetic method is more reliable (70% of success), but is also expensive ($80,000). In both cases of failure by electronic or magnetic methods we have the opportunity to finish the project by the reliable mechanical method with additional cost of $120,000. In a classic decision theory we are choosing the path bringing the expected payoff of $20,000 which is better than 0 (nothing) for decision not submitting proposal. The preferable chain of decisions and events is indicated by the bold lines in Fig. 2.21.

{Prepare proposal $\to$ Try electronic method

$\to$ Use mechanical method}.

Monte Carlo computer simulations of this case will give more informative answers with probability distributions of payoff for each decision in addition to the expected payoff. Then we may use decision criteria of Return-to-Risk calculated as expected value of payoff divided by its standard deviation.

In the business game *NewProDev* choice between different strategic decisions is influenced by the players' behavior more than by statistical justification. Teams represent interests of specialized departments with different experience and resources for the new product success. Besides, the time pressure is an essential factor for decision making and design itself. It is explicitly defined as delays in informational and material flows which may have a technical or behavioral nature. The most essential result of the game is elevation of players on the steps of knowledge from one to the next round of the game. From the accumulation of knowledge presented by the **repeating** of the traditional mechanical method, players go to the **learning** which is required for the improved magnetic method and to the exploring of the **new paradigm** of electronic method. Analysis of the game includes finding expected delays, learning rates, parameters of utility functions, costs and revenues estimates.

NewProDev game can be played as a field game for an experimental mission. It requires from teams designing prototypes and mock-ups of proposed products and defending their proposals before a competent jury. The game organized at a particular corporation takes two or three days necessary starting on Friday at the plant. On this day formed teams are working on the product concept and production scheduling in their offices. On Saturday teams are making mock-ups of proposed products in a workshop. The same day or on Sunday they present their proposals to the competent jury. Jury should include potential customers and suppliers of components. In the jury of consumer products we include members of the families of participants, so that everybody is happy over the long weekend. Corporate bosses receive fresh ideas and families have fun. The results of the game are presented spectacularly and emotionally by the competing teams.

The educational version of the *NewProDev* game takes less time and material, but also can produce entertaining and tangible results. Teams of students demonstrate creative design prototypes and interesting constructions of product mock-ups when the problem is clearly formulated. A more detailed model of this game will be presented in Chapter 8. The events of acceptance, rejection or rework of the product which are presented in a field game by the expert judgments are replaced by Monte Carlo simulations.

2.5. PROBABILISTIC MODELS AND MONTE CARLO SIMULATION

Random events are the natural components of business games, representing some not entirely explainable influence on the players' consequences on their decisions. Some of these events are external "happenings", absolutely out of the players' control, for example, the emergence of a new competitor in the industry. Such events are introduced to the game by the instructor as Cases or Situational upgrades. Some other events like the appearance of new customers on the market might be possible, but not a guaranteed result of our decision of reducing price. These events may be represented as a roll of a die, picking of a card from the stack of "chances"; or an event generated by the computer. The random numbers are playing leading role in gambling, that is why such a tool has the fancy name "Monte Carlo". For the entertaining games, generating random events is an essential component. But for business games with well-justified model random events form a smaller influence on the situation. So generating random numbers is necessary to present variation of some variables around the expected trend. For example, the level of businesses' financial efficiency is primarily dependent on quality of players' decisions. The fluctuations of business efficiency then is introduced from a matrix of transition probabilities for a random numbers generator.

The *uncertainty* in business games should be generated mainly from the process of the game; and only partly externally by introducing cases and generating random events. Business games do not produce any material results, they just facilitate learning. Rules of game simplify economic regulations, but should be close to the reality. Business games are also *fictitious* in material as a virtual environment: people and objects are represented by tokens; processes are described by charts and results are recorded in tables.

The type of probability distribution which is behind the business game events might be theoretically proven and its parameters should be statistically verified. But still in most games these events are presented as all equal by a choice from the stack of cards. This pattern starts in simplest form of the flipping coin with 50:50 outcome for each of two events in the previous example of the *NewProDev* game. The throw of die provides for each six outcomes probability of 1/6. The mechanical wheel of fortune generates more equally possible events, but may differentiate their probabilities by the sizes of its sectors.

Most technological and ecological activities are thoroughly studied and may be introduced by theoretical models. Fluctuations of product quality and deviations of environmental conditions are likely to be Normally distributed. Productivity variation and differences in educational levels of employees rather follow LogNormal distribution. Time between consecutive communications and transportation events is usually distributed exponentially. Monte Carlo simulation may be applied after verifying theoretical hypotheses with the sample data. When we have no such solid theory behind, we may find out statistical patterns of variation as soon as additional data is collected. Chapter 1 illustrated such a process applied to the study of structural properties of team development. Dynamic characteristics of organizational behavior are still less studied because of difficulties in measurements of teams' development parameters.

In the game *HELLO* we used Supply Chain SIMulation (SCSIM) model to generate events, such as product demand and transit times. They were obtained from corresponding probability distributions. Random variability of events is justified theoretically by the type of the process because of the absence of data for the system which was under design. Therefore statistical properties of some variables were hypothetical, but parameters were realistic. For example, shipping times were presented as the constants plus exponentially distributed delays. The sizes of transport queues were presented by the Poisson distribution. Productivity of the factory was assumed LogNormally distributed and quality of supplies as the Normal distribution. This was done in the only way possible for the design of a new system. The combination of theoretical assumptions about the type of distribution and statistical estimates of their parameters is the most valid

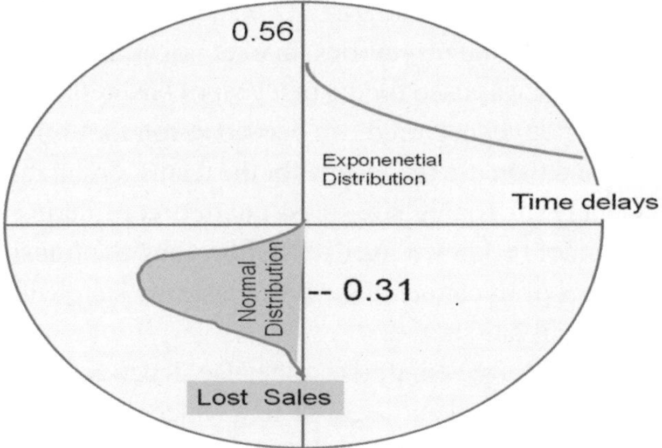

Fig. 2.22.   Combination of two sources of supply variation.

source of random numbers generation. An example of such combination is illustrated by Fig. 2.22.

There are two sources of the variability of supply: quality of supply measured in the percentage of lost sales and accuracy of delivery measured by the delay over scheduled time. The average number of lost sales per day happens to be 0.31 and assumed to be Normally distributed. Average delay in supply was 1.8 days and supposed to represent exponential distribution. So the parameter Λ (lambda) of the Poisson distribution is the inverse to the average delay.

$\Lambda = 1/1.8 = 0.56 -$ probability of zero delays (no one delay for the day).

The parameters of interrelated distributions define the probabilities for the rest of possible delays and lost sales. Assuming the independence of accuracy in supply and lost sales we may generate combinations of both of them by multiplying corresponding probabilities.

There are different approaches to the games simulating existing systems about which we have some information and to the designed system. We have no statistics for the new system and rely on hypothetical or analogous data. Only after the actual system starts functioning may we perform hypothesis tests on the system parameters to see if there are statistically different with our assumptions.

For the beginning of the game *HELLO* we need to formulate several initial values for size of initial inventories, market prices and available investments. SCSIM model was used for the first year of business initialization. If a steady state had not yet occurred, we needed to run the simulation for an additional year, and then use the results for the teams' orientation. The simulation was actually run for eight business quarters considering seasonality of demand. It cannot be known in advance how long the transitional stage will be. The graphs of dynamics show when a steady state with repeatable patterns in the output has started.

The situation with free enterprise zone also depends on some statistically unpredictable political and legal factors which were presented by the introductory cases. Therefore the results were seen as scenarios presented by teams in the graphs and reports of the simulation of the production flows through the supply channel. The following business results were reported by the teams (see Table 2.6).

Mathematical models of economic processes are either theoretical or statistical because real economics does not allow deliberate experimentation. Business games demonstrate the influence of social, psychological and emotional factors of economic decisions. Games are opening bounds of rational behavior first by introducing elements of utility theory and then by using developments of cognitive psychology and lately by meeting environmental concerns. The approach of *satisficing* decisions offered by Herbert Simon [Simon, 1955] is valuable as most instrumental for business games. The latest developments in this direction concentrated in studies of making decisions under uncertainty related to the lack of information in a limited time.

Theoretical behavioral economics now is supported by the experimentation available for creative professors on their students. Some of them are developing *Neuroeconomics* going in depth of human brain using MRI scanning in different situations [Siegfried, 2006]. The case studies approach provides information on *heuristic* tools of decision making. The stochastic component of game model includes prefabricated external events introduction at random like Community Chest cards in the *Monopoly* or regular updating of stock market situation as in the *Glo-Bus* game. Timing and extent of their impact may be determined by mechanical random events generators like dice or by roulette wheel. They represent artificial uniform

Table 2.6. Business results reported by the teams in *HELLO* game.

Results	Parameters of model	Random variables	Decision variables
Revenue	Elasticity of demand	Retailer selling price	Finished production and inventory
Cost of purchased goods	Fixed costs	Supplier selling price	Inventory of components
Gross margin	Interest rates		Reporting quarterly orders
Production cost	Marginal productivity	Variable cost	Batches of production runs
Transportation costs	Transportation rates and times	Travel accidents	Shipping volume
Sales order handling cost	The cost for a sales orders handling	Lost sales	Unit orders
Order-processing cost	The cost for a facility rent	Delayed orders	Purchase orders placed
Inventory cost	The size of warehouses	Lost and spoiled inventory	
Back-order cost	Penalty rates	Litigation cases	
Total cost	The sum of the fixed and variable costs		
Net profit contribution	Taxation rates		

or triangular distribution with limited list of discrete events. For business games we prefer a computer generator with specified probabilities distribution justified by statistical evidence. For example, supply delays in the game *HELLO* were generated by exponential distribution; fluctuations of inflation rates in the *Career* game are presented by the Weibull distribution.

Uncertainties of different kinds may make game players creative or frustrated. Videogames designers noticed that Americans are more excited by games of chance than by strategic challenges [Bates, 2001]. Random events better be theoretically proven or statistically verified to support the allocation of resources in the game. External sources of uncertainty like case introductions disturb and sometimes disrupt the learning process. The best learning experience during business games is obtained by internal process of decreasing uncertainty from mistakes, miscommunications and conflicts.

Essential features of a game are proportions between strategic and statistical uncertainties, and between externally and internally generated events. External strategic uncertainty is presented by the introduction of situational intrusions. Their timing may be regular or random itself. In *Monopoly* game they are presented by the "Community Chest" and the "Chance" stacks of cards. Players experience double randomness: first from the outcome of throwing dice, and if they land on a question cell, the second is about the event from the deck of cards. Internal sources of strategic uncertainty arise from insufficient knowledge of structure and rules of the game, about motivation and decisions of the other participants. External statistical uncertainty might be also represented by a random allocation of resources between roles or over time. When games start with equal assets for each player, the uncertainty is generated by the throw of dice allowing participants to advance around the board. Card games generate statistical uncertainty by random distribution of cards between players. Videogames generate random events and numbers as predefined by the designer, but not necessarily announced to players' probabilities. In the flow of the game players may accumulate the data converting strategic uncertainty into statistical knowledge.

The uncertain phenomena are supposed to be explained to players before or in the course of the game. Evaluation of individual behavior and results of team participation should not depend much on unexplainable events. Business games should be built on explicit models and explained probabilities instead of blind *risk* of unfortunate event or pure *luck* generated by the dice, cards or computer.

> "One of the trickiest aspects of game design is achieving just the right balance of skill and luck. In some instances, though, a recognition of the role luck plays is healthy. It can keep a trailing team from becoming demoralized and keep a winning team from resting on its laurels"
>
> [Orbanes, 2002].

The examples of processes generating random events during a business game are presented in Table 2.7.

Table 2.7.   Examples of random events generation.

Business process	Type of model	Examples
Availability of resources	Combinatorial model	Allocation of cash funds
Quality of product	Normal distribution	Interruption of supply
Quality of service	Binomial distribution	Lost customers
Fluctuations of production	LogNormal distribution	Productivity of an operator
Trends in supply and demand	Markov chain matrix	Seasonality fluctuations
Delays in product development	Exponential distribution	Returns for changing project
Customer's expectations	Poisson distribution	Number of defects
Market prices fluctuations.	Weibull distribution	Inverse variable generator

The introduction of statistical uncertainty in a game should be done gradually and according to the level of players' education. Otherwise some of them might be overwhelmed by the stream of random events and start to play blindly. In games simulating production or service control it is natural to include variation in the description of technological processes. We used in *Shell Game* and *Cellulose Aircraft, Inc.* introductory exercises with statistical analysis of production runs results. They are useful for initial involvement in the game and for visualizing the sources of uncertainty. In the short games like the *Simkin's Drill* and *Out of Control* some random functions are prefabricated for the saving of time for the optimization of management decisions.

2.6. OPTIMIZATION MODELS

Three types of decisions which were outlined before, would be routine, innovative and inventive. Routine decisions are based on players' experience, innovative decisions are supported by optimization models, and inventive, radical proposals — by individual creativity and collective brainstorming. Routine decisions are modeled by decision trees. Methods of facilitation creativity will be presented in Chapter 7. Optimization models for justification of innovative decisions are popular in economic literature as more mathematically elegant. The concept of optimization is based on assumptions of clear definition of players' goals and full knowledge about their resources. But because most decisions are made in limited time and on incomplete information, optimization provides just the first version of decision which should be clarified with the help of experience and creativity.

Fundamentals of ***optimization*** models originated from Russian economist Leonid Kantorovich [Kantorovich, 1939] and Dutch mathematician Tjialling Koopmans [Koopmans, 1971], who were awarded for that with Nobel Prizes in Economics in 1975. Kantorovich first applied microeconomic models for the business enterprise level and developed the duality principle. These models are mainly applicable for the business games and management simulations of medium-term horizon. Computers provided optimization of economic models and managerial decisions with quick and precise solutions. But business reality is far from basic assumptions of complete and accurate information. There are also multitudes of criteria and motivations which mathematical models cannot reflect. Business games are not so formal in decision rules and more attractive than optimization algebra and computational numbers crunching. The euphoria of optimization was pushed away in the 1980s by the more practical concept of ***satisficing*** proposed by Herbert Simon [Simon, 1955] who was awarded the Nobel Prize in 1978. Since then a rational combination of optimization and satisficing concepts was established. Optimization became a leading tool for control and management functions on the business enterprise level while satisficing principle — for executive decisions on corporate level and for the governance in Systems of Systems.

An optimal decision in a business game should be defined by the clear criteria of *maximization* of some outputs with limited inputs or *minimization* of inputs for getting specified outputs. These models are based on the concept of ***duality*** as the requirement of presentation in the model of both sides of the business situation. For example, in business game *ReActOr* we represent both sides of the problem of minimizing costs of production for the plant and providing maximum revenue from the sales. A problem which is primal for production management defines the dual problem for sales department and vice versa. Neither of them can exist without the other like two sides of a coin. The correspondence between primal and dual optimization problems is illustrated by Fig. 2.23.

The diagonal of the chart outlines borders between primal and dual problems and indicates that there is no priority between them. The primal is just one which is formulated first, then the dual is also completely defined.

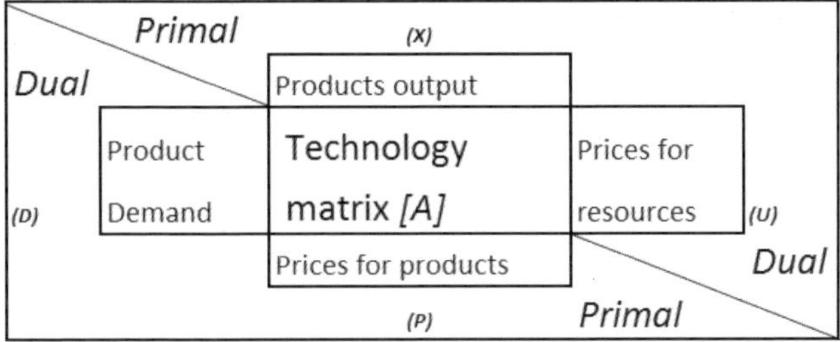

Fig. 2.23. Correspondence between primal and dual optimization problems.

The validity of the optimization model is in the balancing of primal and dual problems. It represents the ideal situation of production completely satisfying demand and revenues covering costs and bringing profit. In the basic linear case for the individual enterprise these conditions are as follows:

<table>
<tr><td align="center">PRIMAL</td><td></td><td align="center">DUAL</td></tr>
<tr><td align="center">Maximum revenue</td><td></td><td align="center">Minimum cost + Profit</td></tr>
<tr><td align="center">$\sum_i p_i * x_i$</td><td align="center">=</td><td align="center">$\sum_j b_j * u_j + d_i * u_i$</td></tr>
<tr><td>Subject to constraint on available resources:</td><td></td><td>Subject to constraint on products demand:</td></tr>
<tr><td align="center">$\sum_i a_{ij} * x_i \le b_j; x_i \ge d_i$</td><td></td><td align="center">$\sum_j a_{ji} * u_j \ge p_i; u_i \le 0$</td></tr>
</table>

Technological matrix [A] consists of elements a_{ij} representing the amount of resource j necessary to produce the unit of product i. Output of each product x_i is expected to be equal to demand for this product d_i. This model might be extended by including the time scale and geographical locations. With addition of time we will include amounts of inventories of products and resources moving from one period to the next. With addition of locations we may consider transportation costs and supply chain networks. These extensions also allow us to add more economic variables such as transaction and opportunity costs, property evaluations and rents, etc.

For the *HELLO* game we used the integration of the optimal management solutions into satisficing decisions for the governance of supply chain. Integrated System of Systems models are combined as the network of production, warehousing, distribution, transportation and other systems. Every participant of the network considers sub-optimization of its results for cooperation with the players representing other businesses.

Business games require a combination of variety of models for simulation of different systems. We will start in the next chapter with overview of basic models of field and board games. The full range of system engineering design of the games on new product development will be presented in Part 2 of this book.

FIELD AND BOARD BUSINESS GAMES

Card version of *Sim City* game

3.1. FIELD GAMES

The most realistic is the game organized around a physical model of the system like in a sports stadium. Children like to play around the sand castle on the beach. Generals are playing war games in situation rooms around the sandboxes or surrounded by the maps as virtual fields. Politicians are playing their games around globes. Industrial executives are playing their outward bound games in the Leadership Trust in the really open fields. Game starts when teams and/or players are assigned to different roles on the positions around the field and make decisions in command of resources symbolized by figurines moving in the field. The difference for business games is that the goal of physically destroying the enemy is substituted with economic competition. Unlike political or war games, business games belong either to the Zero-Sum (losses balanced with gains) or to the Win-Win (everybody wins) types of games. In the first case of the *Monopoly* game properties of bankrupt players go to the winner; in the second case of the *Capstone* game every team has an opportunity of progress.

Field games which are organized in a real physical environment or around a sandbox are the most spectacular, but expensive kind of business games. Military institutions, governmental agencies and big corporations can afford such a luxury for training their employees. The most natural are the games organized around a physically downscaled model of the system. Training stands called *Flight Simulators* are essential for preparation and testing operators of complicated equipment in many industries. Games designed originally as work stations for training of professionals are used now for *arcade games* based on playstations. They are placed in areas of public concentration (fast food, shopping malls, stadiums, recreational and entertainment facilities). They can hardly simulate any kind of economic activities, but if connected by a communication network, may support the field business game.

One of the liquor bars on Wall street in New York demonstrates experimenting of interdependence of the customer's demand and price. It constantly adjusts prices on drinks according to the balance of demand and supply. Corrected prices are demonstrated on the electronic tableau that visually provides feedback to the customers. Such a way of regulating a closed market by our definition represents the field business game.

Most field games are organized around virtual models like maps or screens for projecting realistic images of the playing field and resources of the game. The most advanced among them are entertainment *video games.* The presentation of a field may be from the flat 2D simplified map like in *Capitalism* up to colorful animated 3D realistic images of *Roller Coaster* games.

> "Many simulation games attempt to model the real world — and players often rely on real-world common sense when playing them. But all games represent some abstraction and simplification of the real world. How real do you want your game world to be? In *The Getaway*, 40 square kilometers of London were re-created using 20,000 digital photographs — incorporating everything from tourist hot spots to back alleys to overcast skies. All of these provide an instantly recognizable simulation of everyday life in their respective cities."
>
> [Novak, 2008]

Real life-scaled field game accommodates participants inside the physical model of the business environment. Televised reality shows such as the *Apprentice* may be also classified as field business games. Their participants combine in-class introductions to the business problems with field exercises in entrepreneurship in real street market conditions. These games have strict rules and high motivation of participants to business projects with following analysis and team restructuring [Burnett, 2004]. These games are different from console or videogames for "coach" individuals who will be described in the next chapter.

Field games may be played in a real field stadium such as outward bound *Leadership in Management* game that performed with the industrial executives in Leadership Trust (Ross-on-Wye, England). There an open-air playing field models main components of a chemical factory producing colored waters: warehouses for the raw materials and finished products, production lines, buffer product inventories, technological and office equipment. Competing teams of players should organize mixing water with coloring pigments according to the product standards for satisfying simulated demand. Teams of six players should observe technology, safety rules of

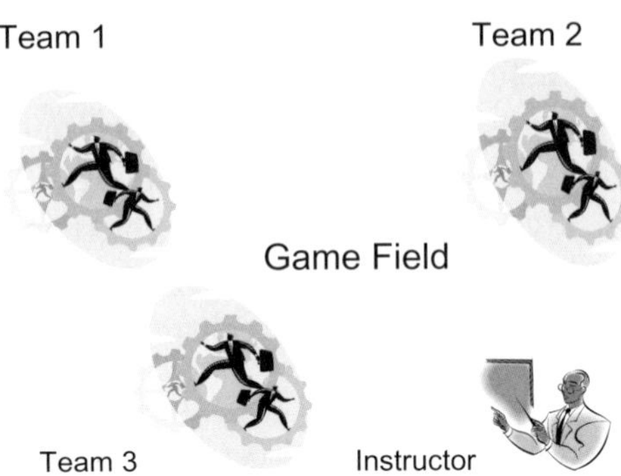

Fig. 3.1.   Architecture of a life-scaled field game.

production and distribution and fill in management documentation. Players
wear safety gear, carry around the factory heavy barrels of water and packages of pigment, fill orders, follow technical documentation and keep cost
records. Quality and quantity of products are clearly visible for the comparison with required colors and quotas. Rejected product literally goes to
the drain with corresponding economic consequences. Players are punished
by the instructors for breaking the production and safety rules. The criteria
of success is objectively measured by the total profit per day of the game.
This game combines intense physical work with management decisions and
accounting procedures. The outcomes include reinforcing personal leadership style, improved skills in communications, observing and reviewing the
jobs. During the game, participants need defining and solving problems on
established objectives by planning, organizing and implementing effective
decisions. Teams are supposed to demonstrate cooperation on the shared
resources, resolve conflicts within a team and establish effective working
relationships.

Most of the field games are organized indoors. Figure 3.1 represents
three teams inside of an industrial playing field symbolized by the gears.

Field games may be organized indoors around sandbox or virtual,
schematic playing fields. These fields may be more or less realistic: maps,
networks, or physical models called "sandboxes" as they were originated
in war games. Allocation of a team for such a game is presented in Fig. 3.2.

A sandbox is situated in the center of a game room and teams of players
are working around the field. Players may have additional satellite tables

Fig. 3.2.   Allocation of field game participants around the sandbox.

as the workstations for meetings, for keeping their documentation and computers. The playing field reproduces the system in a scaled physical model or as a detailed chart for demonstrating situations. Projector screens, posters on walls and easels may complement the playing field with permanent or changing information. Each team's workstation should have a view of the sandbox to observe the current situation. The locations of materials, information and places for discussion of decisions may be in different rooms. Field games are usually served by several instructors equipped with computers connected to the projectors and networked with the players' workstations. Sandboxes are specific to the type of business game: scale physical models of production processes and flowcharts for technological applications; organizational charts and decision trees for management simulations; market structures for economic systems; landscapes or maps for environmental systems and the flowcharts and visual images for social systems. Such large-scale games are usually organized for the corporate executives with a presence of the jury including consultants, academics, industrial and government officials.

Field games are played in rounds reproducing weeks, months or years of business activity. These games became possible in the Soviet Union in the 1980s for the economic restructuring during *perestroika* policy introduced by President Gorbachev. We used as the prototype the *Red Weaver* business game of the 1930s, but with the opposite mission: instead of restructuring industrial plants to the military production as before World War II it was conversion of defense industry to consumer goods and services on open market principles [Bazilevich, 1993].

Virtual fields of a game now may accommodate the images of players, their ***avatars***. It may be a figurine representation of the players, their portraits, or three-dimensional animated alter egos. Avatars on Internet forums serve the purpose of representing users and their actions, personalizing their contributions to the forum, and reflecting their beliefs, interests or social status. Some forums allow the user to upload an avatar image that may have been designed by the user or acquired from elsewhere. The players may select an avatar from a preset list or create their own cartoon or photographic images. The *Cybertown* Internet chat first introduced in 1995 three-dimensional avatars. It is a subscription based, family friendly, online community living in a virtual ghost town. Users are able to have jobs within the community, thus gaining virtual money which may be used for buying or renting houses and for buying goods. Videogame *City of Heroes* offers avatar creation process, allowing players to construct anything from traditional superheroes to aliens, medieval knights, monsters, robots, and many more.

The avatars became a useful participants of the new trend of ***alternate reality games (ARGs)***. ARG simulates and stimulates fulfillment by the players some useful actions in the real world. The *Chore Wars* game motivates players to keep the house or office clean and tidy by rewarding their avatars:

> "The more chores you finish, the more experience points and virtual gold you earn, and the faster you level up your avatar's powers. But *Chore Wars* isn't just about tracking your avatar development; it's also about earning real rewards. The game's instructions encourage households to invent creative ways to redeem the virtual gold in real life. You could exchange the gold for allowances if you are playing with your kids, or for rounds of drinks for roommates, or coffee runs for workmates, for example. My husband and I share a single car, so we use our gold pieces to bid on what music to play in the car whenever we're driving somewhere together."
>
> [McGonigal, 2011]

The *Nike+* ARG encourages players to accumulate points for physical exercises, and the *Lost Joules* game rewards energy-saving behavior. In the game *Extraordinaries* players enthusiastically search for opportunities to carryout heroic missions for their community. This may be the locating of the nearest defibrillator for a person in cardiac arrest or repair shop for a broken car. ARGs are gathering virtual communities from the family and friends up to the global multiplayer communities fighting hunger, diseases and illiteracy.

We used avatar images for the players in the *Career* game which is an active social system simulation in a virtual field [Bazilevich, 1982]. The game is organized inside the classroom with tables and/or wall posters and computer screens representing Education, Work, Family and Recreation areas of a person's life. Each network diagram presents available states and allowed transitions between them. Arrows connecting states are provided with gates or switches describing conditions of transition. If person wants to get a certain job, education is required (gate) or that person is expected to be of appropriate age (probability). The personification of avatar is real, but may be fictitious if the player does not want to share with the other players intimate details of one's biography or plans for the future.

The *Career* Game might be played as an explanatory forecasting model for a group of players or exploratory tool for an individual. Every participant of this game plays two roles: *expert* as a member of one of the teams (Education, Work, Family, or Recreation) and the *avatar* exploring its own available paths of life. The model of this game is the Markov chain of states represented by the matrix of transition probabilities. It is visualized by the graph of possible transitions network.

The visualization of the system's structure or of processes in the system organizes the game in the most efficient way. Workstations or side tables are needed for players, teams and game organizers to keep documents, calculators and computers. Structure of allocation of the teams in a game room is presented in Fig. 3.3.

Arrows in Fig. 3.3 present recommended to a player routes between teams following precedence or prevailing influence of some areas on the others. Obviously, all of them are interdependent, but some of them have temporal, logical or social prevalence. The choice of route between teams depends on personal plans and is up to the choice of each player, although sometimes it occasionally depends on the availability of the next team at the moment when a player leaves the preceding team, possible diversion

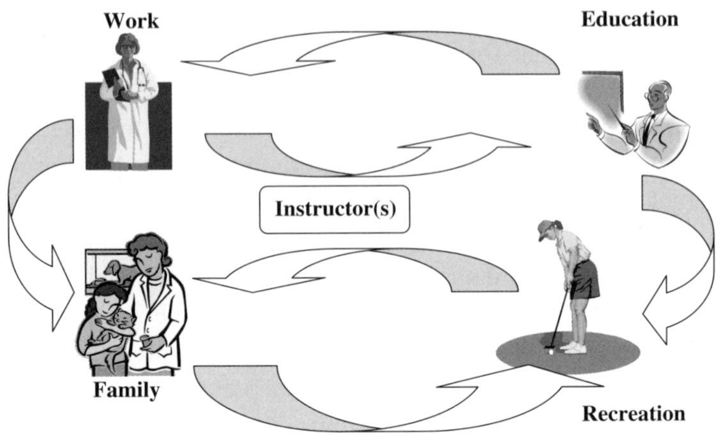

Fig. 3.3.   Interconnections between areas of activity in the *Career* game.

like in real life. For example, a certain level of education opens different opportunities for work and entertainment, so players are recommended to visit "Education" team before going to "Work" and "Recreation" teams. But individual stories may justify the opposite way between work and education if a present employer sponsors a player's education. Some players decide to look first for a job while the others begin with establishing social contacts. Family and Recreation areas are definitely interdependent, so the chart represents it by two counter flow arrows allowing to player visit appropriate teams in an any order. Practically during the game in this case players go to the team which is free to serve them. This flexibility of this game procedure allowed us to make experimentation for the statistical analysis which was presented in Chapters 1 and 2.

The model of this game as a network of states represents several lines of progress inside each activities' area with indication of conditional, unconditional and random transitions between states. For example, transition from the state of single to the married person depends unconditionally on age, while the requirement of meeting the bride is conditionally dependent on religion, age, location and much more. After a while the setting of a separate housing becomes possible depending on the family income. A model of each area of activity is displayed as a network diagram at the work station of the appropriate team. Team members may expand the network

Area of Activity: RECREATION

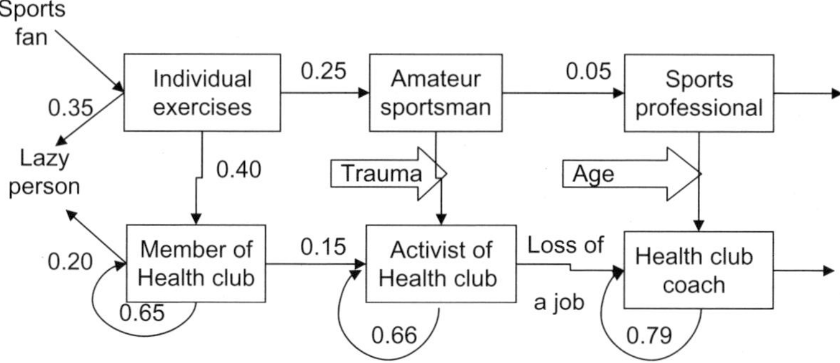

Fig. 3.4.   Fragment of RECREATION area diagram for *Career* game.

according to the additional research, from observed in the game transitions or by collecting data in the area of activity. Games in a college may be better prepared on information from the admissions and alumni offices, fraternities and sororities. Most such information we collected during the games in our off-campus graduate classes in corporate training centers. Students were requested to record their experiences of actual transitions in the real life before the start of the game. Transition chart displays four to six lines of activities in each area with six to eight states progressing on each line. Expert teams may expand diagrams with the post-its on the poster or with new nodes and arrows on the computer charts. The fragment of such diagram is shown in Fig. 3.4. Rectangles represent states, arrows show possible transitions, and symbols on arrows formulate conditions or probabilities of transitions.

The probabilities of transitions during one year should be calculated before the game. They should be specific and based on the college retention rates and alumni statistics. For the game with undergraduates we usually make it prepared as a course research project. The game may be organized with participation of graduate students or professionals of the same industry. There are so many individual circumstances in a player's life, therefore each appropriate team is supposed to use their expertise besides following the model of the game.

The most popular and spectacular field games belong to the *Sims* series beginning with the *SimCity* game. Originally it was a 3D sandbox computer toy, but it has become a business game for a large community of competitive players. The majority of *SimCity* players are male students in the 14–25 age group. Now other demographic groups, especially girls and women are having the choice from many *Manias* about fashions, recreation and family life. We used to ask students in the beginning of management and economic courses to bring to the class their favorite card and board games, or demonstrate videogames they like.

The Sims game gives the best examples of virtual 3D areas of life, with realistic sound effects and animation. The *Sim City* is based on architectural and engineering models that allows to organize a variety of competitive, cooperative or just introductory business games. Among *Sims* there are several games with industrial contents:

> "*SimRefinery* is a simulation of the refinery operation, for orienting people in the company as to how a refinery works. It wasn't so much for the engineers as it was for the accountants and managers who walked through this refinery every day and didn't know what these pipes were carrying."
>
> [Wright, 2010]

The distinctions between different types of games become negligible. The field games are becoming digital, and some videogames may be offered in card and board versions. The same *Sims*, for example, are now offered as card games around the board.

3.2. CARDS AND BOARD GAMES

Card and Board games are played around the table or on the computer screen as a building up or simulation of the abstract or real system. Card games are mainly built as procedures of collecting or eliminating cards by exchange between players using an empty table just for the display of cards. Board games usually also include display of cards as part of the game, but require cards to form required structures. In business games cards are used to represent some resources, events, characters or processes available to players. When a card is opened, a new chance or just additional information about the game situation is revealed for one or for all players. Cards represent this information by text, charts and pictures. A board of business game besides the cards, may accommodate different tokens and other items that serve as symbols of some items, persons or processes. Card and board games are strictly regulated by the rules defining distribution, placing and exchange of cards; team structure and moves allowed or required to form by the players; rewards and punishments for breaking the rules. Number of players in teams is usually small (two, maximum eight, typically four). The time of one game may vary from a few minutes to hours or in some games is indefinite.

Many games designed originally in field or electronic format now are offered in as a card or board games. *Sim City,* for example, as the card game is illustrated on the cover page of this chapter.

There are hundreds of recreational and gambling cards and board games. We will not discuss here so-called "salon" games or tarot cards used for fortune telling. Business board games are able to simulate operations, growth and development of technological, environmental, economic or social systems. The players can represent the similar roles in a competitive game or play different roles in a cooperative game. They may play individually or in small teams according to the organizational chart of a business. The game provides visualizing of a structure or process by a board used for assignment of roles, for allocation of resources and for tracking progress of the game with the cards and tokens. The table for the board should be large enough to place the cards and accommodate players' documents and laptops. Otherwise the classroom needs satellite tables for individual players or teams.

A standard class of 20–30 students is usually split in 3–4 teams of 5–8 players each for the short board game or in 2–3 teams for the medium size game. Recommended allocation of three teams in the classroom to play competitive board game is shown in Fig. 3.5.

The basic information consists of naming segments of simulated system or roles of players who are facing each other across the board. For example, every team in *Words-in-Sentences* game may have fixed or rotating operational and management responsibilities. Structure of board for the assigned roles of Manager, Quality controllers, Word producers and Sentences assemblers, is presented in Fig. 3.6.

This game is a valuable exercise for the "warming-up" class, especially when students of different specialties meet together for the first time.

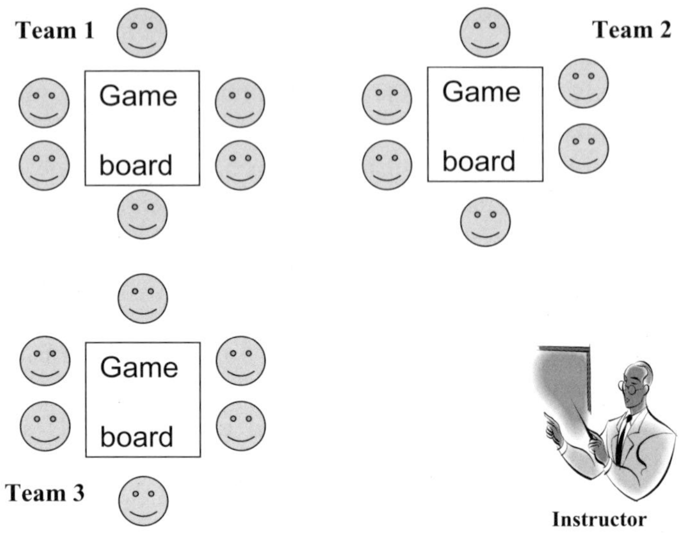

Fig. 3.5.   Allocation of players for the card or board game in a classroom.

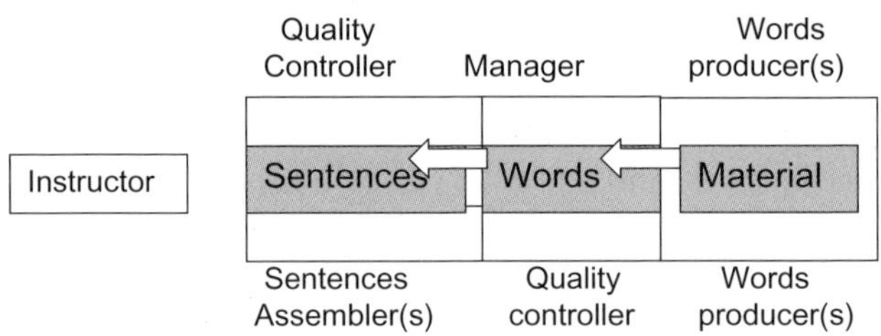

Fig. 3.6.   Allocation of players around the board in a team of *Words-in-Sentences* game.

During the standard class time (45–75 minutes) they may play 4–7 cycles of the game giving everyone the opportunity to test their leadership ability by rotating roles around the board. Each team starts with the same initial resources and follows the same procedure (see Fig. 3.7 representing flowchart of the game).

Game boards may represent information with different levels of detail: as a minimum defining structural allocation of the roles and up to procedural flowcharts and artifacts symbolizing the game situation. Specifics of a board are different for competitive, cooperative or integrative games. Game starts with the spliting of a class in teams and with assigning players to different

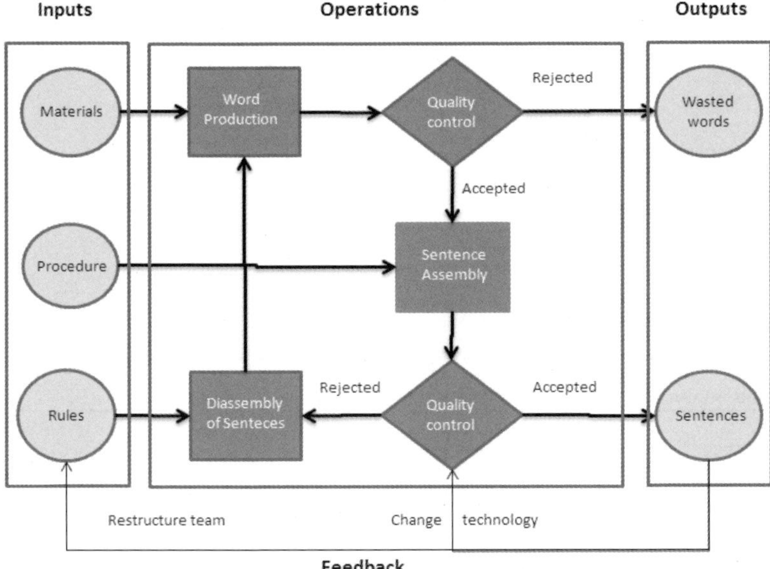

Fig. 3.7.   Flowchart of *Words-in-Sentences* game.

roles within the competing teams. The results of the round of the game are recorded in a team protocol containing the name of the team (preferably funny), names of players (real) occupying certain places around the board, date and number of the game round. The initial information is the word which provides teams with the raw material. The word should be shorter if you limit the time for the round or long enough to generate dozens of words. In this illustration we use the word TECHNOLOGY which is reasonably good for the round 10–15 minutes long (Table 3.1).

The score for the team represents amount of final product minus 1/3 of unused words as a wasted material which could be used for the average 3-words sentence. This game shows advantages of the assembly-line organization of production and job specialization. It also reveals leadership ambitions, management abilities and creativity of players. During the game we may measure learning rate and the cohesion of the team.

The most popular short business game, *Beer Game*, represents the organizational structure of the Supply Chain with roles of Factory, Distributor, Wholesaler and Retailer. Players at one table form a team competing with other teams of the same size. A place occupied by a player at the table

Table 3.1.   *Words-in-sentences* game team protocol.

Team .... *PINK*.	*Players:* *Manager* ...... *Jiby* ....
Date .*08/31*	*Quality controllers* .. *Sam, Issac*. ....
Round . .*1* .	*Sentences assemblers* .... *Andy, Liv*. ....
	Words producers ..... *John, Fred, Kyle* ....

Raw Material: TECHNOLOGY

Unused words	Accepted Sentences
1. then	1. Glen got one note
2. on	2. Con loot Chloe (not accepted)
3. hole	3. Let no hen go
4. net	4. Notch the log
5. not	
6. hot	
...	

Score = {(number of accepted sentences) – 1/3 (number of unused words)} = 3– 6/3 = 1

defines a player's role for the whole game which lasts about an hour. Each cycle of the game represents a week of business activity which includes placing orders for a product, revising inventory and transporting goods down the supply chain. During the class time it is possible to simulate up to 52 weeks of yearly business activity. The board of the game defines roles assignment for four to eight players. One side of the board represents downstream material flow of product from factory to consumer. The initial resources allocation of product inventories is shown on the board by the tokens (black dots on the chart below). The other side of the board represents upstream information flow of orders for neighboring links of the supply chain. Initially supply chain is balanced for the demand of four cases of beer per week reflected in the orders of size 4 all across the chain (Fig. 3.8).

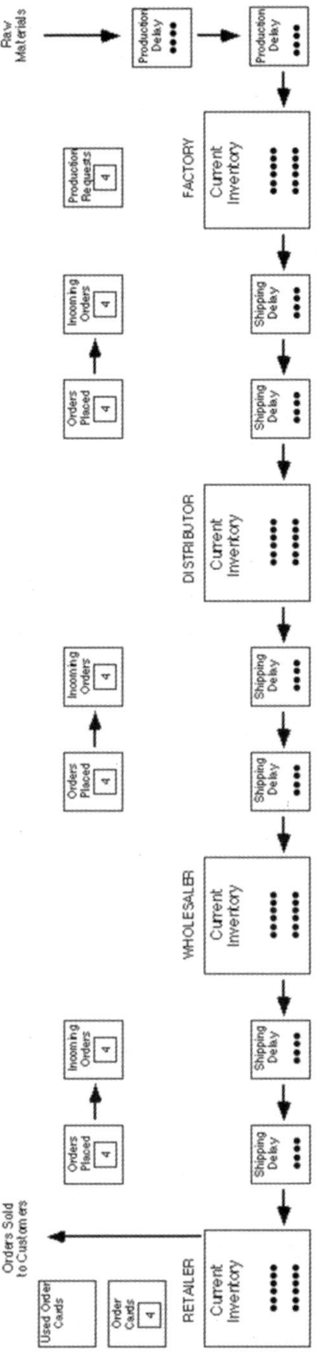

Fig. 3.8.   Starting resources allocation on the board of the *Beer Game*.

Beer Game demonstrates "bullwhip effect" of delays in material and information flows on the performance of different links of supply chain. It is an amplification of production rates and of inventories upstream of supply chain in response to changing demand. In the worst position is the factory which is forced to change drastically production from week to week to support inventories which meet fluctuations of customer demand. Such a serious responsibility ignites tensions between players in each team trying to balance the supply chain better than other teams competing for cost effective strategies.

Integration of learning and fun might be achieved even as part of teenager's culture. We designed board business game "*Obla-di, Obla-da*" by microeconomic interpretation of the Beatles song story. One player, Desmond, who "… runs a barrow in the marketplace" simulates **Industry** role of producing food and jewelry. Another player as his wife Molly who "…is a singer in a band" who simulates providing **Services**. Both of them are simultaneously playing roles of households consuming food and jewelry and providing labor and capital for businesses. The number of players may be increased from two to five including **Retired** Desmond's mother and **Working** Molly's father as well as the local **Banker**.

The model of this game is presented on a sliding transparent charts of demand and supply curves for the goods (Food and Jewelry) and factors of production (Labor and Capital markets). The game board includes simplified erasable tables of balance sheets and income statements. Natural limits of curiosity and patience for kids allows several rounds of the game from a three months to five years, each round requiring 15–20 minutes. It allows them to play this game during a high school lesson. In the Advanced Placement Economics high school class, it is better to play this game in several weekly cycles to give students time to analyze and present results.

Interesting business games for individual households and small businesses are developed by Robert Kiyosaki for the popular "Rich Dad, Poor Dad" seminars.

> "In order to survive financially, and feel secure financially, people need to develop financial survival skills before they enter the real world. If they do not have these skills before entering the real world, the real world has other lessons about money that it wants to teach your child. And today that includes the school system. Not only are young people leaving school

now with credit card debt, many are leaving school with debt from school loans. It is important to teach your child about money management as early as possible. The best way to teach those skills is by playing with your children, for it seems that play is how God of nature intended all young to learn …"

[Kiyosaki, 1990]

Entertaining material for the games is published by Lewitt and Dubner in their unusual economic analysis called "Freakonomics" [2007] and "Superfreakonomics" [2009]. But we did not try yet to develop business games simulating prostitute or terrorist markets.

The choice of a business game should correspond to the horizon of play: Short-term games are more detailed in roles with diversified products and resources. Most business games are based on medium-term horizon of several years. Long-term games are aggregated and time-compressed played by the competing individuals or teams. Participants are performing the same roles with the same or randomly generated starting resources. In the *Finance* game each player gets an initial sum of money. In the *Career* game for college undergraduates or high school every participant starts from the similar situation of a college graduate. The same game for every graduate student starts from the different position one actually holds in life. Such personalized games often better be played with fictitious characters, avatars to avoid revealing sensitive information, creating conflict or frustration. *Monopoly* is organized around the board representing different properties and processes of real estate business. Players use game money, cards representing resources (real estate addresses), cards representing opportunities (community chest), random events (chance) and tokens for houses, hotels and for players identification. The pace of movement around the board is generated by the throw of two dice. The *Monopoly* game became a favorite family pastime entertainment and is used by educational institutions in economics classes.

We transformed a middle-sized role playing exercise *Shell* [Ward & Schwarz, 1995] as a business game around the board representing four work centers: red, blue, green and yellow (see Fig. 3.9).

The work center operator colors the appropriate layer of the blank shell — paper card with 12 layers of different succession and proportions of four colors. Each of the 24 cards represents a job requiring different

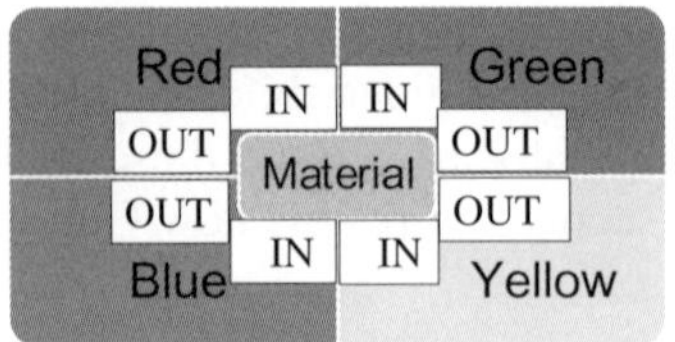

Fig. 3.9.   Board of *Shell* business game.

operations with a different due date of completion. So the game begins with building a schedule of processing jobs. During the game the schedule may need intermediate correction according to the actual productivity of different work stations.

Shell Game may be played in two basic arrangements: (1) as a cooperative field game for the full class split in four teams representing work centers around one playing field; (2) as a board game for several competing teams, each team around a separate table. A specialized team for the field game includes operator, dispatcher, timer, recorder and material handler. This option is concentrated on accurate timing and quality control of the jobs. Results of the game include control charts and learning curves. The game may be repeated for experimentation with different scheduling rules. The board option of the game is a competition between several teams with main concern on productivity. The team includes four operators, manager, quality controller and dispatcher. Results of the game are time charts reflecting shipments of jobs to customers. First, the field option requires more class time; second, the board option requires more material and instructor's control. Courses of logistics and operations management may afford playing both options of this game. It has a good learning contents and a great fun for such a dull topic as short-term scheduling.

The other exercise *Cellulose Aircraft Inc.* [Benoit and McDougall, 1995] we extended into the business game by placing students around the board representing assembly line (Fig. 3.10).

We made the enlargement of this game by adding the intermediate role of quality controller. The original exercise defined this role to keep measurements of defects as if it was a continuous variable which justifies application of control charts based on the properties of the Normal distribution. But quality control charts for the results of acceptance testing

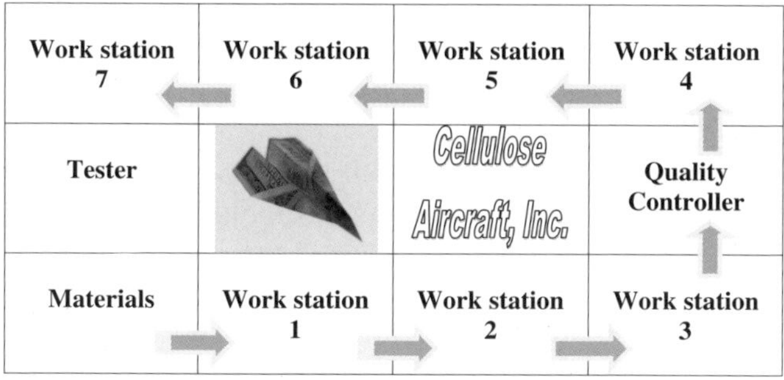

Fig. 3.10.   Board for the *Cellulose Aircraft Inc.* business game.

actually binary (accept or reject) decision, so we transformed the control charts to the parameters of the Binomial distribution. The game may be also extended by comparison of individual craftsmanship with batch production and assembly line as it was presented in Fig. 3.7 for the *Shell Game*. It also could be played as a cooperative field game or competitive board game. Additional registration of time gives data for calculating learning rates of different production arrangements for individual players and for teamwork. The other modifications of the game are possible by variation of rules and procedures which we will review in the next section. Board business games which attract attention of players as entertainment might be used also as educational and socializing tool. So some of our games students are using as a pastime recreation in their homes, fraternities and sororities.

Several board business games of the *Zodiak* family are offered by the company "Paradigm Learning Inc.". Games *Impact5: The Business of Leadership Game* and *The Game of Business Finance and Strategy* allow small teams of learners to run a fictitious company for three business years. The *Zodiak* game helped Expedia managers to understand how organizations earn and spend money. Going beyond basic financial literacy, the game strengthened their understanding of what it really takes for a company to make a profit and generate cash:

"*Zodiak* is a one-day, high energy classroom learning experience that is fun, fast and effective. The use of unique discovery learning techniques, including game boards, simulations, stories, audio clips and small team exercises, keeps interest high and learners engaged. The program can be used to build the financial literacy and business acumen of executives, managers, team leaders, employees, sales professionals, human resource professionals and more."

[Harrington, 2002]

Agricultural business games are still the most popular product on the board games market. The list of farm games includes dozens of board and videogames:

"Farm Games: *Alice Greenfingers, Alice Greenfingers 2, Barnyard Sherlock Hooves, Chicken Chase, County Fair, Dairy Dash, Enchanted Gardens, Family Farm: Fresh Start, Fantastic Farm, Farm Craft, Farm Craft 2, Farm Frenzy, Farm Frenzy 2, Farm Frenzy 3, Farm Frenzy 3: Ice Age, Farm Frenzy 3: Madagascar, Farm Frenzy 3: Russian Roulette, Farm Frenzy Pizza Party, Farm Frenzy: Gone Fishing, Farm Mania, Farm Mania 2, Farm Tribe, Farmer Jane, Finding Doggy, Fisher's Family Farm, Funky Farm 2, Garden Dreams, Green Valley: Fun on the Farm, Grimm's Hatchery, Harvest Mania To Go, Kelly Green Garden Queen, Little Farm, Magic Farm, My Exotic Farm, Orchard, Plants vs. Zombies, Ranch Rush, Ranch Rush 2 — Sara's Island Experiment, Ranch Rush 2 Collector's, Edition, Supercow, Tropical Farm, Virtual Farm, Wandering Willows, World of Zellians, Youda Farmer, Youda Farmer 2: Save the Village, Youda Survivor.*"

[BigFishGames, 2010]

Life on the Farm board game became a Winner of 2006 Teacher's Choice Award. It enhances critical thinking and money handling skills, with players racing against each other, trying to buy enough cows to "Retire" first and win the game. Students from Cornell University had so much fun with it that they used *Life on the Farm* as a fundraiser for their school. *Life on the Farm* board game is acclaimed the Winner of the 2002 Award of Excellence, by Education Clearinghouse [Education NEWS, 2003].

3.3.   RULES AND PROCEDURES OF GAMES

A business game starts from the appropriation of roles, allocation of resources, introduction to rules and explanation of procedures. During the game we need to exchange information between players and to evaluate their participation. The game ends with the players and teams' presentations of strategies and with the analysis of results by the instructor. Some games include physical activities of changing places, moving furniture or just relaxation exercises. For example, field business game *Leadership in Management* requires from participants carrying around physical objects of a chemical factory. Business game *Career* simulates real life by intense moving of players between the teams equipped with tables, computers and posters representing main areas of social activities.

Roles appropriation may be fixed, random or rotating. Fixed roles are recommended for strategic games in executive education and for professional designers. College students feel comfortable in random assignments at first and then in rotation of roles.

Resources in a game might be also allocated evenly or randomly and presented either physically (water and paints in *Leadership in Management*), by scaled models (LEGO bricks in *supply chain* games) or symbolically (coins or chips in *Beer Game*). Flowcharts are preferable to written rules and procedures for support dynamism and professionalism of the game. Running scores and analysis of results should be natural and objective. They should be quickly visualized with PC screens or posters.

Rules regulating actions of players in business games are supposed to be close to real regulations of economic life. Because of unlimited variety of moves available to players, most rules are expressed as prohibiting, not permissive ones. The basic *Capstone* game rule is:

> "You can change your Official Decisions as many times as you want prior to the end of the round. When the round is processed your Official Decisions become final."
>
> [Capstone, 2003]

Rules impose limits on resources and bounds for decisions. Rules should be explicit and unambiguous, fixed for the whole run of the game. Instructor usually needs to interpret some rules for educational purposes, but not so often. Observing of the rules is better controlled by cross-team examinations in addition to the instructor's control. Games as artificial and artistic designs cannot anticipate all possible improvisations demonstrated in each run of a game. This is why feedback is necessary to clarify rules and procedures from run to the run of the game. Such corrections should be avoided during the game, especially on the player's complaints. Participation of the same players in several runs of the game in different roles helps to edit rules and to carry over accumulated experience. We recommend avoiding the presence of other people around the game because it diverts attention of players and affects their behavior. The advice of the observers may be considered only after the end of a game. The jurors may be allowed to interfere in the game with the purpose of accreditation of some players. The game can be used to test the character and professionalism of some players by planting in a team of specially prepared provocative players.

There are three levels of rules: general, operational and implicit rules.

General rules reflect underlying formal relations of the game. In the business games these rules are based on economic and legal regulations. Rules of the games like *Capstone, CyberMarket* and *MarketSim* prescribe interaction between customers, producers and distributors; regulate accounting procedures and statistical calculations. These rules also regulate the access of players to the relevant information:

"General Rules

1. Your instructor controls the simulation pace, processing schedule, class events (e.g., Peer Evaluations, Scoring Criteria) and availability of results.
2. You must download a new starting condition file (Conditions.prn) for each round.
3. Play begins each simulated year on January 1. Previous year's reports reflect the industry status as of December 31 of last year.
4. Any team member can upload decisions. It's up to your group to assign decision responsibilities. The Web site tracks the decision upload history.
5. When uploading decisions you will see a message on Step 4 that reads 'You have successfully made changes...' **If you don't receive this message you have not properly uploaded your decisions."**

[Capstone, 2003]

Operational rules ensure orderly behavior of players. Different business games are regulated by certain rules of players' and teams' interaction. For example, moves (decisions) in the game may be simultaneous or sequential. Decisions may be declared orally, presented in writing or typed into a computer. The emergence of the variety and uncertainty is higher if decisions are simultaneous and lower if they are sequential. Operational rules may be adjusted to the game environment. For example, information protection in a standard classroom may be enforced by prohibition of some players to talk. In a specially organized playroom illicit communications are prevented by the screens. Operational rules support observing the schedule and order of a game:

> "Operational rules are the "rules of play" of the game. They are what we normally think of as rules: the guidelines players require in order to play. The operational rules are usually synonymous with the written-out "rules" that accompany board games and other non-digital games… The constituative rules of a game are the underlying formal structures that exist "below the surface" of the rules presented to players. These formal structures are logical and mathematical."
>
> [Salen and Zimmerman, 2004]

Implicit, unwritten rules require etiquette, good sportsmanship and respect to the instructor and to the other players. These rules depend on the context of the game, organizational and cultural climate, level of responsibility. If the results of a game will be considered for the rewards and promotions, the players will be cautious in their manners; if game is just explanatory, they will be more relaxed. Specifics of the business game are most clearly expressed in operational rules. They are defined by the real interaction between economic agents and/or management structures:

> "If you uploaded decisions for a single Product or Functional Area, you now have an opportunity to download a new Decision.prn file that has *all* the current decisions (yours and your teammates'). To do so, click the Download Official Decisions link on your Welcome Page.
>
> [Capstone, 2003]

Rules of the game also provide provisions against human errors. The system's analysis of factors influencing variation of technological and economic processes may include following groups of errors [Eisner, 2002]:

- Human (operator and controller errors)
- Instrumental (measurement errors)
- Platform (structural errors).

Game participants deal with uncertainty and pressure from different levels. The game should look like a real business environment. The uncertainty varies in a range from full, perfect information to restricted data

Table 3.2.   Main human errors causing problems in a game.

Source of problem	Safeguards
Forgetfulness	• Double checking all work • Checking at regular intervals
Misunderstandings	• Standardizing work practices • Checking in advance • Clearly instruct players • Written documentation of practices
Identification	• Training • Attentiveness • Vigilance
Inexperience	• Training • Skill building • Work standardization
Inattentiveness	• Discipline • Work standardization • Work instructions
Cheating, plagiarism	• Mutual control • Investigative software "turnitin"

(statistical uncertainty and down to absolute absence of information of strategic uncertainty). Pressure on the player is provided by the instructor, by peers, by timing and by responsibility. They all facilitate human errors of different kind (Table 3.2).

Bending the rules and cheating is more likely among undergraduate students than in MBA classes. Our experience shows that mutual control between players is more efficient than instructor's inspection. It is essential to avoid disciplinary remarks from observers unless they are the jury members. Their comments are better discussed after the game ends and all participants are no longer under stress.

Instrumental errors are essential for business games dealing with large amounts of information. The designer of the game should test variables at possible extreme values to avoid unexplainable results. The probability of numerical errors increases for the graphical inputs in the game even if processing is computerized. The most likely is inaccurate interpolation on

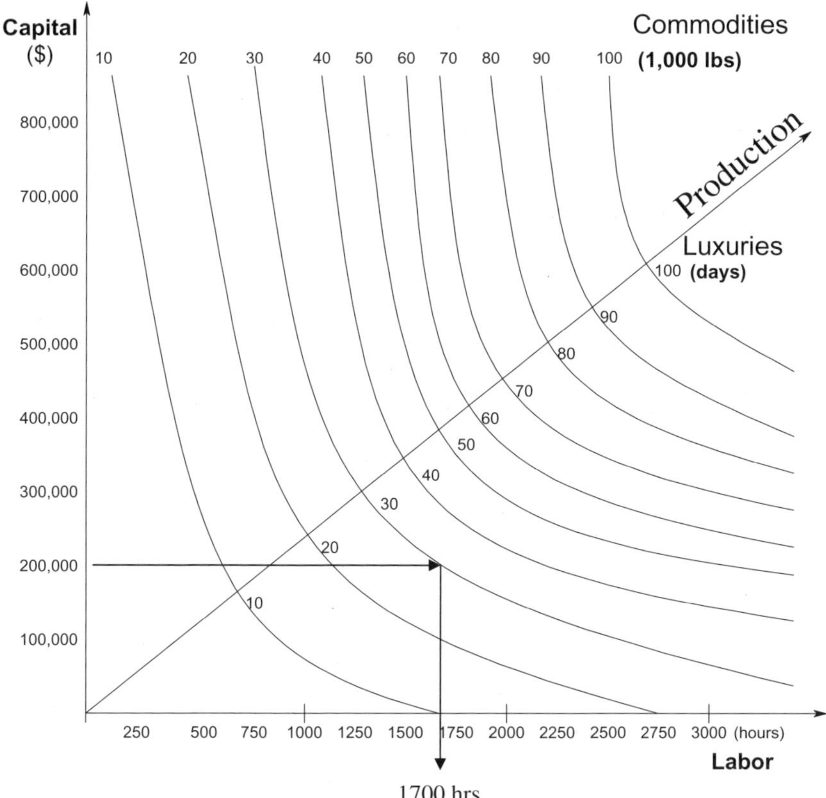

Fig. 3.11. Interpolation on the production function graph in *CyberMarket* game.

curves such as production function or derivation of 2-dimensional charts from 3-dimensional models (Fig. 3.11).

Platform (structural) errors are the most dangerous fundamental mistakes in a building game model. They may be avoided by testing the game with different groups of players. Computer gaming industry established high standards for their products and designers themselves are much aware of the customer's satisfaction:

"Game testing involves playing the game before it's release to determine whether or not it *playable* — bug-free, consistent, and entertaining... If a tester doesn't feel a product is playable, a producer will often take this information very seriously — and have the development team make any changes necessary to pass the playability test... Testers focus on the game's: "fun factor," usability, logic, and functionality."

[Novak, 2008]

Games for accreditation and professional testing should be especially carefully prepared and documented to avoid complaints and even legal consequences from the disgruntled players. In some runs of such games we found out that the participants were more concerned with the creation of personal image than with the results of the game.

Most card and board games recently were digitized for computers and playstations for projection on the screens. We will review them in the next chapter.

COMPUTER GAMES

The most popular videogames

4.1.　ELECTRONIC (DIGITAL) GAMES

Digital or electronic games were first developed for training military personnel using mainframe computers. In the 1950s military bases in Hawaii launched SEGA (Service Games) on electromechanical machines. Later, most of their ideas were implemented into commercial arcade games and flight simulators. At the same time, programmers of mainframe computers started to entertain themselves by designing games like *Spacewar* [Novak, 2008]. Now entertainment out-of-pocket expenses by all US homes, digital (electronic) games are more costly than attending live events such as concerts or sporting events, movies and theaters (5.4%). If we add 5.3% of cellular phone-related payments on entertainment (besides just calling) and 4.9% of videogames costs, they are exceeding 10% of family entertainment budget [Nilsen, 2010].

Massive mainframe games were introduced in the Ukraine's capital Kiev in the 1970s by the Cybernetics Institute of Soviet Academy of Sciences. It was a nationwide televised agricultural business game *Cybernetic Fitotron* for simulation of growing crops in a simulated environment. (Fitotron is a physical model of an agricultural field with the control of temperature, humidity and lighting.) The game combined biological and microeconomic business models connecting decisions of players with a product yield. The model included production functions describing how harvest depends from natural, technological and managerial factors. Natural inputs included climate (soil structure, temperature, humidity); technological factors were represented by fertilizers, equipment, watering; and management decision variables were cultures rotation, scheduling of seeding, cultivating, and harvesting. The game started in 1976 with over 9,000 individual subscribers and teams. This number was reduced to just 100 of the best players in 1980 after 20 sessions of the game. Sessions of the game were televised nationally every other month. Players were mailing their decision sheets that were analyzed by the computer programs and commented on TV and in the newspapers by leading scientists [Ivanenko, 1982].

The same team of programmers and TV producers later launched a similar game, now about city developments, called *Urbanistics*. This game attracted the first 1,073 teams in 1979 and eliminated them to 200 finalists in 1985. They proposed original long-term development projects of the national capital's "satellite" cities with given environmental, demographic and industrial parameters. The success of this experience inspired them to offer the game on national economic development which was not accepted by the Soviet TV executives as ideologically unpredictable.

Western game designers were also interested in simulation of agricultural business on the farmer's scale. There are hundreds of videogames presenting all branches of agricultural and food industries. They present farming life, fishing, hunting, products processing and distribution. The earliest publications of such board games are recorded in the early 1900s on the *Herefordshire Farm Game* [Taylor, 1975]. Much later *The Farming Game* was published in 1979 originally as a board game simulating the economics of a small farm. It simulates the real life difficulties of running a farm. The whole family of *Farmers' Market* games teaches the selling of products such as eggs, milk, beef, and corn. It also teaches players to combine ingredients to sell freshly-made waffles, barbecue, ice cream, fruit pies, and more. It recommends attracting new customers with a band, and increasing the price of your food with blue ribbon contests. It allows creating markets in the city, in the desert, at campgrounds, on the pier, and at many other exciting locations. It is up to the player to build a bustling farm-fresh marketplace in the *Farmers Market* game. Some digital games are listed as farming simulations, but actually expand to the social problems. 11 million people a day now play *Farmville* [Smith, 2010]. The *InLiving* game is a mobile phone game to help young people think about the future.

> "The game allows the player to manage their own virtual home and learn about personal finance, education and employment in a fun and engaging way. In the process, they develop more realistic expectations of tenancy, and principles of the game can be emphasized in conversation by housing association staff"
>
> [Innovation-exchange.org, 2010].

The most advanced are digital games simulating business management functions: marketing, sales, forecasting, etc. The *Marketplace* games are a family of business simulations for undergraduate, graduate and executive level business courses. This simulations deliver a realistic hands-on learning experience. The simulations are designed to fit both the distance learning and the classroom format [Cadotte, 1990]. The *Marketplace* simulations range from marketing games introductory courses on the undergraduate level, to games for marketing strategy. This family of games is designed for the business and economics courses at the undergraduate, MBA and EMBA levels.

These games started with individual players, later involved small groups of players, and now whole communities of players called gameworlds participate in these games. The first videogames were installed in public places (arcades) and at homes as console games. Then as personal computers became widely available, computer graphics quickly progressed and videogames entered family homes and individual offices. They are now portable and may be played in flexible schedule asynchronously on laptops, iPods, iPads and even on cellular phones.

The few economic applications are primarily related to the speculation on the stock, money and commodities markets. *The Stock Market Game* and *Wall Street Survivor* simulate trading in a fictitious market. The *Wall Street Survivor* makes trading easy and has educational information to help beginners in stock market trade. Since 1977, more than ten million students have participated in *The Stock Market Game* program, and more classrooms sign on every year. Today the program is available in all 50 states and worldwide. The other areas of such games applications are domestic business and family finances.

Business games which are applied to the new system design, need initial competitive equilibrium values. Game experimentation on the convergence of prices and quantities in supply chain System of Systems will be described in Chapter 10. The model for calculation of such values was outlined by the duality approach bridging together game theory with business games. The theoretical model balances prices and quantities of supply and demand. In the game behavior of buyers and sellers is simulated by bidding on the commodities following the rules of real markets. *Gazillionaire* is the most sold game that LavaMind LLC makes, and second is *Profitania* followed by *Serpengo* and *Zapitalism*. Pareto chart of the proportions of sales between different games of the family is presented in Fig. 4.1.

Gazillionaire accounts for over 50% of LavaMind's profits. *Gazillionaire* is the leading game in the portfolio of LavaMind LLC (see Fig. 4.2).

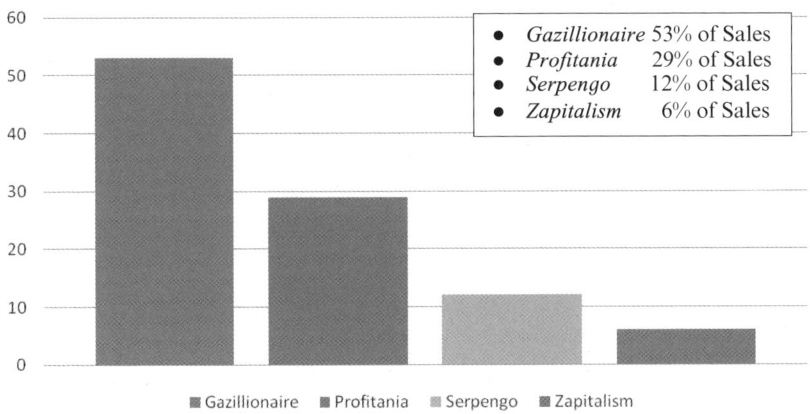

Fig. 4.1.   Pareto chart of the *LavaMind* games.

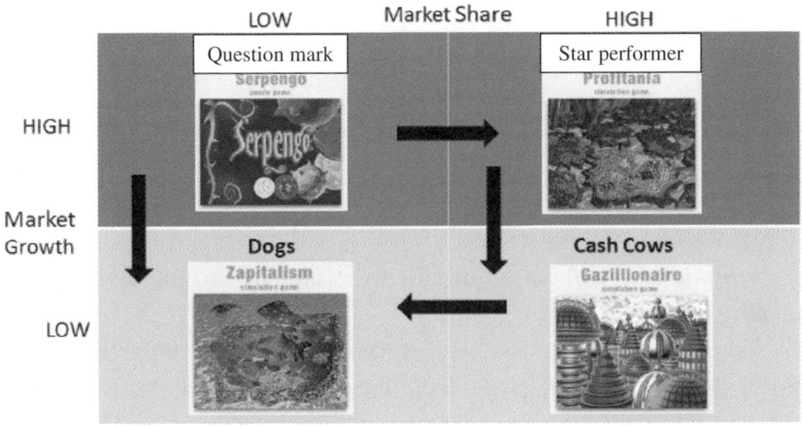

Fig. 4.2.   Portfolio matrix of the LavaMind family of games.

The portfolio represent games at different stages of their life cycles: *Serpendo* at the introductory stage, *Profitania* at growth, *Gazillionaire* reached maturity and *Zapitalism* is going out of the market (Fig. 4.3).

The comparison of *Gazillionaire* with other games of the same type shows opportunity for improvement before the game will go into decline. The first concern should be decreasing number of players. The Quality Function Deployment (House of Quality) analysis requires changes in the

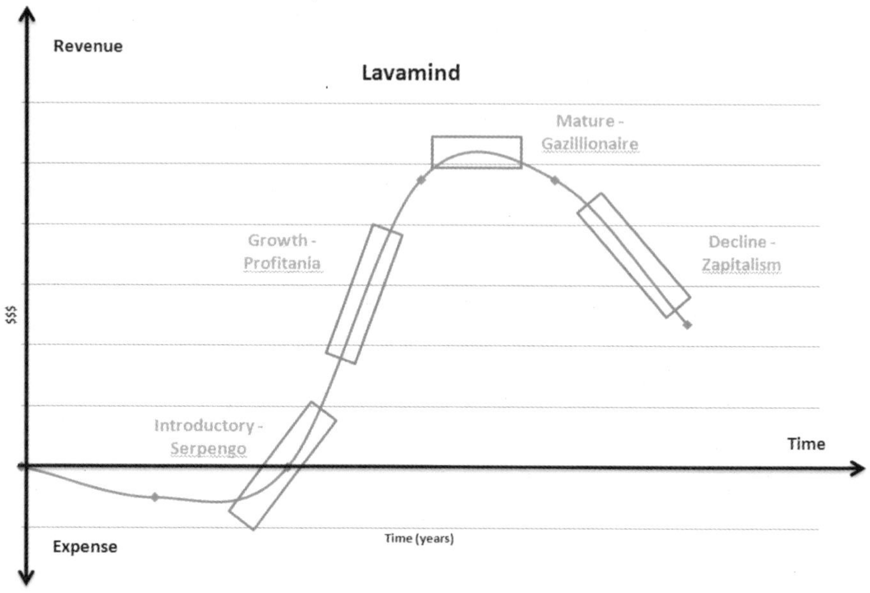

Fig. 4.3.   Life cycle positions of *LavaMind* games.

contents of the game. As we see from Fig. 4.4, the highest rating (63) for the *Gazillionaire* technical requirements is attached to the diversification of scenery.

A more detailed analysis of necessary improvements of the digital game might be done with the help of a fishbone diagram. It structures the factors which may affect attractiveness of the game to the players. Such a diagram outlining main and secondary factors of the *Gazillionaire* game is presented in Fig. 4.5.

The fishbone diagram for *Gazillionaire* structures the main factors of profitability as the spaceships, measurements, materials, and net worth. The spaceship can lose fuel, have empty cargo space that is not being sufficiently used, and cannot pickup passengers which will not bring you a profit. Also you cannot upgrade the ship too early if you do not have enough money.

The contents of digital games began with sports, then included adventures, and are now about races. Many educational games are related to biological and medical applications. According to the most prized scientific

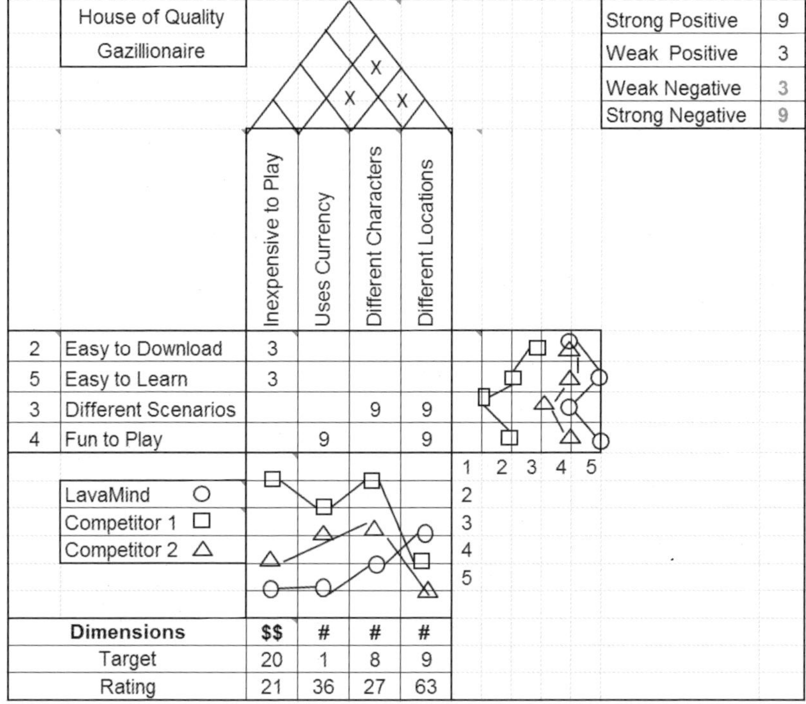

Fig. 4.4.   QFD (House of Quality) for the *Gazillionaire* game.

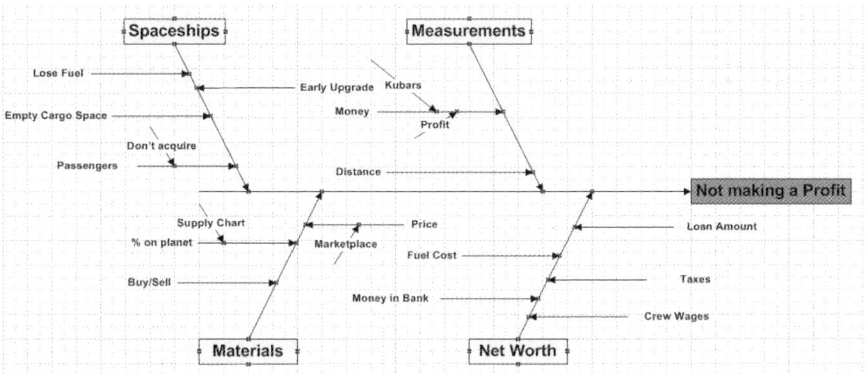

Fig. 4.5.   Fishbone diagram for analysis of *Gazillionaire* game.

achievements of the last century the top ten most visited educational games are as follows:

"1. The Blood Typing Game
2. The Laser Challenge Game
3. The DNA — the Double Helix Game
4. The Pavlov's Dog Game
5. The Diabetic Dog Game
6. The Lord of the Flies Game
7. The Electrocardiogram Game
8. The Immune System Game
9. The Control of the Cell Cycle Game
10. The Split Brain Experiments Game"

[Nobelprize.org, 2010]

Electronic games also applied to the teaching of foreign languages as a role playing by visualizing and animating everyday topics. Special language programs like Rosetta Stone allow the interaction of a student with the instructor anywhere by using their PC, iPhone or iPod. Most language schools include exchange programs with foreign countries, where students play games with native speakers.

Most contemporary electronic games like *Second Life* and *Sims* are played in virtual worlds containing elements of economic activity. Therefore, they may be either classified as business games, or become a part of a business game. Most educational videogames are designed to learn geography, history and mathematics. But such edutainment games in the 1990s lost competition with purely entertaining adventure games. Most talented designers of education games went to work with the companies making games based on popular books, movies and TV sequels [Novak, 2008]. But Jeannie Novak and other games designers are still optimistic about the future of educational games:

"There is a large market of adults in colleges, universities, research institutions, vocational schools — even in corporations — who would benefit from games that serve an educational purpose... An interesting educational application might be online distance learning. Most online classrooms consist of discussion threads — which enhances social interaction (as it does in online multiplayer games). Instead of posting only discussion threads — which greatly enhances lateral learning but does not involve constructivism (learning by doing) — students could be playing online multiplayer games that incorporate real-world simulations, such as economics, archeology, automechanics, music, marketing … even surgery!"

[Novak, 2008]

Novak's expectations of the revival of educational games has started to happen. Public interest in the economic applications of games during recessions is increasing. People escape to virtual spaces from the problems of reality. The *Monopoly Revolution* is the remake of the classic *Monopoly*, many mods (modifications) of games like *Tycoons* and new games such as *Credit Crunch* were offered during 2010 [The Economist, August 2010].

Research and educational games started to attract attention of geeks demonstrating creativity in science and engineering. University of Washington circulated online computer game *Foldit!*

"…in which players score points by squeezing proteins into the most chemically stable configurations. Proteins, which are the building blocks of life, come in long chains of molecules that work properly only once they have folded into their final, three-dimensional shape. Figuring out how they fold correctly is thus crucial to understanding biochemical processes, and to creating new drugs."

[Nature, 2010]

Programs like "Quest to learn" for New York schools are now financed by the Bill and Melinda Gates as well as other foundations. They introduce games like *Codewords* integrating subjects of Mathematics and English.

"Students have been called upon to balance the budget and brainstorm business ideas for an imaginary community called Creepytown, for example, and to design architectural blueprints for a village of bumping little creatures called the Troggles."

[Corbett, 2010]

The variety of personal digital devices leads to the transformation of all games into electronic video format. Most original card and board games have been transformed now to an electronic format, but sometimes at the expense of losing social interaction between players. Online version of the *Monopoly Tycoon* is a PC game that makes strategy and speed into determining factors for winning the game. It eliminates the element of luck represented by the dice rolls of the original game. The game uses the same Atlantic City properties as its basis, but the game revised their values close to present real estate prices. The game also allows for solo and multiplayer online play. The *Monopoly Casino* is also a PC game; it simulates a casino full of *Monopoly*-based adaptations of various casino games. This program was released in both standard and "Vegas" editions, each featuring unique games.

4.2. VIDEO GAMES

The first videogames were played with a console as simulations of aggressive strategies in sports, wars or adventures. Since they are usually placed in public places, such entertainment is also called ***arcade games***. An individual player races to get to some destination, to hit some aim, to occupy some space or to kill a virtual enemy. Games for several players acting simultaneously are also expecting to achieve the same result from each participant. The game environment is colorful and dynamic: the screen display provides every competing player with the same information. The game is accompanied by music and sound effects. Sony Playstation, Microsoft Xbox and Nintendo are the most successful tools in a highly competitive industry of digital entertainment with console games. Such game starts from an equal allocation of resources and the same roles and propagate on higher, tougher levels as a player succeeds. The boom of these coin-op arcade games was during the 1970s.

Until now, just a few games were able to build interactive business environment. These are mainly Japanese and German simulations of competition in financial markets. A few of them are translated in English, for example, the German *Game Tycoon* that simulates videogames production. But Japanese influence on American games market is more noticeable even visually in computer graphics like *Anime*. On the other hand, many US and UK game designs are translated into most world languages. The game *Fast Food Tycoon*, playing the owner of pizza business, is adjusted to a dozen of cities starting with New York through Moscow and Tokyo. Business games like *Capitalism* and *Beat the Market Online* which originated in USA are also popular in Japanese and Chinese versions.

Eventually videogames start to apply for economic and business education. *Glo-Bus* is an international business game that is used in many American colleges. *Business Strategy Game* is published by McGraw-Hill for students competing in the Business Strategy Invitational. There are many websites supported by game designers that offer a variety of videogames. Some of them are specialized in economics and management applications. Capital Connections sells games like *Profit & Cash,* Andromeda Training is the creator of the *Income-Outcome* game, the Ninth House developed the *Insight* video simulation for management training.

Videogames are either computer or microprocessor-controlled systems. Computers can create virtual tools to be used in a game between human and simulated opponents. A player of videogame uses one or more input devices, typically a button/joystick combination (for arcade games); a keyboard, mouse and/or trackball (computer games); or a controller of a motion sensitive tool (console games). Recently more devices such as paddle controllers, motion and voice activated sensors and floor pads have been used for input. In computer games, the evolution of user interfaces from a simple keyboard to mouse, joystick or joypad has profoundly changed the nature of game development. It is also necessary for business games quantification of variables. Videogame industry designers hope to include elements of business in the contents of their entertainment games:

> "Most [video]games have no business component, or they have a very simple shop interface for purchasing items. A few games are focused mostly on business as a simulation. However, very few games feature anything more complex than the simple store concept. But business can be a source of money and power, of risk and reward. And even in games with other types of main focus, putting in a business component can add variety and new options and challenges."
>
> [Perry, 2009]

Very promising for business games are interactive smart boards. They allow players to demonstrate game material on the board and transform contents by a combination of computer control and touch-screen input. The SMART Notebook software makes it possible for teachers to create content rich, dynamic lessons that address specific student skills. The collection of interactive whiteboard games for educators on PBS KIDS includes such games as *Curious George, Super Why* and *Arthur.* Students enjoy participating in these collaborative, fun and engaging experiences, while following a standard school curriculum. Most of them are designed for the development of basic language and mathematics skills.

There are many genres of video games; the first commercial video game, *Pong*, was a simple simulation of table tennis. As processing power increased, new genres such as adventure and action games were developed that involved a player guiding a character or avatar through a series of obstacles. This "real-time" element cannot be easily reproduced by a board game which is generally limited to "turn-based" strategy; this advantage allows video games to simulate situations more realistically. Additionally, the playing of a video game does not require the same physical skill, strength and/or danger as field representation of the game, and can provide either very realistic, exaggerated or impossible physics, allowing for elements of a fantastical nature. Many games present races, physical violence, or simulations of sports. A computer can, with increasing degrees of success, simulate human opponents in traditional board games such as *Chess*, leading to the progress of such games that can be played at progressing levels. *Deep Blue* supercomputer after several attempts defeated chess World Champion Gary Kasparov. New software started winning less formal games such as *Jeopardy* from the best human players.

In computer simulations, the game provides a virtual environment in which the players may be free to do whatever they like within the rules of the game. Some games that have no opposition, like the *Sims*, should be considered "computer toys", or creativity "God games" which cannot be lost [Crawford, 2003]. Will Wright, the most famous videogames designer, in an interview with The Times, expressed his belief that computers extend the imagination up to the emergence of the "metabrain":

> "Any human institutional system that draws on the intelligence of all its members is a metabrain. Up to now, we have had high friction between the neurons of the metabrain; technology is lowering that friction tremendously. Computers are allowing us to aggregate our intelligence in ways that were never possible before. If you look at *Spore*, people are making this stuff, and computers collect it, then decide who to send it to. The computer is the broker. What they are really exploring is the collective creativity of millions of people. They are aggregating human intelligence into a system that is more powerful than we thought artificial intelligence was going to be."
>
> [Wright, 2007]

The closest to our definition of business games are the *Roller Coaster Tycoon* videogames series. They are educational business strategy games, designed to simulate development and operations of amusement/theme parks. Players are in charge of managing the park and its employees, creating or demolishing rides, adjusting terrain and scenery, and controlling prices of rides and choice of vendors. *Roller Coaster Tycoon*, the first of the series, generated much popularity and sales, leading to the creation of *Roller Coaster Tycoon 2*. However, the second game did not generate as much revenue, but still maintained interest. With interest in the product already established and new technology available to enhance the game, a third installation was designed and produced.

Roller Coaster Tycoon 3 maintained the objectives of managing an amusement park and generating profit, while keeping their "peeps" happy. Like the previous versions, it features Career Mode, where players play scenarios with specific goals to reach in order to grow higher in ranking (Apprentice, Entrepreneur, and Tycoon), and Sandbox mode, where players are given an empty plot of land with unlimited funds to build their own custom parks. New to the game are gameplay features, such as the CoasterCam, which allows the players to "ride" the rollercoasters, and the MixMaster, which allows the player to coordinate firework shows with music. Other new developments were made on the "peeps." They now can arrive in groups in variation of gender and age. Enhancements were also made on the simulation of the environment, showing day and night cycle changes, as well as sunshine and rain. New technology also allowed the game to be made with 3D graphics instead of the isometric viewpoint seen in the previous versions. Players can now rotate and zoom the view of the park to any degree.

Roller Coaster Tycoon 3 is an educational, strategy simulation game. It simulates the design, building and management of amusement parks. Its main customers are video game players interested in business construction and money management. Consumers are attracted to its new 3D graphics and weather simulation. The game has the ability to simulate rain, sunshine, night and day. Developers, designers, and programmers tried to create the game close to real-life scenarios. The more new technological enhancements made to the game, the more interest is generated from consumers. As new technology develops, it asks the question if more advanced games

Market Share

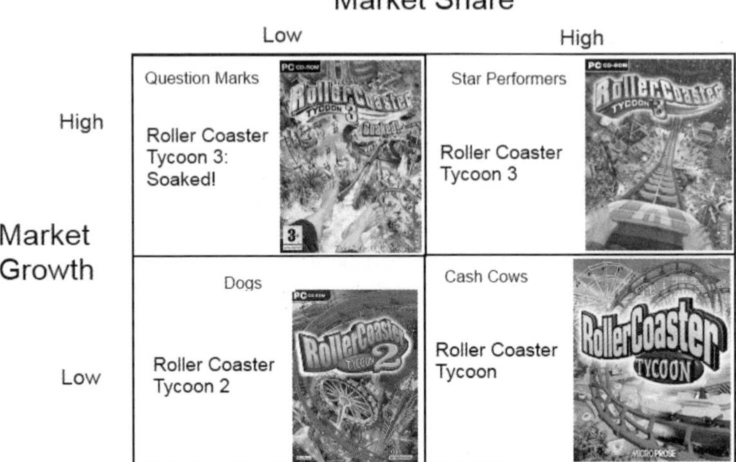

Fig. 4.6.   The *Roller Coaster* games portfolio matrix.

would be designed. Technological advances could lead to more graphics and sound effects that can be added to the game through expansion packs in new versions of the *Roller Coaster Tycoon* series. The following Portfolio Matrix (Fig. 4.6) illustrates the family of *Roller Coaster* games.

We found simulations like the *Roller Coaster Tycoon* useful for business and management education. The designers of these games are helping us by including in each new version of the game elements of economics and management. Table 4.1 presents development of three generations of *Roller Coaster* games in detail.

Roller Coaster Tycoon 3 experiences a typical game "hype cycle" that looks like the same as the LavaMind products illustrated in Figs. 4.3 and 4.7.

Unfortunately, designers did not introduce a new advanced version of the game with capital modifications before decline started, so potential customers migrated to the other games. Introduction of the DeLuxe edition of the game stabilized demand in 2006. But for many of the entertainment products life is different, called a "hype cycle": from a fast growth of demand right after the introduction. It followed by a relatively short peak of inflated expectations to a long maturity stage [Schell, 2008]. Overall demand forecasting is an important tool for companies during the life cycle of a game. Applying basic trend formulas for similar products may be an

Table 4.1.   Three generations of the *Roller Coaster Tycoon* family of games.

	Roller Coaster Tycoon	**Roller Coaster Tycoon 2**	**Roller Coaster Tycoon 3**
Release Date	March 31, 1999	October 15, 2002	October 26, 2004
Developer	Christ Sawyer	Chris Sawyer	Frontier Developments (with Chris Sawyer as a consultant)
Publisher	Hasbro Interactive	Infogames	Atari
Expansion Packs	— CorkScrew Follies (Added Attractions) (1999) — Loopy Landscapes (2000)	— Wacky Worlds (2003) — Time Twister (2003)	— Soaked! (2005) — Wild! (2005)
Compilations	— Roller Coaster Tycoon: Gold (Totally Roller Coaster) (2002) — Roller Coaster Tycoon: Deluxe (2003)	— Roller Coaster Tycoon 2: Combo Park Pack (2003) — Roller Coaster Tycoon 2: Triple Thrill Pack (aka Totally Roller Coaster Tycoon 2) (2004)	— Roller Coaster Tycoon 3: Gold (2005) — Roller Coaster Tycoon 3: Platinum (aka Roller Coaster Tycoon 3 Deluxe Edition) (2006)

(*Continued*)

Table 4.1.   (*Continued*)

	Roller Coaster Tycoon	Roller Coaster Tycoon 2	Roller Coaster Tycoon 3
Updates/Differentiators Comparison	— Isometric graphics — Only rides that have tracks could be built underground	— Isometric graphics — More robust system for building structures (ability to lay each piece of wall and roof individually) — Flexibility in scenery — Allowing rides and shops to be fixed at any elevation — New gameplay features: import user-created scenery items, bulldozer, scenario editor, etc.	— 3D graphics — Rotate and zoom the view of the park to any degree — New gameplay features: CoasterCam & MixMaster — Variation of "peeps" in gender and age

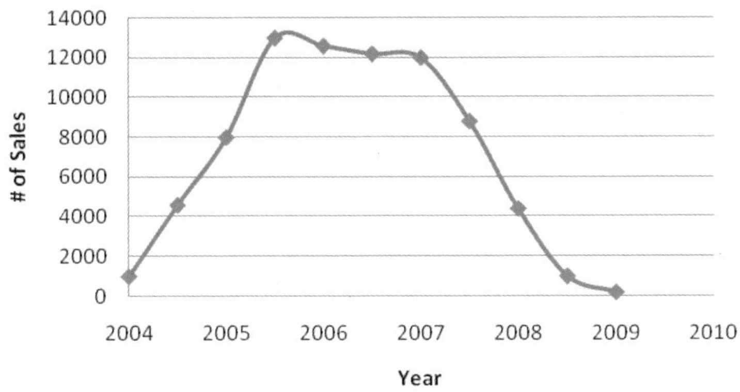

Fig. 4.7.   Life cycle of *Roller Coaster Tycoon* 3 game.

accurate way to predict when the decline will start and a new game should be introduced.

Medium-term forecasting is a typical component of business games. The *Capstone* and *NewProDev* model the best time for the introduction of new products to the market. Other steps of upgrading and marketing strategies can also be taken to extend a game's life span. From the earliest days of networked and time-shared computers, online games have been part of the young nerd's culture. Early commercial systems such as *Plato* became famous for their games and for their strictly educational value. The *Plato* family of games was written by John Daleske as project coursework for an education class in the spring of 1973. The first version of the game, *Empire I* was a strategic turn-based game for eight players. Each player had ships, industry, and budgets. Players have to keep the budget up to build more ships, maintain industry to help pay for it, provide raw materials to turn into goods and trade.

This was the earliest example of an online, multi-player, inter-terminal computer game. Games prior to this were either two player or one player against a computer. But each new version of the game was less about economics and more about wars in space. *Empire II*, written in the fall of 1973, was substantially different and much more tactically oriented. Each player managed a starship and could fire torpedoes at each other. Silas Warner liked the earlier version, and with Daleske's permission resurrected it under the name *Conquest*. Usage logs from the *Plato* system at the

Computer-based Education Research Laboratory at University of Illinois at Urbana-Champaign indicate that between 1978 and 1985, users spent about 300,000 hours playing *Empire*. It was not the most popular game; twice as many hours during the same period were spent playing a dungeon adventure game called *Avatar*. But *Empire* is still available and widely played by tens thousands of visitors [<www.cyber1.org>, 2010]. *Avatar* is an early graphics-based multi-user highly interactive role-playing computer game, created on the University of Illinois' Control Data Corporation *Plato* system in the late 1970s. It has graphics for navigating through a dungeon, with chat style text for player status and communication with others. It can currently be played online via Cyber1 or the NovaNET system. What makes this game popular is the high level of interactivity with other players and the sense of community that the game develops.

Modern videogames are played using an Internet connection; some have dedicated client programs, while others require only a web browser. Some simpler browser games appeal to specific demographic groups (especially to women and the middle-aged men) that otherwise play very few video games. Women are increasingly becoming active online gamers. They usually get involved in the game themselves while supervising their playing children. The computer game is the most established of all sectors in the emerging new media. Games like *Designer's World* and *Dream Life* are becoming popular among teenage girls. These games allow the player to build a fashion business producing clothes and apparel, organizing fashion shows and managing company finances [Bednar, 2006]. The media of these games is transformed from the traditional one way to an interactive play. This is the phenomenon that is broadening the market of video games. It is an obvious example of the ways in which online and offline space can be seen as "merged" rather than separate.

The characteristics of media audiences have been changing due to social changes and economic development. They are becoming active and interact more than ever before. The players of the games in this phenomenon are just like the social formation in our society. They are self-organizing, creating their own social norms. They are subject to regulations and constraints through the code of the game and sometimes through the policing of the game by those who run it. The values that are governed vary from game to game. Many of the values encoded into game spirit reflect social and cultural values, but games also offer a chance to test alternative values in fantasy play. The players of the game in the new century are now apparently expressing their profound self through the game. When they can play with their anonymous status, they are more confident to express and to step out from their position. A game offers new experiences and pleasures based in the interactive and immense possibilities of computer technologies. That brings us to the development of interactive computer simulations as the trend into the future.

Students learn at different rates and in different ways. Computer technology supports instructional strategies by creating new routes to learning and addressing multiple learning needs. The differentiation of instruction is possible by using the wealth of digital resources that challenge and engage all types of intelligences and learning styles.

The computer game designer Chris Crawford attempted to define the term *game* as creative expression of art:

1. *Entertainment* if made not for money.
2. A piece of entertainment is a *plaything* if it is interactive. Movies and books are cited as examples of non-interactive entertainment.
3. If no goals are associated with a plaything, it is a *toy*. If it has goals, a plaything is a *challenge*.
4. If a challenge has no "active agent against whom you compete," it is a *puzzle*; if there is one, it is a *conflict*.
5. Finally, if the player can only outperform the opponent, but not attack them to interfere with their performance, the conflict is a *competition*. However, if attacks are allowed, then the conflict qualifies as a *game*.

[Crawford, 2003]

Crawford puts to the first place entertaining ability of games. Then goes requirement to players to be interactive, goal-oriented, in which players can communicate and compete with each other. This functions are perfectly performed by on-line games.

4.3. ONLINE GAMES AND INTERACTIVE COMPUTER SIMULATIONS

Web-based simulations are used by many online computer games. They are also used in e-learning through quick illustrations of various principles to students by means of interactive animations. Distance learning provides an alternative to installing expensive simulation software on a student's computer, or as an alternative to expensive laboratory equipment. A web-based simulation can either take place on the server-side or on the client-side. In a *server-side simulation*, the numerical calculations and the generation of graphical output are carried by the specialized academic and consultancy groups, which provide the clients with the graphical user-friendly interface. For example, server-side scripting such as PHP or CGI scripts, interactive services based on Ajax or AnyLogic application software remotely accessed through a Java. In a *client-side simulation*, the simulation program is downloaded from the server, but completely executed by the client, for example using Java applets, Flash animations, Java script or other similar software. Server-side simulation is not scalable for many simultaneous users, but places fewer demands on the user's computer performance and web-browser plug-ins than client-side simulation. The term online simulation sometimes refers to server-side web-based simulation, sometimes to symbiotic simulation, i.e., a simulation that interacts in real-time with a physical system.

New possibilities for the multiplayer online games are opening with the introduction of cloud computing. This is an Internet-based network of servers that share software and data among computers on demand. Cloud computing is a natural evolution of the widespread adoption of virtualization, service-oriented architecture and utility computing. With the upcoming cloud computing technologies, almost unlimited resources can be used for new simulation approaches. For instance, there are multi-agent simulation applications which are deployed and act independently. This allows simulations to be scalable close to infinity. A cloud computing conceptual diagram is presented in Fig. 4.8.

Cloud gaming opens new opportunities for online gaming that allows the direct streaming of games onto a computer of a player from the game company's server. This allows access to games without the need of a console and makes the capability of the user's computer almost irrelevant, as the server is the system that is running the processing needs [BBC News, 2009]. The controls from the user are transmitted directly to the server, where they are recorded, and the server then sends back the game's response to the input controls.

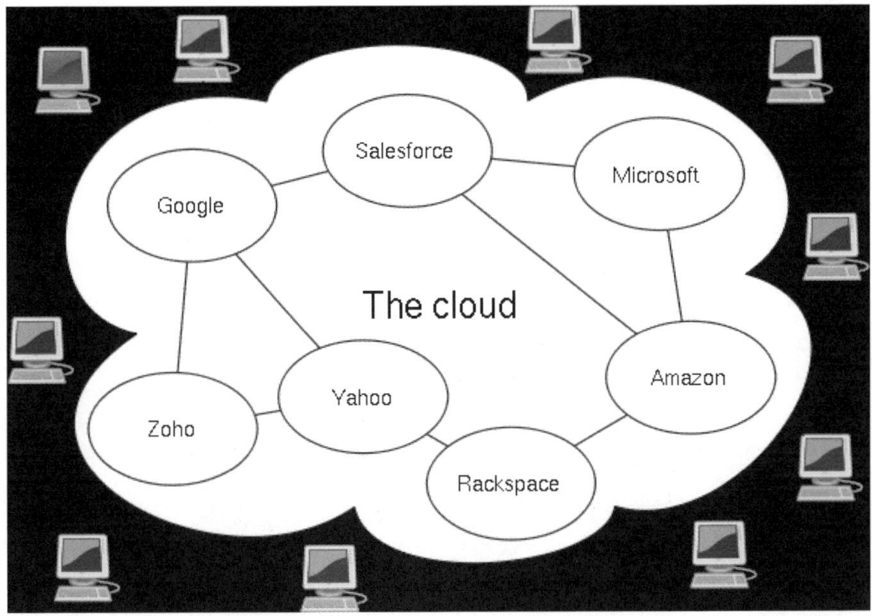

Fig. 4.8.   Cloud computing conceptual diagram.

Among a few online games directly related to business we may find games simulating different markets and manufacturing such as *MacMulti* which is about the oil industry. Players make decisions about extracting, processing, selling or buying oil. The choices facing a player are presented in the following *MacMulti* game flowchart (Fig. 4.9).

Interactive computer simulations as digital games are also used for the presentation of economic systems. They are more informative than console games. The most popular is *SimCity*, it simulates development of city infrastructure in realistic detail. The advantages of digital games are in the fast handling and presentation of a large amount of information; visualized processing of texts and images; networking communications; and the integration of all sorts of media. Modern online games are played using the Internet for downloading of software and for networking with other players. These games assemble the entire communities of fans. This is the best model for presenting either worldwide competition or cooperation between amateurs and professionals in the design of products, processes and systems.

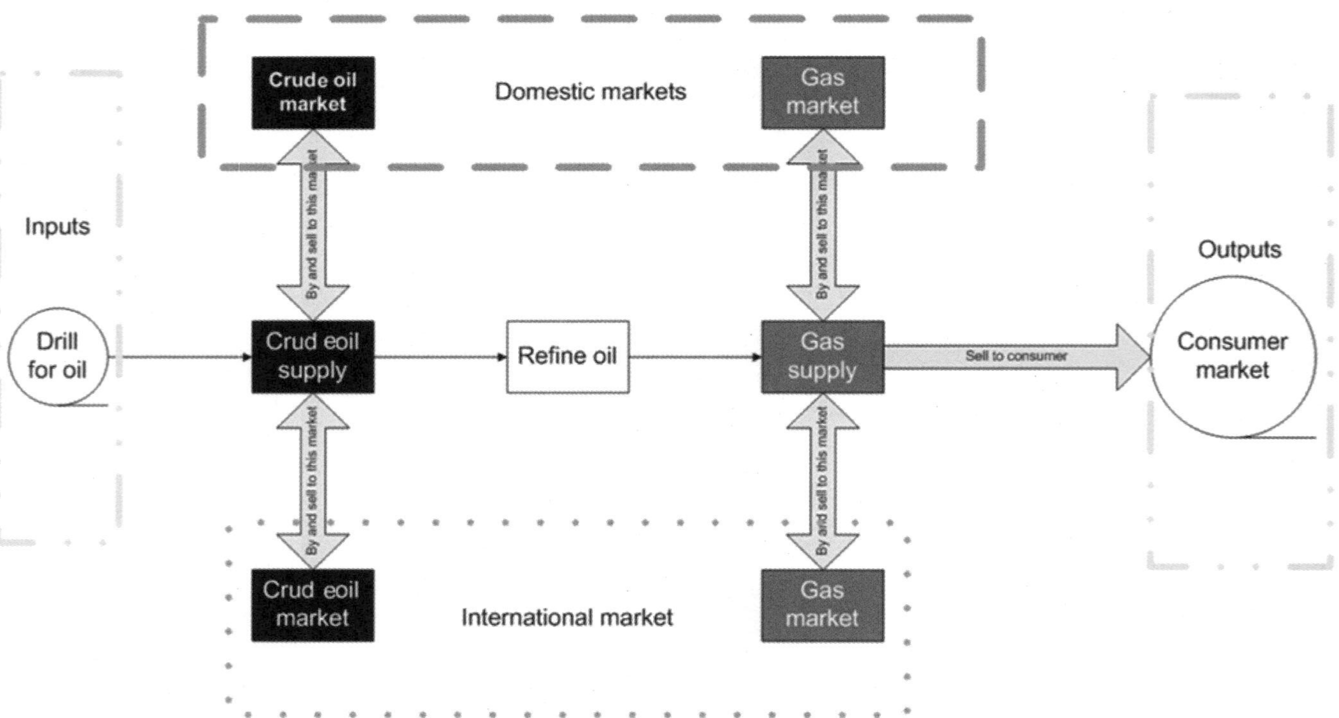

Fig. 4.9.   Flowchart of *MacMulti* game.

One of the most advanced games for computer simulations called *MarketSim* is designed in Youngstown University [Ruffer and Usip, 2005]. It demonstrates to the student two basic types of closed economic systems: starting with a Barter Economy and finishing with a Monetary Economy. *MarketSim* is designed to help students gain a better understanding of economic theory by having them take on the roles of consumers and producers in a simulated economy accessed via the Internet. Exchanges are made by students posting and accepting offers at terms that they choose. Students must participate in a game simultaneously, any student who is inactive for more than an hour will be logged out of the game. Students who are logged out or who exit the game by closing their browser will not be able to re-enter the game. The instructor controls the pace of a game by choosing when to start a new period.

MarketSim includes two simulations: Jeremy's Market and Adam's Market. Jeremy's Market is a barter economy. At the start of each period, every household is allocated 100 hours of time which can be used to produce goods or consumed as a leisure time. The households can exchange goods by posting and accepting offers to trade. The households have an incentive to trade because groups of households are assigned different production and utility functions. Authors recommend that classes play Jeremy's Market after covering consumer choice theory. Students should also be introduced to simple one-factor production functions before participating in the game. Students will finish the game with a better understanding of consumer choice theory, opportunity cost, and gains from trade.

In Adam's Market, firms and money are introduced. As in Jeremy's Market, consumers are allocated 100 hours at the start of each period. Each student is responsible for the actions of a consumer and a firm. Consumers can sell hours of labor time to firms, that the firms use to produce output. The firms can then post offers to sell the output to the consumers. Instructors can choose to make the simulated economy more sophisticated by allowing firms to purchase additional capital, change industries, and issue bonds.

For the simultaneous play version designers recommend that instructors should play Adam's Market at least twice to gain a player's experience. The first game should use the "short-run economy" option (a four-period game). Students would be ready to participate in the game after covering profit maximization topic. Playing Adam's Market is recommended after entry/exit and capital investment is introduced. The final option includes a bond market for classes that have the time to cover financial markets. Students participating in the simulation should have a better understanding of profit maximization, price determination, market structure, labor supply, and labor demand.

> "Designers of *MarketSim* believe that it has several advantages over experiments:
>
> - Students can participate in the simulation outside of class, minimizing the amount of class time dedicated to the simulation.
> - The software tracks students' choices, so the program can be used with classes of several hundred students.
> - Students have access to worksheets so they can successfully make choices in a sophisticated economy.
> - Since students participate in the simulation over the Internet it can be used in distance-learning classes."
>
> [Porter and Shueller, 2005]

Simunomics is a multi-user online game service that allows to play business games in most common JavaScript-enabled browsers. In the game, you will create a library of licensed digital objects that depict physical objects such as land, buildings, employees, inventory, and currency and you will obtain a limited license for the right to use such representations within the game.

An interaction between the teams develops a superstructure of the game. The most popular games are developing superstructures in a natural way by socializing in a local geographical areas or in a cyberspace. This way emerged *Monopoly* and *McMulti* Game Clubs in some communities. They are meeting regularly for entertainment or for competitions. The Internet opened communities of gaming around such games as *Beer* and *Gazillionaire*. Some games are becoming international global edutainment tools.

4.4. GAMES THAT CONQUER THE WORLD

Several foreign-made business games were mentioned before, but their number is huge and growing. Large number of games developed by US designers in most cases find customers not only in English-speaking countries, but all over the world:

"Game industry revenues, which some have estimated exceeded \$30 billion per year worldwide, have surpassed film box office and music concert revenues in the United States alone — making games the fastest-growing segment of the entertainment market, and an excellent career advancement. According to an industry impact study conducted by the International Game Developers Association (IGDA), in several countries, exports from game sales represent one of the highest exports — and well over 100,000 people are employed worldwide in the game industry."

[Novak, 2008]

Games are the pioneers of computer education in poor communities and developing countries, among most conservative cultures. Some of these cultures are embracing new games and toys, some are resisting foreign influence. The most acceptive to the "western" games are the Japanese with a lot of appeal to the population of local nerds. India and South Korea are leading in the number of new games on their markets. The Japanese like in many other areas of life demonstrate more creativity than their western mentors. Among the games that came out of the western games industry are:

- Highly realistic flight simulators, vehicle sims, war sims, and any kind of simulation of anything inspired by real-world mechanics, behavior and history.
- Freeform, "sandbox" games like *GTA* and its clones, *Spore*, *The Incredible Machine*, *Civilization*, *The Sims* and other management games.
- Non-linear adventure games (with an emphasis on exploration and freedom) like the *Ultima* series. *Fallout 3* and *Fable II* serve as a modern examples.

Japanese game designers are especially creative with game aesthetics. Their systems *manga* and *anime* are used by game designers all over the world. Japanese games also express the desire to reduce and simplify the world into comic book representations. This applies to gameplay as much as graphics: the reduction of skill and learning into statistics and "level ups"; gameworld attributes into "hit points" and stat bonuses; boxing and fencing into rigid "moves" and "specials". Japan excels at making "arcade-style" games, because of their cultural knack for funneling complicated, abstract concepts and mechanics into easily understandable icons, quantifiable values and symbolism. But still the Japanese industry needs Western developers as was proved by the annual 2010s Tokyo Games Show (TGS). This event has shown that, more than ever before: Western developers and publishers are collaborating with Japanese studios. *Capcom* developer says that TGS showed "everyone's making awful games". *Lost Planet 2* was "too Japanese" to appeal in the West. The last decade has seen the balance of power in the gaming industry shift westward. The American company Microsoft succeeded in the console wars, while British Rockstar North and California's Infinity Ward have been responsible for phenomenally successful series like *Grand Theft Auto* and *Call of Duty*.

The second most active videogames developers are in South Korea. They introduced games ideas of their national culture, creating games with a collective spirit. In the game *Lineage* players are defending their castle from siege. Such games train players in building organizational structures, in supporting team work and in sharing risks and rewards. South Korea regularly organizes widely publicized games congresses and competitions, popular TV shows. Games have also became a part of national culture as game parlors are installed in almost every housing block or apartment complex. Government supports with services and, via the education system, professional game development by subsidizing game industry start-ups. South Korea started the World Cyber Games in an olympic fashion of competing teams from all over the world. Their participation is colored dark in the map (Fig. 4.10).

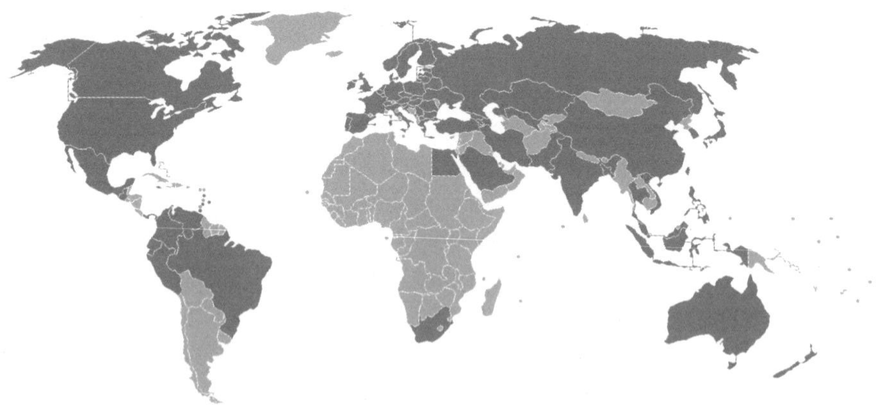

Fig. 4.10.   Countries participating in the World Cyber Games 2010.

The World Cyber Games (WCG), or "Cyber Games Festival" was organized in 2001 by the Korean company World Cyber Games Inc. It was supported first by Samsung and later by Microsoft. The official motto of WCG is "Beyond the Game". WCG is the largest gaming festival celebrated once a year. More than one million virtual visitors come every year. Each participating country conducts preliminary rounds before sending the finest gamers to represent them in this final major event. In 2007, over 700 athletes from over 70 countries came to Seattle, with Spike TV being the WCG's official media partner. In March 2009, WCG debuted its first reality television show, WCG Ultimate Gamer. In WCG tournaments of 2001–2009 South Korea won five times, US won two times and Germany and Holland winning once. Singapore has monthly Business Board Games Meetups. Each person is charged $6 as a fee for the event. Free soft drinks are available at the meetup. In the 2010 season they are playing *Cashflow 101*. 646 groups participate in these Meetups around the world including more than one hundred thousand members in 379 cities of 11 countries.

Communist China elevated games even higher than their capitalist rivals. The base of the game industry was laid out by the Internet cafes with hundreds of PCs in some of them. That gives access to the electronic toys for millions of hungry people. They use the information access to get goods in an eBay-like market. In November 2009, the WCG was held in Chengdu, China. 600 participants from 65 countries were competing for $500,000 worth of prizes. The current record of World Cyber Games was established in November 2008 in Cologne, Germany with 800 participants

Table 4.2.   Medal tally in the 2010 World Cyber Games.

Rank	Team	Gold	Silver	Bronze
1	South Korea	3	2	3
2–4	Brazil, U. K., Germany	1	1	0
5–8	Australia, Ukraine, Sweden, USA	1	0	0
9	Netherlands	0	1	2
10	Japan	0	1	1
11–13	Austria, Denmark, PR China	0	1	0
14–17	Russia, Slovakia, Poland, France	0	0	1

from 78 countries. The prize money that was shared there by the teams was $470,000. Results of 2010 World Cyber Games which were held in San Francisco, USA are given in Table 4.2.

Electronic games and other Internet-based products generated the whole new geek-speak vocabulary facilitating international communications. A new Skype symbols for actions and emotions called Emoticons are presenting new iconic language. This language of Millenium generation game culture widely presented in their text messages on cellular phones, iPhones and iPods.

The variety of card, board, field and electronic games opens wide choice for school teachers, industrial instructors and college professors. The opportunities of using some of them will be discussed in the next chapter.

CHOOSING A GAME

Portfolio matrix of *Roller Coaster Tycoon* games

5.1. LEVEL OF EDUCATION AND GAME TYPE

The choice of a business game from advertized and published material depends on many factors: mission of the game, the size of class, the dynamics of system and the influence of random events on the business. There are three types of business game functions:

> ***Entertaining*** for generating interest in the study of systems and enterprises;
> ***Education*** for the learning of system properties;
> ***Experimenting*** for the design and testing of new systems.

Most business games are supposed to be able to carry all three functions in different proportions (see Fig. 5.1).

The electronic game industry made several attempts to design educational business games for kids. The game series *FleetKids* is aimed to teach kids about money and includes *Windfall* (manage a factory), *Play Ball* (manage a baseball team) and *Frontyard Fortunes* (learn to start your own business). The *Lemonade Stand* web game teaches basic business calculations. The *Gazillionaire* game introduces players to deeper business concepts such as overhead costs, profit margins, market capitalization with the difficulty increasing from the elementary to the college level. The most successful series started in the 1990s from the Nintendo game *Wall Street Kid* based on a series of Japanese games. It teaches children to invest $500,000 of seed capital in the New York stock market. In the case of success the game offers different ways to spend additional money earned. The player is

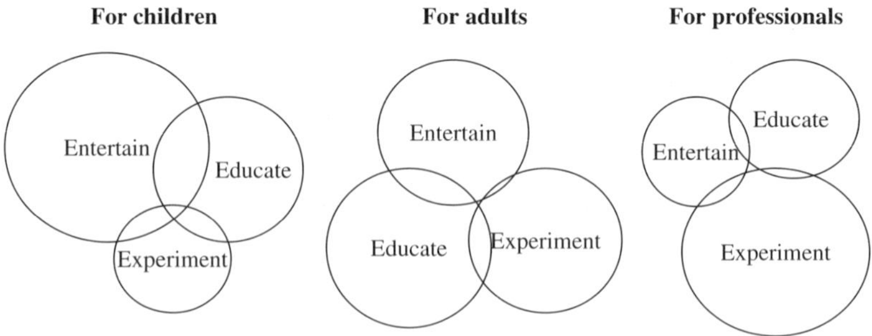

Fig. 5.1.   The proportions between different functions of games.

supposed to buy houses, yachts and even castles to get the ultimate reward: the marriage to his girlfriend.

The largest variety of modifications for all ages, nations and demographic groups is offered by *Monopoly*. This extremely popular business game balances all three of the described above missions. *Monopoly* teaches real estate economics in an entertaining way. It has also transformed itself during the 80 years with a return to commercial success at every technological or economic modification. Every new technological or business innovations ignite a so-called "hype cycle" of game life [Schell, 2008]. The first wave was after patenting it in 1935, then in the 1970s after aggressive advertizing on TV and radio. Significant growth was seen after patenting a Nintendo edition, and the last spectacular success was on 75th anniversary of the first edition as it was illustrated by Fig. 1.1.

Although entertainment is not a primary function of business games for adults, this capacity is becoming more essential for the distraction of kids and teenagers from meaningless, time-killing videogames. The ability of some games like *Monopoly* to become a pastime for family and friends proves the necessity of modification of full-scale business games for younger audiences. Our experience with the development of *"Obla-di, Obla-da"* version of the *CyberMarket* game shows that it is more difficult than the design of a "serious" business game. Entertaining games for children should be faster, more colorful, animated, portable and safe. There are few business games of this type. Among them is our game *Aquarium*, another is the modification of the *Career* game for high school teenagers [Bazil, 2003] and *Cashflow for Kids* [Kiyosaki, 2002].

Business games may be integrated with other kinds of playing, for example, solving quizzes and puzzles. The introduction to economic education of *MarketSim* and *CyberMarket* games is based on basic econometric exercises. The usual practice of the entertainment industry is the offering of toys and souvenirs that complement the release of new movies and books. Some games are also commercially supported by toys and vice versa, when toys remind us of the game characters and scenery. We found jigsaw puzzles helpful for ensuring the correct placement of cards on the game board. Toys are especially attractive to kids who may spend additional time for the activities like solving auxiliary problems. Music and art, especially cartoons, are an essential part of entertainment games. They can also illuminate business games. Housewives and seniors are often attracted by gambling which may also be a part of a business game:

> "An Entertainment Software Association survey showed that men and women over 18 make up 69% of the gaming population — and that the average age of players is now 29 years old. A full 25% of players are over age 50."

> [Novak, 2008, p.56]

The educational role of business games had been proven through the experience of several generations of high school and college graduates. But still these games are mainly departmental, functionally restrictive exercises without using the main advantage of business games: interdisciplinary integration. This quality of games is achieved by the few business schools that use multifunctional games such as *Capstone* and *Marketplace*. We are working on the next generation of a platform for modular business games which cover a life-long continuous education (see Part 2 of this book, "Design your Own Business Game").

The least recognized role of business games is experimental. The games are the only tools that model real human behavior in technological, environmental, economic and social systems. Business games allow the testing of different versions of system design in a short time and at a small cost with convincing conclusions. Moreover, participants of such experiments may become active developers of the game and experts in simulated systems. This is proven by the "open-source" approach of software development and the furnishing of customized game contents [Edery, 2009].

After defining the primary function of a game we should formulate its mission. Missions of entertaining games range from an introductory social function like building trust to the psychological intent of elevating team spirit. These games are usually short, require minimum hardware and are well presented in popular books and manuals [Scannell, 2007; Tamblyn and Weiss, 2000]. They are usually called "icebreakers", or "humorous training games". If the educational goal prevails, it requires a game for the development of the basic knowledge of science, technology, economics and management. Educational games are longer and more complicated. Additionally, they require a long-term commitment to a study program and may require interdepartmental consent or school-level approval. The most challenging is the choice of a business game for experimentation purposes. It should be based on a theoretically sound model and carry the responsibility for the purity of experimentation on the choice and composition of the participants. As with any scientific experiment, it must be reproducible with accurately documented results.

The *Countdown: A Strategy Game for Project Teams* is a project management game that enhances the knowledge and skills of project teams. It was developed by Paradigm Learning in collaboration with project management experts. This game uses a variety of discovery learning techniques. This project management game engages and energizes learners as they explore the concepts, tools and behaviors of effective project management. The program targets project managers as well as project team members and can be customized to specific projects.

In Chapter 1 we presented some results of experimentation with the game *Career*. This game was built on the universal Markov chain model with parameters specified for a particular school or demographic group of players. Therefore, the results of this experimentation have to be compared either within the dynamics of the same institution or with a similar population of players. The other game, *TranSport*, that has universal applications, we used for experimentation with more general conclusions about different strategies and learning rates. The board of this game is presented in Fig. 5.2.

This game might be played on different levels of uncertainty and cooperation. Rules for a transportation system game may restrict players from the information on resources of the other players (closed cards) or reveal them (open cards). Players may be following an individual gain of placing cards themselves and preventing others from finishing (individual criteria), or be asked for faster game finishing as a whole team (collective criteria). Figure 5.3 shows comparisons of four possible combinations of game rules corresponding to four different transportation systems.

Results of the game are presented in reports comparing efficiency of each organizational model and the learning rate in different conditions. The results of experimentation on scale from extreme competition to full cooperation are presented in Table 5.1.

The analysis of this experiment shows that cooperation/competition factor significantly influences the average time and much less affects

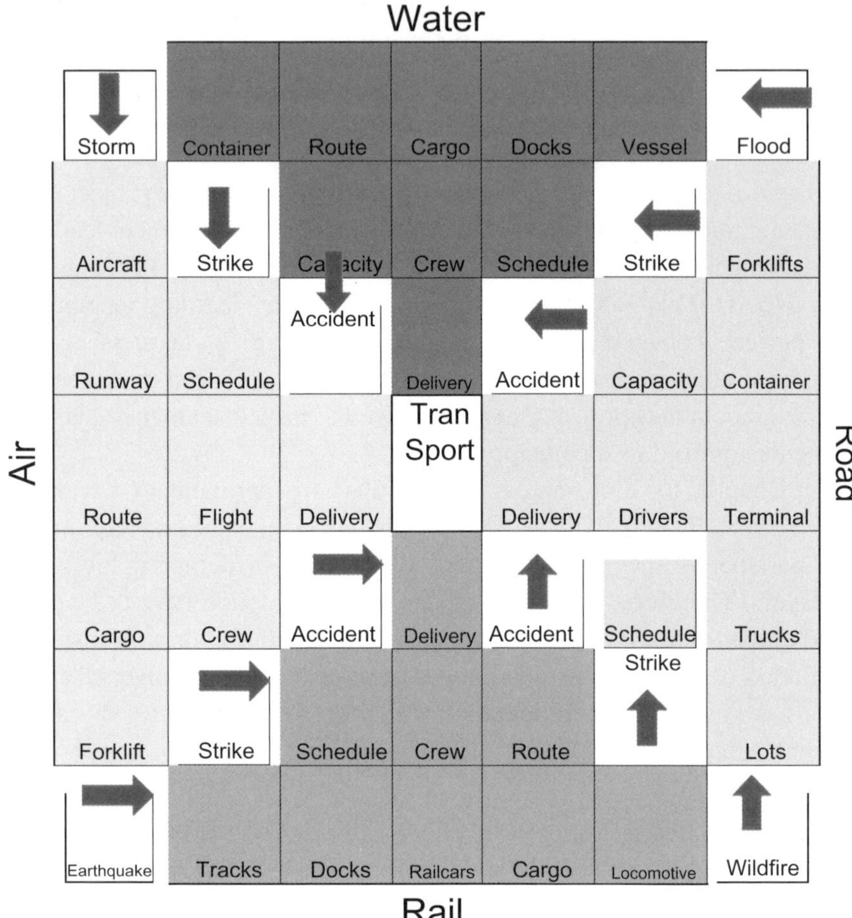

Fig. 5.2.   The board of *TranSport* game.

learning rates. The influence of the uncertainty level is opposite: less on averages and more on learning rates. Cooperation drastically decreases average time. The increasing uncertainty facilitates the learning progress. The most significant difference observed between competitive and cooperative modes of the game in the total number of missed moves (30:12).

Closed cards

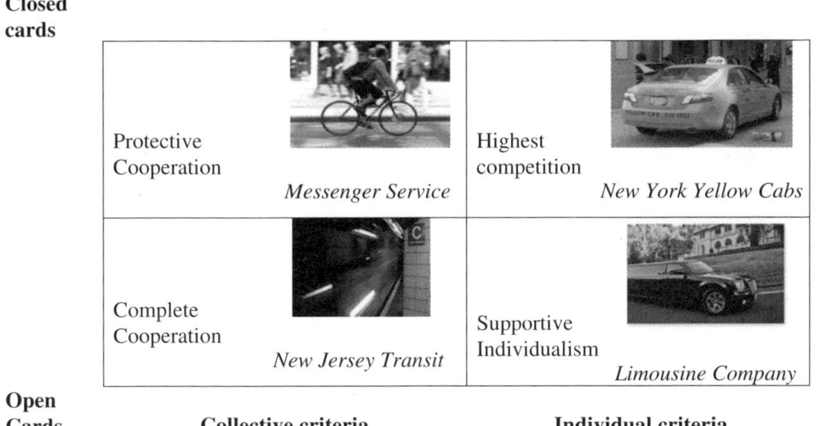

Fig. 5.3.   Organizational settings for *TranSport* game experimentation.

It shows that players behave negatively mainly by preventing competitors from opportunity to move instead of constructive strategies of success.

We experimented with a number of players of the *Monopoly* game. When compared three, five and eight players, we found out that the fastest learning rate is for three players (76%) and the slowest is for eight players (94%).

Figure 5.4 shows learning curve for three players.

These experiments also show that average time of play is shortest for the small size of a team of three players, and longest for the medium size of five players with the largest team of eight players falling in between. So the best combination of small average time and fast learning shows up for the three players game.

5.2.   CLASSROOM GAMES

The best start of the class where you plan to use business games is by asking students to bring to the class their favorite card and board games or demonstrate a videogame. You may choose some of them as modules of business

Table 5.1.   Results of experimentation with *TranSport* game.

Transportation system			**Team**	**Black Hat**
			Timer	____________
GAME REPORT			*Players*	____________
				____________
Date__/__/__				____________
				____________
				____________
Cycles	**Runs**	**Missed moves**	**Time**	**Analysis**
Closed cards, Competitive	1	2	12:00	Average 459 sec
	2	3	7:04	
	3	4	5:35	Learning rate 66%
	4	2	5:15	
Closed cards, Cooperative	**Runs**	**Missed moves**	**Time**	**Analysis**
	1	3	1:17	Average 58 sec
	2	1	1:00	
	3		:39	Learning rate 87%
	4		:55	
Open cards Competitive	**Runs**	**Missed moves**	**Time**	**Analysis**
	1	5	3:45	Average 218 sec
	2	7	3:36	
	3	4	3:28	Learning rate 85%
	4	3	2:41	
Open cards Cooperative	**Runs**	**Missed moves**	**Time**	**Analysis**
	1	2	1:09	Average 62 sec
	2		1:11	
	3	6	1:40	Learning rate >100%
	4		1:31	

games. Many business games for high school and college students are used only by individual instructors and are not available to others because they are not published or just improvisational. A large variety of educational games is offered by specialized companies and educational consultants. Choosing games from adverts is not easy: many of them are not described in detail, so instructors are hesitant to spend their time and money in advance for an unclear result. References in professional publications, demonstrations at conferences and workshops are the best ways for the choice of the game. The most informative are blogs containing remarks of players.

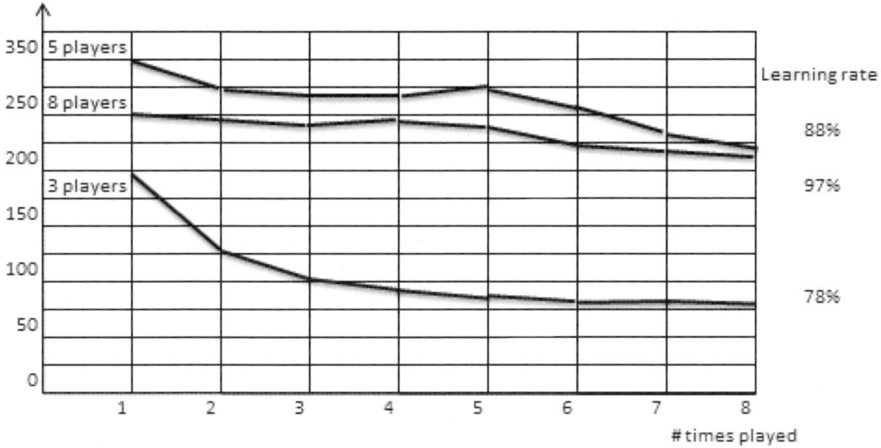

Fig. 5.4.   Learning curve for *Monopoly* with three players.

Many games are industry, area or culture specific and are too detailed or naturalistic to be used as a platform in different environments. On the contrary, general purpose games advertized as "strategic" are actually adventures in fantasy worlds. Success of the game often depends on the personality of the instructor and hardly may be repeated by the others. Many videogames are displayed on websites of training consultants who help to choose, download and test the game.

Table 5.2 represents some of the most popular business educational games from the smallest and quickest to the largest and longest.

Business games for economic and management education programs should be carefully planned as an integral part of class schedule. The ideal is the development of comprehensive business game covering the entire course or several complementing disciplines. These are games such as *Capstone* for an Executive MBA program or *CyberMarket* for a Microeconomics class. But most business games are designed to cover just one or a few topics of the single course, to be allocated along a semester schedule by the professor. The game can be in the beginning of the course, inside the appropriate topic or as a conclusion of the class. Some comprehensive games like our *Finance SoS* may be used as tests and exams.

Business game *CyberMarket* is able to produce different results. First, the educational result is knowledge of the basic microeconomic models.

Table 5.2.   Examples of business games for college education.

Name of the game	Level	Structure	Model and procedure	Schedule
Pyramid of Businesses	All	Teams of 4–6 students	Filling in the board with cards representing businesses	10–20 min per round
Words-in-Sentences	Under-Graduates	Teams of 5–8 students	Generate words and assembly sentences according to processes flowchart	1 hour class
Shells Game	Under-Graduates	Teams of 4–6 students	Production of colorful cards on four specialized workstations	1–2 hours
MarketSim	Under-Graduates	Class of 20–30 students	Production and sales of products and services in closed markets	Synchronized web exercises
Beer Game	All	Teams of 5–10 students	Production and distribution stages of Supply-chain process	1–2 hours
Monopoly	All	Teams of 2–6	Real estate and city utilities trade in randomly generated events	2–3 hours
Cashflow	All	Individuals	Family budget as income statement and balance sheet	3–4 hours
Career	All	Individuals	Forecasting individual professional career and/or life	1/2 hour per a year of life
Glo-Bus	Graduates	Teams of 4–6 students	Production and trade by industry in regional markets	6–8 hours
CyberMarket	All	Teams of 5–7 players	Production and sales of products and services in a closed market	5 sessions 1–2 hours each

(*Continued*)

Table 5.2. (*Continued*)

Name of the game	Level	Structure	Model and procedure	Schedule
Capstone	Executives, MBA	Teams of 4–7 players	Development, production, marketing and sales of electronics	5 sessions 3 hours each
Leadership in Management	Executives	Teams of 6 players	Team building games and field production process simulation	3–5 days
upTick	MBA students	Unlimited community	Financial strategy on stock market	No time limit

Then, understanding of the relation between structural and behavioral variables of an economic system. These results could not be achieved without the emotional and artistic involvement of students. Here are some of their remarks at the end of a Microeconomics course based around the *CyberMarket* game:

- *I had no idea Microeconomics could be so much fun. I feel that I learned so much, and I also enjoyed working with the class and professor tremendously.*
- *The Business Game really made the objectives learned come to life.*
- *Very informative exciting subject if put into perspective of Business Game — colored up a dry subject to the point of enjoyment.*

[Bazil, 2003]

One of the student's reports of *CyberMarket* game is attached in the Appendix. It illustrates a deep involvement and creative approach to this game.

The size and especially stability of the class participation is crucial for the choice of a game. A game with specialized functional roles cannot be successful every round of play by the students representing new unfamiliar responsibilities. On the other hand, a game requiring creative decision making is performed better without carrying over the knowledge of routines accumulated by predecessors. Teams without specialized roles suffer less because of the changes of players. Introductory games are better if they are less structured; it gives a player a chance for experimenting with different roles. The rotation of roles between rounds of a game may be one of the organizational devices of learning, but it should be controlled and infrequent. For coordination of games within a course we may schedule the exchange of players between teams. For example, the role assigned to a student in the *Shells Game* is better performed if it is similar to one's professional choice in the *Career* game. The free choice of roles is useful for the exchange of experience with other teams. The scheduled rotation may be necessary for equalizing the size and competence of teams, but it is difficult in the case of fluctuating class participation.

The structure of a game should be balanced with the size of the class and the psychological limits of communication. With a reasonable size of three to five members in a team, a class of 20 to 25 students may be split into five to seven teams to ensure a competitive superstructure of the game. If the mission of the game is functional, the same class may be divided in a smaller number of teams. Experimentation games may use a variety of structures.

Videogames are no longer an exclusive pastime for young guys. Retired people are spending less of their golden years playing traditionally recreational games like *Scrabble, Checkers, Poker* or *Chess*. More seniors and women are involved in videogames today. They have a choice between playing by themselves, with the family and friends, and in community clubs where they also socialize. But financial institutions that chase for their time and money still use promotional seminars rather than games about family economics.

Teachers of economics, especially at the high school level, may be also not scrupulous seducing students by easy ways of making money on the real markets. Many financial games are built on the simplified models of ideal markets:

> "One can easily imagine an exciting simulation game that includes the real-world possibility of prices first rising irrationally, only to fall when investors lose confidence. Students might buy and sell stocks as quickly as they can, passing the hot stock to someone else — until the bubble bursts and the stocks are worthless. For some purposes like teaching math, stock market games provide a dose of reality. Brad, a sixth grader in Pasadena,

California, points proudly to the stock chart he keeps at home: "It wasn't math; we used percentages and multiplication to figure out how much we made." It might be too much to expect schoolteachers to pass up such an easy way to spice up a humdrum class. Certainly, the lure of a compelling game, along with glitzy corporate-sponsored lesson plans, is attractive to overworked teachers. But if students are to learn how the economy actually works, then teachers need to use stock market games with great caution, supplementing them with alternative activities to show the real world of unequal resources, impotent small shareholders, and reckless speculative bubbles."

[Maier, 2010]

It is the responsibility of the teacher to clarify the border between the virtual reality of the game and real life. There is an efficiency criteria between choosing of the proper game and the final analysis of results. For example, the business game *upTick* has been developed and used at the Harvard Business School. Six other business schools have been involved in *upTick's* "Beta Test" program, each with similar success. A Penn State professor's comments on *upTick* efficiency are below:

"*upTick* takes students closer to experiencing real market situations than can be accomplished using traditional cases or by examining how markets reacted to prior events (e.g., discussing past situations by looking at market data around the event on Reuters or Bloomberg.) Through *upTick*, students get the chance to be in the seat of the decision makers rather than just observing the decisions that were made. As a result, they seem to gain a much greater understanding of how financial decisions are made and how markets function."

[Haushalter, 2007]

A former Wall Street businessman, Mark Zurack, after becoming a professor found that *upTick* successfully brings a realistic trading environment into the classroom. His students enjoy participating in the simulations because they bring concepts about securities pricing, trading and risk management that they have learned about in a more traditional manner to life [Bloomberg, 2011]. Finding an appropriate to your needs game is easy with the Internet search. However, there may not be an available game, and then a teacher needs to modify the published one, or design their own game. That is the purpose of the second part of our book.

5.3. MANAGEMENT SCIENCE/OPERATIONS RESEARCH

As it was shown before, business games development in the second part of the 20th century was inspired by war games. This knowledge was carried by the Operations Research (OR) personnel from military OR units. Commissioned OR officers come to work from the defense to the civilian industries. These specialists in military strategy were well qualified in sciences and had a taste of work in multifunctional teams. The spirit of teamwork was encouraging whole OR groups to stay together after the end of World War II to form OR departments in industry and academia. Later these groups were merged with Management Science (MS) specialists forming an OR/MS community in companies and universities. Many of these specialists became industrial consultants or formed institutions like the famous Rand Corporation. The founders of game theory John von Neumann, Oscar Morgenstern and John Nash worked at Rand. Rand's gaming activities started from the design of policy strategy simulations for the US government, logistics for industry and even to preschool education in California [Karoly and Bigelow, 2005]:

> "The origin of the business simulation game dates back to 1955. In that year, the Rand Corporation developed a simulation exercise called *Monopologs* which focused on U.S. Air Force logistics. *Monopologs* required its participants to perform as inventory managers in a simulated Air Force supply system, thus providing decision-making experience without the risks associated with the consequences of a wrong decision. The Air Force continued the use of *Monopologs* for many years and reported it to be a highly successful training device."
>
> [Jackson, 1959]

Mathematical models of academic OR/MS eventually converged with industrial applications of classic Scientific Management (SM). SM was formed in the first half of the 20th century as an engineering approach to the management [Taylor, 1911]. The "father of SM" Frederick Winslow Taylor after getting recognition as an industrial consultant had fallen out of favor with powerful labor unions. By the 1930s his time and motion studies were used only to manual "blue collar" jobs at Ford's car assemblies. Taylorism was revived in the 1980s for the research of "white collar" and especially "gold collar" jobs. The term "Gold collar" was coined by professor Robert Reich when he was the Secretary of Labor in Bill Clinton's administration [Reich, 1998]. "Gold collars" are the professionals integrating high academic qualifications with fine manual or psychological training. Examples of "gold collars" include surgeons, pilots, astronauts, operators of complex equipment and stock market brokers. They are especially in need of and get training at flight simulators and business games.

Computerization of decision making in the 1970s started integration between OR/MS academics and SM practitioners. The new generation of scientists in the 21st century finished integration of the two communities by combining their achievements under the umbrella of System Engineering. The main component of system thinking was developed within a strong community of System Dynamics [Forrester, 1961; Senge *et al.*, 1994; Sterman, 2000]. All these achievements unite business games designs with the new opportunities of computerization and visualization of business processes.

Vladimir Lenin, the Russian leader in the 1920s, was so impressed by Taylorism that he incorporated it into Soviet industry under the name "Scientifically Organized Labor". Taylorism and the mass production methods of Henry Ford thus became highly influential during the early years of industrial development of the Soviet Union. In the 1930s, war against Germany was looming over the USSR. Accordingly, factories started running exercises of training managers to convert plants from civilian into defence production. From the contemporary point of view these "industrial experiments" were actually the first field business games [Gagnon, 1986]. The first *Red Weaver* game was based on Taylor's methodology and war games. The engineers designed new products and technology while managers and workers supposed just "storm" production output. In 1950s business games activities resumed in the USSR and in the US independent of each other [Greenblat, 1988].

Scientific Management equips business games with many practical tools you have seen in previous chapters. These include organizational charts and statistical diagrams, flowcharts and technological schematics, control charts and cost analysis. These tools are necessary for the introduction of players into the game situations and for the analyses of game results. OR/MS provides business games with the strong support of optimization models and game theory. In addition to science, a game needs artistic support to be entertaining and engaging. The means for integration of art and science in business games will be discussed in the following chapters.

The contemporary Systems Engineering (SE) approach to business games is focused on the system as a whole, but treats the separate parts of the system differently before integrating them into a global model. SE also recognizes the fact that we should handle systems as a whole. So business games for real Multi-Dimensional systems we base on the *Holarchy* platform. Development of System of Systems (SoS) we propose as a series of games or *metagames* on the *SimSoS* platform. The disaggregation and integration of SoS may follow either spatial or temporal dimensions. Industrial applications follow the life cycle model of the system and economic systems are represented by the business cycles. Finally, social systems are the most complex, and cover all of the above including the human behavior which might be simulated by the business games.

Human factor study very closely related to the basics of the Utility Theory which we will present in the next section.

5.4. UTILITY THEORY

Contemporary Game Theory scientifically clarified classic Utility Theory that was born two centuries ago in application to gambling. Gambling is a $60 billion dollar annual revenue industry in the US alone. Americans spend ten times more on casino gambling and lotteries than they do on going to movies [Gardner, 2003].

> "Americans love to gamble. At least 50 million Americans patronize the businesses in this sector every year. Indeed, some Americans love to gamble so much that they are clinical — some 5 million are diagnosed as compulsive gamblers, suffering from addiction. These are the kind of people who are prone to lose everything they have gambling — like the former owner of the Philadelphia Eagles, who lost $20 million, including control of the Eagles, during a particularly bad losing streak in Atlantic City, New Jersey."
>
> [Gardner, 2003]

Decision theory as one of the scientific management tools, also operate with measurements of utility. That integrates the Homo Sapiens' model of behavior based on criteria of business profit only with emotional Homo Ludens into the practical Homo Economicus. Businessmen do not always behave rationally. Statistical analysis of gamblers and studies of the activity of stock brokers formed empirical utility models. Eventually this formed basics of the universal utility theory as applied to financial decisions of businesses and households. Now society also expects from businesses and population more social and environmental concern. Sometimes these responsibilities are lowering profits and incomes. Accordingly, the contemporary utility theory justifies the rational balance between individual gain, collective achievements, environment protection and support of social values.

Utility Theory in business games translates material and monetary gains and losses into the measurement of individual motivation and group satisfaction. Although feelings of happiness or distress are highly subjective, the proportions between them for the same person or social group are quite stable and measurable. They may be predicted hypothetically and evaluated experimentally. Social utility concept was introduced by Utilitarians in the 19th century. They postulated that society should aim to maximize the total utility of individuals, aiming for "the greatest happiness for the greatest number of people". The revival of this doctrine for economics belongs to Alfred Marshall:

> "Utility is taken to be correlative to Desire or Want. It has been already argued that desires cannot be measured directly, but only indirectly, by the outward phenomena to which they give rise: and that in those cases with which economics is chiefly concerned the measure is found in the price which a person is willing to pay for the fulfilment or satisfaction of his desire."
>
> [Marshall, 1920]

The first problem of utility theory is the choice of variables for the measurement of business success, individual happiness, nature protection and social justice. Players in a business game don't have real money at stake. Professor Sterman recommends in the *Beer Game* a small incentive for the winning team as a collection of $1 from each player in the cash prize pool. We sometimes offered a real beer as a prize to this game to the winning team in our off-campus graduate classes. Some instructors of the

MarketSim game, which is a story based on bread and wine, offer a bottle of wine as the prize to the winner. For undergraduates we recommend using non-toxic prizes such as professional publications or expensive textbooks.

The primary result of the game is the learning which includes the evaluation of the progress in a simulated enterprise. The learning rate defines the optimum length of the game to get the maximum knowledge out of a variety of situations. Short-term profits are often gained at the expense of long-term efficiency, and team results might be undermined by individual selfishness. Utility Theory does not yet reflect the delays between a player's decisions and results of the game. The other underdeveloped part of the theory is the evaluation of the individual's input into the collective success or failure.

The first problem of utility theory is the quantification of variables. Technological and environmental applications of business games are using natural scientific and engineering measurements. Economic applications are historically advanced with the money and time variables. But social and ecological events need to be quantified according to their intensity which is impossible to measure instrumentally. We need to transform subjective judgments of different individuals or social groups into numerical evaluations.

Scales of such measurements begin with two alternatives, like a business decision "Yes or No" for acceptance or rejection of an offer, or a customer's decision of buying or ignoring the product. The next step in scale clarification goes up to three levels. An additional neutral level of indifference in between of the extremes becomes the option. Game Theory uses preference statements of "better", "worse" and "equal" for comparison of scenarios. Project management uses "Optimistic — Most likely — Pessimistic" estimates of time for a job. Psychology professor from Cambridge University Edward DeBono introduced Yes-Po-No scale with the additional level of agreement Po (Possible) in between of answers Yes or No [DeBono, 1967]. Figure 5.5 shows ordinal scales for measurement of customer's satisfaction. Two different scales for transformation of subjective judgments into ordinal numerical evaluations are compared in Fig. 5.5.

The most popular are the scales of 5 to 10 steps with 1 denoting the end of the worst statement. We find it misleading to represent negative judgments in positive numbers. That is why we recommend "minus-zero-plus" scales for the measurement of game progress in scales presented

<table>
<tr><td colspan="7">Non-linear progressive scale</td></tr>
<tr><td></td><td>Strongly
Dissatisfied</td><td></td><td>Indifferent</td><td></td><td>Strongly
Satisfied</td><td></td></tr>
<tr><td>Absolutely
dissatisfied</td><td></td><td>Slightly
Dissatisfied</td><td></td><td>Slightly
Satisfied</td><td></td><td>Absolutely
Satisfied</td></tr>
<tr><td>-9</td><td>-3</td><td>-1</td><td>0</td><td>+1</td><td>+3</td><td>+9</td></tr>
<tr><td>- 2
Absolutely
dissatisfied</td><td></td><td>-1
Dissatisfied</td><td>0
Indifferent</td><td>+1
Satisfied</td><td></td><td>+2
Absolutely
satisfied</td></tr>
<tr><td colspan="7">Linear scale</td></tr>
</table>

Fig. 5.5. Ordinal scales for measurement of customer's satisfaction.

in Fig. 5.7. Then the evaluations of performance by players and teams are more consistent with human ability to differentiate emotional impressions. For the technological and environmental applications when polar points of the scale are extremely valuable, nonlinear scale is preferable. Japanese quality control tools in industry use progressive exponential scales apparently for the same reason. That approach, called Taguchi quality control, prevents large deviations from the target by the scale of quadratic proportions. As we will show below, the most justified by the Utility Theory are exponential scales.

Project management estimates of a time necessary for the job require continuous evaluations. The most convenient is the transformation of judgments of experienced professionals into the variation of continuous Beta or triangular distribution. It gives accurate interpolation between three evaluations of triangular distribution (optimistic, most likely, pessimistic). Figure 5.6 illustrates the appearance of this distribution in evaluation by a player of a time for a completion of a job.

Utility theory differentiates three types of players: risk averse, neutral and risk takers. The majority of individuals and especially teams are risk averse and conservative. A smaller proportion belongs to the neutrals and only a few are risk takers. The neutrality assumes that a player's reaction is proportional to the results of the game. Experiments with simple lottery games show different degrees of deviation for the conservative and risky individuals. Risk averse persons are more excited about initial modest gains, risk takers are more excited by the large amounts of gain. So if the straight

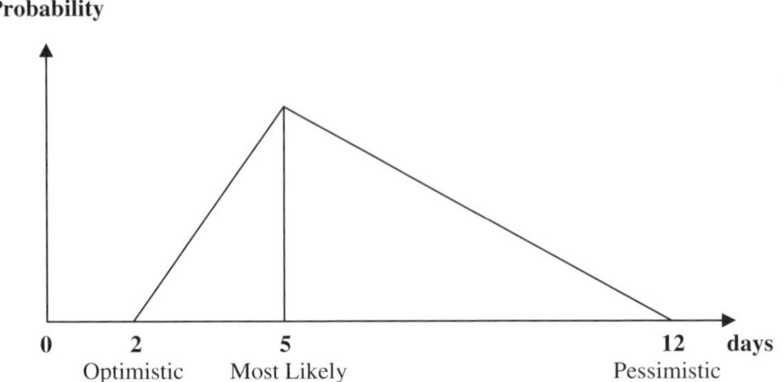

Fig. 5.6.   Triangular distribution of the estimates of time for a job.

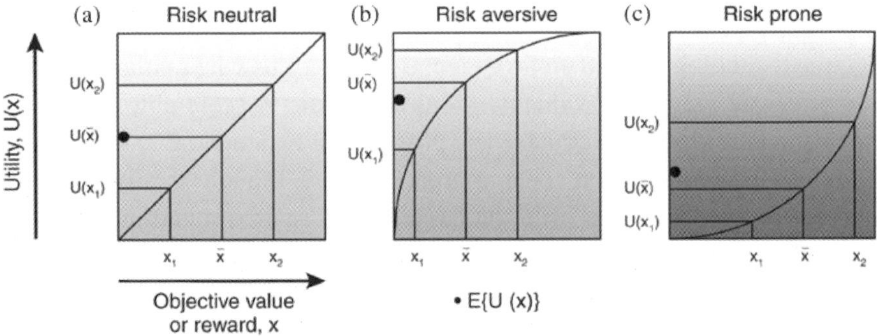

Fig. 5.7.   Three types of players: (a) risk neutral, (b) risk averse, (c) risk prone.

line represents neutrality, then risk avoidance is presented by the curve above it, and risk prone — by the curve below it (Fig. 5.7).

The universal mathematical model of utility explains intensity of the reaction not only to the gains, but also the degree of deviation from neutrality in the distress of the loss. The main driver of businessmen reaction is the amount of resources at their disposal. It is represented by the exponential utility function

$$U(x) = 1 - e^{\wedge}(-x/R),$$

Where x is the amount of gain or loss in a game, R is the limit of loss at stake for the player.

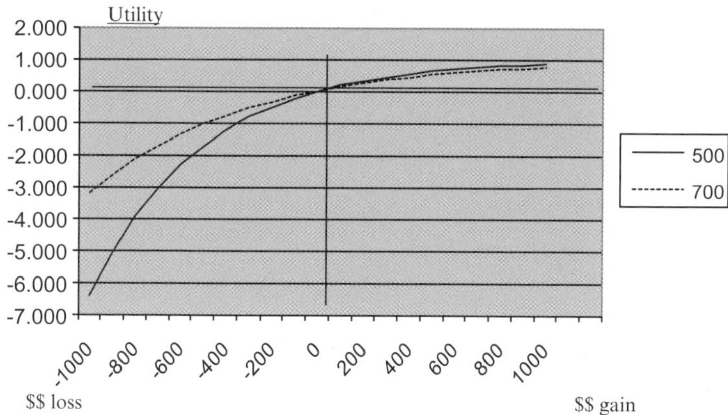

Fig. 5.8.   Utility functions of risk averse persons with different amounts at stake.

The influence of parameter R on utility function is illustrated in Fig. 5.8 for typical risk averse players.

A player with a smaller sum to risk is more sensitive to losses (left part of the solid curve) while both are close in their reaction to gains (upper parts of both curves are close). Utility function is a relative presentation of the level of satisfaction (or distress) on the ordinal scale. It measures relative happiness or distress, so we may say that a loss of \$500 for the first (poorer) player is about three times more distressful than the loss of \$250. For the richer player it will be the same proportion for the loss of \$700 compared with \$350. Contemporary Utility Theory may reflect by more complicated models some other factors such as charity donations and sharing of collective gains/losses between members of the team.

The utility functions are therefore an essential tool for evaluation of business game results. The application of them will be illustrated in the following chapters of this book.

Part 2

DESIGNING A BUSINESS GAME

As many business games go unpublished and unpublicized, it is a challenge to find an existing business game for specific purposes. The ambition to develop one's own game is also a temptation. There are two main challenges in developing a game; first it is not a good idea to oversimplify an advanced subject. The second danger is the creation of an overly complex and unmanageable game. Therefore, it is better to begin with a simple model that can be expanded if time and resources allow. Additionally, we also warn against the computerization of games before they are tested in a paper version.

The architectures of business and entertainment games are opposite. Recreational games start with the story where participants play characters. Meanwhile, business games give a framework that players use to develop their own stories. Yet in both cases, players can develop their avatars.

The purpose of a **Holarchy** platform is the visualization of roles, procedures and resources of participants. The medium for games is the "playing field," for example a game board or the computer screen. It displays organizational charts and decision processes. Examples of these are material, energy and information flowcharts. The movement of cards or tokens on this field symbolizes business processes.

The **SimSoS** game platform was developed for the design of new systems and the testing of new procedures. SimSoS is based on System-of-Systems and Game Theory. The SimSoS platform integrates systems projects and saves time for managers in testing different options. It is also necessary for faculty of all levels of education for teaching economics, management and systems engineering.

THE PURPOSE OF THE GAME

Board of *The Game of Life* (1860)

6.1.　TECHNOLOGICAL SYSTEMS

We start with technological and environmental applications of business games because these systems are based on solid scientific and engineering models. To become a business game they must be complemented by economic and managerial components. Sound technological or environmental contents naturally generate economic variables reflecting new enterprises of the time. That is why the first business games were created as simulations of agriculture and construction. Board games in the beginning of the 20th century were designed for the blooming trucking industry in the US. They were regularly patented starting from the 1920s to today [Stoll, 1920; Goetemiller, 1938; Michel, 1984]. Later, in the 1930s, new realities of contemporary life added components of economic development to board games such as the *Landlord's Game* and *The Game of Life*. These games may be considered the beginning of the modeling of social systems of wealth distribution and power structures. Business games reflect emerging industries and business problems of time. In 1980s energy crisis was reflected by the games that applied to the oil industry — *Windfall: the Oil Crisis Game, Oil Barons, Black Gold (Oil Imperium)* and others. Communications and environmental applications appeared at the end of the 20th century [Jarvis, 1995]. Complex problems of the early 21st century require business games that integrate problems of System of Systems engineering.

Entertainment games reflect the culture of the time. Most of them are based on popular literature, cinema and television stories. In some cases they are affected by the economic situation and social events. They also reflect man-made catastrophes and ecological disasters presented in a realistic industrial and geographical scenery.

So-called "serious" games such as *Flight Simulators* are used for military training exercises, by police, fire fighters, medical and other emergency professionals. Players are required to perform the vital operations in a virtual scenery with visual, mechanical and other effects reflecting situation and the consequences of their decisions. These simulators are also necessary for training and testing operators of fast, dangerous and complicated technological processes. Examples of such applications are the transportation, energy supply, telecommunications and other hi-tech industries and

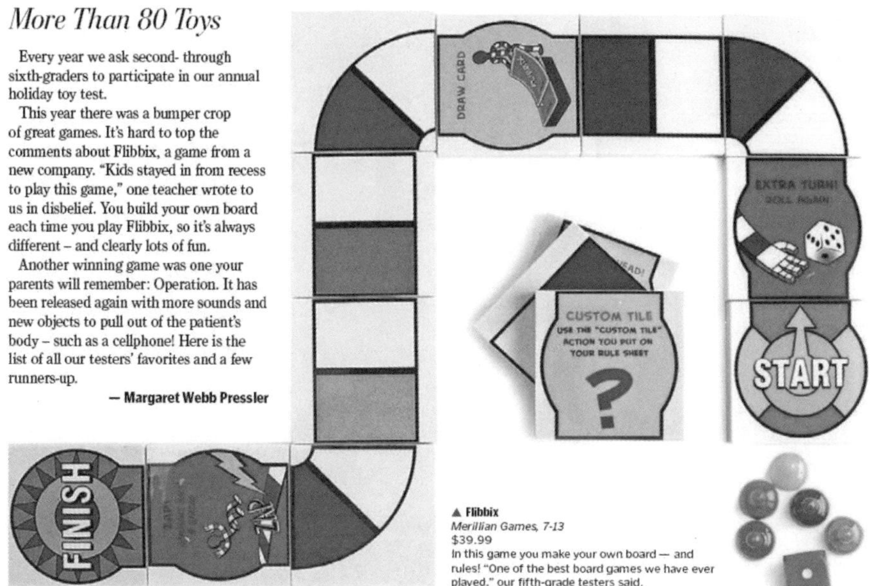

Fig. 6.1. The flibbix game board.

services. The introduction of management functions is the next step for technological simulations such as the *Highway Construction Game*.

All simulations are becoming more realistic by adding the scale of time that is similar to the development of new technologies. Board games started with 1-dimensional (1D) *Flibbix* that is flexible as a snake (see Fig. 6.1).

This snake swallowed its tail becoming a squared cycle like in the classic *Monopoly* or in a circle as in the newest version of *Monopoly Revolution*. The movement along such a chain represents the position of a player in the game. Evolution of games may be illustrated by the construction and military applications which have the longest history. It started thousands of years ago from 1D *Jenga* game and was converted into 2D *Tetris*. Recently they were modified into 3D *Tower Bloxx*. The next generation of construction games appeared from the biology for the building of new protein structures. The *Folding@home* game required from players to go into higher-dimension structures (3D + time scale) on Sony Play Station 3. Now modernized *Foldit!* game may be considered a 5D game (4D + player's creativity) for PCs [McGonigal, 2011]. So the designs of technological

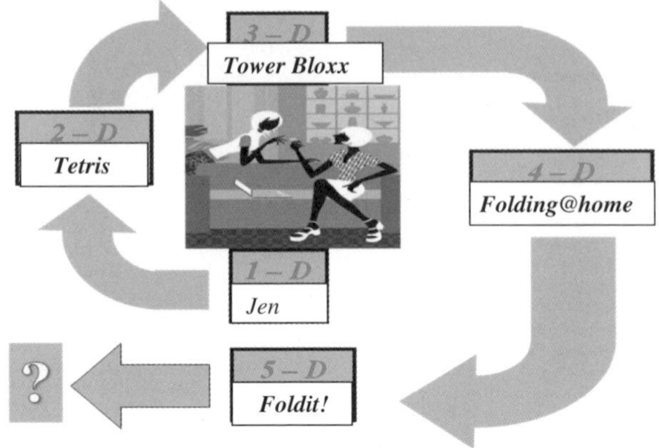

Fig. 6.2.   The spiral of development of technological games.

business games follow a spiral of evolution with radical changes accelerating from centuries into years (Fig. 6.2).

Technology of games starting from millennia old *Jenga* have already passed several generations of development starting with wooden blocks and evolving to computer images. Today there are several business games based on 3D LEGO blocks such as the *SIEMENS Supply Chain Simulator*. The *Lego* family of tools exerted influence on technological game designs by allowing interlocking constructions. Higher order structural models of networks and maps naturally prevail for the presentation of transportation and construction environments. Adding new dimensions for economic applications is possible by using 2D and 3D matrices. These models are reflecting operations, growth and development of production processes and services. The 3rd spatial dimension is now possible to visualize in holographic software.

Most innovations in games as in other new designs are the combinations of old components by new available technologies. These processes are described by Steven Johnson and Kevin Kelly in their books [Kelly, 2009; Johnson, 2010]. The process of innovation as a combination of market expectations and technology capabilities is reflected in their lively discussion:

"KELLY: As I started thinking about the history of technology, there did seem to be a sense in which, during any given period, lots of innovations were in the air, as it were. They came simultaneously. It appeared as if they *wanted* to happen. I should hasten to add that it's not a conscious agency; it's a lower form, something like the way an organism or bacterium can be said to have certain tendencies, certain trends, certain urges. But it's an agency nevertheless.

JOHNSON: I was particularly taken with your idea that technology wants increasing diversity — which is what I think also happens in biological systems, as the adjacent possible becomes larger with each innovation. As tech critics, I think we have to keep this in mind, because when you expand the diversity for a system that leads to an increase in great things and an increase in crap."

[Wired, 10/2010].

It is not always possible to find among the published business games one which exactly fits our purposes. Accordingly, it is better to look for a prototype rather than creating a game from the scratch. We found many parallels and analogies between business games and other types of games in gambling, sports, entertainment and the military. The earliest business game of the 1930s, *Red Weaver* and the management simulators in the 1950s *AMA* (designed by American Management Association) and *Monopologs* (by the RAND Corporation) were directly influenced by predecessors of the 19th century as the German military game *Kriegspiel* [Edery, 2008]. Now the choice of prototypes is a hundred times richer. Military war games became an example of the competitive environment undergoing a process of change. It allows decision makers to simulate how different organizations can adapt to the change. Richard Clark, CEO of Merck and Co., considers competitions very useful:

> "I am a strong believer in if you're going to develop a vision or a strategic plan for the future of a company that you have to engage the organization in doing that [roles-playing simulation] ... it can't be just the CEO or top ten executives sitting in a sterile conference room."
>
> [USA Today, 2006]

We also apply models of technological and biological developments to business games to simulate ecological, economic and social systems. The early generations of business games had a strong technological component prevailing over business decisions and economic analysis. These games were designed by engineers who usually patented them as the products with appropriate technical documentation. For example, there are dozens of patents registered on trucking board games since the 1890s with plenty of geographical and technical details. They visualize on the board a chain of events ("states" in mathematical terminology) along the traveling routes on a real or fictitious road network. The events, equipment and personnel are represented with hundreds of cards and tokens. The engineers who naturally pay attention to technical details, are not accurate in economics.

Simplification of economic calculations is acceptable for board games, but it must maintain realistic proportions between different costs and prices. For example, the *Trucking Simulation Game* [US patent #4,426,084, 1984] requires $1,000 for any of the following events: Tire repair, Damage a fence, Pay toll. Some of those expenses are extremely high ($25,000 for a speeding ticket) or ridiculously low (Buy a speedboat for $1,000). Transportation costs include most of storage, handling, moving and documenting expenses, yet again in unrealistic amounts. Vacation in Switzerland is priced $500,000 while the holidays in New York City would cost a trucker $800,000. Few truckers could afford at that time a world cruise for $850,000, unless they belonged to the corrupt administration of teamsters' unions. All of these recreations look too expensive especially in 1984 prices. But the game is extremely detailed in its elaboration on the game board (see Fig. 6.3).

These games require a huge amount of cards representing all imaginable events that truckers may encounter, from meeting a bear on the road through the company's bankruptcy. Playing such a game may take hours and days without much learning occurring. For example, the event of bankruptcy just happens as bad luck, not as a result of bad management or mistaken business decisions. These "happenings" are generated either by dice, a deck of cards or by the "wheel of fortune" with equal probabilities for either dramatic or insignificant events. The similarly patented later *Trucking Business Simulation Game* [Patent #4,643,430, 1985] was even more technically elaborate. But it has even less economics and is not realistic in many details, including the equally possible an event such as meeting a bear or a policeman on the road in Florida (see Fig. 6.4).

A typical example of a particularly detailed and specific engineering in materials and equipment is found in the *Highway Construction Board Game* [Whitney, US Patent # 5,456,473, 1995]. It introduces dozens

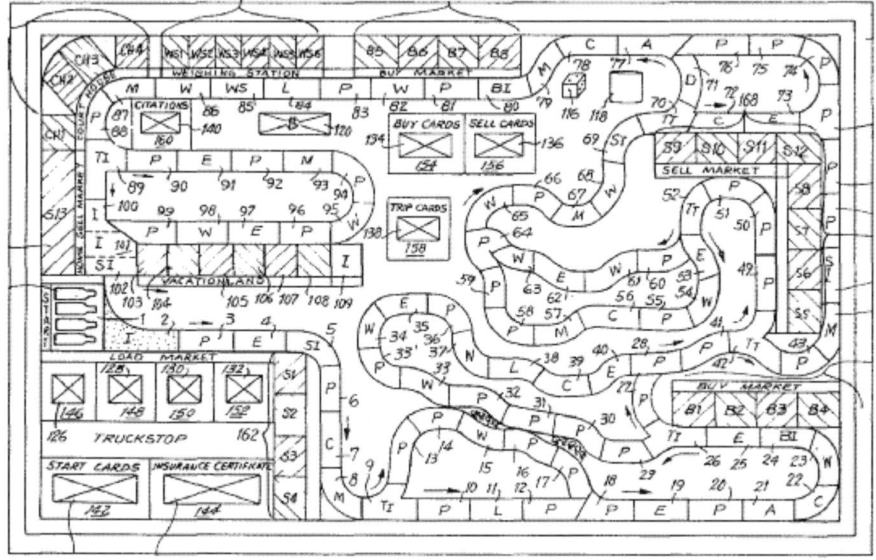

Fig. 6.3.   The board of the *Trucking Simulation Game*.

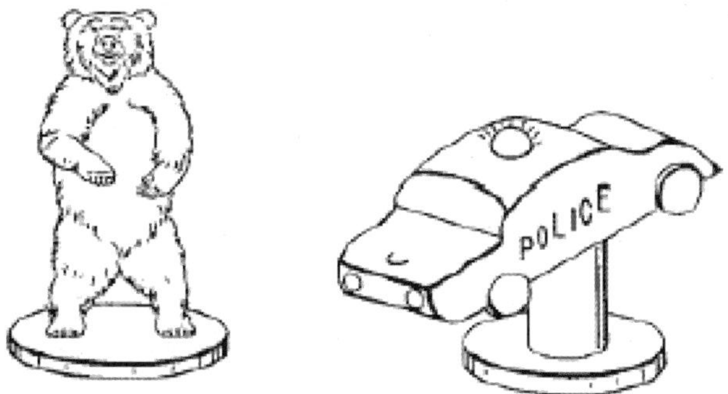

Fig. 6.4.   Game pieces for the *Trucking Business Simulation Game*.

of cards and tokens representing deterministic (technology), stochastic (market availability) and strategic (decisions and auctions) factors. The game is intended for the simulation of construction technology process for two to four players. It includes the main elements of a real life, a modern highway construction project: 48 equipment tokens, stocks of play money, stacks of cards representing predetermined or random events. The process of the game is sequential, including technology management and control of operations, which is typical for the construction industry. Designers of the game even included such socio-economic details as use of prisoners' labor.

Meanwhile such essential economic parameters like costs and income tax are not related to the level of production. They are given as fixed payments of $500 at a moment randomly generated by a deck of cards. So such accurate technological and ecological parameters without accurate economics give to such games very low business value. Technology games are so industry specific and detailed, that make them difficult to customize for economics and management courses. Therefore, it is preferable to find some basic game platform which can be furnished with details that time and resources afford.

Technological businesses of the 21st century became so integrated that we need radical changes from traditional to network-centric modeling. We are using for that purpose a System of Systems (SoS) approach [Boardman and Sauser, 2009]. We developed the gaming platforms *Holarchy* for simulation of existing SoSs and *SimSoS* for the testing of new SoS designs. The business game *TranSport* includes several transportation systems: Rail, Road, Water and Air transports with several levels each. Technology levels represent the main required resources. The next, management levels, represent different combinations of resources necessary to complete the delivery of goods and passengers. The third level represents economic results of transportation (Fig. 6.5).

The highest level of governance of the transportation SoS is not presented on the board explicitly. It will be shown in Chapter 10 as simulation by the interaction of game designer teams in the Situation Room. This structure of the game board is the same for the *Holarchy* platform used for simulation of existing SoS. It represents a vertical hierarchy within each sector of industry with horizontal integration between them. The universal properties of technologies generate sets of events that require management decisions. The interdependence of resources ignites external events according to their joint probabilities represented in transition matrices.

For example, if a system requires long-term resources, say warehouses, then they are constant through all rounds of the game. Medium-term resources like handling and storage equipment can be changed according to a player's decisions in a round of the game. Short-term decisions like changing the means of transportation into piggyback or fishyback combinations

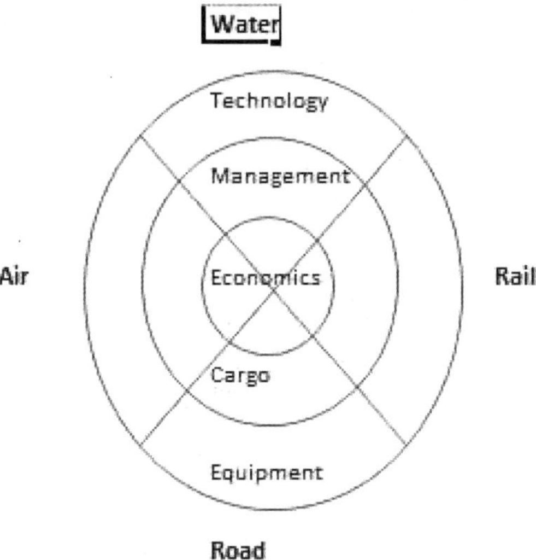

Fig. 6.5.   Four systems at three levels of *Transportation System of Systems* game board.

or other freight consolidations are represented by combinations of different means of transportation. External uncertainty may be represented by a traditional stack of situational cards or by video clips. The unexpected interventions should play a minimal role, and if they are necessary, they should disrupt the situation to the same extent for all players. The exclusion may be made for a game with the primary purpose of simulating extreme events like natural disasters or international terrorism. The primary drivers of the game should be the decisions of players themselves who may use their resources for the support of their own system; otherwise they may be sold or exchanged with other players. The internal source of system uncertainty as the interference to the other systems, is represented by the trump cards. The secondary role in generating uncertainty belongs to the probability of random events which are explained by a stochastic model. For example, breaking down a machine should be generated not just by a pick of a bad luck card, but as the probability function of equipment reliability according to its age and quality of maintenance.

Events of every upper level of the board are becoming possible after the underlying levels ensure necessary conditions. For example, delivering cargo on time depends on a readiness of the proper combination of all the resources required for that technological operation. The most significant advantage for the *TranSport* business game is that it reflects cooperation and competition between different means of transportation. The choice of decisions may be based on technical parameters (speed of movement), technological (capacity of complementing equipment), ecological (level of pollution), economic (budget limitations) or social (human relations).

The structural complexity of a game grows exponentially with the increasing number of interdependent systems. The number of levels may exceed five as was illustrated in Chapter 1, Fig. 1.5 for maritime SoS. That provides SoS models with appropriate complexity that satisfies the Ashby Law of requisite variety [Ashby, 1956]. Models should reflect structural complexity, dynamics of systems and behavioral adaptability of the players. So from the linear functions we need to go to curves, from uniform statistical frequencies to complex probability functions, from one-dimensional to multi-dimensional distributions, from simple lists of events to the 2- and 3-dimensional transition matrices, from static to dynamic models. This is especially essential for the generation of random events when we explain to players different sources of uncertainty. Instead of pure luck or misfortune from a stack of cards they are presented as a result of a mistake, miscommunication or mismanagement. The process of building up models and refining procedures should go parallel with the testing of each completed version of a game.

The most advanced technological games like *Sim City* are modeled on a scientific base of system engineering, geography, geology and biology. These games may be played individually, being actually complex evolving computer simulations. They represent systems of such size, complexity and dynamics that can only be learned from management simulations or business games. Possible sequence of events in techno-socio-ecological SoS overwhelms individual human vision. It needs computerized teamwork representing so-called counterintuitive behavior. Technological components of business games are also useful for visualizing the enterprises in familiar animated images. The games are necessary for the learning of a system thinking for the controlling technological processes. These games teach how managerial decisions affect economic efficiency and trigger ecological consequences.

6.2. ENVIRONMENTAL SYSTEMS

Business game designers may be attracted to environmental systems not only by the beautiful appearance of Mother Nature and engineering marvels. These systems also give the opportunity to use theoretical models of biology, meteorology, geology and other natural sciences. These models combine deterministic and random components that are accurately presentable by the computer graphics and probabilistic functions. Dramatic events like transportation accidents and industrial equipment failures may be forecasted as stochastic processes. We already discussed them in technological applications of business games as the results of accumulated human negligence. But environmental games also include unpredictable natural disasters like earthquakes, floods, draughts, etc. The attractiveness of landscape, infrastructure and architecture allows a colorful background for game scenery. Environmental impact also enriches scenarios of economic and especially technological games.

One of the earliest elegant environmental games was called *The Island* [Kavtaradze, 1980]. It was designed as a card game for the simulation of interaction between nature, industry and community in preserving the environment. The idea was in presenting a closed environmental system in a game as a 2D pyramid of cards. It represents the natural food chain feeding each consecutive upper level with a lower level. This structure of the game was originally a pyramid in just three levels: plants, herbivorous animals and predators. It can be played on the blank table, but we recommend it to be presented on a board with empty cells. When players use just a blank table building up this pyramid may not be accurate. Figure 6.6 illustrates the final arrangement of cards in the game.

The Island model is actually a 2-dimensional model of medium-term growth of an environmental system. The first level presents vegetation as a food for herbivorous animals that are placed on the second level. The total amount of 100 grass units supports life of ten hares. Each couple of hares needs at least 20 units of grass to survive. The hares themselves become a food for two carnivores living on the third level. Three trump cards represent environmental hazards: for the first level they are the wild fires destroying grass, for the second level they are fertilizers poisoning herbivores and for the third level there is a hunter who shoots carnivores.

The growth of each upper level of the pyramid is provided by the bottom level, but hazard cards (with a red arrow) may destroy a corresponding level of the pyramid. Players begin with a random allocation of cards at hand and make moves around the table. Vegetation cards should be placed first at the lowest level of the pyramid. As soon as the quantity of grass is enough to feed a family of hares (20 grasses), a card of two hares might be placed on the board. A hazard card can be placed on any move, killing all the species of the corresponding level. Cards from the destroyed level and from all levels above, which it feeds, return to the players. Hazard card stays on the table for the rest of the game and cannot kill the level again, so this level starts to grow once more. The placement of a hazard card represents the accumulation of environmental knowledge that prevents the repetition of the same distraction in the future.

The winner is a player who first gets rid of their cards. The success of a player depends on the initial set of cards at hand and their strategy of placing cards. Strategy of destruction by hazardous cards gives to the player a short-term individual advantage, but slows down the natural growth. This strategy may backfire due to the reaction of other players affected by such an action.

The quantity and power of cards should be consistent with the complexity of the environmental system. For example, the three levels game that was demonstrated in Fig. 6.6 is good for two or three players dealing with 12 to 20 cards. For more players number of cards may be increased

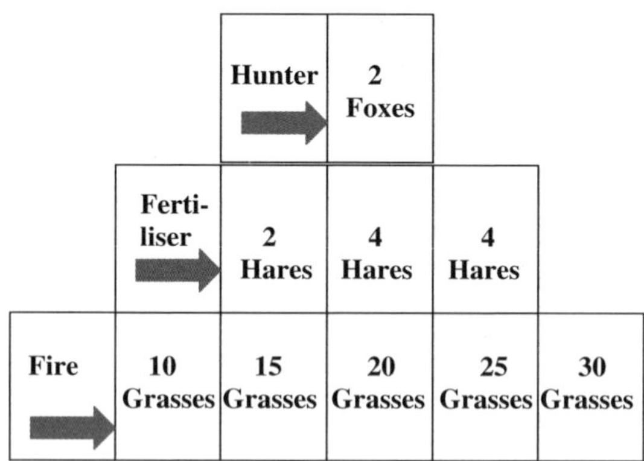

Fig. 6.6.   Environmental pyramid of *The Island* game.

by decreasing value of each card. It is necessary to provide up to a dozen cards for every player initially. The example of ecosystem of four levels: (1) nutrients; (2) vegetation; (3) herbivorous; (4) predators. The elaboration of each ecosystem and especially using different kinds of species on every level increases the quantity and variety of cards. Such a structure requires more time for each round of the game and accommodates a larger number of players.

The number of levels in the pyramid and the power of the cards may be unified or differentiated, representing actual proportions between components of the ecosystem. For example, the bottom levels can represent the food ingredients of soil and microorganisms; the next levels represent grass and other vegetation. The following levels can represent herbivorous animals; and the couple of top levels will represent carnivorous animals and predators. This game may simulate many different ecosystems: a river, lake or sea; a meadow, mountains or steppe; the bushes or a forest. Then game will become more realistic, complex, thus accommodating a larger number of players and will take more time. Originally, *The Island* was designed as a card game, but we recommend the use of an underlying board as for all card and computer games. The displaying of cards on the board forms the game pyramid in a more accurate shape and prevents cards from being misplaced. The board also helps to organize role assignments, resources allocation and processes control.

We also designed several modifications of this game by changing the rules. Giving some cards universal meaning allows their placement into certain cells with a different effect. Trump cards may represent not only negative destructive capacity, but may become a positive constructive factor if placed in another cell or at an other time. For example, the "Fertilizer" card on the first level of pyramid increases vegetation, but on the second level poisons hares. The "Hunter" card placed before the foxes appeared does not harm them; it thus simulates training by firing at empty cans. More complicated decisions and consequences emerge when we deal with multidimensional games which will be discussed later.

Moscow State University professor Dimitry Kavtaradze and his students designed the Green Backpack of 20 simulation games, toys, and interactive posters on ecological and environmental problems for education of sustainable development:

"Green Backpack ... starting from CD-ROM with the manual "Training & Game", "Econet ABC" demo and background of principles of Education for Sustainable Development. User gets access to: "Eco-Mobil" toy, posters "ABC Biodiversity", "Make Decision- Stop the Desert", "pH at Home and in the Nature, 10 board games that based on the "match boxes" — all of them designed by students of IU ("Who is Warmer?", "Who is Faster?", "Earthquake in Matchbox", "Noise in Human Life", "Risk in Human Life", etc. Simulation Games include *"The Island"* (card game), *"Development Without Destruction"*, *"Ecological Construction Set"*.

[Kavtaradze, 2006]

We combined three, four or more of such 2-dimensional pyramids of *The Island* cards on the table board [Bazilevich, 1992]. Each side of the board represents identical or different interdependent ecosystems. We also used it as System of Systems *Holarchy* model for technological, economic and social systems. The model as 3D board of $6 \times 6 = 36$ cells representing four of the same pyramids is illustrated in Fig. 6.7.

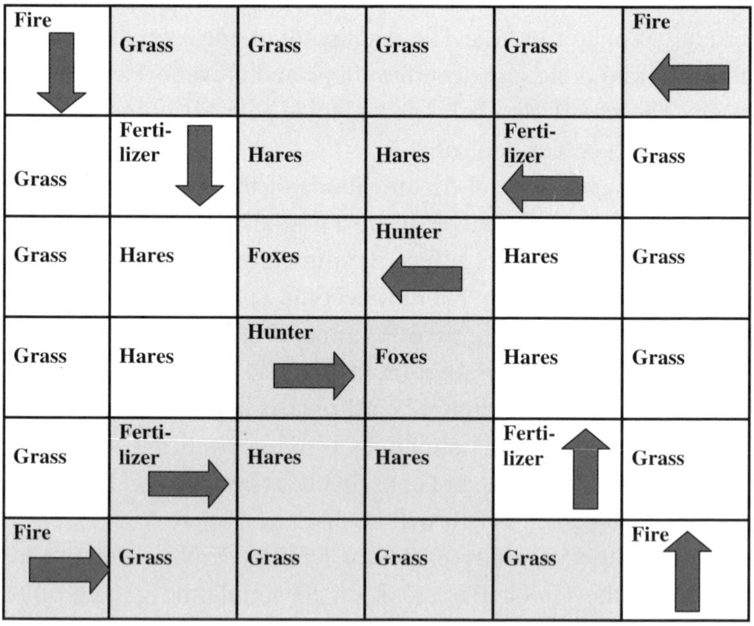

Fire ↓	Grass	Grass	Grass	Grass	Fire ←
Grass	Ferti-lizer ↓	Hares	Hares	Ferti-lizer ←	Grass
Grass	Hares	Foxes	Hunter ←	Hares	Grass
Grass	Hares	Hunter →	Foxes	Hares	Grass
Grass	Ferti-lizer →	Hares	Hares	Ferti-lizer ↑	Grass
Fire →	Grass	Grass	Grass	Grass	Fire ↑

Fig. 6.7. Game board structure for 3-dimensional version of *The Island* game.

The original *Island* game is so simple and clear that it did not require a corresponding board, although we still recommend using the board to keep the simulation better organized. It is also useful for the kids and teenagers to explain the correspondence between natural images of objects and their titles and properties. This game can be used for the study of many basic subjects, especially languages and mathematics. The multidimensional version of this game opens opportunities of simulation of more complicated real ecosystems and environmental Systems of Systems. This composition does not just enlarge the game and makes it rich and real, but allows it to reflect the emerging synergy of the interaction between systems. Then, the underlying board is useful for organizing game on the table or on the computer screen.

The board representing four interrelated ecological systems (River, Lake, Fields and Bush) on the 5×5 board for the game *Pyramid of Nature* is presented in Fig. 6.8.

The Holarchy approach makes a qualitative step into SoS representation of four interrelated ecosystems: River, Lake, Field and Bush. The

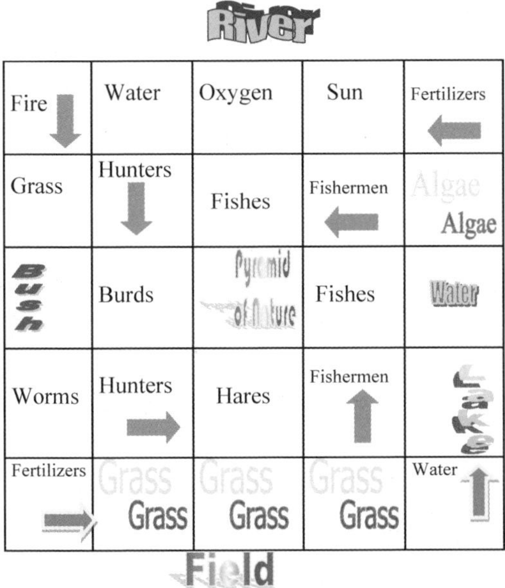

Fig. 6.8.   Holarchy board of *Pyramid of Nature* game.

interference is reflected when the same card which is just a component of one system becomes a trump card for the other ecosystem. The placement of such cards have more than one option. The choice of the cell also modifies the properties of the card. It may be positive in one ecosystem and become destructive for the other. Fertilizer, for example facilitates growth of grass and bushes while it destroys river and lake populations. According to a *Holarchy* SoS model we do not denote the strict meaning of cards unequivocally. It gives to the players a choice of the card placement according to the time and to the location of other cards.

The cards may be neutral, positive or negative; constructive, communicative or transformational. For example, the "Water" card is just a component of the first levels of the River, but when it is placed in the first level of the Lake side, it becomes the positive trump card which increases the rate of water supply to the lake. In other versions of the game, it may be a negative trump card representing a flood. Hazardous "Hunter" in the Bush and Field and "Fishermen" in the River and Lake each have a choice between two different environments. They even become harmless as just firing exercises if trump cards are placed before the corresponding level is filled. Similar transformation of the role happens for the "Fertilizer" as positive for grass growth to the negative for water flora and fauna. For the such a free interpretation of the rules of the game some cells or even the full board may not keep names or images giving players a choice.

The board cannot represent a system in full detail. It can be a blank grid if the game is used for the study of a scientific subject. Then the board becomes a representation of the structure of an ecosystem. The appearance of cards and the cells on the board should be different, so that the players see easily which parts of the grid are covered. The same game for the testing of knowledge should have an opposite edition, so that players are required to identify images of creatures by covering them with corresponding names. The best protection from the misplacing cards is provided by using jigsaw or color cards, by Lego bricks.

The pyramid structure may be transformed for the different size and complexity of systems. The set of five, four and six systems are presented in Fig. 6.9.

The variation of numbers of systems and levels of every system gives the opportunity of reflecting properties of many ecosystems and SoSs. It

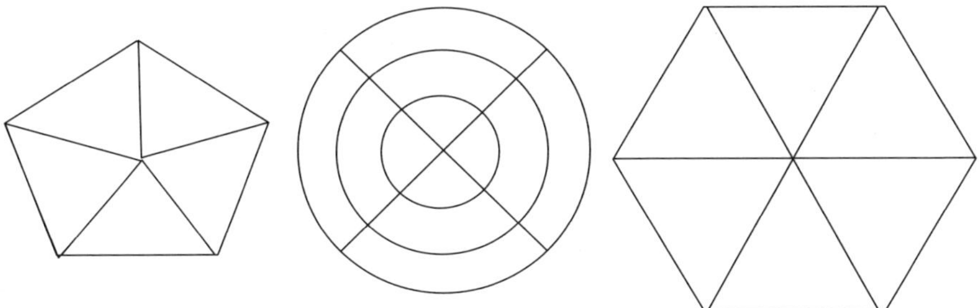

Fig. 6.9.   Three alternative configurations of *Holarchy* game boards.

may be a rigorous scientific model or a simplified introductory image. The number of players and even the size of the table affects the structure and the size of the board. The connection of several players by the intranet allows them to play synchronized games. Then players make independent decisions at every set of the game.

The appearance of the board may be customized for different purposes. Games for different kinds of players: kids, teenagers, students, should have different graphics. The images of components may be just printed names, photos, and cartoons. For kids we choose easily recognizable photographic or cartoonish images of the ecosystem components. The adults may operate with just names printed on cards. But the board of *The Nature* game for teenagers is more attractive in cartoons as shown in Fig. 6.10.

Teenagers can identify the type of component by the cartoons or by even more abstract images. Small children may expect a more realistic game appearance. So we use for kids the most simplified version of cards and board as photographic appearances. The example of the board for ecological game *The Aquarium* is presented in Fig. 6.11.

Boards of different sizes and shapes allow the representation of systems of different complexity and structures. The proportions between the number of levels and the quantity of components on each level may be different. The players may have the same interest of building the whole SoS; or be responsible for a system; or just for the level of a system. It may require a definite allocation of cards instead of their random distribution.

The square board may vary in size from minimal $4 \times 4 = 16$ cards for two players; to the most recommended 7×7 board for four players dealing

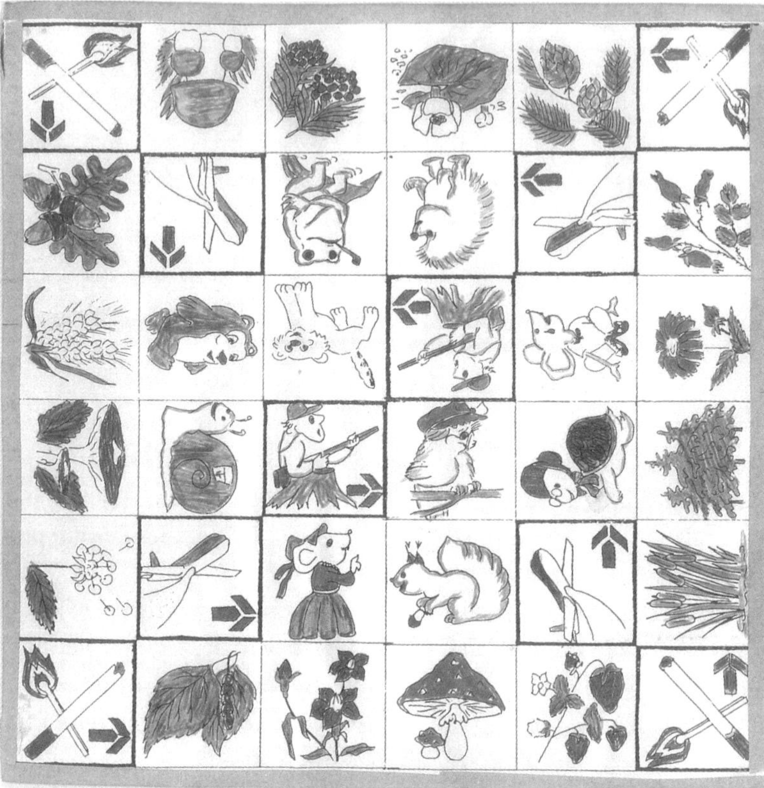

Fig. 6.10.   Game board: *The Nature* for teenagers.

48 cards. The larger boards with more players may represent ecosystems in more realistic detail. But the time for the game grows exponentially with the size of the board, so if a 5×5 game requires three to five minutes, a 7×7 game takes 20 to 30 minutes to finish. The time required for a round of a game also depends on the level of uncertainty and the rules of the game. For the most complicated *Finance SoS* game we use a large 8×8 board with 64 cells for four to eight specialized players. The *Holarchy* platform may be used for teaching foreign languages or scientific terminology; biological and medical courses; geology and meteorology; abstract logic or general philosophy.

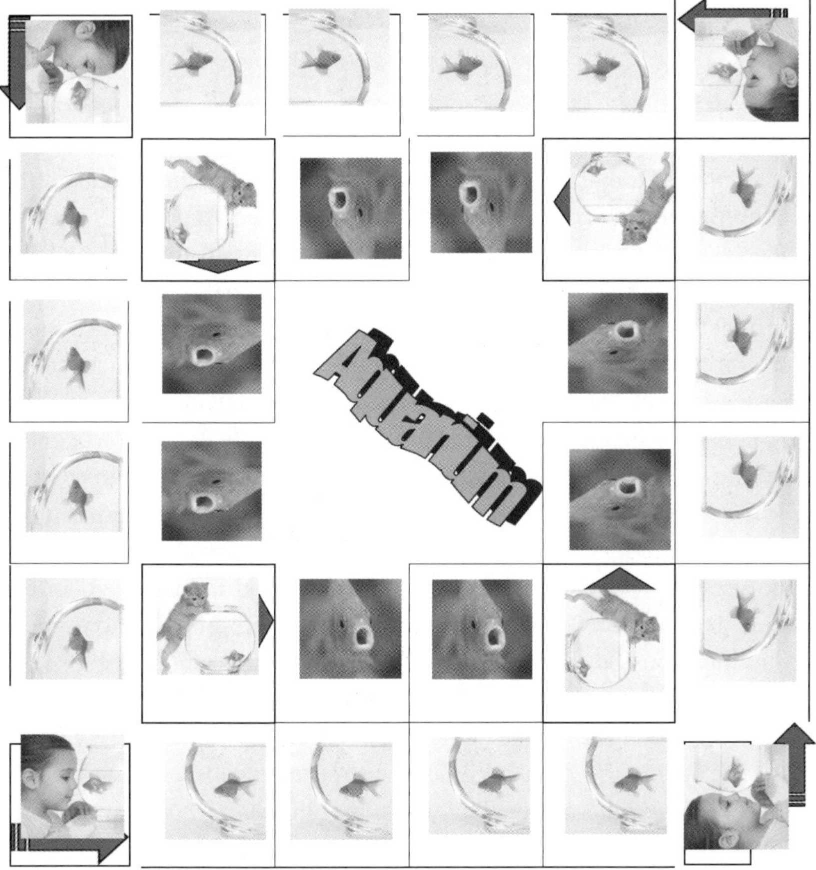

Fig. 6.11.   Game board: *The Aquarium* for kids.

The design of edutainment version of the game may be supported by board cells identical to the cards, but in black-and-white or in faded colors. Then players will have fewer chances to place a card in a wrong cell, so play goes correctly and faster. For the players of higher education levels cells of the board may contain just a printed name and cards to present corresponding images, or vice versa.

The rules of the game that we discussed in Chapter 5 may be amended for card games: Do not sneeze, or cards will fly away!

6.3.   ECONOMIC SYSTEMS

Economic systems are more complicated for the presentation by business games because they are less tangible and spectacular than technological and environmental systems. The term "economic" is too wide and covers business games from the global market down to the efficiency measurement of technological, environmental and social processes. Economics plays different roles for the simulation of existing systems versus forecasting human behavior in designed systems. In the existing system economics is a monetary reflection of technological, environmental and social processes, an essential tool for training. Examples of the first type of game are *Cyber-Market* and *MarketSim*, that simulate established businesses. The games experimenting with the design of new systems entirely depend on economic opportunities and reasoning. Examples of the second type of games are the *Roller Coaster Tycoons* that simulate development of new enterprises. The videogame *CakeMania* opened the whole series of *Mania* games representing the growth of small businesses in the fast food industry and in retail services. The *Tycoons* videogames started with presenting economics of entertainment business development. They now cover many other industries from *Fast Food Tycoon* to *Tycoon City: New York* and up to *Railroad Tycoon*. The contents of these games are prevailing over the purely random events. The *Monopoly Tycoon* game relies more on the speed and creativity of players than on the roll of dice. Ultimately *Game Tycoon* simulates the game industry itself.

The content of business activities for economic SoS's may be represented by technological and ecological systems. Their hardware is in physical or virtual playing fields, sandboxes or in specialized situation rooms. Purely economic and social systems may be represented using statistical data and by mathematical models. They may be visualized either through organizational structures and maps, or by flowcharts of procedures and decision trees, or by processing diagrams of rules and regulations.

Most economic business games are representing financial markets. The most advanced economic games like the *upTick* game developed at the Harvard Business School, teach decision making in interdependent financial systems [Edery, 2009]. The game requires playing at least 20 hours a week to give the MBA student a comparison of five different trading strategies. It overcomes simplified initial images by a creating system thinking of counterintuitive rules of mass competitive behavior. Yet the majority of computer games are designed for advising individual investors by anticipating stock market trends. Games like *FINANSIM: A Finance Management Simulation* [Greenlaw *et al.*, 1979] were historically the earliest of the "serious" economic business games and they prevail on the commercial game market today.

Games for college education are supposed to give students basic knowledge of a market economy. The business Game *CyberMarket* [Bazilevich, 1992] has been developed to integrate topics of a course in Microeconomics for students of Business, Management and Engineering programs. The purpose of the game is to understand the dynamics of a closed economic system. Students who play the roles of **Businesses** make decisions supporting sustaining growth of manufacturing and services. One student plays the role of the **Government** representing economic regulations and coordination of business strategies. Students playing **Households** illustrate the distribution of wealth, representing different spending or saving patterns of consumption. The closed economy as a whole is represented by a team of four to nine students. If team consists just of four players, the Government role is substituted by the democratic agreements between two Businesses and two Households.

The behavior of an economic system is simulated by the dynamics of the interactions between businesses and households in production and factor markets. Each team begins the game from the same initial position introduced by statistical tables and charts describing the main relationships of a fictitious economy with realistic parameters and proportions. In the beginning of the game, volumes of production and consumption of products and services are balanced. Factor markets (labor and capital) are also balanced by given wages and interest rates.

Structural proportions and technological restrictions of a simulated economy are typical for contemporary industrialized countries. The models of this game are the classic microeconomic functions expressed algebraically, graphically and in MSExcel tables. A model of the game includes 3-dimensional Production Functions and Consumers Utility Functions. During the *CyberMarket* game students derive from them 2-dimensional

     Business Games

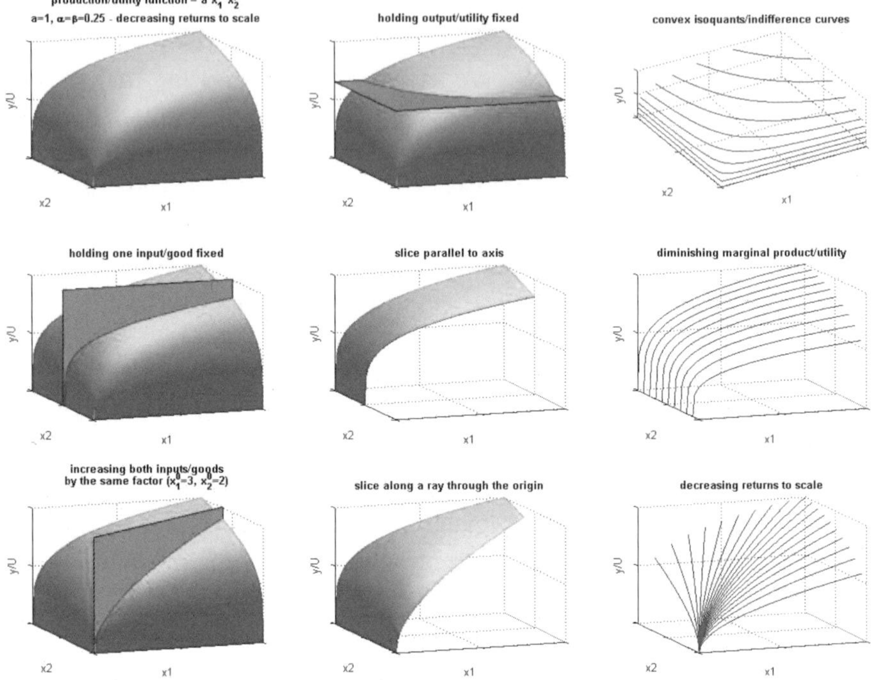

Fig. 6.12.   Production function for business in the *CyberMarket* game.

Supply and Demand Curves and carry on calculations of the main parameters of business efficiency and consumers satisfaction.

In most cases we prefer graphs (remember the second component of **ViVaT** game feature, **Vi**sualization). An example of a 3D production function for business is presented in Fig. 6.12.

Teams are playing several years of economic activities spending on each year as a cycle of the game up to one hour, depending on the computational means and the depth of analysis. The game requires at least one personal computer for every team. Each team can deliberately or via a chain of random decisions, demonstrate a certain pattern of economic policy — from command to a laissez-faire doctrine. After three to five cycles and at the end of the game teams make multimedia presentations of the results of the game. Every student writes a report describing history of their roles, decisions, achievements and mistakes. Finally, a professor compares strategies chosen by different teams and demonstrates their strengths and weaknesses. The game procedure is as follows:

"1. Explanation of the purpose of and rules of the Game. *It takes 20–30 minutes if the Game is at the end of the course (recommended for engineering students). Otherwise the full lecture may be given in the beginning of business and management classes.*

2. Allocation of students between teams, selecting their names and assignment of roles within teams. *It is essential to combine teams of the equal strength and similar structure (avoiding strong differences in gender structure, academic power and in cultural orientation of teams). The name of the team may reflect the general idea of its strategy, for example,* "Japan" *for a thrifty, fast-growing economy, or* "Nowhereland" *— for the random search of a strategy by "trial and error".*

3. Describing the position of each player and studying their functions. *It may take from ten minutes for the economists, up to an hour for engineers. Each student finds out the statistics of the role, fills out the starting year data in the corresponding tables and positions it on functional charts.*

4. First slow training cycle representing decisions for the following year. *It takes up to an hour to give an explanation of the main links of the economic structure and functions connecting the variables. This stage should not be hurried, even if all of the tables and functions are tabulated in the computer. It provides an initial understanding of interdependence of different sectors of an economy and relationships between their performance.*

5. Simulation of cycles for the subsequent three to five years. It can be given as a homework with following analytic session for the next class. *It gives the possibility to verify the correctness of computations fulfilled by different teams, to discuss different strategies and outcomes and to announce "situational" changes, for example, the introduction of taxes or legal restrictions.*

6. Final discussion of the results of the Game with a prizing for the winners. *This discussion should compare the behavior of similar sectors of economies presented by different teams. The students show the resulting charts of data and analyze dynamics and efficiency of simulated economy (rate of growth, profitability, etc.). The winning team and best performers may be awarded by the corresponding literature encouraging their interest in the further research of the problems risen in the discussion.*"

[Bazilevich, 1992]

Table 6.1. Options of business game *CyberMarket*.

Level	1 Beginners	2 Low	3 Medium	4 High
Contents	Entertainment	Exploratory	Explanatory	Educational
Participants	High School, Social Sciences	College, Humanities	College, Economics	University, Microeconomics
Structure	Small teams of 2–5 students	Teams of 4–5 students in random roles	Teams of 5–7 players in rotating roles	Teams of 5–7 players with permanent roles
Time	5 min /round up to 5 cycles	10 minute rounds up to 5 cycles	20 minute rounds up to 7 cycles	30 minute rounds up to 10 cycles
Tools	Posters, stickers, transparencies		Tables, charts, calculators	Personal computers

The *CyberMarket* game opens wide opportunities of applications for different purposes and audiences. At minimum, it is a short demonstration of an economic system structure and dynamics. Then it may be developed into an deep analytical system simulation of different economic strategies. The *CyberMarket* game was played in different educational and academic institutions on various levels. High school students were entertained by the competitive interaction while teams of executives were deeply involved in the discussion of their own corporate future. The data for the game should be simplified for beginners and may be real for advanced studies. Different options of the Game are presented in Table 6.1.

An example of an introduction to the role of a retired household in the *CyberMarket* business game is presented in the following instruction (Table 6.2).

Such a short introduction always needs additional explanations by the instructor in the first round of the game. Later, during the game most questions are usually resolved within a team. It is very helpful for undergraduate classes where the structure of a team changes through rotation of the roles.

The business game *CyberMarket* opens various educational and analytical opportunities. Due to typical competitive spirit and entrepreneurial

Table 6.2. Introductory instruction for the role of retired.

Team __________	**Household**	**RETIRED**	
Your family budget		2010 Actual	2011 Plan
Net income including:		**$50,000**	
Wages for labor ($10/hr × 1,000 hrs)		$10,000	
Dividends ($800,000 ∗ 0.05)		$40,000	
Less			
Purchases:		**($50,000)**	
Commodities ($1/lb × 10,000 lbs)		($10,000)	
Luxuries ($1,000/day × 40 days)		($40,000)	
Income tax (20% of $50,000)		($10,000)	
Plus Social Security benefits		**$10,000**	
Savings		**0**	

(Student_____________)

You are paid 5% as dividends on common stock of your investments ($800,000 × 0.05) = $40,000 from businesses and wages $10/hr for 1,000 hrs for the part-time work ($10 × 1,000) = $10,000. You decide yourselves for the next year how much of these resources to offer to businesses, and how much of goods and services to buy at the prices which are established by the market. If you, the RETIRED, ready to pay higher price than the WORKING for the same product, then you will buy all that you requested or all that is offered by businesses, whichever is the smallest. Your offer of capital investments and labor may be accepted by businesses in a similar way: whatever is cheaper for them between your and the WORKING's offers, they will take.

attitude, it gives a live demonstration of economic behavior. In undergraduate classes, we also expect that students demonstrate their ability to apply liberal arts knowledge into their individual reports and into team presentations. Some reports were even written as a poetry and some teams presented results in the spectacular way. Example of multimedia presentation based on the features of Hawaiian economy is reproduced below in the Appendix. (The fun of the presentation and especially in the artistry of a team are lost in black and white slides reproduction).

> "Results of the Game are presented in individual written reports, in a yearly team reports and in the final team presentations. The essential feature of the materials presented — is the visualization including tables, graphs highlighted by such illustrations as icons and cartoons. Some teams introduced in their presentations elements of role-playing, video clips and even puppet show. Integration of playing and learning is the most powerful tool of early childhood education. It unfortunately eventually transforms into the boring process of mechanical memorizing at the college level. Our experience shows that it is still possible to revive the learning process for the economics and management classes on the contemporary technology. Stevens Institute of Technology supports the efforts to integrate study, research and business activities under the *Technogenesis* approach."
>
> [Bazilevich, 1992]

Every player makes an independent decision on the next year's strategy. Players of the households make decisions on how much of their resources they are willing to spend. They type their offers of labor and capital as their individual plans for the next year in MSExcel tables. Responsibilities of their roles also include decisions to buy certain volumes of goods and services. Players of businesses make yearly decisions on volumes of output of goods and services and calculate required amounts of resources (labor and capital). The strategy of economic growth can be discussed by the team before making individual plans.

The flowchart of the game is presented in Fig. 6.13.

Each player prepares final five-years report containing individual results and analysis of the achieved goals. Every team prepares a powerpoint presentation to the class illuminated with the history of economy development based on the chosen scenarios. For example, it may be a history of closed mini-country or literary story. The most popular among undergraduates are space communities from videogames, and among graduate students real geographical or corporate images. The game may allow teams to interact, as if simulating their participation in a global economy. Then it includes negotiations on prices and volumes of traded resources and products.

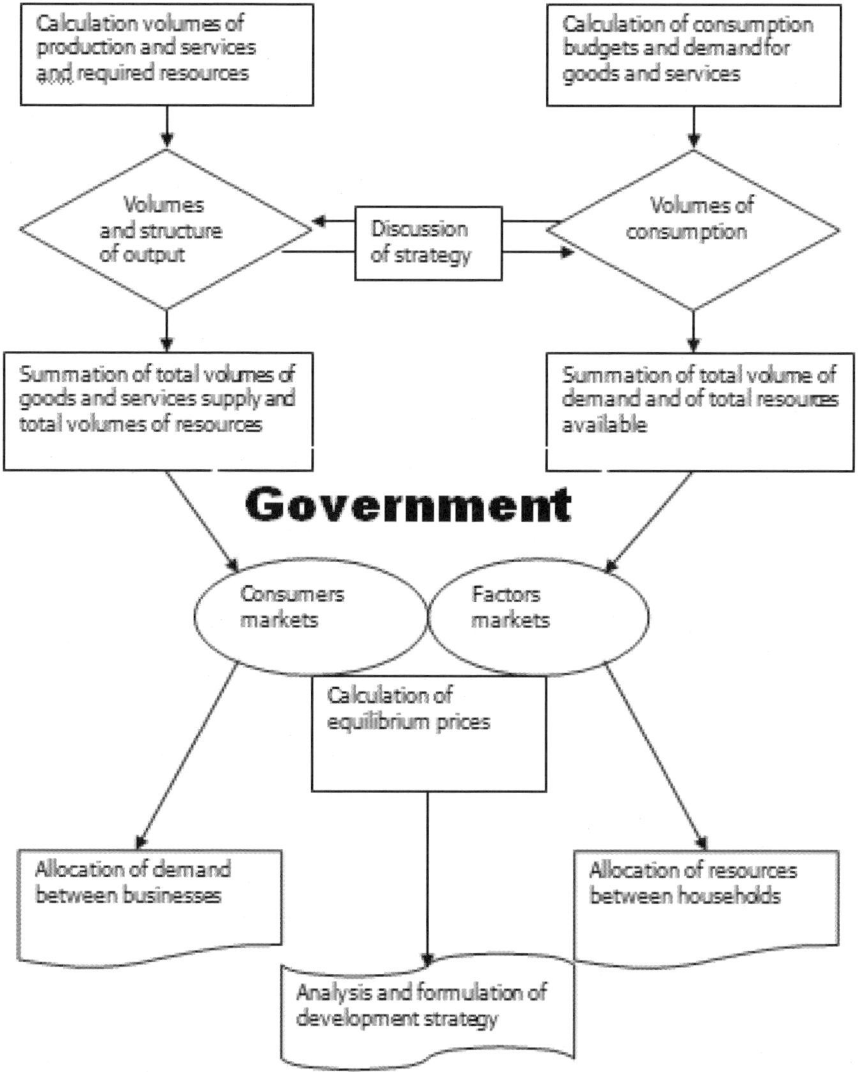

Fig. 6.13.   Flowchart of the *CyberMarket* business game.

Table 6.3.   Contents of final individual report of results of a player.

Final report	Team . . . . Player	
Time	**Role**	**Exercises**
Initial position in 2010	**Industry**	Supply and demand curves derivation
Results of 2011	**Industry**	Average and marginal costs calculation
Results of 2012	**Working**	Elasticities calculation
Results of 2013	**Retired**	Marginal rates of substitution calculation
Results of 2014	**Services**	Utility estimates and budget balancing
Results of 2015	**Government**	Production Possibilities Frontiers

Long-term results

	Strategy applied	Dynamics of main variables
	Lessons learned	

References (additional literature)

Every player reports to the instructor basic statistics of performance during the years of simulation. Table 6.3 gives just a structure of such a report.

Teams then makes multimedia presentations of economic development based on a story of their choice. The creativity demonstrated by students of the stories' choice and presentation appearance is amazing. Scenarios vary in the range from a secluded monastery on the island up to the planet in outer space. Presentations vary from standard powerpoint reports to poetry and up to the animated video based on dynamics of the simulation. Examples of individual game report and team presentation are given in the Appendix. There are the stories based on succession of roles which participants played from year to year of simulation. They include decisions made, their justification and results, evaluation of influence on and from the other players. Students demonstrate in this report the amazing creativity in storytelling and in graphic illustrations. Some students use real-life examples, the others literary narratives, some create imaginary scenery of an island, country or planet.

The final results of Business Game *CyberMarket* are demonstrated on the posters to the class in aggregated variables as presented in Table 6.4.

Outputs of products and services by businesses are presented by Cobb-Douglas production function:

$$P = A^* L^\alpha K^\beta$$

where

P — total production in units per year,
A — total factor productivity,
L — labor capital input with elasticity α,
K — labor capital input with elasticity β.

After several rounds of game students are allowed to use Cobb Douglas Production Function Calculators from the Internet. Before that they are required to study formulas and parameters of production functions and use appropriate graphical functions for interpolation as was explained in Fig. 3.11.

Players in roles of businesses are motivated to maximize the profit form sales of commodities and luxuries. Preliminary optimization of production at present market prices they can make using linear program model outlined in Section 2.6. After several rounds of the game they may use for more accurate solution anticipated prices from the markets forecasts.

Utility functions for households are presented in exponential form illustrated by Fig. 6.12 according to the model:

$$U = 1 - e^{-a\{(f/F)+(j/J)\}},$$

Table 6.4.   Final team report in the *CyberMarket* game.

| Variables | Team .... | | | | |
	2011	2012	2013	2014	2015
Products Commodities (1000 lbs) Price ($$) Luxuries (days) Price ($$)					
Factors Labor (hours) Wages ($$/hr) Capital (1000 $$) Interest rate (%)					
Capital gain (Spending), $$ Working families Retired					
Profit (Loss), $$ Industry Services					
Comments _______________________________________					

where

U — utility of consumption in ordinal scale,

a — risk aversion factor,

f — actual and F — desirable consumption of commodities,

j — actual and J — desirable consumption of luxuries.

Utility estimation also may be supported by some of Internet calculators. Players of introductory level are provided by the graphical utility functions for qiuck interpolation. The shape of utility function for households is presented in Fig. 6.14.

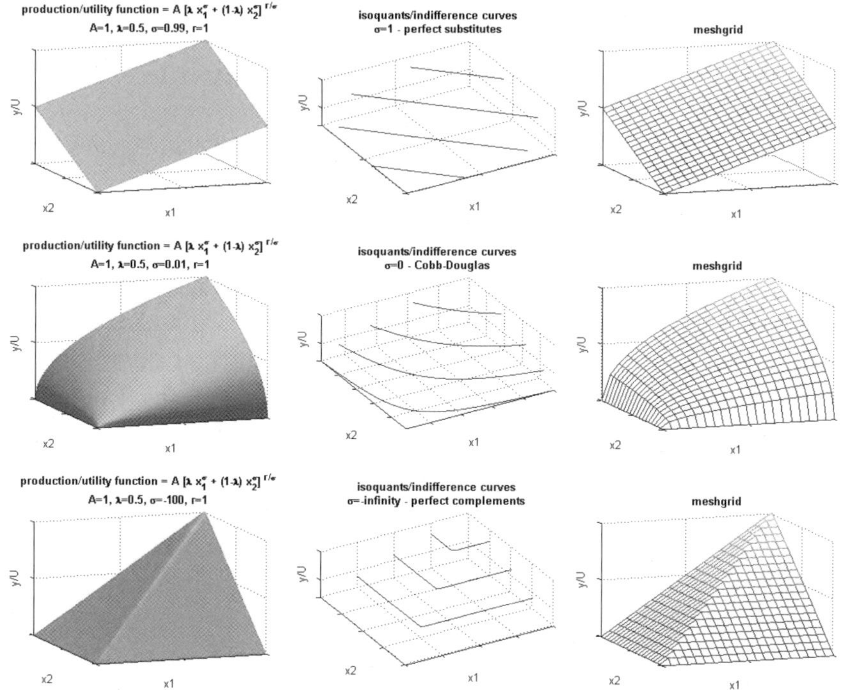

Fig. 6.14.   The shape of utility function for households.

Robert Kiyosaki created a school for family economic education. The "Inventor, Entrepreneur, Educator" as he introduces himself, provides practical financial advice presented through personal stories. Kiyosaki's TV presentations and promotional seminars created a community of amateur real estate speculators. Kiyosaki teaches how to generate an income by investing in a real estate and businesses. Kiyosaki defines "assets" as things that generate cash inflow, such as rental properties or businesses — and "liabilities" as things that consume cash, such as houses, cars, and so on. He has published a series of "Rich Dad, Poor Dad" books. The book "Cashflow Quadrant: Rich Dad's Guide to Financial Freedom" [Kiyosaki, 1998] summarizes his experience of investing in housing and business markets:

"It is a book written for...

- people who are ready to move beyond job security and begin to find their own world of financial freedom.

- people who are ready to make deep professional and financial changes in their lives.
- People who are ready to move from the Industrial Age to the Information Age."

[Kiyosaki, 1998]

Basic principles of his ideology Kiyosaki expressed in a series of board and computer business games for adults and children named *Cashflow* [Kiyosaki, 2004]. In the *Cashflow* games there are two stages: the first, "Rat Race", when the player aims to raise their passive income level to where it exceeds the character's expenses. The success in the first stage allows to raise to the second stage, "Fast Track". The winner is determined among the participants of the second stage. To win, a player must get their character to buy the "dream" or accumulate an additional $50,000 in monthly cash flow. The board of the game is presented in Fig. 6.15.

The game requires the players to fill out their financial statements: a Balance sheet reporting on a player's assets and liabilities, and Income statement as Profit and Loss statement. Player can borrow money from the bank to raise enough cash for the down payment on an investment

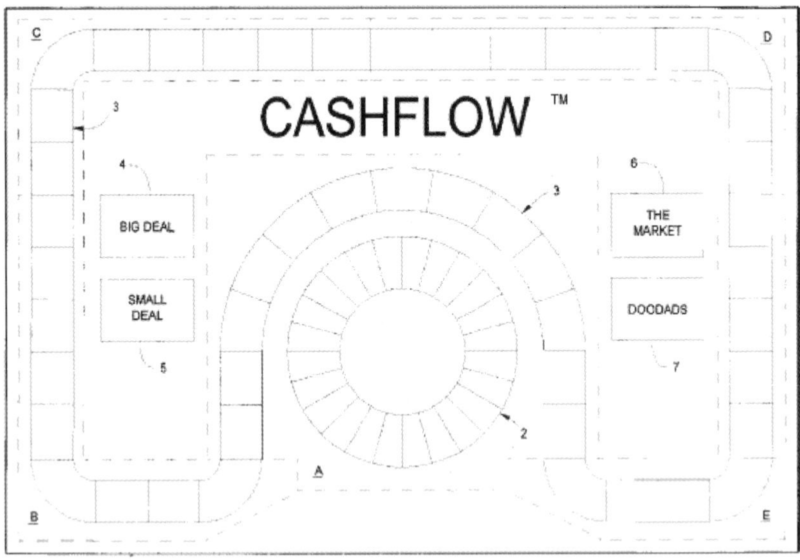

Fig. 6.15.   The board of *Cashflow* game [US Patent #5,826,878, 1998].

property. The game demonstrates to the players what is happening with their money; show how assets generate income and what their expenses are. The *Cashflow* games were designed to be played by more than one player. The best interaction occurs when three to six people are playing. It coincides with our experiments with the *Monopoly* game presented in Chapter 2.

The *Holarchy* platform provides the clearest visualization for the structure of a SoS. For the most complicated *Finance SoS* game we use 7×7 or larger boards for four players or teams. Every player is assigned to one of the systems: Bond, Commodities, Real Estate and Stock market. The team holds full responsibility for the development of the whole economic SoS (Fig. 6.16).

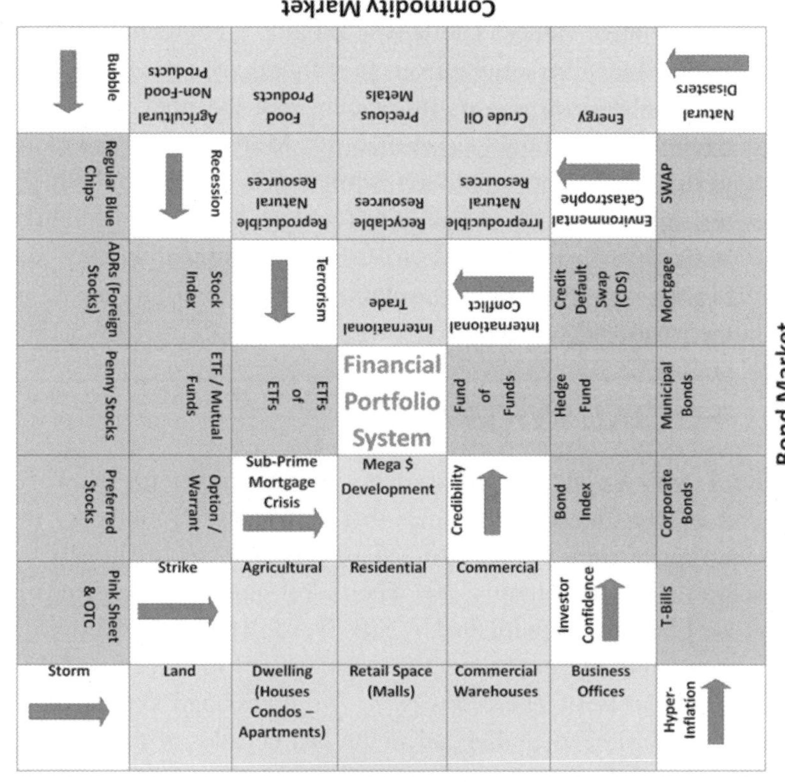

Fig. 6.16.   Finance *SoS* game board.

The changes in a structure of the board allows representing financial markets of different size and complexity. By the changes in team roles and by elaboration of the rules we can simulate how different regimes and regulations change developments of the markets.

The *Finance SoS* game may begin with random or predetermined distribution of cards. Random distribution represents an initial situation on freely developing markets that gives to every individual player equal opportunities of success. The team option of the game assumes predetermined allocation of cards simulating mature diversified markets. The team responsible for each of the markets can influence the other markets and carry on negotiations for the trade of assets with other teams. Then the cards change their initial values according to the balance of supply and demand. The component and assembly cards have initially positive values and trump cards have negative values. The moves should be consecutive around the table board and may be simultaneous in a digital version of the game.

The specialized team wins by placing first the final resolution card which symbolizes reaching market maturity. Motivation for the individual players is in the fastest accumulation of assets. The strategy of both, players and teams, is in getting rid of liabilities (cards in hand) and build up assets (cards on the board). The evaluation of results of simulation may be based not only by declaration of a single winner, but on more differentiated criteria of relative wealth accumulation.

6.4. SOCIAL SYSTEMS

The term "social systems" covers many economic systems. However, we interpret it here for business games that represent non-monetary interactions between people. These restricted aspects of social life mostly include personal relations and family life. The oldest among these games is *The Mansion of Happiness* published by S.B. Ives in 1843. It had a strong message encouraging players follow the moral way of life (see Fig. 6.17).

The popularity of *The Mansion of Happiness* and similar moralistic board games has been challenged in the last decades of the 19th century when the focus of games became materialism and competitive capitalistic behavior. *The Game of Life* which was published in 1860, had the same fate of modernization in its moral values in the later versions. The game

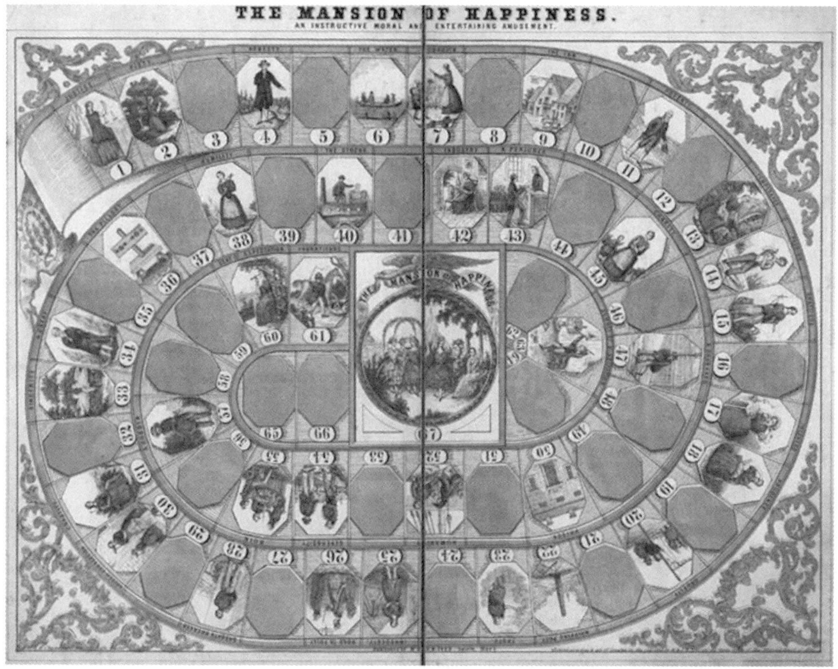

Fig. 6.17.   The *Mansion of Happiness* game (1843).

was originally created by Milton Bradley and called *The Checkered Game of Life*. Later versions of *The Game of Life* during the past 150 years were published in board, cards, computer and mini-arcade editions. Bradley's game did not include dice, as considered a requisite of gambling, using instead a teetotal with a six sided top. [Wolverton, 1998]. The object was to land on the "good" spaces and collect 100 points. A player could gain fifty points toward this goal by reaching the "Happy Old Age" cell in the far diagonal corner, opposite of the "Infancy" corner where one began. The original form of the board now *The Game of Life*, is presented in Fig. 6.18.

The version of *The Game of Life* a century later consists of a linear track on which players travel by spinning a small wheel located in the middle of the board with the spaces numbered 1 through 10. The board represents mountains, buildings and other objects, making the playing area a three-dimensional virtual sandbox. Playing pieces (pawns) are small, colored plastic automobiles which come in six different colors. Each pawn has holes

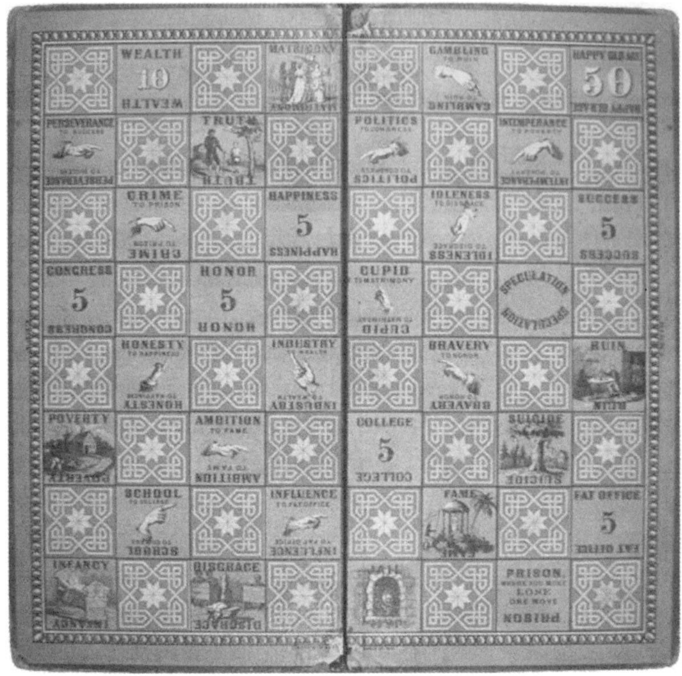

Fig. 6.18.   The original 1860s *The Checkered Game of Life Game* board.

in the top in which the blue and pink "people pegs" are placed throughout the game as the player "gets married" and has or adopts "children".

Some "early modern" editions have up to eight automobiles. Each game also includes a setup for a bank, which includes play money (in denominations of $1,000, $5,000, $10,000, $20,000, $50,000, and $100,000), insurance policies (automobile, life, fire and/or homeowners' insurance depending on the version), $20,000 promissory notes and stock certificates. Other tangibles vary with the game version. A children's commercial version of the *Game of Life* simulates linear movement of individual along a flibbix snake presenting different life events with discrete steps generated by the rotation of the teetop in the center of the board (see Fig. 6.19).

In 1998 Hasbro produced a CD-ROM version of this game that added computerized moves and short animations to the game. The players were also given the option to compete over the Internet. However, luck plays too large a role in determining the winner of the game. The random allocation

Fig. 6.19.   Childrens' commercial version of *The Game of Life*.

of the Life Cards is the prime determinant of the winner. The aspects of
the game where a user has to make a decision, such as attending college
or purchasing insurance, have a very small effect on the outcome. Still the
game does not reflect the essential realities of life such as opportunities
available to people of different gender, race and social background.

The rules of actual life also changing faster than different modifications of this game. What was written in the 1970s is no longer the truth
today:

> "Everything now being equal in the Land of Opportunity (that's what
> employment laws say, don't they?), it should seems safe to predict that
> the future chief executives of America's four million major corporations
> will start turning up in a ratio of one woman to every two or three men. Yet
> the odds against a woman becoming chief executive officer of AT&T, Gen-
> eral Electric, Xerox, IBM, First Boston Corporation, Bank of America,
> Pillsbury, Revlon, CBS, or Sears by the year 2000 are so astronomical
> that, in real terms, she has almost no hope."
>
> [Harragan, 1977].

Although family obligations still make it a challenge for a women to
enter executive ranks, during the last decades we observed a drastic growth
in the number of women in high executive and governmental positions.

At present there are many economic and social programs designed to help women and minorities to advance in business and public service. However, a new study finds that a generation of advocacy to break the "glass ceiling" is not proving successful. Yet women who do progress are relegated to jobs that often do not lead to CEO positions, and others are mired at the middle-management level [Cappelli, 2006].

Social systems hardly can be presented in images resembling some physical objects. But still, models of social system are supposed to be an abstraction isomorphic to the system. In most cases we are dealing with just a conceptual models of SoSs. Some of such games are built on images and stories of individuals familiar with the appropriate system. Central parts of the game model play practical rules and procedures. They may be preferable to theoretical models that are usually hypothetical. The business game *Career* is an example of our game that balances structural and procedural models.

The game *Career* was developed for the simulation of several years of a professional life during and after graduation from college. It shows the consequences of different decisions taken by the individual in areas of Education, Work, Recreation and Family. For young people, (high school students or college undergraduates) it demonstrates the interdependence of events in the abovementioned areas of life. For mature students, (graduates, managers or executives) the Game gives participants a chance to test their real-life strategic decisions.

We played the business game *Career* for many years in universities and business schools in different countries [Bazil, 2002]. It may be adjusted to many management-related courses and to different professions and cultures. The game has versions for different sizes of the class and various degrees of computerization. The basic version of the Game splits a class of 20–25 students into four teams of "experts" in following areas of life (Fig. 6.20).

The game is played over one to two hour classes for several weeks. It gives enough time to introduce the theoretical material between sessions and at the same time keeps the emotional spirit of the game alive. Meetings with professionals during or after the Game also facilitate realism. Having teams of students with different backgrounds, as well as professional and

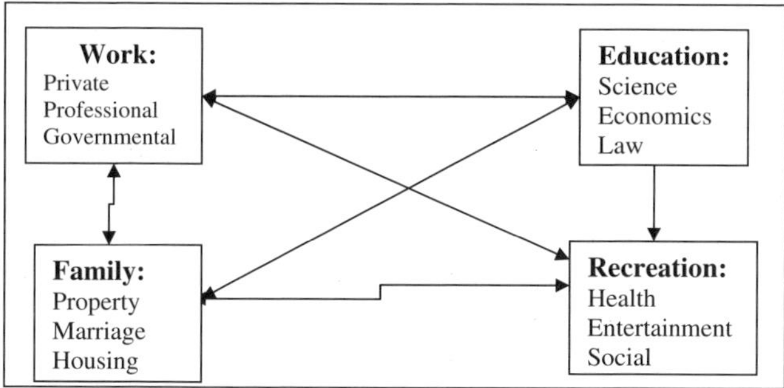

Fig. 6.20. Four interdependent areas of activities in *Career* Game.

cultural experiences can also mimic reality better. There are four options of the Game aimed at different goals:

- To teach course-related topics by using illustrations of real-life cases. For example, human resources problems of leadership; motivation or business ethics for management courses; Markov chains or Bayesian decisions for Operations Research, random processes for Modeling and Simulation;
- To demonstrate the advantages of teamwork and to encourage creativity and competitiveness through dynamic simulation of business successes or failures in a particular field;
- To forecast individual life development in interrelated areas of study, work, social or family activities. This helps a college graduate to make conscious choice for application to the first job;
- To diagnose an individual's ability to perform a professional, managerial or social role, especially for professions based on interpersonal communications, as a part of personnel assessment procedures.

The *Career* game was originally developed for the simulation of human resource topics in different management courses. The game demonstrates the interdependence of progress between four areas of activity: Work, Education, Family and Recreation. An example of the initial classification of activities for the game version for an "International Business" course is represented in Table 6.5.

Table 6.5.   Activities represented in business game *Career*.

Area of activity	Directions of activity	Examples of international activity
WORK	Business Management	Joint Venture Executive
	Professional	International Project Leader
	Private Entrepreneurship	Global Consultant
	Governmental	Embassy Information Manager
	Other	Religious Missionaire Abroad
	*.....................	*.....................
EDUCATION	Arts, Humanities	Studying Foreign Language
	Management, Economics	International Business School
	Science, Engineering	Foreign College
	Politics, Law	Peace Corps
	Other	Corporate Internship Overseas
	*.....................	*.....................
FAMILY	Relatives	Marrying Foreigner
	Housing	Renting Space with Foreigner
	Other Property	Buying a Boat
	Alternative Way of Life	Gay/Lesbian Festival
	Other	Keeping Foreign Mistress
	*.....................	*.....................
RECREATION	Sports	International Competitions
	Health	Catching a Tropical Disease
	Entertainment	International Travel
	Arts, Crafts	Exhibition Abroad
	Social Work	International Hospitality Club
	Other	Foreign Pen Friend
	*.....................	*.....................

*Fill in with your example(s)

Unlike the moralistic intentions of first business games simulating
social systems, you may see the presence of some immoral realities of
life which cannot be even considered before. These details of real life we
omit from the teenagers' versions of game, but they are necessary for the
games with adult students. The moral values and preferences are changing fast in the modern society which requires regular updating of a social
game's contents. The player's participation in different expert teams may be
predetermined by an instructor in order to create the most competent teams,

but during the game it may be allowed for players to change teams. We also experimented with a random initial allocation of players requiring only a minimal size of every team to be able to support the area activity. Such an approach works better with classes where we have limited preliminary information about each individual.

One cycle of game simulates the yearly changes in a person's life. Every student goes around the class recording individual changes approved by the appropriate teams. The pace and succession of movement between workstations of teams that represent different areas of life may be different. A procedure of the game is strictly regulated in undergraduate classes, but might be loose for the graduates. The number of years of a career simulation may be different for every player. It also varies for the participants who happen to land in some inescapable or terminal state, for example, getting into disability or jail. But student may explore some life options available to escape even such a specific situations.

Every participant of the game keeps a record of his/her own positions in those four areas of activity starting either from the current situation or from some hypothetical set of states in the future. The game can be played for oneself as *avatar* or for some other real or fictitious person. The game may require some privacy precautions, especially in a class or training group inside the business or closed community. The players are not required to present their true data and intentions. But they usually display real information about themselves considering that otherwise the results of the game will only have hypothetical conclusions. So the *Career* can be classified as a simulation game with perfect present information, but with statistical uncertainty based on a stochastic model and strategic uncertainty of players' strategy.

Every visit of the player to the team starts with a person's request for a desired transition. The team then studies a person's history and can make a decision on the person's request immediately if the transition is unconditional. If a girl is pregnant, she is definitely supposed to become a mother the next year unless we play this game with medical students who may define the probabilities of miscarriage. But in most cases the team must approve or disapprove the requested transition either collectively by vote if transition is conditional, or by random event generator if it is probabilistic. The typical example is the decision of passing student to the next college level as based on university retention rates. The decision of the team is final for this year with the clear explanation of requirements for changes available in the following steps of the game. It usually ignites changes in the other interconnected areas of life that are considered by the corresponding teams. For example, to get a certain job a person must get the required professional certification (unconditional requirement), or perform voluntary work (facilitating condition), or reach a certain age (conditional probability).

The intermediate document for every player is the protocol consisting of transitions between different states filled in at each team for every year of life (Fig. 6.21).

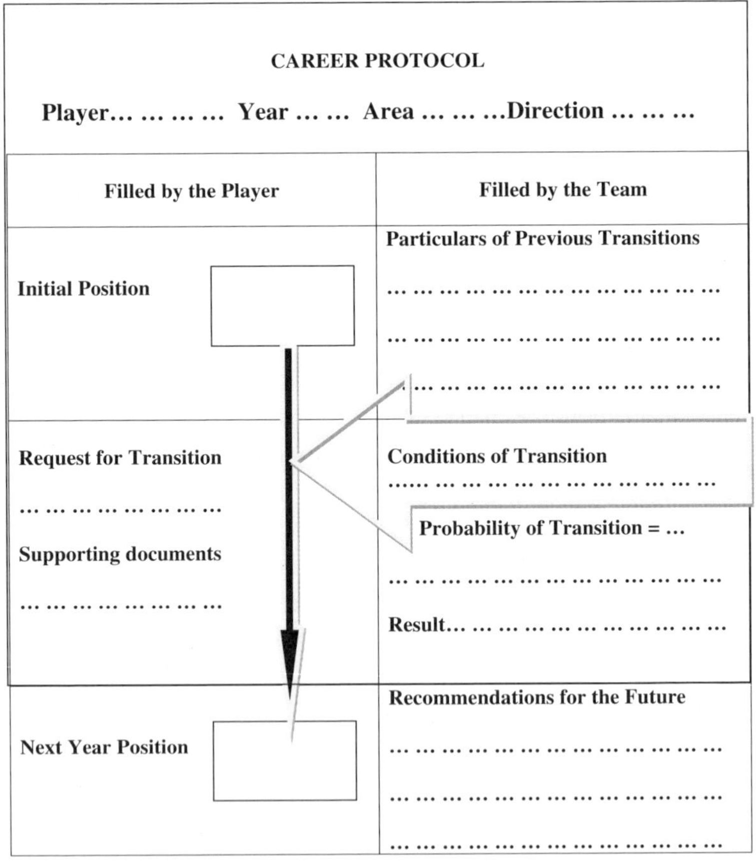

Fig. 6.21.   Intermediate protocol for a year in the *Career* game.

The team that is responsible for the area of life studies the upper part (initial position) of a person's protocol and asks relevant questions. Then the team demonstrates to the player the possible career transitions available to the player and the player formulates one's request for the next year in the central box. If the transition is conditional, the team formulates requirements in the central section of the protocol. If a transition has a chance to occur, the team defines the probability of transition and generates the outcome of the event as it happens or rejected. If the answer satisfies the player, it becomes the final answer, but the player may challenge the team's decision. Then team may offer to the player to try other chances or explains opportunities for the next year. The last sections of protocol are filled as the explanation of additional opportunities and conditions of further progress in this area of life. But such extensive work with every player slows down the game and can be used as an exception or if the team is not busy with other players. Teams register the successful transition on their working network chart or add new positions if they were not included before. The team should try to classify new positions of a particular individual as general as the others previously included in the model. For example, if a player requested in recreation area intension to buy a hot air balloon, it will be classified as the same position as "Buying a boat" which requires the check of the financial status of the player in the WORK area and time budget in the FAMILY. Such information is supported by the players in realistic documents like income statements, resumes or graduation certificates.

During the game every player fills in an individual Career Path Chart and prepares a report on their life story. At the end of the game, every team makes multimedia presentation of results with an analysis of typical career developments.

Presented examples of business games for simulation of operating, growth and development of technological, environmental, economic and social systems allow us to show in the following chapters the principles of their design. The methods of a design depend mainly on the initial concept of the game: to demonstrate experience, verify a theoretical model or simulate a new enterprise.

THE IDEA OF THE GAME

Board of the *Nature* game for kids

7.1. THE SOURCE OF THE GAME

The first decision in designing a new game is its purpose. This will be its place in a learning process among other tools of study. The best, but the most complicated case is when a game integrates the whole field of professional education. The introduction of an interdisciplinary game is possible in specialized industrial business schools and corporate training centers. These schools are problem-oriented and not divided into academic departments like the universities. Such games are intended for advanced interdisciplinary system studies. Developing these games requires joint efforts of instructors and industry specialists. Because active professionals and executives are busy, the involvement of recently retired ones is especially beneficial. Game designers get a feeling of actual problems and retirees are happy to be useful.

The team of designers of such a game should eventually grow by including teachers, industrialists, system analysts, artists and software programmers. The role of a project leader may not be permanently performed by the same person. This responsibility should naturally drift from a sponsor of the project to the idea generator, then to the scanner and finally to the product champion. A business game project usually requires considerable time with a serious commitment of school resources. The introduction of such a game should be done by testing its modules with the students or external professionals.

At the opposite end of the business games scale are games for a short illustration of a particular topic in a course of study. The design of such a game is possible by the individual instructor. Its first purpose is for the use in their own class. The critical feature of such games is the portability, affording fast deployment of the game's hardware in a classroom. The ideal case is that it is a videogame that requires every student to bring a laptop to class. An instructor must first test the "paper" version of the game before implementing a computer version. The students themselves are usually willing to become participants of game design. They are particularly active in the choice of the story and of the aesthetics of the game. In some universities, these classes become a game of games development [Claypool, 2005].

Most business games fall in between these extremes. These games may cover a whole university course or a complex system and require several class sessions inside a standard school schedule. In a business school or in a corporate (industrial) center, a game can be run in several consecutive days of training. The optimal schedule of the game is a "sandwich" course, alternating lectures and exercises with sessions of the game. The design of the game may be carried out by a small team including the instructor, a teaching assistant and some students. A game eventually becomes digital through the computerization of problem modules.

The business games are the logical conclusion of the development of several stages of active methods of teaching. First situations and cases are included, then system analysis, and finally management simulation (Fig. 7.1).

Many economics and management courses are furnished with situations and cases. The most popular for MBA classes are the Harvard Business School (HBS) Cases. Teaching through cases is historically done at HBS by discussing business cases in class, with a professor as a moderator and facilitator. There is an Education Representative role in each section whose role it is to develop an appropriate learning environment and effective relationships between the students and faculty. HBS students represent

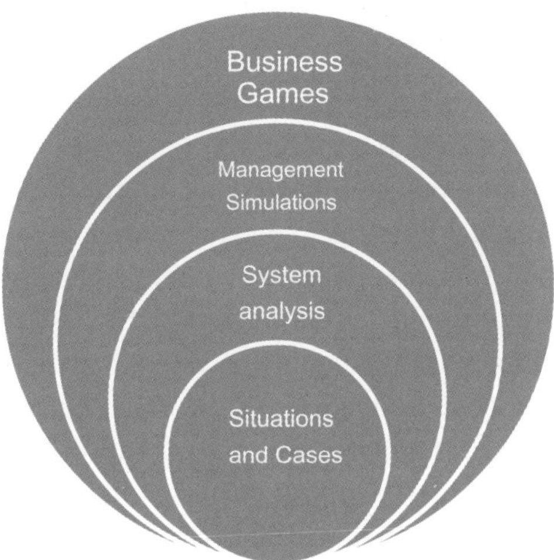

Fig. 7.1.   Nested view on relations between active methods of teaching.

a broad range of industries, undergraduate schools, ethnic backgrounds, geographies, and cultures. Yet most HBS cases are related to top-level executive strategy problems of large corporations. The entire collection includes over 13,000 case studies with new cases constantly being added. The list of the most popular published cases according to Harvard Business Review (HBR) includes the following:

- Airbus A3XX: Developing the World's Largest Commercial Jet (A);
- Petrolera Zuata, Petrozuata C.A.
- Meeting the Diversity Challenge at PepsiCo: The Steve Reinemund Era
- Cirque du Soleil — The High-Wire Act of Building Sustainable Partnerships
- HubSpot: Inbound Marketing and Web 2.0
- Supply Chain Optimization at Hugo Boss (A)
- Symbian, Google & Apple in the Mobile Space (A)
- Sanctuary Soft: International Expansion Strategies
- U.S. Subprime Mortgage Crisis: Policy Reactions (B)
- Barbara Norris: Leading Change in the General Surgery Unit

[HBR, 2010]

The list above represents a wide range of cases from small business units up to the global economy. Each case description contains dozens of text pages, tables and charts. It requires several days of individual study and several hours of discussions in a class. That approach is one of the pillars of the American "critical thinking" educational ideology.

The most advanced business schools and technical universities extend the discussion of cases into system analysis. Sloan School of Management (SSM) at Massachusetts Institute of Technology (MIT), unlike HBS, approaches the executive education differently. The SSM is focused on action learning, it requires that students apply concepts learned in the classroom to real-world business settings. Courses are taught using the case method as well as management simulations and team projects. The academic level of coursework is considered extremely rigorous by business school standards, with a greater emphasis on analytical reasoning and system analysis than most MBA programs. The competitive programs in systems, enterprises and technology management are also offered by the Stevens Institute of Technology, the other oldest American engineering college. As of 2006, there were about 75 institutions in the US that offer 130 undergraduate and graduate programs in systems engineering and technology management.

Management simulations are the next step in teaching methodology. Finally, some universities, business schools and many corporate training centers integrate all of these tools into business games. Many of them are also included in professional training, videogames, Management Flight Simulators (MFS) and Learning Laboratories (LLabs). This approach corresponds to the industrial trend of using "off-the-shelf" products and outsourcing services.

Many videogames can be used as modules inside a "serious" business game. They are especially valuable as introductory exercises for igniting a student's interest. They do not require as much class time if students become involved in playing them outside of class. Some of these games can be adapted to different courses of study. The design of entertainment videogames is well publicized, documented and supported by open source software or freeware [Salen, 2004; Schell, 2008; Novak, 2008]. They contain good inspirational and technical material for business game designers. Students may be also involved in developing of these games. A module or the whole game can be outsourced to professional consultants or to specialized companies that might be found in the magazine *Game Developer*. The trend of player participation in game modification is used by videogames designers as a testing tool as well as for developing new options of a game.

Industrial simulators were originally designed to train pilots and operators in control of complex industrial assemblies and systems. Flight simulators are necessary to teach and test professional and amateur pilots before allowing them to fly a real plane. The original simulators had black and white wireframe graphics, and featured a very limited scenery. They provided a very basic simulation (with only one aircraft simulated). However, it became one of the most popular Apple II applications of the 1980s. Later, the more advanced *Microsoft Flight Simulator* improved the virtual environment by providing better views and speeds. It represents control of over 60 types of modern airplanes. The flying area now encompasses the whole world, including over 24,000 airports. Extremely detailed scenery represents major landmarks and an ever-growing number of towns and cities. Although landscape details are often patchy, a variety of websites offer scenery add-ons.

The Sloan School of Management at MIT initiated the development of Management Flight Simulators (MFS) starting with the *People Express Management Flight Simulator* [Sterman, 1994]. The prototype of the game was the story of the rise and fall of a real airline: People Express. A player in the game makes decisions about buying and leasing aircrafts, hiring personnel, establishing fares and providing service. The next generations of MFSs that were designed at MIT now are used for learning how to manage corporations and economic systems. Among them are:

- *B&B Enterprises Management Flight Simulator* [Sterman *et al.*, 2000],
- *Commercial Real Estate Management Flight Simulator* [Bakken and Sterman, 2002],
- *International Oil Tanker Management Flight Simulator* [Bakken and Sterman, 2004].

Learning Laboratories (LLabs) approach was initiated by Peter Senge from the same System Dynamics Group in Sloan School of Management at MIT. It is the simulation process based not on a physical model of the MFS, but based on a virtual System Dynamics model of a system. It was first offered for the corporate management training practice at Saturn, Ford Motors and AT&T companies [Gerber, 1992, Simon *et al.*, 1995]. The Saturn program manager Fred Simon recollects the experience of training with LLab:

"In retrospect, the flight simulator was interesting, and it gave us a threshold from which to talk about systems issues. But the noncomputer-based parts of the learning lab had the most impact. They gave us ways of talking more directly and effectively about our issues. ... The learning lab wasn't structured like the training environment we were used to... It was uncomfortable that the boss was learning with us; that he didn't have the answers; that we were going to figure it out together. And yet it was exciting, because we could see that we were all going to be in on this together."

[Simon, 1995]

The experience of designing advanced digital entertainment games is valuable for business games; a game should not be a closed system. It is natural for a model of an economic system to evolve in the same fashion as all other systems. Digital game designers try to find the elements of economics in entertainment games as well:

> "Game *economies* are systems in which resources move around — either physically (from place to place) or conceptually (from owner to owner). Resources can be money, troops, characters, weapons, property, skills — anything that players can "own" in the game (information, too!). In an FPS [First Person Shooters], a primary resource is often ammunition that can be found or obtained by stealing it from dead opponents. This resource is consumed by firing weapons. Health points are other resources that are consumed by being hit — and are restored with medical kits. Since resources interact with each other, players can't produce too much or too little of them — or the economy will be thrown out of balance… *Ultima Online* was originally designed to have a completely self-contained, closed economy with a fixed number of resources. Players, acting in a way that had not been anticipated by the developers, hoarded objects without using them. Resources were depleted, which caused an inflation in the game economy (in which the hoarders could charge ridiculously high fees for these objects). Developers eventually had to do away with the closed system and adopted an open economy in which new resources were spawned."
>
> [Novak, 2008]

We will follow the classic model of a product life cycle for a business game development explanation. (see Fig. 7.2).

The design of the game as the first half of the life cycle consists of the game idea implementation in hardware and software. An introduction of the game requires the training of instructors in wetware. In contemporary terminology, wetware includes besides know-how as explicit rules and procedures also implicit live experience in playing and conducting the game. When the game is introduced, it experiences a "hype cycle" of life typical for electronic games: an immediate growth of interest going to the peak of popularity and then stabilization at the maturity stage. Very few games stay at the maturity stage long as the market offers a stream of new games. Even a successful game needs regular modifications to accomodate new information technologies. Business games based on academic

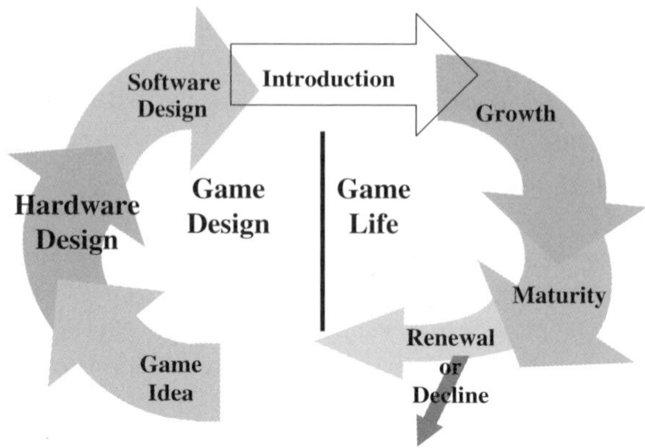

Fig. 7.2.　Stages of a game life cycle.

theories have a life as long as the underlying theory or academic school stays respected.

The proportions between stages are different for specific games. Field and board games are mostly implemented as the hardware; digital games as the software. The most valuable component of business games is wetware: rules, processes and know-how. The wetware is more complicated than hardware or software because it regulates less predictable human behavior. Wetware should be regularly updated and clarified during each play of the game. It is especially essential to adjust the appearance and music of the game for a young audience. The design of a game requires scientific intelligence, engineering creativity and artistic imagination.

At the first stage of the design we need to clarify the idea of the game expressed in clear terms and concepts. The natural initial point is the mission of the game as either an educational tool or a forecasting device. A well-designed game may be able to fulfill both missions. Figure 7.1 presented in nested view of a game as a shell covering all other tools of learning. Therefore, the concept of a business game might be based on any of the predecessors: cases, systems or simulations. The game may be a stream of cases requiring players to make decisions in a changing environment. It can start as a system model used for the practical interpretation of system behavior. It can be also a statistical analysis of management simulations. Each of these starting points requires different types of knowledge.

The natural source of business cases is practical experience in the industry. This is the main feature of the earliest so-called "serious" business games implemented by the Rand Corporation in *Monopologs* and by ABSEL in *Capstone* games. The models of System Dynamics are implemented in the *Beer Game*; and System of Systems Engineering in our *TranSport* and *Finance SoS* games. Classic *AMA* management game and MFS simulation devices gave birth to the family of *Management Flight Simulators* at MIT. But the best business games are using all three sources of material: cases, models and exercises. The initial idea of every one of these games required genuine creativity from their designers.

So the idea for individual business game design may be ignited by one of the three possible sources:

- Case studies and class exercises
- Management Flight Simulators (MFS)
- Theoretical models of life- or business-cycles.

These components must satisfy the repetitive nature of games by being short and concise. The most natural way of game development starts from a "basket" — the collection of small similar case studies for practitioners or class exercises for students. The MFS as a source of situations may be available for the corporate executives or government officials. Corporate training centers and governmental institutions may support expensive MFSs. Theoretical models may be used after testing of their validity in practical situations. But most business games are usually combining all three components in different proportions and in certain order. Educational use of business game is likely to start with the model illustrated as cases by the instructor, illuminated by students' behavior and interpreted by professor. Games for corporate personnel training naturally start with cases and proceed to MFS or forecasting with the life cycle models. MBA students may start with HBS cases demonstrations followed by the business cycles scenarios.

The game development process is a continuous change of game generations or modifications to keep the games family portfolio as a mix of games on different stages of their life cycles. Then customers will upgrade their interest in the business game subject getting wider choice and more

                    Business Games

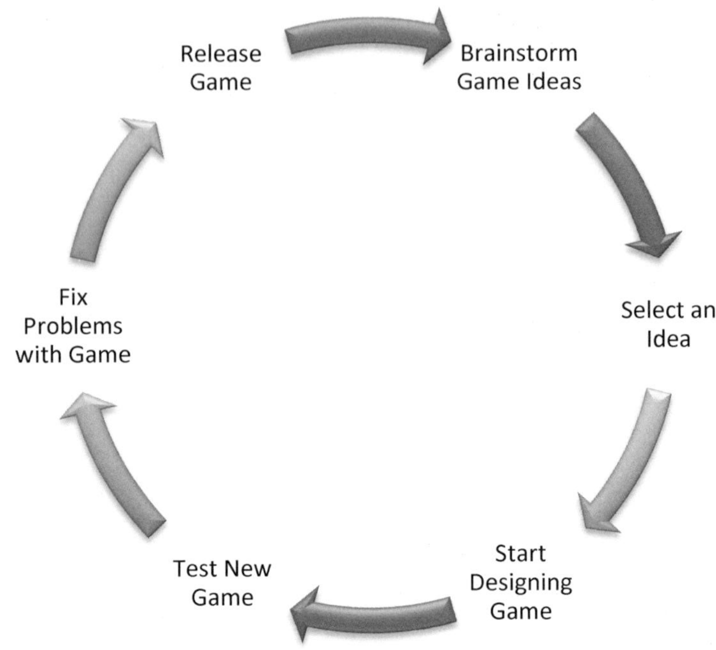

Fig. 7.3.   Continuous improvement process of game designs.

advanced features. The process of continuous improvement for the family
of games is illustrated by Fig. 7.3.

This is a long-term cycle for development of the family of games.
Game development is a hardware design and software development process
by which video games are produced. The following steps highlight the
development of a games such as *Gazillionaire* or *CyberMarket*.

The first step is to decide on the concept of a game which comes from
brainstorming for different ideas. Next is the beginning of the design stage
we must see how the game will look like. Next comes the testing of the game
prototype to see if it will get the approval of the future customers. Next is
fixing the problems with the game before it gets released. And lastly is the
release of the game to the public for purchasing and playing. The chances
of game survival depend first of all on its idea originality. The idea of a new
game may be generated in a creative mind.

7.2. THE SOURCES OF CREATIVITY

According to the model of knowledge development presented in Chapter 1, creativity is the highest stage of the learning process. Paradoxically it is demonstrated more often by the least experienced people: children. Psychological studies estimate the peak of human creativity between 3, 14 and 18 years of age (Fig. 7.4).

The latest studies of child psychology are moving estimates of a peak of creativity down to three to four years of age [Sandhu, 2006]. Japan leads the trend of use the earliest demonstration of creativity with special subjects for kindergarten students. Then from age six to twelve the Japanese education system gives to kids the first stage of compulsory education including English for children. Almost all Japanese children enter at this stage with increasing number of those who have already experienced kindergarten. So the general improvement of standard of living for the Japanese population has resulted in some of the highest standards of education in the world. About 93% of children enter high school, and nearly all of them graduate. Japan also has one of the highest university enrollment rates in the developed world (40% in 2000), and a huge number of state and private universities to serve the population. Japan is also a world leader in electronic and video games development [Novak, 2008].

In the 1950s Japanese started publishing a translation of the Russian children's magazine "Young Designer" in search of fresh ideas which were not recognized in Russia itself. In the 1960s Japanese were heavily involved

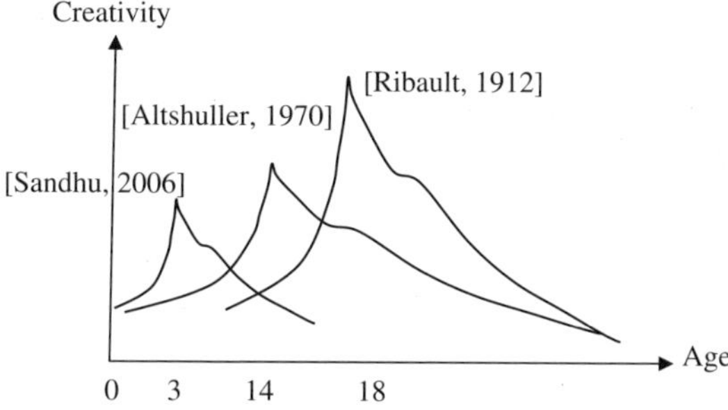

Fig. 7.4.   Creativity curves in relation to age.

Table 7.1.   The process of developing knowledge in products and game designs.

Results \ Process	Repetition	Analysis	Creativity
Experience	Reverse engineering	Modular design	
Learning	Technology transfer	Incremental innovation	Invention
Changing paradigm		Radical innovation	Discovery

in the reverse engineering of products and games from the West. The purpose was to deduce design decisions from end products with little or no additional knowledge about the procedures involved in the original production. This way Japanese designers developed their own capacity to improve foreign design [Chikofsky, 1990]. And now they became the leading developers in the world of new videogames. Now Red China and South Korea are catching up in the gaming industry by exploiting industrial espionage and reverse engineering. They include many samples of Western gaming software and wetware [Novak, 2008]. This process fits in our model of developing knowledge introduced before in Chapter 1 in Table 7.1.

In Part 1 of the book we presented several business games that may be just adopted for your class by the reverse engineering. The other games may be adapted to your specific requirements by including new modules. Now we will present different tools for the reinforcing of your own creative powers.

Assuming that you are the curious person (otherwise do not try to teach others!), we may offer you possible ways to facilitate your natural creativity. One is psychological activation of your mental process. It might be achieved individually or collectively. Creative ideas sometimes are stimulated in artists with coffee, alcohol, or narcotics. We consider it as not acceptable for the university professors. Scientists are reaching such a state of mental activity either by thinking about their problems day in and day out until a solution appears, sometimes even in a night dream, or in intensive discussions with colleagues. We also know about less stressful ways of ideas generation recommended by Steven Johnson by systematic recording and revising observations. He describes collecting and sorting ideas using modern information technology like Microsoft tag applications on your smart phone [Johnson, 2010]. Professional designers of computer games call the short and concise concept of the game as "the pitch". A pitch may be generated by the popular among digital games designers brainstorming "the silly cow exercise". It is a warm-up session of a designers' team visualizing on post-its conceptual ideas of a new game [Osterwalder, 2010].

There are many organizations with great ideas of creativity promotion for the education and research. One of the leading ones is TED that started in 1984 as a conference bringing together people from three worlds: *Technology, Entertainment, Design*. Since then its scope has become ever broader. It helds two annual conferences — the TED Conference in Long Beach and Palm Springs (USA) each spring, and the TED Global Conference in Oxford (UK) every summer. TED includes the award-winning TED Talks video site, the Open Translation Project and Open TV Project, the inspiring TED Fellows and TEDx programs, and the annual TED Prize. TED conferences address a wide range of topics within of science and culture. The speakers are given a maximum of 18 minutes to present their ideas in the most innovative and engaging ways they can. Past presenters include Bill Clinton, Jane Goodall, Malcolm Gladwell, Al Gore, Gordon Brown, Richard Dawkins, Bill Gates, Google founders Larry Page and Sergey Brin, and many Nobel Prize winners [Guardian, 4 July 2010].

The collective ways of generating ideas called brainstorming may be just improvisational or methodical. Game ideas may be ignited during the free discussion or during the organized and managed meetings. They may look like focus groups or Delphi sessions. In a focus group participants are asked questions towards a concept of product, service, advertisement, or packaging. The first focus groups were created at the Bureau of Applied Social Research by associate director, sociologist Robert K. Merton [Kaufmann, 2003]. The Delphi method is a systematic, interactive forecasting method which may be also used for generating game ideas. The experts answer questionnaires in two or more rounds. After each round, a facilitator provides a summary of the experts' forecasts from the previous round as well as the reasons they provided for their judgments. During this process the range of the answers will decrease and the group will converge towards the "correct" answer. Finally, the process is stopped after a pre-defined convergence criterion (e.g., number of rounds, achievement of consensus, stability of results) and the results of the final rounds determine the idea [Rowe and Wright, 1999].

For the purpose of business game ideas by generation by systematic ways are preferable. Among them are such analytical methods as lateral thinking, morphological analysis and TRIZ (Russian abbreviation for the Theory of Innovative Problem Solving) [Terninko *et al.*, 1998].

Lateral thinking developed by Edward De Bono recommends search in a systematic way for ideas in the neighborhood of any starting proposal. By scanning the likely possibilities we sooner or later will run into real opportunity of solving the problem [De Bono, 1985]. Morphological box is a device for reducing the number of possible solutions by the elimination of unacceptable combinations of factors. Morphological analysis was designed for non-quantifiable problems [Zwicky, 1969]. TRIZ offers an even more detailed structural search of an idea by formal mapping it in multi-dimensional space of available materials and technologies [Altshuller, 1988]. The last two methods are especially valuable in the technical stages of hardware and software design. Generating of the idea is better performed by the methods of search for a new combinations of factors. This approach is popular among videogames designers. They either take ready scenario of a popular book or movie or create a fantastic world as an unusual combination of familiar things.

Different combinations of basic features are available for the business games ideas. Put the components of a game on separate cards, shuffle them and pick up combinations of them at random.

First dimension is the type of environment: technological, ecological, economic or social as we discussed in the previous chapter. The second is the scale and scope of business: Small, Medium or Large; Local, National or Global. The next is organizational level: the whole business enterprise or its functional, product/service specific or regional aspect. The next is the type of game: card (board), digital or field game. The choice of degree of computerization may be the last decision about the idea of the game. It will become clear after a preliminary, "papermade" design of the game is finished. For example, it happens to be ecological impact on the medium business field game. It may be a good learning tool for the environment awareness class in a county community college.

And finally, what is the most essential for a success of a game?

Catchy name, colorful advertising!

There are examples of fancy names for some computer games closest to the business online simulation: *Gazillionaire, Tycoons, Civilizations, EverQuest, Gran Tourismo, Math Blaster, Ultima Online, upTick*. The names of business games are usually not spectacular, just reflecting the object of simulation: product for technological applications, process for environmental and model for economic. Still some games are attractive like *Megastore Madness or Vacations Mogul*. The most compelling are sceneries of games for social systems like *The Game of Life* or *The Romance of Rome*.

7.3.   THE STRUCTURE OF A GAME

The defining factor of the game structure is the size of the class and a time assigned for the game. The larger the class, the more essential is its structuring to keep the game organized. Then it does not need frequent interference from the instructor to keep it on schedule and to regulate communications between players. Small class size gives more opportunities to improvise both for the instructor and for the players. The shorter time allowed for the game, the more disciplined should be all participants to fit in the game schedule. The game, organized by daily/weekly sessions, allows instructors just the opposite: to reassign the teams, refurbish the environment and readjust the rules from one session to the next. It also gives extra time to prepare intermediate documentation, process new information and to make preliminary analysis. This is especially essential for the games in graduate schools and corporate training centers where players have powers to interfere in the instructor's conduct during the game and to complain to the authorities in between and after the sessions. To minimize such a consequences we should keep players busy mentally and physically by organizational means as well as by the rules and procedures which we will discuss in the following chapters.

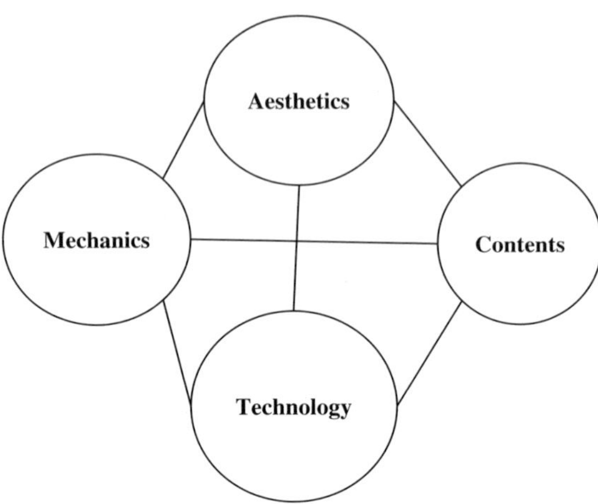

Fig. 7.5.   Four leading elements of a game.

Professional game developers accumulated huge experience in design of entertaining videogames. Their approach might be used for the design of business games with appropriate modifications. It first of all is related to the architecture of the game which is universal for all types of games. The best of practically tested classifications of game elements is proposed as ***elemental tetrad*** by Jesse Schell, one of the leaders of entertainment games industry [Schell, 2008]. It consists of four following elements (see Fig. 7.5).

These four elements may be interpreted for business games architecture as the following:

- **Mechanics**: These are procedures and rules of the game. They should be derived from the industrial technology, ecological studies, economic theory, organizational behavior and other social sciences. They will be the bases of corresponding technological, environmental, economic and social business games. We will refer to them as ***models*** in theoretical terminology.
- **Contents**: This is the sequence of events that unfolds in your game. It may be some project management stages, years of professional life, family history, growth of the business or large scale industrial development. Economic classes are usually refer to such a material as ***business cases.***

- **Aesthetics**: This is how your game looks, sounds, smells, tastes and feels. Business games mainly operate with formulas, tables and charts, but should also use arts to generate positive emotions. The more of such a feelings the game ignites, the better. The story descriptions and results may be illustrated by diagrams, photos and cartoons. Appropriate video-clips and music are also recommended. We will refer to these materials as to the *software.*

- **Technology**: The medium of the game should be artifacts, like cards, boards, posters, tokens. Computers may present corresponding images on the screen besides being the main processors of game models defined above in the aesthetics as software. The *hardware* then will be a material support of the game including first of all computers.

This classification is to some extent a simplification necessary for practical applications. The other multidimensional interpretations of these elements will be later used in the system approach to business game designs. It will correspond to the duality as organizing principle of system optimization.

Game architecture and dynamics of simulated system should reflect the complexity sufficient to Ashby's Law of Requisite Variety [Ashby, 1956]. There are five possible options of interaction between space and time in computer games. Inside the next quotation we added our business games examples:

(1) **Linear**. A surprising number of games are arranged on a linear game space where a player can only move forward and (maybe) back along a line. Some well known linear game spaces: *Monopoly, Words-in-Sentences.*

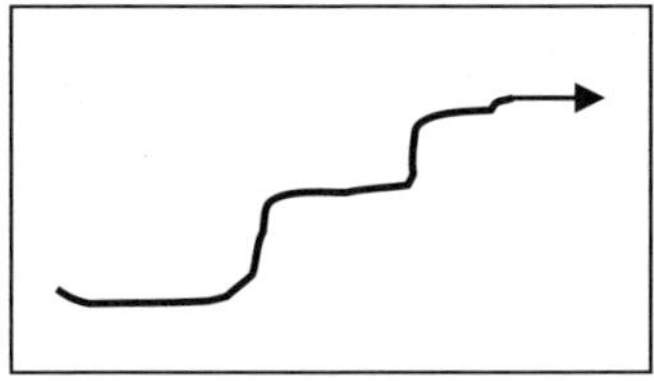

(2) **Grid**. Arranging your gamespace on a grid has a lot of advantages. It can be easy for players to understand, it makes it easier to ensure that things

line up. Some well known grid-based games:, *Highway Construction, Nature, TranSport.*

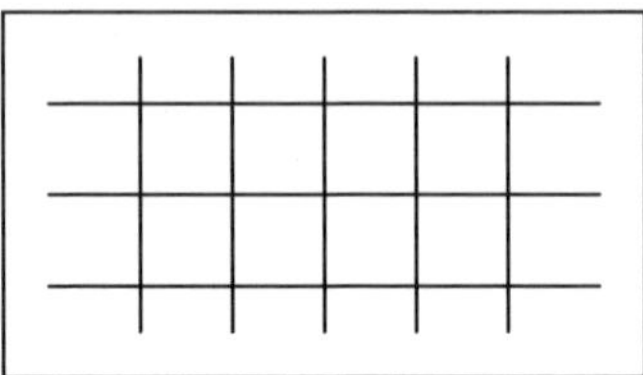

(3) **Web**. A web arrangement is achieved by marking several points on the map and connecting them with paths. Some examples of web-based spaces: *HELLO, Toontown Online, Trucking Business.*

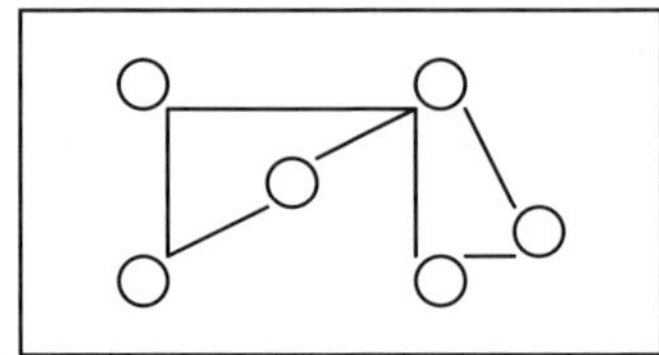

(4) **Points in Space**. This somewhat uncommon type of gamespace is usually for games that want to evoke something like wandering a desert and occasionally returning to an oasis. Some examples of this kind of organization: *Shell Game, Career.*

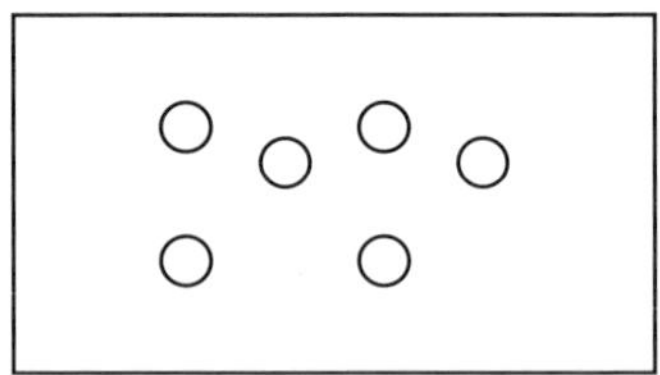

(5) **Divided Space**. This kind of space is most like a real map and is common in games that are trying to replicate a real map. Some examples of games that have divided space: *SIEMENS Supply Chain Simulator, Glo-Bus.*

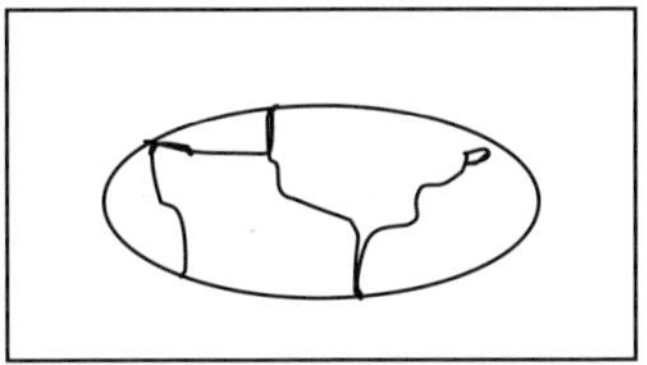

[Abbreviated from Shell, 2008]

It is difficult to find direct correspondence of classes of business games to the entertainment games mainly associated with adventures in space. Business games are based on duality principles of decision optimization. The business game architecture should represent organizational structure, dynamics of business processes and human participation.

The best examples of game structure evolution are games on supply chain systems. There are three business games on the same purpose: *Beer Game, Siemens Supply Chain Simulator* and *HELLO*. Their structural parameters are presented in Table 7.2.

The structures of three games are similar: several interconnected businesses, but dynamics of these games are different. The *Beer Game* is short and simple, the *HELLO* game is long and complex. All three games fulfill two main requirements: (1) increasing difficulty from cycle to cycle; (2) constant visual feedback on decisions of players.

(1) The players in all games are starting with learning rules by slow performance of the first cycle(s) of a game with increasing speed and additional challenges in the following cycles;

(2) The constant feedback loops are providing visual demonstration of changes in game situation. The responses on player's decisions are presented either on the game board, on the multimedia wall or on the screens of PCs.

7.4. BUSINESS GAME PLAYERS AND TEAMS

After the choice of structure for the business game we should decide upon the assigning of roles and allocation of resources in the game. Quite a few business games offer a player a choice between playing as a separate individual or become a member of the "gameworld" — term used

Table 7.2.   Structural parameters of supply chain business games.

Game name	Decisions level	Hardware	Software	Parameters	
				Schedule	Structure
Beer Game	Operations control	Board with chips and paper orders	Hand filling of orders and tables	52 weekly exercises, 2 minutes for each	Several teams of 4–10 players each
SIEMENS Supply Chain Simulator	Management Improvements	Board with Lego bricks assemblies	Flowcharts and statistical analysis	12 monthly cases, 20 min each	2–3 multi-functional teams
HELLO: Help in Economics of Logistics and Location Order	System of Systems Governance	Network of businesses and offices	Simulation and optimization	5 yearly simulations, 2 hours each	6 teams of specialized businesses

by computer games designers. Gameworlds are organized as competitions between independent players or teams. Computer games now often ignite self–organized multiplayer communities which are complementary for game improvement. Educational games are usually designed for a few groups of players with similar structures of the teams. We are also designing games for educational institutions with many participants self-organized in teams, or in a local network of individual players.

Let us look at examples of different business game architectures.

Individual multi-player game *Career*. Fixed number of teams for an unlimited class size.

Each participant of the Game works out the decisions of his/her individual life story and provides expertise for the decisions of others as a member of one of the specialized teams (Education, Work, Recreation and Family). The instructor may offer different ways of allocating students between teams — ranging from the instructor's own decision, especially if the time for game is limited, and up to the full freedom of choosing and changing teams by each participant (provided that the sizes of the teams will be approximately equal). If some professional advice or technical assistance is available, it is better to keep these people (experts, teaching assistants) permanently on different teams. Each team has a workplace at a separate table board. Additional charts illustrating opportunities offered by this area of life should be displayed on the wall, or on the PC screen. Laptops might be used for keeping personal records and illustrating models and calculations.

[Bazilevich, 1979]

Unlimited number of teams of fixed size in the *Beer Game*.

The game can be played with anywhere from four to hundreds of people. Each person is asked to bet $1, with the pot going to the team with the lowest total cost, winner takes all. The game is initialized in equilibrium. Each inventory contains 12 cases and initial throughput is four cases per week... Each player has good local information but severely limited global information. Players keep records of their inventory, backlog and orders placed with their supplier each week. However, people are directed not to communicate with one another, information is passed through orders and shipments. Customer demand is not known to any of the players in advance. Only the retailers discover customer demand as the game proceeds. The others learn only what their own customer orders.

[Sterman, 1992]

Unlimited number of individual players. The Web based *Beer* business game.

The Web based *Beer* business game allows multiple users to play a single game at the same time…In order to play the simulation, you will have to either create a new game, and be the manager of the game, or join a game some other manager has already created… If at least one more of the roles were not filled, we would have to wait for another player to join in the game. At this point, you can enter the simulation by clicking on the "Play Distributor" button… you take the role of a manager of one of the components of the beer supply chain, either the retailer, the supplier, the distributor, or the factory. This will be called interactive role. The computer and other players take the remaining roles… When the simulation begins, the players downstream from the interactive facility will play. Note that any role not filled by a human player will be played by the computer, which will act according to a classical inventory management.

[Li and Simchi-Levi, 2002]

Fixed size of a team for variable class size. Business Game *CyberMarket*.

Essential feature of the game is the competition between several teams of the same size and structure. Initial structure of the Game was based around the board reproducing classical model of economic cycle including two markets: Products and Factors; and two roles of participants: Businesses and Households. There is two or three participants represent Businesses and two to three participants represent households of different types. Besides, team may include role of Government — either performed by one of the students, or simulated by the "Parliament" — conference of team members. It is possible global extension of the game by allowing negotiations and exchange of resources between teams. Teams may make calculations on charts and tables, but usually they are equipped by Personal Computers for the performance of calculations using Excel, for the writing of reports and for multimedia presentations. On introductory levels 1 and 2 of the game general calculations are preformed using prefabricated tables, charts and nomograms for the expedited reporting. Large-scale posters and flip-charts are necessary for the introductory explanations if the LSD projector is not available Video recording is recommended for the team presentations. Instructors are equipped with the PCs to keep records of individual and team performance as well.

[Bazilevich, 1992]

Fixed roles of players in the limited number of teams. *Capstone business game.*
Game is played by four work roles in a team: (1) Product Manager, managing one of the five products in the starting product line with opportunity to invent new products; (2) Segment Manager, responsible for one of the five market segments; (3) Functional Manager, responsible for R&D, Marketing, Production, Finance, Human Resources or Total Quality Management; (4) Competitive Intelligence Officer, predicting the behavior of competitors. The team may work face-to-face or communicate in cyberspace to work out on each round of the game yearly decisions and download them for the revision by the instructors. The model of this game is large in size and interdisciplinary which require support of a team of professional instructors and technical personnel.

[Capstone, 2003]

Individual multiplayer games in this respect are different from the "coach" videogames as games against Nature. The development of network of interacting players is the logical extension of one-player videogames. Such originally purely individual videogames as *World of Warcraft, Habbo Hotel and Sims* has grown into virtual worlds of tens of millions of interactive players. These games assembled a large number of originally lonely coach players into significant social communities which opened huge business opportunities. This new industry transforms individual players in multi-person gamers. They build informal coalitions of customers easily influenced by advertizing industry through *advergames* in *adverworlds*. [Edery, 2008].

Amount of business-oriented videogames increases as many industries and services realize that the advertizing power of games exceeds other media influence on customers. The population of videoplayers has instantly grown from mainly teenagers to the other demographic, especially female and senior age groups. It is a result of widening contents of games to everyday life and due to availability of games everywhere on personal computers, iPhones, iPods, iPads and even on cellphones. Such a game platform as *Second Life* has grown into a virtual sandbox for millions of "avatars" representing unlimited markets of all population groups trading virtual goods for the Lindon Dollars. It even enables most entrepreneural players to convert virtual dollars into real money and goods.

Design and marketing of a videogame is a highly professional activity requiring millions dollars of investment. So first game designers, and then whole information, computer, and telecommunications industries are enormously empowered by involving millions of enthusiasts in the development of their products. Videogame producers now allow the download of game content free for any user through the Internet. So the corporate initial investment in advergames was reduced in some cases from millions to just hundreds of dollars. [Edery, 2008]. Industrial giants like *Ford* and *General Motors* are also sponsoring videogames in exchange not only for advertizing, but even for improvement of their products through dedicated gaming websites. Most platform games become open for the content and appearance development by players themselves who become voluntary designers and advertizers of "mods" (modifications) of videogames.

An opportunity to design mods also may be useful for the development of business-oriented versions of entertainment games. For example, we customized the *GranTourismo* videogame for exercising in economic analysis of the motor racing business. Students are drawing control charts and learning curves, calculate costs and estimate utilities. Most videogames might be used far beyond entertainment for a business simulation. Videogame *Roller Coaster* is a good exercise in economics and management development of different businesses. Popular fast food business game *CakeMania* ignited dozens of mods of the same purpose of small businesses from *BikeMania* to *TravelMania*. They teach enterpreneurship and management improvements, and how to invest in business development.

Previously the success of entertainment games distracted its resources from a few companies specialized in educational business games. Most of them are now out of business or acquired by the entertainment industry giants [Novak, 2008]. Virtual worlds are becoming attractive, being based on popular TV shows, movies or books. MTV Networks launched *Virtual Laguna Beach* and *vHills* worlds based on successful shows of the same titles. So the experience and technology of designing videogames for entertainment is helpful for the development of business games, especially due to introducing specialized game design courses in some universities. They are also provided with very helpful fundamental textbooks written by the experienced game designers [Salen and Zimmerman, 2004], [Schell, 2008], [Novak, 2008].

Stevens Institute of Technology launched an annual contest on the best system design game for students. In 2010 it awarded two first prizes for the videogames and two second prizes for management simulations. Videogames were related to health and military services, simulations presented manufacturing industries.

7.5. DESIGNERS TEAM FORMATION AND LEADERSHIP

The nature of the game influences the professional and organizational structure of the game developers, designers and testers. Entertainment game industry has these three groups of professionally specialized, even departmentalized inside corporation. A business game amateur designer usually combines these functions oneself or shares them with a few colleagues and assistants. Entertaining games industry historically demonstrated classic life cycle of organizational development. First individual game inventors teamed up with friends into small businesses. It corresponds to the "garage" stage of business development model (see Fig. 2.12). Those of them who offered commercially attractive designs were acquired by the toy industry giants like Hasbro. Others were growing independent if their first success attracted venture capitalists or commercial loans. Then they become standard specialized and later diversified corporations protected by patents or copyrights. Now it is a global multibillion industry employing over 100,000 people. The education system itself reacted to support demand of human resources for this industry:

> "In response to this rapid growth, hundreds of colleges and universities in the United States have launched accredited game development programs in the last few years — and textbooks providing support to these programs are in great demand."
>
> [Novak, 2008]

The business games are still in the first, "garage" stage of the industrial development. Management interpretation of each point of life cycle curve illustrates dynamics in the direction by a team structuring. Nuclear teams of two or three enthusiasts cannot be structured, in teams of four members or more the coalitions begin to form according to typical team dynamics. It arises struggle for a leadership and conflicts between groups as a source of the first crisis of business development. A project team seldom exceeds ten members with maximum number of five specialized subgroups (see Fig. 1.14 in Chapter 1).

The game is usually designed by the team including a set of professionals in different organizational and informal roles. There are large teams of professionals that are required for the industrial computer entertainment game designs. We will outline only those professionals which are required for the educational business game design:

"*An executive producer* responsible for production management, proposal and prototype management, and product support. Oversees multiple projects.

The *producer* is responsible for meeting project goals and establishing policies. The producer resolves communication problems with partners (e.g., publisher, developer, hardware manufacturer, licensor).

The *creative director* ensures that the overall style and game content is consistent with the original vision for the project.

A *lead designer* usually supervises the game design team and is also often involved hands-on in the daily game design process.

An *interface designer* determines the layout, content, navigation, and usability features of the game interface.

The *art director* responsible for the style of the game art — including determining the mood, look and feel of the game.

The *tools programmer* designs tools to assist art and design team members incorporate their work into code so it can be included in the game.

The *graphics programmer* (a mix between a programmer and an artist) is responsible for programming solutions to specific graphical game issues.

The *lead tester* usually supervises the testing team and is also often involved hands-on in the daily testing process for a particular game project.

[Novak, 2008]

William Wright's success demonstrated that design of a game itself is essentially an intense teamwork. The structure of the team there designed *Sim City* game in Electronic Arts company is presented in Fig. 7.6.

Assignment of game developers to different roles follows not only professional education, but should also consider their psychological profiles.

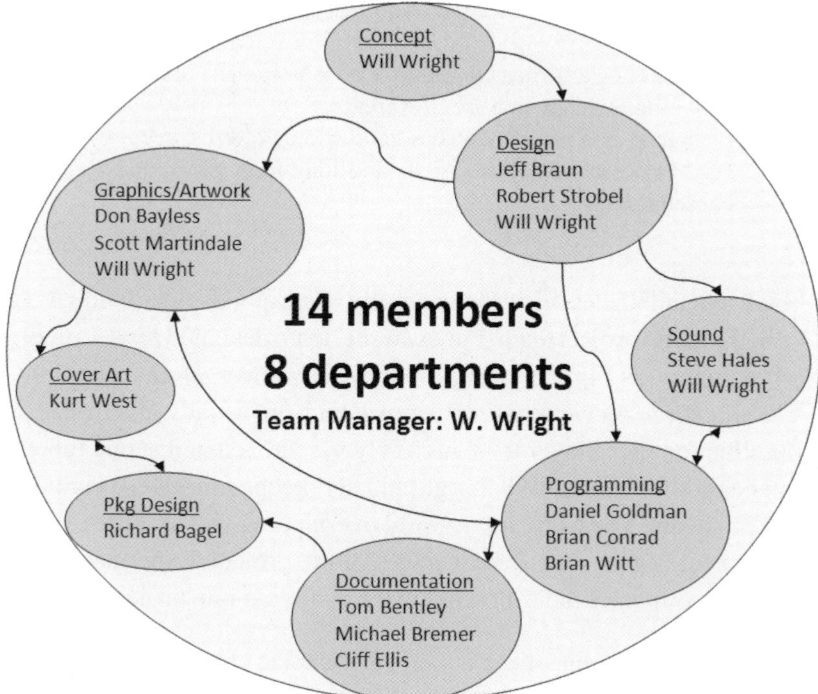

Fig. 7.6.   Professional team of designers of *Sim City* game.

Organizational psychology defines individual roles of members of a project team in terms of information handling in the following way.

"There are nine team roles defined to help the team function more effectively:

- Organizer — a person who visualizes and plans for the whole design process.
- Motivator — a person who takes care of the schedule and goals of the team.
- Pusher — an active person who makes team work faster.
- Solver — an imaginative person who deals mainly with problem resolution.
- Gatherer — a person who is good at collecting information and communicating with other teams.
- Listener — a perceptive person, who can listen and combine the ideas and statements of others.

- Completer — a careful person who specializes in eliminating design defects.
- Specialist — a dedicated person who is extremely skilled and has a lot of knowledge in a specific area.
- Evaluator — a person who has good strategic skills, keeps the balance between immediate needs and long-term goals, and weighs consequences

[Skalak, 2002]

Such a detailed classification generally corresponds to individual characters in the game project team. For example, team designed *SimCity* including 14 members, as Fig. 7.6 shows, so they may cover all nine positions of this classification. As we deal with teams which are usually less in size, it is not possible for each player to be narrowly specialized in just one function. The manager of the team Will Wright himself keeps four out of eight positions in this team. The roles are not only overlapping, but also are changing for the same designer on different stages of the project. Experienced game designers recommend the following mantras for a game project manager:

Mantra 1: "No amount of ego is worth any amount of talent."
Mantra 2: "If you are not having fun making the game, the players won't have fun playing it."
Mantra 3: "Be a leader, not just a manager."
Mantra 4: "Fiction explains gameplay — so gameplay should not have to explain fiction."
Mantra 5: "No plan survives contact with the enemy."
Mantra 6: "It's game and a service."
Mantra 7: "Stable, fast, fun — in that order."

[Novak, 2008, p. 355]

Many game designers' teams are becoming more decentralized, multifunctional and even international. The best arrangement for a design of the games is a situation room with the standard media equipment. Interaction between designers, instructors and players with different backgrounds requires using all opportunities of **ViVaT** approach.

Virtualization is necessary to connect different physical, informational and psychological processes in one space. Architecture of most games, especially computer games, is virtual. It allows us to integrate these components simultaneously to the full ability of every participant. The virtual

Table 7.3.   Means of communication for virtual teams.

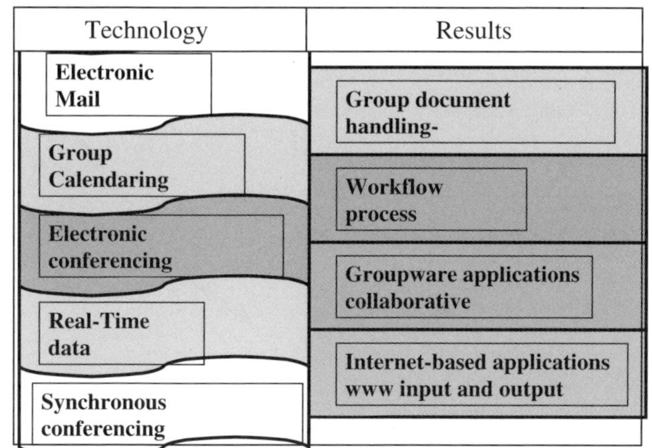

interaction between designers separated by distance, time, languages and cultures may be organized on different levels (Table 7.3).

Most experienced products and processes designers are working out a universal approach to the development of new products and services named "Design of Design" [Brooks, 2010]. The roles allocation between members of a game design team and roles allocation between players of the game are following the same lines. It allows the support of activities called "Game of Game Design" [Claypool, 2005] which joins together game designers and game players in the same knowledge creation model. The difference is that if game design stages take months and years, time which players have is measured in days and weeks. The time pressure and younger age facilitates creativity of players.

The new tools of communication support a strong trend in game designer teams' development from the traditional functional teams to global virtual teams. This is typical for all new product development processes as shown in Fig. 7.7.

Now we may establish correspondence between life cycle of designer's business development and information exchange in their teams on the knowledge creation model introduced in Chapter 1 (Fig. 7.8).

The garage stage of business development works as intense search of innovations and as a learning from the first mistakes on this way. Small

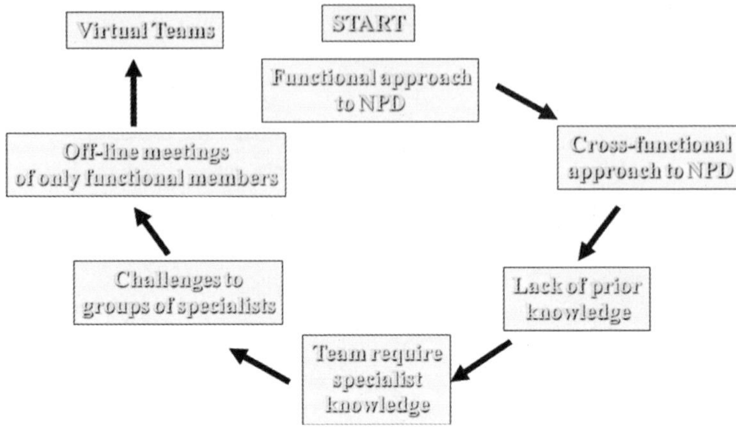

Fig. 7.7.   From cross-functional to the virtual team.

business starts accumulating collective experience. The corporation hires more already experienced people who share their experience with the rest of the enterprise. The correspondence between model of continuous learning process (Fig. 1.9) and the team dynamics (Fig. 1.12) allows measuring by an entropy the synergy accumulation during a game design.

A complexity of the game design management increases with the growth and development of a business. The uncertainty of a choice between two alternative conceptual game ideas is measured in modest bits of information. A larger amount of $3-4$ options correspond to the small business situation and can be measured in nits based on natural logarithms. The choice between a larger variety of $5-8$ options of preliminary designs is better be measured in bytes. The most uncertain corporate situation as a choice between $10-12$ application tools with the information amount to be measured in dits on decimal logarithms scale. We tested this axiomatic model of knowledge development by the experimentation with short repetitive games such as small 5×5 *TranSport* game. Other parameters of discrete structural models of designer teams will become instrumentally measurable with an accumulation of business games design experience. Until now time scale is most natural unit of measure for these purposes.

Time necessary for making decisions during the game design depends on the type of leadership demonstrated by the leader of the design team. The main ability of the leader is integration of individual motivations into

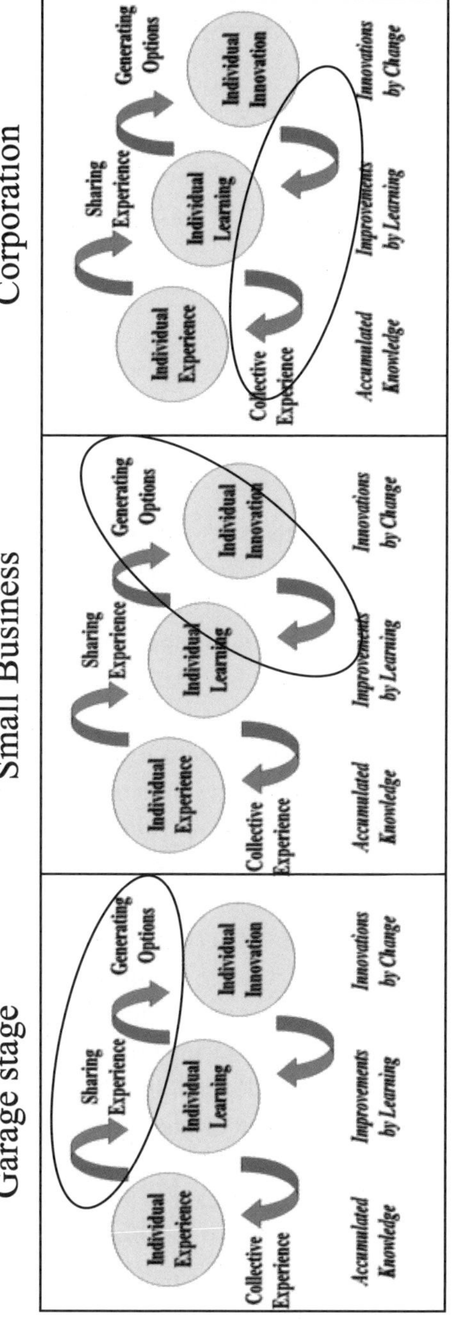

Fig. 7.8.   Information exchange patterns on different stages of game business development.

Table 7.4.   Individual contributions to the team results.

Key individual	Role	Contribution
Innovator	Generates new ideas	Changing paradigm
Scanner	Acquires vast amount of information	Accumulating relevant information
Gatekeeper	Keeps informed of related developments	Communicating information to players
Game Champion	Sells new ideas to others	Connecting to other teams
Team Leader	Plans and organizes the decision process	Organization and inspiration
Sponsor	Helps the team to get what it needs	Providing necessary resources

team spirit. The time to reach consensus partly depends on the size of a team. Educational games are usually designed by relatively small teams of two to five members. Roles assignment in the game follows similar lines as the game design. First stages of team development (forming and storming) require the leader to play a role of either idea generator or of the sponsor (see Table 7.4).

The following stages of the design team life cycle (norming and performing) should clarify role of the leader in his main capacity of adjusting decisions according to the situation. Time and attention of the leader for different functions grows from constant α for control to logarithmic for direction, then linear for instruction and grows exponentially with increasing size of a team because of the requirement of coordination of all communications between members of a team. The relative magnitude of time required for the leader managing the team in different functions is illustrated in Fig. 7.9.

Assume that **Control** of the final result requires α (alpha) units of a manager's time. That time does not depend on number of members in the team, it is constant for each type of a job. The project manager just checks each finished game module.

We are assuming that a project manager is also the leader of the team. Then s/he provides the rest of the team with a **Direction**. S/he demonstrates how to make a job to the first member (deputy, assistant) with a delegation to

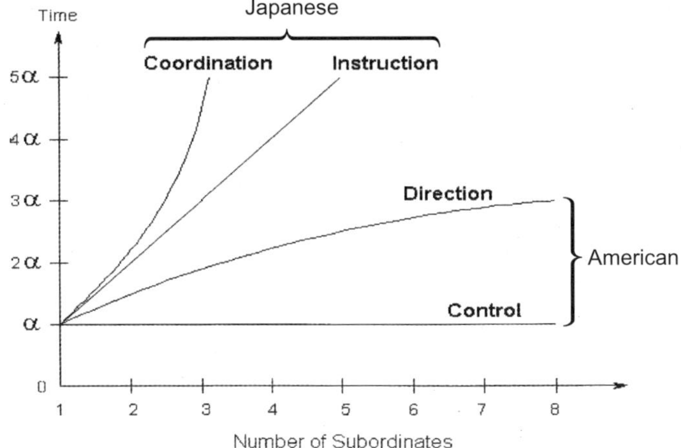

Fig. 7.9.   Relative time consumption for the exercising different leadership styles.

this member a right to manage the next subordinate. It takes the leader time with a larger number of subordinates, but with exponentially decreasing marginal proportion.

$\alpha^*\,(M-1)^{\wedge}(-b^*M)$, where parameter **b** represents learning rate and **M** is the size of the team.

An **Instruction** of each member of the team personally requires the same time α for everyone of them. Then the total time required for the leader is proportional to the number of all other members of the team: $\alpha^*(M-1)$.

The **Coordination** of activities of all members of the team requires manager to control of all communications between them. The time which required for that equals to $\alpha^*M^*\,(M-1)/2$.

The absolute amount of the management time spent by the leader of a team on the first subordinate α is different for each type of decision, but proportions of total time in relation to number of team members are changing from constant through exponential to quadratic [Bazilevich, 1979]. The first two lower lines allow more individual responsibility, leadership which we call "American style". Two upper lines represent more cooperative leadership and we call them "Japanese style" where the leader spends more time on coordination and search of collective consensus. It is also supported by a higher variety and creativity of Japanese games designs.

The inventor of the light-emitting diode (LED), now Professor of Engineering in University of California at Santa Barbara Shuji Nakamura describes two education systems this way:

> " In Japan we are strong in a manufacturing and these require teamwork while in the U.S. the forte is invention. My familiarity is with [American] students primarily, and I can tell you, teamwork is not their strong suit."
>
> [Nakamura, 2004]

So the American education system needs more board games which may substitute alienation of individualism of coach videogames with the teamwork of face-to-face cooperation around the table. American educational industry was also working for many years for the support of the social structure rather than as a learning system. Different levels of educational structure were enforced by the filters of the social funnel. Academic institutions were stratified in separate subsystems of Community colleges, four-year universities, Graduate Schools and Ivy League universities.

Present social, ethnic and demographic changes in Americal society affects academic structures as well. The leadership in industries is shifting from the "old boys" to entrepreneurs, the ownership of assets is moving from the "old money" to the global investors. The management becomes a faceless bureaucracy under the corporate executives which are practically not responsible to shareholders. It breaks "glass ceilings" for entrepreneuring yappies and women. They need fast and practical education tools. The aspiring immigrants also need tools for economic and cultural adaptation. The best results for them are provided by the business games. They integrate decision making by communications with other players with analysing and presenting game results.

During a business game three different components of the learning experience (memory, knowledge and change) should be demonstrated by every member of a team. As we have seen before, teams rarely exceed five to seven members that requires wide and dynamic specialization of players. So we prefer the condensed roles classification presented in Table 7.1.

Different roles should be played by members of a team at certain time and in appropriate situation. The roles assignment should be flexible

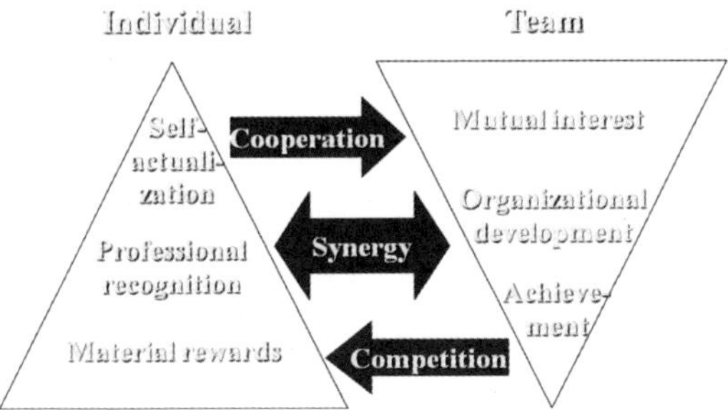

Fig. 7.10.   Correspondence between individual and team motivations.

reflecting not only personal traits and professional experience, but also giving to the player chances to explore different capabilities. An innovator will concentrate on generating new options, the scanner works on collecting relevant information, and the leader should be first of all concerned with the exchange of experience between members of a team.

A team motivation is radically different from the hierarchy of individual needs. We represent needs for the team as the inverted Maslow's pyramid of individual needs. A team synergy generation depends of the success of individuals in a complicated way (Fig. 7.10).

The best team achievements are provided by the integration of the motivations in the middle of both pyramids. There the professionalism of individuals might be realized by the organizational support. The synergy of players' interaction might be generated when the individual interests are balanced with the goals of the team. Material rewards for the individual achievements should provide the right initiative for short-term achievements and for the strategic progress of the team. Competition for the immediate individual success may undermine team spirit. The lack of cooperation between active members of the team may require additional time for finding consensus in team decisions. So the responsibility of the team leader is in supporting everyone without losing team goals and delaying from schedules.

There are many "small" games used for the building teams, trust-building activities and team spirit exercises useful at the forming stage of team development. They are called ice-breakers, or trust building games. These are mainly simple physical or communicative group activities which facilitate forming a team and clarify roles. Such a games might be found for free on various websites and in books designed for use by social and physical trainers [West, 1996; Newstrom & Scannell, 1998]. We also use for this purpose short active class exercises and small games such as the *Learning Curve Cards, Cellulose Aircraft Inc., Paper Puppets* and others accumulated for operations management classes [Heineke & Meile, 1995]. They are readily adaptable to introduce situations of the game and for roles assignments inside the business game.

The extended physical exercises like bicycling, rafting or caving are used for the forming teams in the Leadership Trust (U.K.) field business games for outward bound executive training. Similar exercises are useful for the students as relaxation tools between the runs of long complicated sessions of business games.

We recommend different physical and mental exercises for experimental clarification of roles which different members of a team can play. In the beginning of the *Shell Game* and *Cellulose Aircraft Inc.* board games we ask students to contest for the best product design. Before the digital games *NewProDev* and *HELLO* we usually ask students to analyze knowledge content of different innovative products and services of the same function. For these purposes we use <Davison.com> or other innovations-promoting websites. In most cases students choose for comparison either videogames, or electronic devices, or sports equipment. The graduate students prefer childrens' toys and home appliances. The executives like to anlayze recreational equipment, boats and cars.

The most efficient way of professional education in work place is individual internship under the qualified mentor. The advantage of proper mentoring for the corporate leadership development is well illustrated in the book "Your Career Game" [Bennett & Miles, 2010] by examples of most dynamic young executives in America. This book and many others now use the term "game" in a figurative sense. By showing the irrelevance of formal education for the success in business it indirectly approves business games' value. It exemplified by the best inventors, entrepreneurs and leaders of industry who were rebellious students or even dropouts from universities.

The second **ViVaT** component, **Vi**sualization became the main language of communication between people with different backgrounds in all areas of life. Traffic signs, sports symbols and other images mean the same for people of different countries and cultures. They break language and professional barriers, save time and space. Charts, diagrams and tables became the language of game designers. Colorful views of nature or outer space, impressive architecture and machinery and animated characters are the main attraction of videogames. Business games may also be not just useful educationally, but also attractive visually and entertaining emotionally.

And the last **ViVaT** component, **V**ariation **in T**ime compresses long-term technological, ecological, economic and social processes into short rounds of the game. If arrangement of the situation room is difficult physically or by schedule, the game may become asynchronous. Then individual players or teams are using personal computers connected by a network. Teleconferencing and wireless communications allow the organizing of these games simultaneously from different locations. Virtual games have advantages of decentralized locations and asynchronous schedules, but may be lacking emotional involvement of meeting face-to-face other participants of the game.

Previously made decisions restrict freedom of choice for aesthetics of a game. Card-and-board games can be presented in cartoons and photographic images like Figs. 6.10 and 6.11. The card game technology may be reinforced by a variety of constructions of the board: plain checkers board, jigsaw, magnetic, tokens.

The process of adjusting a game idea to the mission of the game and to expectations of potential players will be detailed in the following chapter as business game hardware, software and wetware.

8

BUSINESS GAME HARDWARE DESIGN

Jigsaw version of *TranSport* game

8.1. GAME DESIGN PROCESS

The first step in game design is defined before formulation of the game idea (concept). The choice of the type of the game between field, board (card) or electronic game is the leading decision for the next stages of hardware and software design (Fig. 7.2). Design of any business game starts from a paper prototype. After testing of a paper draft we may work on professionally published or digital modules of the game. The advanced videogames designers may employ computer aided design (CAD) or special game design software for the design of its modules. Special design software is available from the leading resources for videogames development (GameDev.net or DevMaster.net). The process of videogame development includes the following stages which may be adapted to the business games in the following ways:

- **Concept:** an idea and choice of contents (cases, simulations or models),
- **Pre-Production** (usually not related to business game unless it is commercialized),
- **Prototype:** a copy of hand-made paper version and program modules,
- **Production:** preparation of sets of hardware, software and game documentation,
- **Alpha:** first test with the teams of other games design professionals,
- **Beta:** correction and second test with outsiders (students, executives),
- **Gold:** professional printing of batches of game documents and software,
- **Post-production:** editing and publishing game documentation and instructions.

The advantage of the CAD process for a digital game project is in quick and accurate access to the game databases and to a variety of specialized software. Most of this software is available as appendices to the books on digital game design [Salen and Zimmerman, 2003; Fullerton, 2010]. The databases for business games are supported by specialized institutions and companies, and may not be accessible or compatible. The process of business game design is not absolutely streamlined, it includes many loops of feedback requiring reworks of previous material. The business games also need systematic revising according to changing economic situations, business legislation and organizational structures. The essential part is preliminary decision on proportions between different phases of the game:

"Most [business] games followed such an implied model for learning by providing three phases:

1. Experience: This phase of learning is provided by game play, decision inputs, and team interaction.
2. Content: This phase includes dissemination of ideas, principles, or concepts regarding business practices and principles.
3. Feedback: This phase includes feedback in the form of financial statements, comparative team standings, and participant and team critiques by the professor or game administrator."

[Keys and Biggs, 1990]

These three phases correspond to the first two stages of experience and learning in our model of knowledge formation. They cover experiental business games of earlier generations [Gentry, 1990]. Younger business and edutainment games are the result of new creative paradigms as the third level of knowledge formation.

Business games require such hardware as furniture, equipment and materials which are either specialized for the games or standard supply for educational institutions. Specialized game environments are built in some corporate training centers and business schools. These are situation rooms (war rooms), training stands (flight simulators), environment models (sandboxes), work stations (personal computers). Contemporary games rooms have internal interface (videoscreens, monitors), and they need external services (scanners, printers, copiers, fascimile machines). They are necessary for the generating of game documentation and for submission of game progress, analytical reports and multimedia presentations.

The environment surrounding games is usually a standard school or college room. Universities are built with amphitheaters for the convenience of lecturing. That is not accommodating for business games, especially if they are organized as competitions between teams. The games require a literally flat playing field with sandboxes or chairs around tables. Then the portable game equipment may fit into the rooms. Industrial training centers, specialized universities and business schools can afford furnished classrooms dedicated to particular types of games. The most convenient for

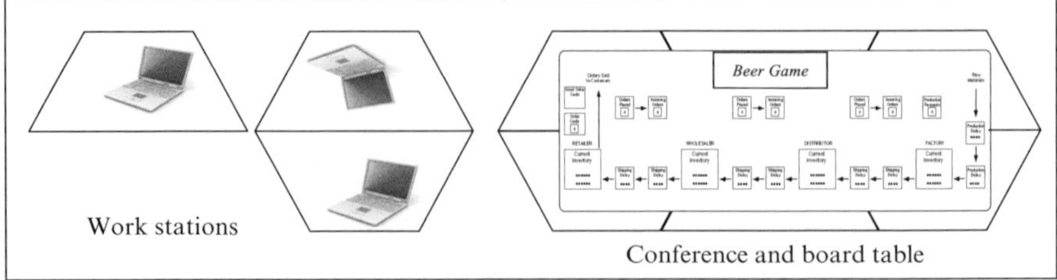

Fig. 8.1. Modular furniture configurations for business games.

the board business games are small modular tables of trapezoidal shape. Some flexible combinations of these tables are shown in Fig. 8.1.

The most advanced field games are organized inside a "firing range" as a physical model of the processes or around a virtual field in a multimedia room. These "situation rooms" provide different universal and specialized hardware. Complicated furniture and expensive equipment need dedicated staff to support them in working conditions. The games also need large amounts of materials and documentation which should be prepared before the game, during the game and after the game. They all should be at hand as needed to prevent slowing down the pace of a game.

The board may be placed on the wall for placing post-ins, pinning or magnetic cards. Contemporary white boards for classrooms are magnetic and very convenient for placing magnetic cards. Some large game boards such as we use in *CyberMarket* game may be combined as separated modules or unfolding wings. Computer screens may display boards for every player, presenting to each individual their available cards through the local area network.

Business games with schoolchildren and undergraduate students may be combined with time breaks for physical exercises. Instructor may use a sports whistle to interrupt an unruly team or to make an announcement. We do not recommend instructors to use microphones to overcome the noise in the game room or to discipline a player. It does not really attract attention and looks like a demonstration of your supremacy over the players. Do the opposite, give a microphone to some of the players for making useful comments. It provides positive motivation to the importance of their work.

The game room should be equipped for multimedia presentations. A printing and duplicating center is necessary in the room or in close proximity. During the team reports symbolic passing of the ball or relay baton may signal the start for individual presentation. Other entertaining elements and gestures are useful for the encouragement of lively presentations. It may be lotteries of time slots for the teams or in the teams, musical or dancing breaks. In our global business games some teams demonstrated national costumes, artifacts and cultural traditions. Do not forget to prepare prizes and gifts for individual or collective achievements. At the end of the game reflection may be organized with food and drinks in the game room, in the café, bar or restaurant nearby. To save time and keep the game spirit alive use the catering service. It is affordable for most executive training centers and business schools.

8.2. DESIGN OF THE GAME PROTOTYPE

The second step of design is expressing the game idea in the prototype. The best approach to it is in generating different combinations of game elements. The games like many new products and services are just an unusual mix of existing elements. For example, you have an idea of designing business game for engineering undergraduate class on new products development topic. The available elements from different blocks of the game architecture according to Fig. 7.5 are:

Technology ideas:
    Card and Board game
    Electronic game
    Field game
Mechanics ideas:
    Sims- or Tetris-like game
    Interactive functions game
    Icehouse or LEGO-bricks
Contents ideas:
    Industrial technology and services
    University teaching and research
    Customer's expectations
Aesthetic ideas:
    Drawings and charts

Photographs and video clips
Pictures and cartoons

The acceptance of such elements may be discussed by the designers after displaying corresponding cards or post-ins into different combinations. It does not need full enumeration of all possible combinations as some components are definitely predetermined. For example, if the game will be in a simulation for a one hour class of economics, field games from the block of technology are excluded. Start prototypes from card and board games which later may be translated to electronic format. If your course has CAD software support you better choose electronic technology from the beginning. It narrows the options of other blocks to interactive mechanics, university teaching contents, drawings and charts aesthetics.

The prototype design phase should be documented in minutes of meetings and in the research memos that you need in the future for design of new games. These data may be required for filing the patent claim or for resolving copyright conflicts. CAD or archive records may be starting point for the new game design or for modifications of the current design. For example, if you have chosen industrial technology contents, your choice is restricted to electronic versions of stochastic life-cycle models. Then the game development process will include stages of idea definition, product/service design, design of operations system and introduction. The progress from one stage to the next will be simulated by events of Success (S), Withdrawal (W), or Rework (R) of results. The process of generating these events according to their probabilities p(S), p(W) and p(R) may be organized by different mechanics: either Sims-like by establishing of connections, or Tetris-like by rotation of objects placing them into required positions.

The Sims-like option of the game model assumes description of model in 2-dimensional drawings or 3D mock-ups. The model of the New Product Development (NPD) process which we used for the *NewProDev* game is presented in Fig. 8.2.

Results of technology, mechanics, contents and aesthetic choices define a structure of the game. The proposed above model of NPD process might be realized in the game implicitly as computer simulation of product design success, failure or return to the previous stage. It may otherwise become a part of the explicit game procedure when the outcome of each stage

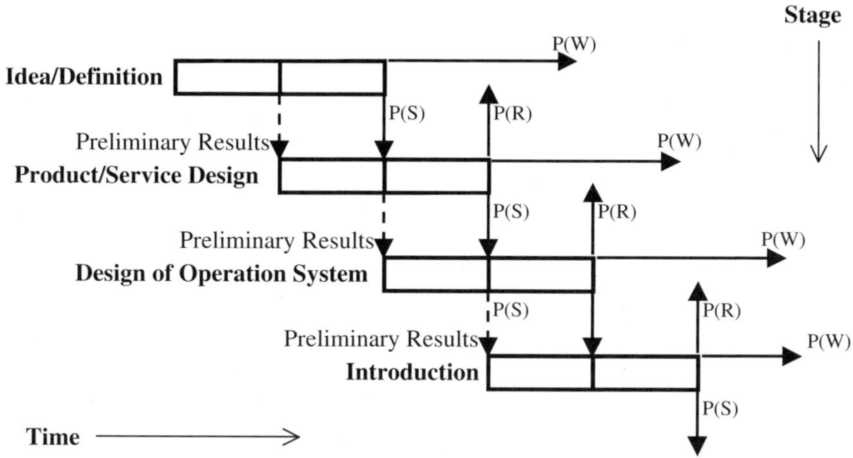

Fig. 8.2.   Stochastic model of concurrency in NPD process.

of the NPD process is determined by the random events generator. The reasons of certain outcome need professional explanation for the team. This converts it into a longer practical field game with detailed specification of the products, processes or services. But as a random process in a game it may be accelerated by the use of the computerized generator of events. Then appearance of Success (S), Return (R) or Withdrawal (W) result of every NPD stage is generated according to the corresponding probabilities *p(S), p(R)* or *p(W)* adding up to 1 (one). Technical realization of the events generation may be different: from the dice cast to the inverse probability distribution software in the computer generator. The choice of generator appearance depends on the time assigned for the game and on the type of participants. Busy executives or advanced students will accept computer output while curious kids would like to play with the top toy spinning.

Dynamics and schedule of the game are defined with rules of a game and its procedures. The details of different game procedures will be discussed in the next section. It is the next essential step in iterative preliminary design. For example, transition from one stage of design to the other will depend on generation of two events: (1) the end of one stage and (2) the readiness of the next stage as shown in Fig. 8.3.

Every stage consists of a research section giving preliminary results and a documentation section giving approval of results. Length of research

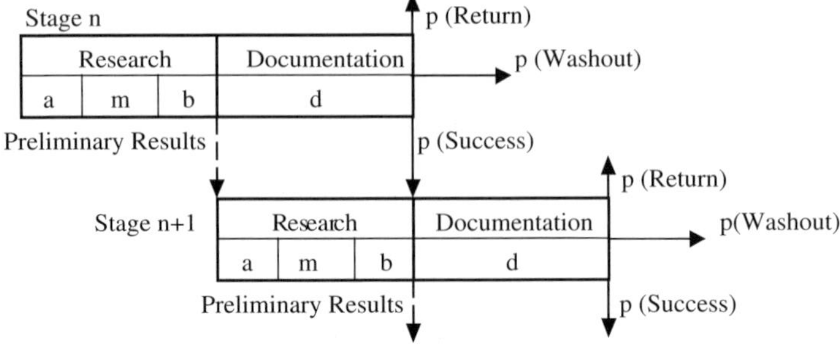

Fig. 8.3. Connection of two stages of *NewProDev* (new product development) game.

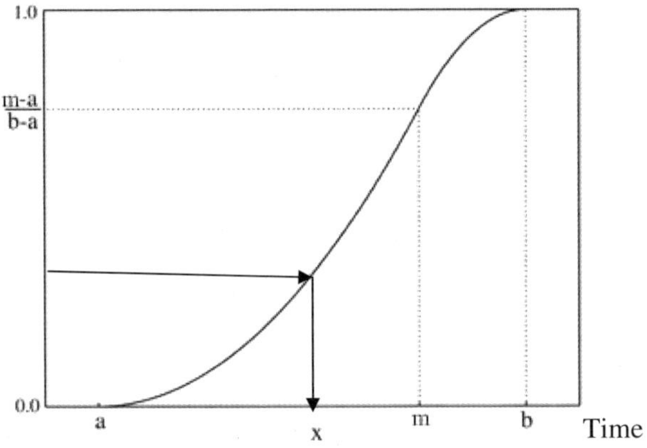

Fig. 8.4. Cumulative triangular distribution.

is statistically uncertain and defined by three estimates of time from a triangular distribution: *a* (optimistic), *m* (most likely) and *b* (pessimistic). Documentation stage time *d* is assumed to be deterministic. It may be either the time assigned to the expertise or required for scheduled meetings of approval body (executive board, appropriation committee, etc.). So the simulation of transition from one stage to the next includes two steps: generation of research time and generation of move to the Success, Return or Washout. The time for research is generated by the inverse cumulative triangular distribution (Fig. 8.4).

Answer of expected time *x* is read on the Time axis according to the probability *p(x)* from the uniform distribution {0 to 1}. The probability *p(x)* might be generated mechanically as a discrete variable by the spin of a top toy or digitally as continuous variable by the MS Excel function *ƒx=RAND()*.

8.3.   RULES AND PROCEDURES

Three types of game rules: general, operational and implicit, that were introduced in Chapter 3, are supporting components of learning process in a different way. We formulate rules and procedures in relation to our knowledge formation model of Chapter 1. This model is applied to the analysis of business games according to three levels of novelty: (1) memorizing by repetition, (2) learning by analysis, (3) creativity by paradigm changing. Different rules are supporting various teaching and research objectives. They also affect motivation of players and teams. We used them for the analysis of games available from publications, patents and websites. Now we will use these models for the synthesis of games as educational innovations.

A business game may be designed on the base of **repetition** of exercises either applied to the different environment or translated in the new hardware. These processes are regulated by operational rules defining small cycles of exercises or cases. The most popular entertainment games from classic *Tetris* to the *Tower Bloxx* attract millions of players by repeating again and again the same simple procedure. Technological games and management simulations may also be based on this principle. The original *Shell Game* is a repetition of shells production in a modified environment. We modified it as a business game by adding elements of control and time management. The *Cellulose Aircraft Inc.* management simulation we extended in a comparison of craft, batch and mass production of paper plane models. This approach is easy to apply to many games using cheap paper or cards, simple children toys and tokens, piecepacks or LEGO bricks.

Repetitive components of business games may be acquired from the laboratory exercises and research experiments of natural sciences like physics and chemistry. Technological courses also contain many exercises which give an opportunity of building games by recording individual or team productivity and quality. Field exercises are also repetitive in classes of construction, biology and geology. Physical education exercises also might be considered as the experimental component of a business game. And the most attractive for students in our classes happened to be entertaining videogames. Any digital game themselves generates data which may be recorded, analyzed and provide players and instructor with feedback necessary for business decisions.

The second level of novelty in design and modification of a game is the **learning** which provides players with the improved designs including new modules of software. It is regulated by the general rules of scientific analysis. The rules allow players to move to the next level of knowledge development. Examples of business games of this type are *Beer Game* and *Siemens Supply Chain Simulator.* During the repetitive exercises of the first level teams form decisions of the next level by adding the elements of managerial analysis. The natural components of such a game are business cases and management simulations. The best business games of this type are designed by the school of ABSEL learning community. Such games as *Capstone* or *Glo-Bus* represent deep economic, organizational and ecological analysis by comparison of different technologies in the chain of business cycles. Our games *ReActOr* and *HELLO* are also use organizational and regional analysis of a product or service life cycles.

The fundamentals of the second level of knowledge accumulation in the games should be built as blocks of the elements of the first level of memorizing. They are usually included as the introductory training sessions explaining rules of the game. After the first sessions of a business game we naturally introduce analytical material of the second level. The *Nature* game was made by adding one or two dimensions to the *Island* simulation. Every business game may also include different tools like musical breaks for players' relaxation. The best time for the physical exercises is in between rotations of players for the new roles.

The highest level or innovation of **changing paradigm** for the game design requires generation of new business concepts. There are few examples of such a game: *Intopia* or *NewProDev*. They review the elements of the second level of simulation and play. It is done in a more condensed or automated data processing paying main attention to the strategic decisions. It saves time for the generating and exploration of new creative options of non-repetitive business development. The *CyberShockWave* and *Career* games are entirely based on new business ideas for combining team development through individual role playing. Players' behavior is restricted just by implicit rules to allow maximum freedom of creativity.

Introduction of rules to the business game might be done with the lectures, printed instructions, video clips, or better by icebreaking exercises or managerial puzzles. The lecture should be accompanied by the handouts requiring active participation of players from simple completion of charts drawing and tables calculation up to the development of their own conceptual models. Printed manuals and prefabricated documents should require the player's input during the reading. It should include exercises, not just yellow highlighting of the text. These are necessary to answer programmed questions and solve small problems. Video clips should be used as complementary and illustrative material provided with some feedback showing the attention involvement. Managerial puzzles are the best introductory tools requiring knowledge of basic principles of control and management with creative thinking.

The proportions between games of different levels of knowledge follow the Pareto principle close to the designs of all new products and services. The ratio between repetitive, analytical and inventive solutions is approximately 10:3:1. We assume that the structure of new games development follow the same proportions as all other innovations. Analysis of 200,000 patents by the TRIZ consultants classified them in five levels. Our more aggregated classification of knowledge falls into similar proportions on three levels (Table 8.1).

There are millions of people playing the *Tetris* game every day. Look over the shoulder of the metro passenger and you will see repetition of the same action over and over again. Thousands of families and clubs are playing *Monopoly* weekly or monthly. Much more difficult is to design and to organize an innovation game. The effort necessary for the design of new games of different types has the reversed proportion, especially if they are built from scratch. But as it was shown above, by incorporating elements of a lower level of knowledge into a higher level we involve students in the gaming process, and hopefully, also in the support of game design and improvement.

The essential part of the games described before were manual and physical activities for recreational purposes. In many cases such actions give faster results than purely mental efforts. The usual paper drawing

Table 8.1.   Proportions between different levels of innovation.

	TRIZ levels of innovation [Terninko *et al.*, 1998]	% of patents	Sum of patents	Our classification [Bazilevich, 1979]	% of games
1	Apparent or conventional solution	32	77	Repetition of patterns leading to a small improvements	80
2	Small invention inside paradigm	45			
3	Substantial invention inside technology	18	18	Learning by analysis leading to radical innovation	15
4	Invention outside technology	4	5	Changing paradigm leading to invention or discovery	5
5	Discovery	1			

or even computer screen search may give less options than just a shuffle of cards. In games with the search of different combinations of the objects, they may be represented by some tangible symbols. It is better than keeping them just as the mental images. For example, in the *NewProDev* game we prepare with players cards symbolizing available parts or properties of the product and recommend combining them randomly in different proportions.

We experimented for this purpose with *Tangram* toys and found out that teams using them as physical objects are finding solutions faster than teams using just paper and pencil and even faster than teams using computers (see Fig. 8.5).

So we recommend using transformers and jigsaw puzzles for igniting creativity among the kids and Rubic's Cube for teenagers. A random search may become more spectacular with using a die or roulette wheel with prefabricated components of the game. This kind of search may also be computerized for the faster generating of options, but it still needs manual sorting for acceptable combinations. In a game of *Words-in-Sentences* teams that use computers have an advantage of generating words, but lose in the assembly of sentences. So the teams using just post-ins and pencils usually win.

Fig. 8.5.   The 13 convex shapes matched with *Tangram* set.

8.4.   GAMES HARDWARE: SANDBOXES, BOARDS AND DISPLAYS

A configuration of game hardware depends on the size of simulated system and mission of the game. It may be as simple as a squared checkers board, or of more complicated shape as the spiral interactive structure which will be described in Chapter 10 for the system design.

A simple game for kids is better presented in a cards and board version. The computer is necessary for presenting the global images based on networks for SoSs. Illustrations of different kind, such as pictures, maps, photos and cartoons create a spirit of creativity and humor, so valuable for the game.

The boards for games may be structured in certain geometrical patterns according with the architecture of the game. The most universal though is the circular or rectangular form of a chain allowing repeated movements in one-dimensional space (states of the player). So the classic *Monopoly* game board was designed for a cyclical movement around the square.

The latest version of the game, the *Monopoly Revolution* game board visualizes the cycle of game by revolving around the natural circle. A change of the board of this game is attractive aesthetically and allows better allocation of resources for players. The historic four-sided board was implicitly assuming four players' participation. A round shape is more universal allowing even allocation of any reasonable number of players and resources.

We demonstrated in Chapter 5 the influence of different numbers of players on the playing time and learning rates. These experiments show that the best number happens to be in the range between three and six players. Hardware design also affects efficiency of a game. The shapes and colors of items should be matching to certain parts of a game model. It speeds up recognizing of objects and reduces misplacing of cards and tokens. Items placed on the board represent players, their resources, events and results of their decisions. Types of artifacts for board games are patented as the *Icehouses, IceTowers* and *Piecepacks* [Looney, 2002]. They include simple items like cards and cubes as well as pyramids and more complex figures. The variety of shapes and colors used for the videogames is unrestricted and depends on the imagination of game art director. Designing of business games is recommended to start with the post-in stickers representing game artifacts. After testing the game prototype they must be substituted by glossy cards and fancy figurines.

The function of the board for business games is manifold. It may reflect a player's progress. It may also be used for indication of players' roles that are written or painted on the sides of the board. It also may contain additional information about the situation; keep stacks of cards for different events, represent money and other assets and liabilities.

A business game starts with allocation of players for different team roles within each of the competing teams. For example, every member of a team in a *Words-in-Sentences* game has different operational or management responsibilities. The linear 1D production process is represented by stickers moving along the arrows. Structure of this game with assigning roles of Manager, Quality controllers, Word producers and Sentences assemblers, is presented in Fig. 8.6.

A checkers board on the table allows representing one more dimension, usually like a geographical map grid. For business games the second dimension usually represents levels in management hierarchy. For example, *Highway Construction* game board has two levels: bottom is available equipment and the next, operations, requiring combination of machinery and materials. (see Fig. 8.7).

Creativity of designers generates elaborate shapes and drawings of game boards. They may be folding, multi-level constructions of cardboard, plastic or metal. But the appearance of the game space might be misleading

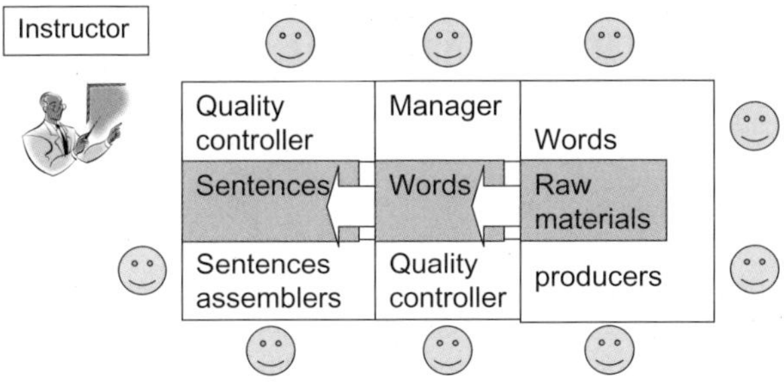

Fig. 8.6.   Allocation of players around the board in a team of *Words-in-Sentences* game.

not only in colorful videogames. For example, patent #5,004,245 in 1991 which claims the 3-dimensional game board like a pyramid actually does not represent additional vertical dimension, but helps to keep cards orderly and provides a useful stereoscopic effect (see Fig. 8.8).

Our games platform *Holarchy* is actually a 3-dimensional structure of system engineering design. The games on this board include three scales: (1) component states of volumes of business activity, (2) organization levels, and (3) stages of system life cycle. Game design on these platforms will be presented in Chapter 10. For example, the *TranSport* and *FinanceSoS* games we organized around the board with technological, managerial and economic levels. The design of the *SimSoS* platform for System of Systems simulation adds a 4th dimension of stages of SoS development cycle.

Field and video games are naturally realistic and it may distract the attention of players from the core, essential feature of the situation. Therefore it is necessary to keep the attention of players to the basic mission and model of the game. Many videogames are attracting players' attention to insignificant details such as *Anime* characters. To avoid that, components and systems on the boards of games for SoS simulation *TranSport* and *SoSFinance* are presented just by the professional terms.

Many business games are based on geographical, architectural or other physical images. It is natural for transportation, communications and environmental applications. Most multinational and global businesses well displayed on maps or as transportation and supply chain networks. The most

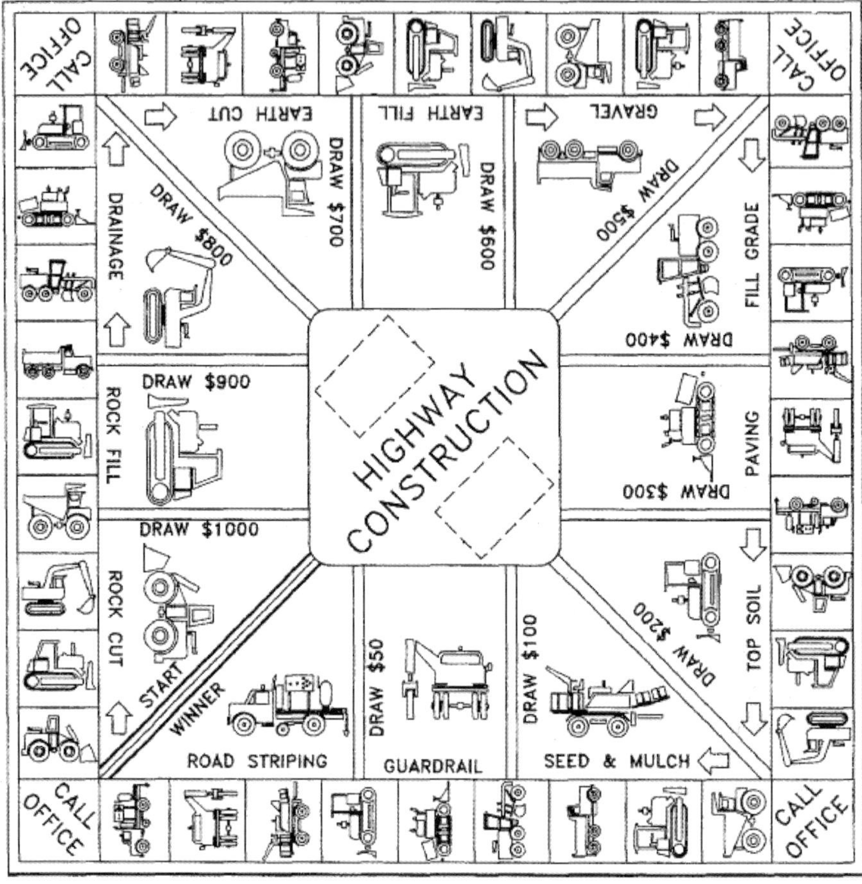

Fig. 8.7.   Structure of the board in *Highway Construction* game.

advanced series of *Sim City* games are visualized as 3D grids of landscape, transportation, infrastructure and architecture.

8.5.   VISUALIZING MATHEMATICAL MODELS

Mathematical models for business games are supposed to be based on solid economic theory. Many macroeconomic theories are biased on such a "dismal science", so the games representing them may be misleading. First

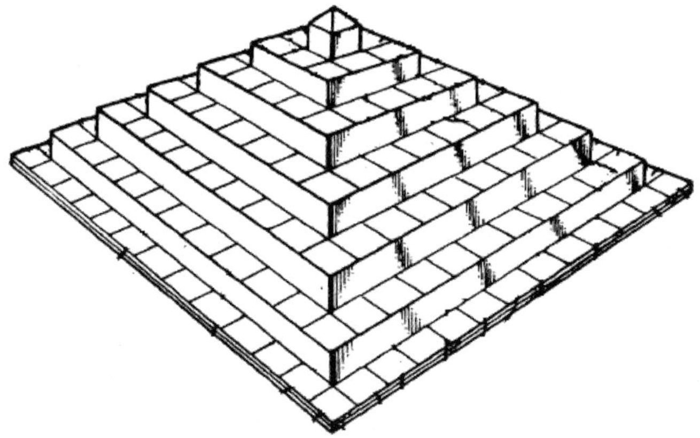

Fig. 8.8.   Pyramidal shape of a game board.

of all it relates to axiomatic economics which satisfies itself with elegant mathematical crystal palaces:

> "Most economists the public encounters are presented as oracles who can tell you, with alluring certainty, where the stock market or inflation or interest rates are heading. But as we've seen lately, such predictions are generally worthless. Economists have a hard enough time explaining the past, much less predicting the future."
>
> [Levitt and Dubner, 2009]

On the microeconomic level business game may rely upon proven theoretical models and reliable industrial statistics. The players are presenting real entrepreneural entities, not abstract economic categories. The *Cyber-Market* and *MarketSim* games are built for the classes of microeconomics around the classic model of closed economic system. It is actually a system with interactive flows of resources and money between two types of markets and three types of agents (Fig. 8.9).

There is minimum of five roles in a team: two specialized businesses called **Industry** and **Services**, two types of households (**Working** and **Retired**) and **Government**. Team may be extended by adding one or two roles of mixed businesses (**Conglomerates**) and one or two roles of **Mixed households** based on multigenerational families. Then a team reaches reasonable maximum of nine players. Product markets are presenting two types of products: commodities and luxuries. The *CyberMarket*

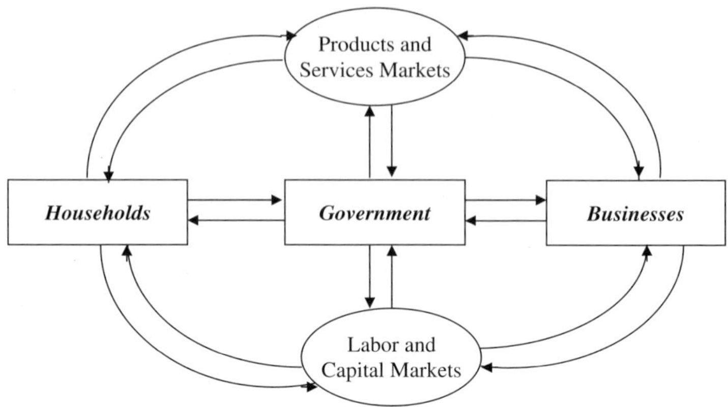

Fig. 8.9.   Virtual playing field for *CyberMarket* game

game demonstrates to the players' dynamics of production, of establishing balance between supply and demand typical for different types of markets and for variable time horizons.

The description of a game model includes analytical, graphic and tabular mathematical models. Among them are Cobb-Douglas production and utility functions, logarithmic cost curves, exponential learning curves, universal S-curves of the business growth. Current data of the game is kept in Excel tables as balance sheets and income statements. Calculation of results may be explicit on the handwritten tables and graphs or hidden behind Excel formulas.

The structure of the board for the introduction to the *CyberMarket* game represents all roles and markets of simulated economic system. So the basic structure of the board looks like Fig. 8.10.

Blocks of the board may be detailed as the diagrams including algebraic formulas and graphs of microeconomic functions. We also recommend illustrating the board with symbols, cartoons and photos, but not to such an extent that it will not leave space for players' documentation and laptops.

Actual appearance of the board may be customized for different kinds of classes. The models of this game are the classic microeconomic functions expressed algebraically, graphically and in MSExcel tables. A model of the game includes 3-dimensional Production Functions and Consumers Utility Functions. During the *CyberMarket* game students derive from them

Production Functions for Industry	Capitals Market	Utility Curves for Working Households
Labor Market	Production Possibilities Frontiers	Luxuries Market
Production Functions for Services	Commodities Market	Utility Curves for Retired Households

Fig. 8.10.   Structure of the board for *CyberMarket* business game.

2-dimensional Supply and Demand Curves and carry on calculations of the main parameters of business efficiency and consumers satisfaction.

The folding board is convenient for introduction to the game by opening one wing of the board after the other during the explanation of stages of the game. Its pages may be with erasable surface to write and wipe out intermediate calculations and drawings. We also use transparent sliding charts which superimpose supply and demand curves, thus finding an equilibrium point of market. This way we get an instant reading of equilibrium quantities and prices of products and services on the appropriate scales without tedious calculations. More sophisticated designs may be implemented on the metal boards by keeping magnetic cards and tokens.

Similar microeconomic functions are used as models for the *MarketSim* computer game [Porter, 2005]. This game simulates build-up of two types of markets: closed barter "Jeremy's market" and open monetary "Adam's market". The barter market reflects two product (bread and wine) production possibilities. Players are maximizing their utilities with constrained labor resources. It requires from the player a comparison of different strategies of production and trade with other players. Production output and utility calculations are based on classical power Cobb-Douglas functions [Samuelson, 1973]. All calculations are installed in software supporting network for interactive class of 20–30 students. Economic functions are graphically illustrated and also duplicated by introductory exercises for players.

The monetary economy game is an extension of the barter economy by adding capitals market to selling bonds. Individual players' criteria is complementing utility for households with business profit. The production activity for each player still restricted to one industry (bread or wine). Each player may switch from one industry to another if he/she finds it more profitable. The amounts of available labor supply and choices between possible strategies are enlarged by the trade of the same two products and resources between players.

8.6. TECHNOLOGY AND AESTHETICS OF A GAME

Technology of a game was defined as handling of the medium of the game. During a game such artifacts as boards and posters, cards and tokens are changing appearance or moving around. That represents game scenery and situation changes, positions, resources and decisions of players. All those objects may be visualized on the computer screen with a graphical software that will be presented in the next chapter. Here we will have a look at the more traditional hardware used for the field and board games.

Objects on fields, sandboxes and boards in the game prototype start with just symbols and names. Then they may be substituted by professional graphs, maps, flowcharts. They will have the same structure, being just graphically improved and color coded. Games for kids are better expressed by easily recognizable photos, cartoons and tokens. The most universal medium for business games are coins, cards or Lego bricks.

The Lego toy company has a rich choice of different bricks and components for construction and playing games. The *Lego Creator* is a computer sandbox game for the PC that involves building with virtual Lego elements. The game objectives are just building something without money constraints. Now the company offers *LEGOGame* combining construction of the game board from the Lego bricks by the moves of players generated by the dice rolling. The goal of the game is to make progress to the center of the board. A player can prevent other players from such a move with the bricks creating blocks in the maze on the board. Dice for such type of games include numerical and situational cubes. For example, sides of one die represent allowable actions by players, or sides of the other die are representing different colors. In addition to the regular bricks in an assortment of colors, Lego includes "Action Bricks" that move or make noise. Such bricks include a Hinge, Propeller, and Siren. There is also a "Destructa Brick" in a form of a no-stud 1×2 tile brick with an image of dynamite. This can be used to destroy models in Play Mode, although they will automatically rebuild when returning to Build Mode. Minifigures can also be used, and can stand, sit (for controlling vehicles), or walk. They too are customizable. They can even be set to drive vehicles to a path or road. In play mode, environments can go from day to night.

A size and appearance of the board depends on the number of players, and even on the shape of tables in the classroom. We experimented with different shapes of the board and detail of game model presentation. The best is a portable folding board with a basic shapes on one side and detailed models and instructions on the other sides of the unfolding wings. The business game for kids, *Obla-di, Obla-da*, has the same structure of the board as the *CyberMarket* game for students, but the board for kids presents all models graphically. The sliding scales and transparencies give to children readable easily answers without calculations. A board for students represents just a structure of economic system, all mathematical models are given in the roles descriptions and in supporting software. The calculations are performed by their computers in Excel. So the board is not overloaded by the information and a table may be used for players' documentation and laptops.

Symbolic models are typical for entertainment games and they are also widely used for business games. Chess men represent a variety of military personnel ranks and resources. The *Monopoly* game uses symbolic figures representing players, houses and hotels. For business games which have no chance of commercialization, objects and events are usually presented on cards. A field and virtual business games are using such symbols as simple tokens. There are coins and plastic chips in the *Beer Game* or Lego bricks in *SIEMENS Supply Chain Simulator*. The *Leadership Trust* field games require from the players to move by wheelbarrows 11-gallon kegs with water as quite perceptible symbols of resources and products along the symbolic production lines painted on the ground.

This kind of field game environment is usually called a ***Sandbox***. Sandboxes may be such as a physical life-sized stadium in Leadership Trust premises, or downscaled 2- or 3-dimensional models of production and supply lines, natural terrain or transportation network. Military and Firemen training centers have full-sized models of terrain and buildings to simulate real physical movements, hazards and communications. Industrial Training Schools have sandboxes of realistic physical appearance of equipment layout inside a classroom. Then players' resources are represented by symbolic tags on the models of equipment, personnel, conveyors, blocks of materials, batches of production, trucks, ships and airplanes. The training center of HESS Corporation displays a scaled model of oil refinery which is used for the simulation of critical situations. Virtual sandboxes are typical environments for videogames. They represent colorful real or fantastic worlds in detail, animated and with the sound effects.

> "Many process sims have often been referred as "sandbox" or "god" games in which there is no goal involved and players can do no wrong. However, the process of building and maintaining systems incorporates the ongoing goals of system balance — whether it ensuring that your roller coaster does not malfunction, that your city does not go into deficit, or that your creature does not (or does) "misbehave". Peter Molyneux and Will Wright are considered the "gods of god games", with their innovative *Black & White* and *Sim City* franchises, respectively."
>
> [Novak, 2008]

The most expensive and complicated game environments are affordable by military academies, business schools and corporate training centers. Interactive computer displays like the one provided by Lockheed Corporation for war games and CNN studios might be named virtual sandboxes. They include flexible multiple touch-screens and score boards. An appropriate hardware is one of the technical requirements that a net-centric game must satisfy prior to the start of the game. The technical hardware such as computers (desktops or laptops) and Internet connections are required for the participants to experience the simulation games.

It is highly desirable that high power computing processors and random access memory (RAM) are embedded within the computer equipment. This would ensure the data and information are transmitted and processed accurately in a timely fashion. Due to multiple participants interacting during the simulation game, the amount of data and information may overwhelm the connected computers. Without adequate processing speed and memory or disk capacity the participants may experience information delay or technical glitches within applications.

The Internet connection is also required to support many business games, where both wireless or land line connections are permitted. The participating workstations are connected via security protocols, such as transport layer security (TLS) and secure sockets layer (SSL). The secured connections utilize TLS and SSL to establish network authentication and communication confidentiality over the network from each participating workstation. Then the information exchange during the simulation would not be tampered [Rescorla, 2001].

The digital version of a board game has an unlimited choice of photo, cartoon or symbolic figures representing game objects. A choice of images of people, animals, landscapes and architecture is growing every day.

Experienced game designers recommend working out initial versions of a new game using "paper technology" meaning handwritten charts and cards. They may be displayed on the board, on the wall or on the easel with post-ins and pins. They can be easily rearranged and replaced during initial brainstorming of designers team on idea of the game. This approach also useful for the working out of aesthetics of the game by the visual comparison of different color and graphic schemes. The appearance of standard technical and economic documents is supposed to be illuminated by different colors and shapes for the faster identification of them by players and instructors. The first prototype of the game may be tested this way earlier and with minimal expense. The roles of testers are usually played by the other games designers. Although it is definitely better to test game modules with outsiders, but for expediting a project, members of this particular game project themselves usually used.

After each test the artifacts of the game prototype may be improved: handwritten sketches become standard charts and typed texts, then they may be printed professionally on cards; paper materials may be replaced by a cardboard, wood, plastic or metal. This approach still keeps development of a game as the cards/board or the field game. Any of them may be computerized to become a videogame. In a former case we may start creating virtual game objects and software controlling their life and interface. The full extent of game project management will be presented in Chapter 9 based on systems engineering principles.

Aesthetics of the game depends on the type of players and technological resources of game designers. All entertaining videogames are using colors, animation and sound effects. It is possible to find the appropriate sound track for business games as well. For example, we used for the musical introduction to *CyberMarket* conceptual model of economic situation for kids the popular *"Obla-di, Obla-da"* song by Beatles:

Ob-La-Di, Ob-La-Da
The Beatles

Desmond has his barrow in the market place…
Molly is the singer in a band…
Desmond says to Molly "Girl, I like your face"
And Molly says this as she takes him by the hand…
Ob-la-di, ob-la-da, life goes on, brah!…
Lala how the life goes on…
Ob-la-di, ob-la-da, life goes on, brah!…
Lala how the life goes on.

Desmond takes a trolley to the jewelry store…
Buys a twenty carat golden ring…
Takes it back to Molly waiting at the door…
And as he gives it to her she begins to sing…
Ob-la-di, ob-la-da, life goes on, brah!…
Lala how the life goes on…
Ob-la-di, ob-la-da, life goes on, brah!…
Lala how the life goes on.

In a couple of years they have built a home sweet home,
With a couple of kids running in the yard,
Of Desmond and Molly Jones…(Ha ha ha ha ha)

Happy ever after in the market place…
Desmond lets the children lend a hand…
Molly stays at home and does her pretty face…
And in the evening she still sings it with the band…

> Ob-la-di, ob-la-da, life goes on, brah!…
> Lala how the life goes on…
> Ob-la-di, ob-la-da, life goes on, brah!…
> Lala how the life goes on.
>
> In a couple of years they have built a home sweet home,
> With a couple of kids running in the yard,
> Of Desmond and Molly Jones…
> Happy ever after in the market place…
> Molly lets the children lend a hand…
> Desmond stays at home and does his pretty face…
> And in the evening she's a singer with the band…
> Ob-la-di, ob-la-da, life goes on, brah!…
> Lala how the life goes on…
> Ob-la-di, ob-la-da, life goes on, brah!…
> Lala how the life goes on.
>
> [Beatles, 1966]

The song gives an introductory story for the business situation which is necessary for inexperienced kids. The model of the game is presented on the game board or on the computer screen in charts and tables. This is different from the similar structure of the *CyberMarket* game where students are introduced to the model of the game first, and then they create the situation around the changing parameters of the game as an individual life and business history. The resulting individual reports and team presentations are included in Appendices to this book and on the website www.bazilconsulting.com.

The children are better at handling real photographic images such as we used for the school versions of business games. Easily recognizable photographic or cartoonish images are also more appropriate for younger kids. The examples of playing cards for the *Aquarium* game for kids are presented in Fig. 8.11.

Cartoonish images are more appealing for the teenagers. The simplified version of the *Nature* game is presented in Fig. 8.12.

The essential part of game aesthetics is its language. The majority of expressions used in business games are supposed to be scientific and

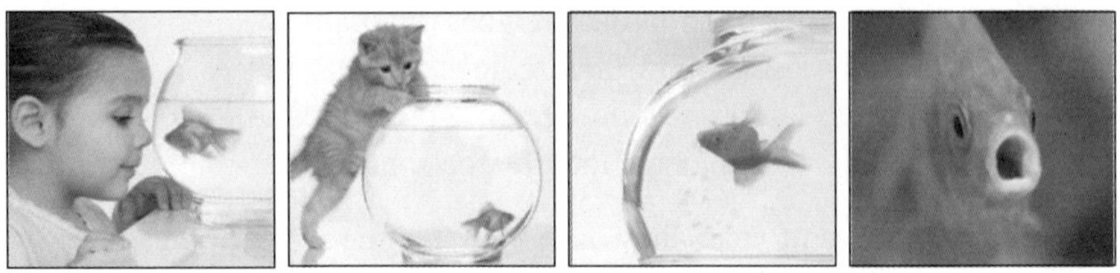

Fig. 8.11.   Playing cards for the environmental game *Aquarium* for kids represents photographic images of the child and the cat (tramp cards); and fish (components cards).

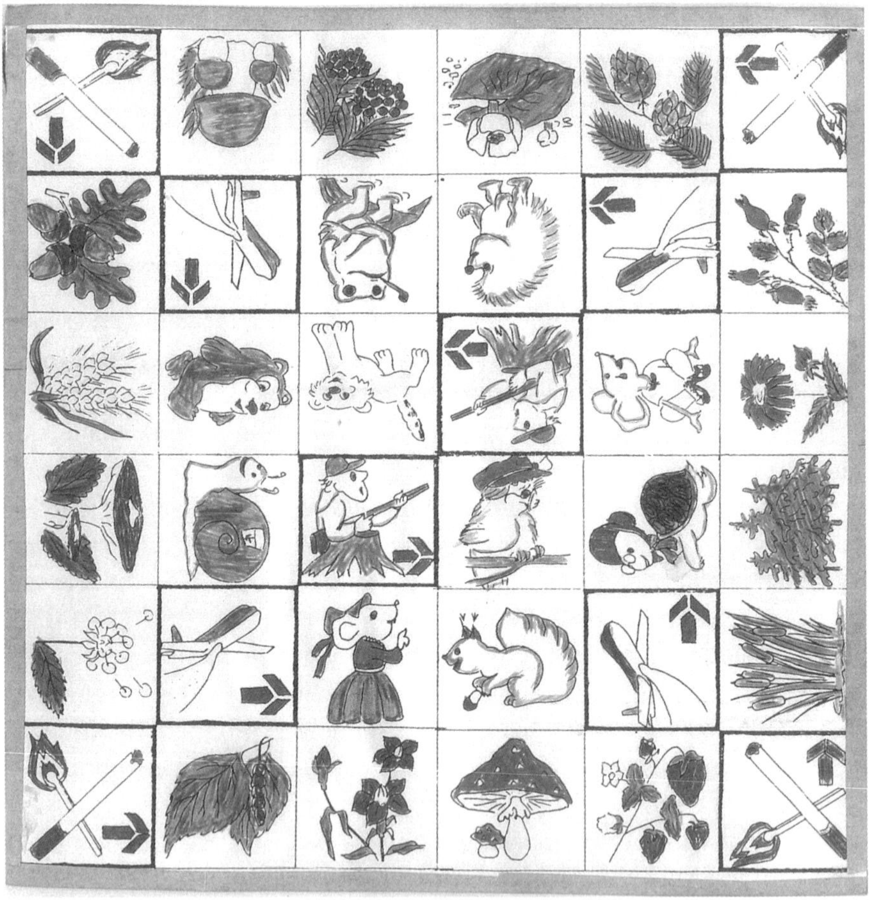

Fig. 8.12.   Cartoonish aesthetics of the *Nature* game for teenagers.

professional. But in many cases we experience influence of everyday street-speak, geek-speak or foreign languages:

> "Although colorful or "dirty" language is often looked down upon in polite society, the truth is that almost everyone uses these expressions. In some sectors of society they are among the most common words and are used to punctuate just about every sentence. To create realistic characters in certain types of games, it's useful at least to know what these words are and how to use them in a sentence. This is not to say that you should or must use them, but you should consider where they are appropriate and then decide who your audience is and what kind of rating you want your game to have."

[Perry, 2009]

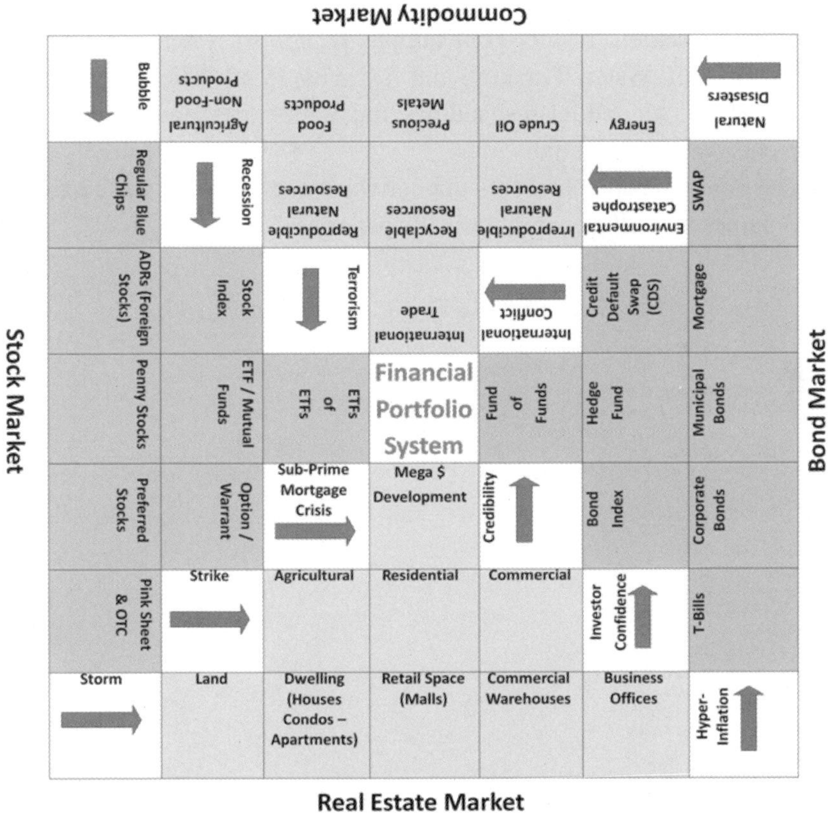

Commodity Market

	Agricultural Non-Food Products	Food Products	Precious Metals	Crude Oil	Energy	Natural Disasters
Stock Market / Regular Blue Chips	Recession	Reproducible Natural Resources	Recyclable Resources	Irreproducible Natural Resources	Environmental Catastrophe	SWAP
ADRs (Foreign Stocks)	Stock Index	Terrorism	International Trade	International Conflict	Credit Default Swap (CDS)	Mortgage
Penny Stocks	ETF / Mutual Funds	ETFs of ETFs	**Financial Portfolio System**	Fund of Funds	Hedge Fund	Municipal Bonds
Preferred Stocks	Option / Warrant	Sub-Prime Mortgage Crisis	Mega $ Development	Credibility	Bond Index	Corporate Bonds
Pink Sheet & OTC	Strike	Agricultural	Residential	Commercial	Investor Confidence	T-Bills
Storm	Land	Dwelling (Houses Condos – Apartments)	Retail Space (Malls)	Commercial Warehouses	Business Offices	Hyper-Inflation

Labels: Bubble — Stock Market — Bond Market — **Real Estate Market**

Fig. 8.13.   Game board for the *Finance SoS* business game.

For the games for students in most cases we use professional terminology or a combination of scientific terms on the board with images on the appropriate cards. This is illustrated in a board of the *Finance SoS* business game in Fig. 8.13.

A preparation of hardware for the board games designed on the *Holarchy* platform is quite easy. We need two identical copies printed on a cardboard: one is for placing on the table, and the other is for cutting off all cards. The jigsaw cardboards may be more entertaining and accurate, but it is difficult to fit pictures and inscriptions to the shapes of the jigsaw cards.

The best design of the board for educational games is 7×7 four-sided field which allows representation of real-sized systems. Then the first level of the pyramid represents basic technical, technological or natural components; the second level represents managerial decisions, and the third level shows economic results. For example, *TranSport* system game has four sectors for Rail, Water, Trucking and Air subsystems. The first level lists equipment, the second level schedules and agreements, and the third level represents consolidated deliveries.

The next chapter represents the software necessary for the support of board games as well as computerized "paperless" business games.

SOFTWARE FOR BUSINESS GAMES

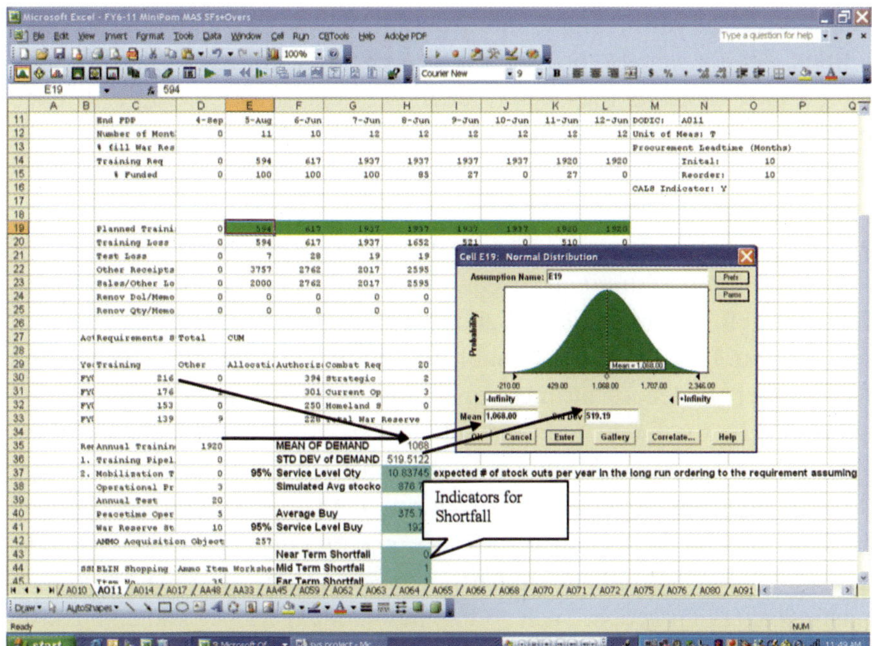

Normal distribution generator for a company training simulation

9.1. CHOOSING A SOFTWARE

Business games can be supported by different hardware and software for each type of education or research. A videogame needs a computer or TV with a console and can be run anywhere individually. Interactive video games may be centralized or networked. Board games are organized for teams sitting around tables. The board is a useful organizational tool for any type of game, not only for cards/board games. The board might be just a simple indication of players' positions or responsibilities. Then it can also be used for the assignment of roles, the allocation of resources and for the display of the current situation. More detailed maps, charts and tables are best placed on posters or screens on the walls and easels. Flowcharts are the best tools for the explanation of processes simulated by a game.

The choice of software depends entirely on the purpose of the simulated systems. The most commonly used software in business games is MS Excel. It is natural for maintaining data and processing financial and other types of information. Excel is also a valuable tool for the visualization of statistics. Many other models of business operations, growth and development are supported by the Excel "add-ins" like Crystal Ball, TreePlan and Solver. Professionals in research, education and industry are using Excel every day. A game with high-level executives during the game data processing may be supported by the technical staff. In some executive games we used the assistance of undergraduate students. It gave students a first-hand feeling of real managerial practice. Such collaboration of experience and enthusiasm is possible by inviting active or retired executives as participants or judges in college business games.

The most extensive use of Excel belongs to the economic applications of business games. The first educational games such as *Capstone* rely entirely upon spreadsheet calculations. Excel tables and charts are used for the introduction of initial information, for processing decisions and the presentation of their results. The algorithms of Excel might be included in game software for automatic calculations. That presents players and instructor with the results of their decisions. The involvement of players in programming of the game can be done initially as the introductory exercises or cases. The model building needs explanation of spreadsheet algorithms as a separate study. It may be required by an instructor on request of some players challenging results. If we need to concentrate players' attention to strategic decision making, calculations should be automated.

A software building usually starts by drawing flowcharts as a part of a game prototype and the most practical tool of model introduction. Flowcharts and decision trees might be developed in different levels of detail. In the beginning of design, and for explanation of the idea of the game to the players, a flowchart should be aggregated. A macro flowchart presenting the model of the *CyberMarket* business game reflects the main decision processes (see Fig. 6.13).

The flowcharts of intermediate levels are an essential part of designing a game prototype. A flowchart establishes a connection between the idea (conceptual model) of the game and technical documentation for software choice and development. The information modules create an interface between different databases and groups of game participants. The databases could be global websites of stocks and merchandise markets. Most of them (Wall Street Journal, Bloomberg, commodities exchanges) are accessible online during a game. Most financial and macroeconomic speculative games allow players to trade stocks in the simulated markets. Stock market games allow players to gain experience or just have fun of trading stocks in a virtual world without the real risk. Players compete with each other in the prediction of stocks movement. Many stock market games are based on real life stocks from the NASDAQ, NYSE and other market indexes. Their designers are trying to intrigue potential customers with suggestive titles *The Stock Market Wants You*, or the National Council on Economic Education's *Learning from the Market* [Maier, 2001].

Global level business games like *Intopia* and *Glo-Bus* are using specially created virtual databases. They represent global markets of high-tech products like electronic components and assemblies of computers or digital cameras. Teams represent companies that compete in main regions of the world (North and Latin America, European Union and Asia-Pacific). Corporate strategy games such as *Capstone* and *BizSim* provide students with virtual databases on CDs or websites for national markets. Games on the functional level of company management are supported by the data on supply prices and production costs. They are either presented to players in prefabricated options or require calculation on microeconomic models.

Flowcharts and decision trees may be useful to explain the procedure of a game. Players usually prefer graphical presentations of the rules and procedures to textual manuals and traditional lecturing. If they need details or definitions, they can use the game's website. The chart might include the inputs, decisions and operations, as well as the player's or team's decisions. They can be permanently displayed on posters or multimedia screens surrounding the game or may be accessible on the computer screens of the participants. Example of such a chart is given for the *Tycoon* game in Fig. 9.1.

Detailed flowcharts of information processing are usually stay "behind the screen" for players unless they are exercises for students in computer science and engineering or a game that supports an accounting class [MicroBusPub.com, 2010]. The example of a detailed information processing flowchart is presented in Fig. 9.2.

This example of the flowchart for computing factorial N (N!) presents N iterations in the exponential process of multiplication of digital numbers M and F by their product $F = F^*M$.

Some business games require specialized tools of process simulations such as ARENA [Evans, 2004] or CORE [Lang and Duggan, 2001, Reiley *et al.*, 2007]. System Dynamics software is presented by STELLA [Fisher, 2010], DYNAMO [Sterman, 2000], VenSim [Kirkwood, 2005] and many other packages. The object-oriented software AnyLogic [<www.XJTechnologies.com>, 2006], NetLogo [Northwestern, 2006] and many others are either free or proprietary simulation software [Swarm, 2006].

From a general perspective, software should be compatible with both Windows and Macintosh operational systems. The systems, such as Windows 2000/XP/Vista might be desirable due to their popularity. However, Macintosh- and Linux-based operating systems must be technically compatible as well [Tannenbaum, 2001].

For different levels of participants there will be different proportions between development of models during the game and the usage of prefabricated modules. Application software should contain systems engineering and operations research modules as functional features, such as context diagram drawing. A Monte Carlo sensitivity analysis and optimization are applicable where system modeling can be constructed with feedback functions [Jeruchim *et al.*, 2000].

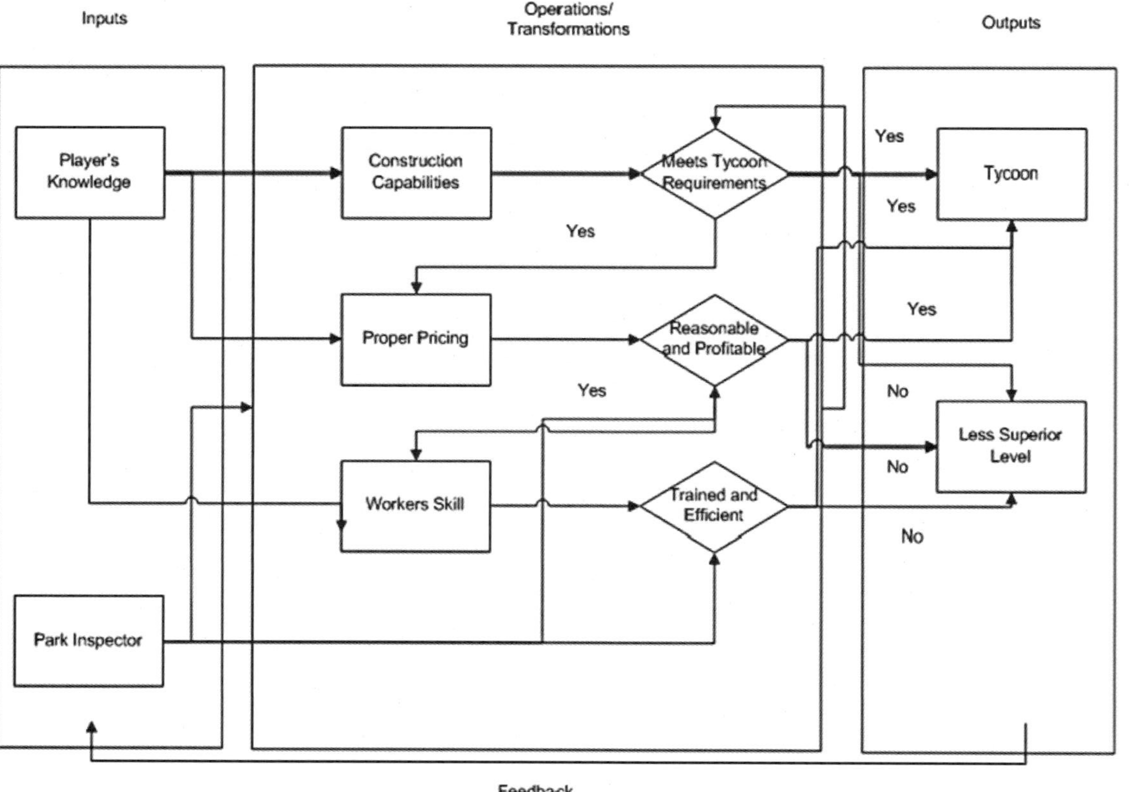

Fig. 9.1.   Flowchart of decisons for the *Tycoon* game.

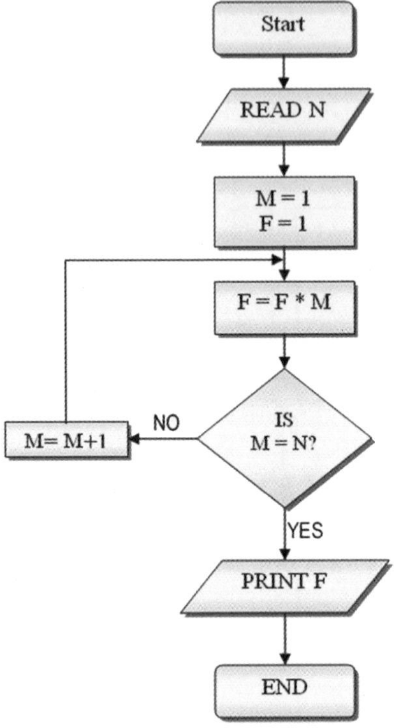

Fig. 9.2.   Detailed information processing flowchart.

Depending on the familiarity and skills of the players, the processes of a simulation can be highly paced. Therefore, in order to record or distribute information in a timely fashion, most documents must be prepared in advance and be ready as templates. These forms should be user-friendly and allow participants to quickly fill in data and information with minimal technical effort. Interactive procedures of programmed learning that are based on decision tree model can visualize results.

9.2.   SYSTEM DYNAMICS SOFTWARE

STELLA and *ithink* are the most popular SD software. They provide a graphic interface of converting the input of stock and flow diagram into equations. Then the model becomes computer readable tables and charts of system dynamics. The company ISEE Systems offers that software free with the tuition:

> "Easy-to-use, STELLA models provide endless opportunities to explore by asking "what if", and watching what happens, inspiring the exciting ah-ha moments of learning. Thousands of educators and researchers have made STELLA the gold standard; using it to study everything from economics to physics, literature to calculus, chemistry to public policy. K-12, college, and research communities have all recognized STELLA's unique ability to stimulate learning."
>
> [http://www.iseesystems.com/softwares/Education/StellaSoftware.aspx]

The following is a stocks and flows diagram of the model that is created in the Model Building & Simulation tutorial demonstration [Fig. 9.3].

Other software packages for design of SD models by beginners comparable with *STELLA* are *VenSim* and *PowerSim.* They have user-friendly interface based on causal loop diagrams. *VenSim* automatically documents

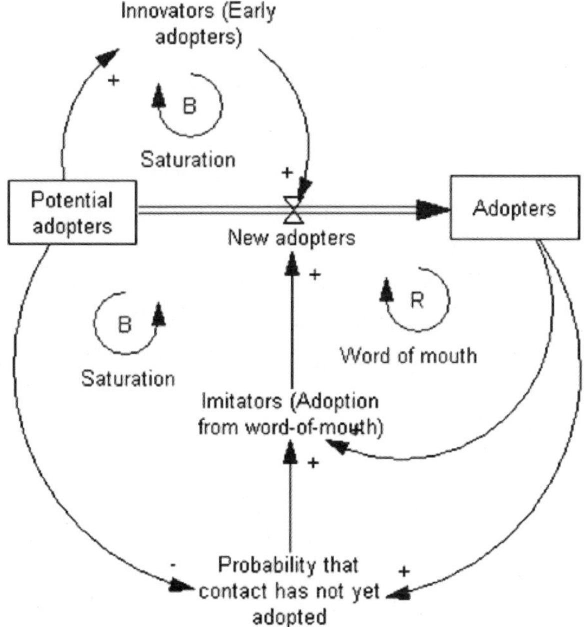

Fig. 9.3.   *STELLA* diagram of innovation dissemination process.

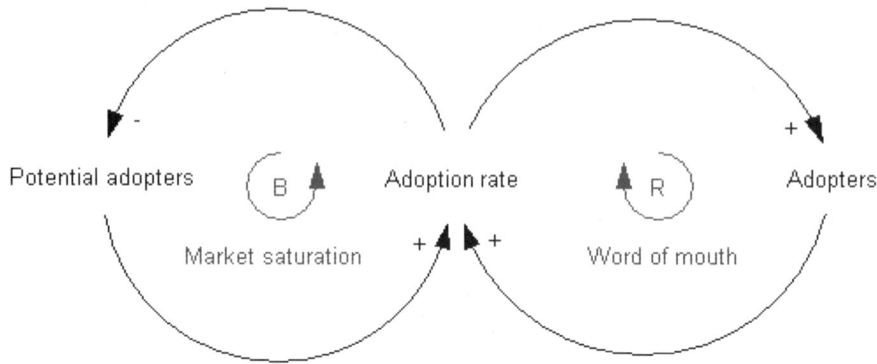

Fig. 9.4. Causal loops of innovation dissemination process.

an SD model and creates trees that allow one to trace cause-and-effect relationships through the entire model. It offers statistical and graphic features
and allows one to create menus, output screens and texts. At the professional
levels *DYNAMO Plus* and *DYNAMO for Windows* are packages for building
extremely large (up to 8,000 equations) models with advanced interfaces
and custom-designed reports similar to balance sheets and other real-world
formats [Senge, 1994]. The starting point of these packages is the creation
of a causal loop diagram for the same innovation process that is illustrated
in Fig. 9.4.

During the last decades, SD software has been improved and modernized to include colorful graphics and animation. A snapshot of an animated
demonstration of SD output is presented in Fig. 9.5.

The faculty and alumni of MIT Sloan School of Management have
developed a whole family of the *Management Flight Simulators (MFS)*:
business games that are based on the following SD causal loops archetypes
[Senge, 1994]:

1. Fixes that Backfire
2. Limits to Growth
3. Shifting the Burden
4. Tragedy of the Commons
5. Accidental Adversaries

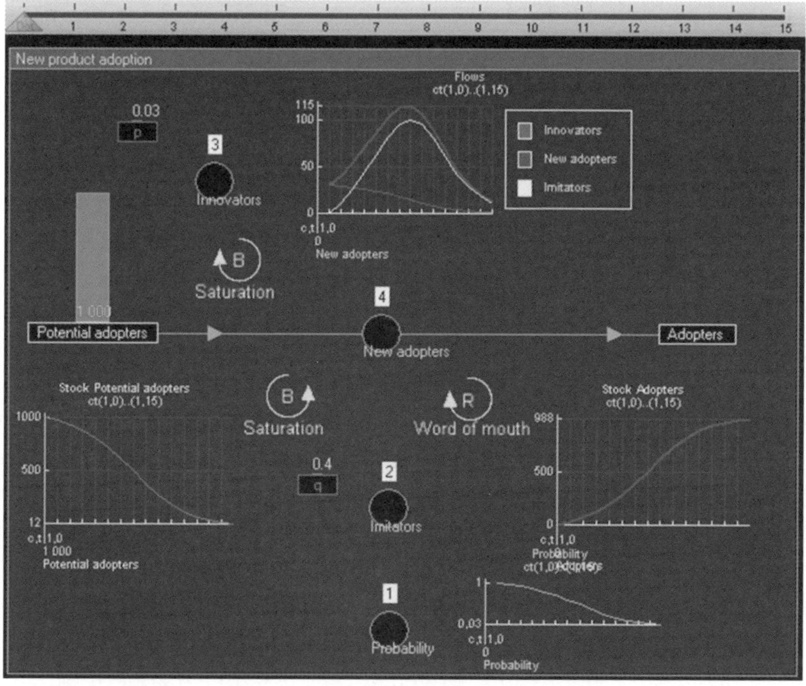

Fig. 9.5. Screen shot of output for innovation process statistics.

9.3. MONTE CARLO SIMULATION BY CRYSTAL BALL

The term "Monte Carlo Simulation" originated in gambling as a process generating random numbers at a roulette wheel. Random numbers are the main drivers of events in entertainment games. A generator of random numbers defines how many steps the player makes along the game path. It is also a tool for the generation of external interferences in many business games. However we limit the application of such an artificial source of random events for business games. In business games the internal uncertainty of events is better than external "happenings". Besides, if random events are picked from a stack of cards, it means that all of them have the same probability. Such an application of uniform probability distribution is not proven theoretically or justified statistically. Uniform distribution also represents the highest possible level of uncertainty that complicates for the players building up a conceptual model of the game by trial and error.

The process of generating random events can be performed either by a physical device (coin, die, card or roulette wheel) or by a computer. A visual appearance of random events is spectacular. They have even become predictable to some extent as all possible outcomes are visible on the wheel. Their probabilities may be known, such as in the throw of a dice. Any justified probability distribution may be generated by a computer. Yet a computer generator may not allow players to see all possible events at once. It is the generator of events in a video game, but the source and probability law of random events in most such games are not explained. So the player has limited opportunities to exercise a forecasting function of management.

Monte Carlo random events generators as mechanical devices are valuable tools of game dramatization and aesthetics. A minimal size generator is an coin flipping. The "ideal" coin provides 50:50 chances for two different events (unless it is from the "Indecent Proposal" or "Batman" movie). The next level of uncertainty is generated by the throw of a die with four, six or more sides that represents uniformly distributed numbers or events. Such ancient devices of random number generating are still a matter of patenting for technological applications of games.

Devices like a roulette or "Wheel of Fortune" are more diverse in reflecting larger numbers of possible events. They also permit assigning different events unequal probabilities (Fig. 9.6).

Computer programs are more flexible in the choice from a variety of probability distributions, but still they do not always provide ideal outcomes. Excel software in particular generates "pseudo-random" numbers and some of the simulation runs may be visibly far from ideal (see Fig. 9.7.).

Some other theoretical distributions may be assumed behind the random events appearance for business game players. Poisson distribution is the most appropriate for the Markov process with a small average probability for discrete random events. Such a model of uncertainty is typical for production, transportation, communications and many other technological processes. For the continuous variables such as quality measurements, biological and environmental parameters, a Normal distribution is justified. Customer satisfaction of services expressed alternatively (accept-reject) should be represented by binomial distribution.

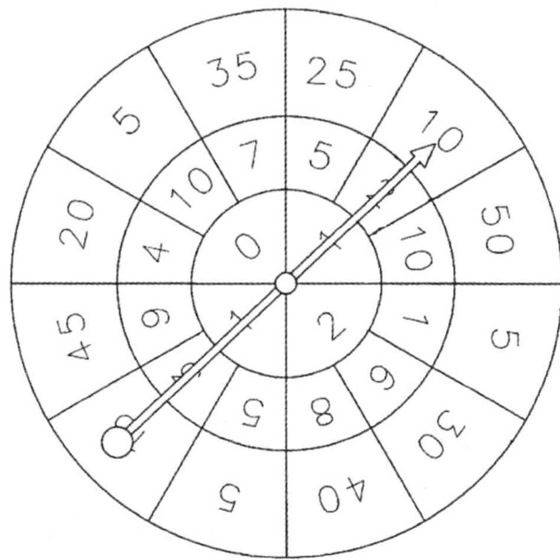

Fig. 9.6.   Random generator with uneven probabilities of events.

100 Random numbers						Bin	Frequency
0.2943	0.9313	0.2723	0.5250	0.0448		0	0
0.7753	0.4825	0.9689	0.1531	0.8936		0.1	11
0.5056	0.2687	0.3811	0.0972	0.3766		0.2	11
0.8142	0.0914	0.8557	0.0971	0.1475		0.3	13
0.9220	0.6347	0.7717	0.3962	0.5603		0.4	9
0.1834	0.2467	0.9091	0.7311	0.1486		0.5	10
0.1887	0.4523	0.4381	0.0229	0.8934		0.6	6
0.8113	0.1326	0.6394	0.6754	0.8111		0.7	6
0.6566	0.8098	0.0581	0.4720	0.0101		0.8	9
0.7488	0.5990	0.5128	0.9613	0.9500		0.9	13
0.4409	0.4480	0.6970	0.2442	0.1362		More	12
0.9333	0.6592	0.6383	0.8255	0.8511			
0.2829	0.4647	0.0500	0.6839	0.6305			
0.1157	0.5246	0.2068	0.2295	0.1980			
0.1397	0.0570	0.5268	0.7302	0.6226			
0.2989	0.2299	0.2628	0.8972	0.8660			
0.2004	0.0108	0.3933	0.2520	0.2726			
0.5694	0.5453	0.7957	0.4064	0.0592			
0.1256	0.6460	0.8340	0.1549	0.5296			
0.1588	0.2520	0.2911	0.6785	0.0834			

Fig. 9.7.   Results of *Excel* random numbers generator.

Table 9.1.   Probabilities of triangular distribution for two dice.

Sum	Probability density		Cumulative probability
	Fraction	**Decimal**	**0**
2	1/36	0.028	0.028
3	1/18	0.056	0.083
4	1/12	0.083	0.167
5	1/9	0.111	0.278
6	5/36	0.139	0.417
7	1/6	0.167	0.583
8	5/36	0.139	0.722
9	1/9	0.111	0.833
10	1/12	0.083	0.917
11	1/18	0.056	0.972
12	1/36	0.028	1.000
Total	1	1.000	

The learning process in business games should be mostly supported by the internal uncertainty generated by the decisions and interactions of the players. The introduction of external events should not be completely occasional but also explained as a random process from a certain model. The majority of entertaining board games represent the game progress as purely random dynamics. In *Monopoly*, the movements of each player around the game board is generated by the throw of two dice. That statistically represents triangular probability distribution (see Table 9.1).

Fig. 9.8 illustrates the odds of moving around the *Monopoly* board after throwing dice. The probability of getting sum of seven is the highest, so experienced players could choose the appropriate decision to increase the chances of landing on the desired cell.

Monte Carlo generated inputs describing biological, technological or demographic processes which represent large number of events (number of species, production output, active population). Then the output of such a process is a frequency chart provided by the Crystal Ball software (See Fig. 9.9).

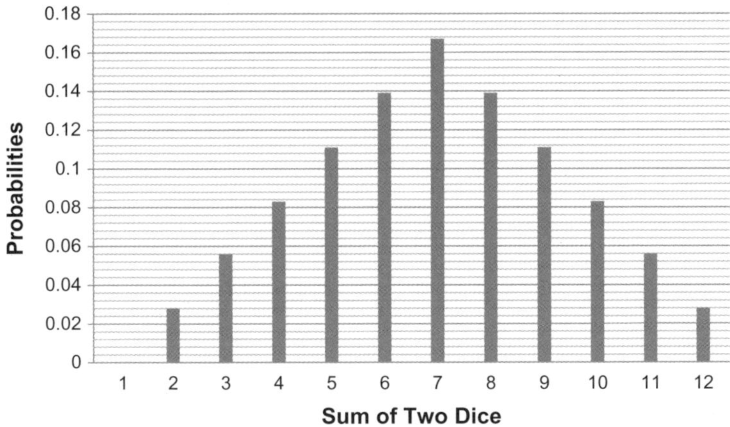

Fig. 9.8.   Triangular cumulative probability function of throwing two dice.

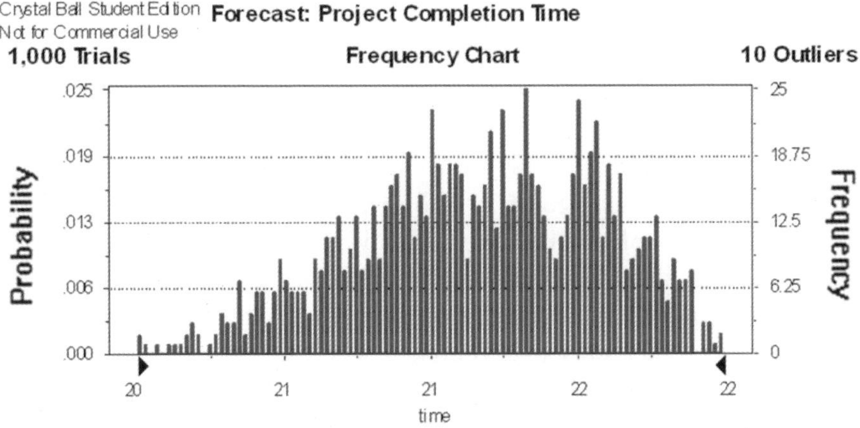

Fig. 9.9.   Monte Carlo simulation result for probability of the game event.

Generating random numbers and events from the probability distribution is acceptable in the case when it is theoretically justified. For example, the widely used Normal distribution may be applicable to physical and chemical processes and may hardly approximate economic and social parameters. For business games a Normal distribution may be used for demographic parameters as it is shown in Fig. 9.10 for human resources forecasting of the large corporation.

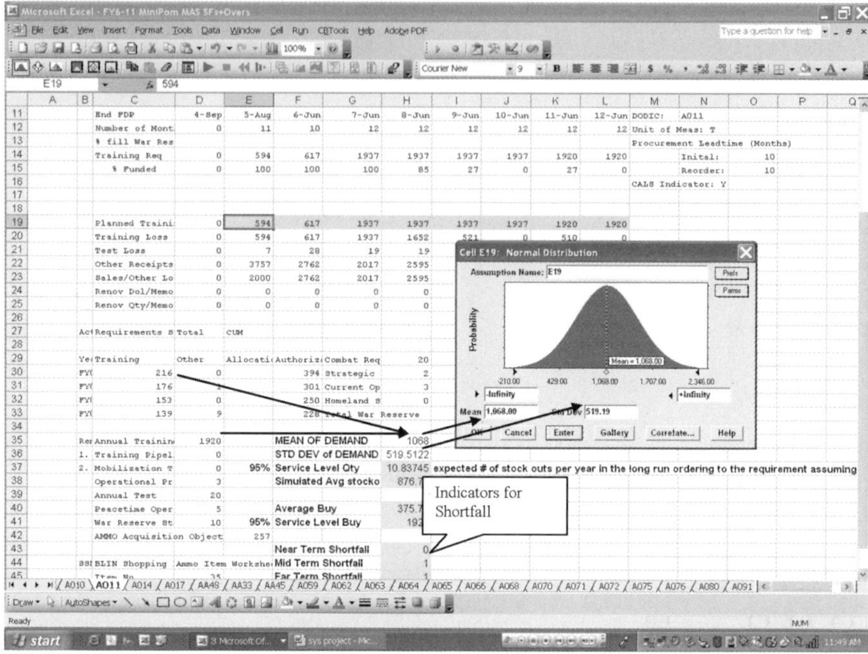

Fig. 9.10.   Normal distribution generator for a company training simulation.

In a game with just a few rounds of play, generating significant events as a very small sample does not provide players with a "level playing field". The rare events should be the same for different teams, then their results will be comparable. Otherwise the losers may just blame a bad luck while winners will get no knowledge from their success.

9.4.   AGENT-BASED SIMULATION BY ANYLOGIC

Agent-based Simulation (ABS) is the most universal tool for the representation of a system operations on a short-term time horizon. The ABS is also a good computational tool for medium-term simulations of a growth models in ecological and economic applications. That is why it is a valuable module of simulation of technological and social processes in business games. The ABS is also a reliable tool for the forecasting of human behavior in different environments. The ABS visualizes formation, changes and disappearance of individuals and groups of population. Specialized Any-Logic software presents simulation results in statistical charts and tables, in cartoons and photographic images, and in dynamic animation. AnyLogic is a good analytical tool for the interpretation of the so-called "counterintuitive", unexpected behavior of complex systems.

ABS operates as a discrete sequence of steps and events when every iteration predicts changes based on the current state of the system. The proper definition of spatial and temporal resolution is essential for this type of simulation. It complements the choice of time scale based on delays in System Dynamics models with the scales in space. Individual transitions might be aggregated in group or crowd behavior in economic and social systems. The term "agent" covers not only people, but many other independent objects (i.e., business, software models, etc.) that are supposed to learn from a changing environment and change their behavior. The essential properties of the agent are:

- **Autonomy**, the ability of making independent decisions
- **Heterogeneity** — agents are identical
- **Active** — agents pursuing own goals
- **Reactive** on changes in environment
- **Interactive** in communications with other agents
- **Mobile** in space
- **Adaptive** — capable to change if necessary.

The formal definition of agents always needs a detailed description of their properties. For business games purposes where, where agents are usually people, we recognize their features of ownership, leadership, productivity, etc. The advantages of ABS are in the generation of emergent behavior in a specified business environment. This way ABS can substitute some natural (physical) experimentation which takes a longer time or may be unacceptable. Emergence of a surprising behavior of self-organization, adaptation, chaos, etc. between agents increases system complexity. The classic example of this phenomenon happens in the neural networks as a result of the interaction between a large number of relatively simple identical components. The aggregate complexity is of particular interest to business game designers in two respects: (1) for building supporting software modeling basic modules of the system and (2) for explaining the surprising behavior of players in the teams.

(1) ABS serves as a basic module that represents the system growth and changes. For example, in the *NewProDev* game ABS can represent the demand of a product offering in place of a team that is playing customers. Although in business games the explicit representation of each type of agent is preferable, it may be substituted by the ABS model.

(2) ABS may provide a meaningful explanation of emergent team behavior because of interactions between players that are uncontrollable by the instructor. For example, a group of individually disciplined students may start obstructing rules of the game to speed up or simplify procedures. That is known as the "crowd effect" especially likely among teenagers.

The interactions between individual agents are complicated, non-linear, discrete (i.e., dramatically changing their behavior). Collective behavior is especially difficult to predict in heterogeneous and complex systems of several types of components. It may be the interaction between operators and managers, or between the leader and other members of the team. A complexity increases with a growing level of agents' knowledge through the adaptation, analyzing and to creativity. Correspondence between different tools of experience formation and level of knowledge may be presented in Table 9.2.

The essential property of ABS is the representation of stochastic behavior of agents and their aggregates. Random changes in a business game are not desirable, yet they happen just like they do in real life. They may be unexpected both for the players and for the instructor, but preferably should be statistically justified. The probabilities of basic processes may be theoretically proven, supported by experience or by the data collected during the game. The probabilities of secondary, especially managerial properties then become the result of an ABS simulation. Finally, an agent-based approach is flexible, particularly in relation to business games. ABS can be defined within different environments (i.e., company, city, supply chain, transportation network, information system).

Table 9.2. Correspondence between types and results of agents learning.

Type of knowledge [Kavtaradze, 1998]	Sources of knowledge	Results [Bazilevich, 1979]	Examples
Instincts	Genetically inherited	Memorizing	Assembly line control control
Imprinting	Patterns recognition		control
Training	Elementary exercises	Analysis	Supply chain management
Education	Understanding principles		
Gaming	Simulating reality	Changing paradigms	New product development

We should also consider some limitations of ABS. First, there are some simplifications in assumptions necessary. Unlike real life and explicit business game simulations, agents of the same type are supposed to be identical. Their actions, reactions and interactions are strictly regulated and are supposed to be completely rational. Their motivation and targets are supposed to be constant and objective. That is the major difference compared with real individuals and especially collective behavior that is driven by mood, fashion, mistakes and misunderstandings. These discrepancies could be eventually corrected through the regular use of business games and management simulations which build a bridge between social sciences and economic reality.

ABS models are useful for the creation of scenarios in the basic processes of business game environment. In a technological system ABS simulates overall results (productivity, quality) instead of physical production performed by players. In social applications, an ABS model may update the behavior of separate homogeneous groups. It can predict trends in supply from many small vendors or aggregate demand of a large consumer market.

Building these models is recommended in cooperation with the system analyst and practitioners (system stakeholders) to verify the reality of the assumptions. The ABS model starts with the classification of agents in

Table 9.3. Interaction between agent and environment.

	Agent	
Environment	**Of the same type**	**Of a new type**
Existing system	Actual stakeholders of the system with validation of empirical statistics on homogeneity and stability	Playing roles of potential stakeholders in hypothetical situations
Designed system	Playing roles of new stakeholders in different scenarios of system structure and rules	Abstract concept of possible groups of stakeholders in hypothetical system

relation to the environment. The purpose of the game may be either analysis of an existing system or the design of a new one. In this respect ABS simulates agents behavior either in a familiar or in the new environment; interacting with similar or with different agents. Then possible combinations of agents with environment are presented in Table 9.3.

Initial classification of agents into different classes of objects allows computers to handle their initial and emerging properties. Then agents' actions, reactions and interactions form certain informal networks and formal organizational structures. Types of networks which possible for agents are presented in Fig. 9.11.

Systems of different structure may be simulated by business games of different missions. Control of an existing centralized system (assembly, subsystem) may be simulated by the card, board, or corresponding digital game. Management of decentralized systems may be represented by a

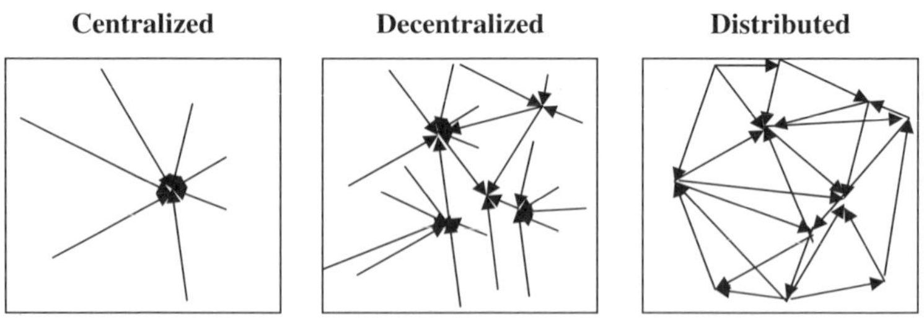

Fig. 9.11. Types of emerging system structures.

Closed system			
	Assembly or technological system	Individual business and technical enterprise	Module of ecological system
		Business Association and technological enterprise	Market, supply chain and social network
Open System	**Centralized**	**Decentralized**	**Distributed**

Fig. 9.12.   Organizational settings for the business games simulating existing systems.

few teams of functionally specialized players. Governance of distributed System-of-Systems is possible to display by the field game of professionals or executives.

The differences in approach to simulation of existing systems are explained by many factors, most of which are related to the degree of system openness. The border between closed and open system is blurry, so classification is just conventional. The first approach to the classes of systems is presented in Fig. 9.12.

The latest developments in software engineering are related to using games for designing games themselves:

> "Many projects currently used in Software Engineering curricula lack both the "fun factor" needed to engage students, as well as the practical realism of engineering projects that include other computer science disciplines such as Software Engineering, Networks, or Human Computer Interaction…. Specifically, a set of game-centric, project-based modules have been developed that enable students to: (1) actively participate in the different phases of the software lifecycle taking a single project from requirement elicitation to testing and maintenance; (2) expose students to real issues in project and team management over the course of 2-semester project; and at the same time (3) introduce students to the different aspects of computer game design. Preliminary results suggest the merit of our approach, showing improved class participation and performance."
>
> [Claypools, 2005]

Other experienced digital designers also recommend system approach to the design of such complex products as games. The Artificial Intelligence (AI) approach is offered in the book "Introduction to Game AI" [Kirby, 2010]. Famous programmer Fred Brooks even proposes universal tools that he applied to the software engineering in a book "The Design of Design" [Brooks, 2010]. We also encountered with a similar idea in "The Game of Game Design" earlier [Claypool, 2005].

The design of new systems and enterprises is the mission of the entirely different class of business games presented in Chapter 10.

BUSINESS GAMES FOR SYSTEM DESIGN

Game board for *Finance SoS* game

10.1.   BUSINESS GAME FOR SYSTEMS DESIGN

Business games are powerful tools for systems engineering education and research. The valuable capacity of business games is in the fact that they provide an interdisciplinary approach to the design and deployment of systems. The games that have been presented thus far, such as *NewProDev*, can be applied to the design of components and assemblies. A business game for design of a system should integrate science with engineering tools and the simulation of human behavior in a system. The human factor is represented by the players of different professions and cultures in multifunctional teams. The design of such a game itself follows the system's life cycle from the concept to production, to operation and to disposal. According to the definition of the International Council of Systems Engineering (INCOSE), business games are part of *systems engineering management*. Systems engineering as a professional activity combines art and science and therefore needs the selection and training of designers:

> "Because systems engineering is both an art and a science, many of the skills and abilities needed to be highly effective in complex systems are not learned in school; they are gained through experience. Processes and tools are very important, but they cannot substitute for capable people. Following processes and using tool sets will not result automatically in a good system engineer or system design … Capable and well-prepared people make the difference between success and failure."
>
> [Ryschkewitsch, 2009]

A systems engineering approach to business game design requires solving technical, artistic and behavioral problems. A game as designed includes hardware and software. A game developer needs an accumulation of wetware during game testing. The wetware was earlier defined as "know-how", and now includes besides rules and procedures of the game also knowledge, experience and the imagination of game designers and instructors. Business game designers must prepare for the players interesting scenarios and cases expressed in attractive images and procedures.

> "When you strip away the genre differences and the technological complexities, all games share four defining traits: a *goal, rules*, a *feedback system*, and *voluntary participation*."
>
> [McGonigal, 2011]

All of the traits listed above are related to entertainment video games, particularly the last one, voluntary participation. Although an individual's participation in a business game may be obligatory, a player is free to choose a team, role and strategy. The goal and rules of business game are forming a base for wetware. Feedback is always provided by the structure of a system as a cornerstone of systems engineering.

Systems engineering as an art and a science includes training of creative approaches to business game design. In addition to artistic skills and scientific professionalism, designers need an understanding of the players' motivation. Business games are the best tools for the demonstration of artistic and psychological skills of players. The psychological component requires the application of behavioral economics and behavioral systems theory. There are still a few publications on recent research in both of these fields. The development of behavioral economics was outlined in Chapter 1 as a slow and contradictory process [Simon, 1987]. Behavioral systems theory which can be used for business game design is even less advanced [Cotroneo, 2001; Rapisarda and Willems, 2006]. Therefore, business games themselves may facilitate an understanding of the behavioral aspects of complex systems. This will promote faster training of professionals in systems design.

The structure of the system defines most of the functional requirements of the game. The players in a business game may participate in six organizational mechanisms. The opportunities of developing SixCs capabilities of game wetware are presented in Table 10.1.

Table 10.1. Opportunities of different organizational mechanisms of business games.

Level of involvement	Organizational mechanism	Capabilities of business game participants	Opportunities for behavioral knowledge development
Control	Individual	Competence	Improving professionalism
	Team	Cooperation	Learning tacit information
Management	Hierarchy	Coordination	Transfer implicit information
	Network	Competition	Generating creative decisions
Governance	Holarchy	Connectivity	Imprinting generic information
	System of Systems	Communication	Initiating entrepreneurship

Table 10.1 outlines the capabilities that are prevailing in the appropriate organizational structure. Every structure provides wetware formation in different proportions. Every level of organizational integration facilitates certain behavioral capabilities. Individual study enriches professionalism and leadership enforces cooperation within a team. Work in hierarchy supports coordination and participation in a network ignites competition spirit. Holarchy and System of Systems are training executives in governance functions. The concept of a business game should clearly specify the choice of an organizational mechanism that corresponds to the development of the required behavioral capabilities.

A concurrent system design goes through the number of consecutive prototypes with coordination between subsystems. During this process customer requirements should be satisfied by the integration of hardware and software. The principal customer of a system should be also involved in the design of the games that support the design, deployment and maintenance of the system. During different stages of the system life cycle, customers should play an active role first in system model concept, and then in the system requirements.

The most recognized in systems engineering is the spiral process of iterative clarification of system design. The game for the planning of that process that contains several sessions of *NewProDev* game we will call *System Design Metagame*. The concept of such metagame is illustrated in Fig. 10.1.

The metagame contains several cycles of prototype design and business games rounds. It starts from the formulation of a system concept during the collective brainstorming sessions of designers and customers. After the approval of a concept, the customer formulates system requirements. The next stage is risk analysis performed by the customer and the first prototype of the system hardware proposal by the designers' team. During the first run of the *NewProDev* game the software design must be simulated. This stage also clarifies an operational concept of the system according to the customer's requirements. The joint participation of customer and designers in the game starts accumulation of the wetware. Then, the team of designers can satisfy the requirements to the system using system engineering tools. They also decide the inclusion of software modules from previously developed systems.

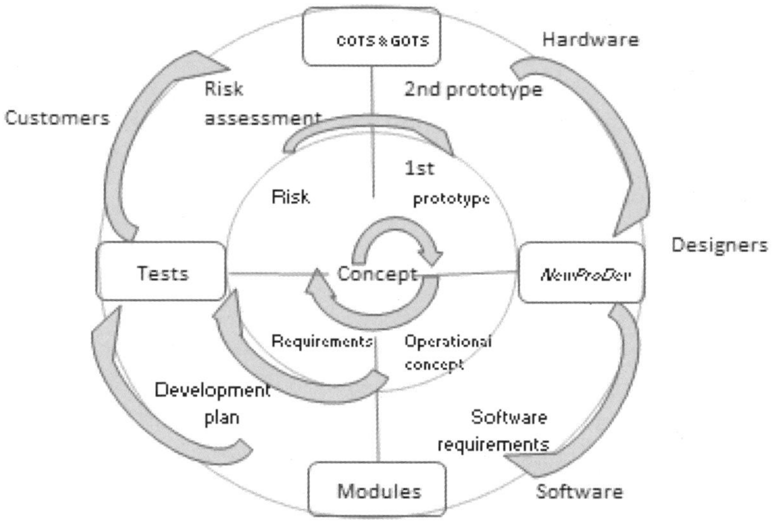

Fig. 10.1.   Spiral model of the *System Design Metagame*.

The first stage of the metagame concludes system concept correction and the formulation of the requirements plans for the subsystems. The game coordinates designers with the customer for the clarification of the system structure of the 1st prototype of subsystems. It includes acceptance of test requirements worked out together by the designers, test engineers, and the customer. They determine that all of the high level hardware require-ments will be user-friendly, especially the computer interface. This may require including business game consultants that specialize in ergonomics and psychology. The goal is the design of control of the technology with the feedback at every level of the system. An operator needs software which supports optimal processes. It includes the interaction with computer oper-ating systems, supply of tools and components, monitoring machinery. An assembly supervisor who manages operators is expecting software for the optimal production and service support. A subsystem manager requires software providing optimal business decisions. Building trust between all of them is the most essential result of the wetware among participants of the metagame. The customer expects the reliability of the system; the designers are primarily concerned with the manufacturability and the compatibility of the components.

After customers' approval of the system's operational concept, the second stage of the metagame begins. It includes the formulation of the operational plan, tests, and risk assessment. Teams evaluate the time and resources necessary for the design of the second prototype of the system. This stage of the game concentrates on the architectural model of the system for the evaluation of compatibility and reliability of the components, modules and subsystems. Designer teams evaluate the subsystem's expected cost, reasonable schedule, and the quality built into their components. They should use the *NewProDev* game again for the simulation of subsystem designs in conditions of uncertainty. The players now keep the balance between technological concerns of the system developers and process concerns of the users. The second stage of metagame may start with two teams representing all designers and all customers in a *Scrum* process.

The closest prototypes of a metagame are the processes called *Scrum* and *Scrum-ban*. They were originally defined as a new holistic approach that would increase speed and flexibility in new commercial product development [Takeuchi, 1986]. In this process project phases overlap significantly and are performed by one cross-functional team that uses analogy to a *Rugby* sports game. The participants of the *Scrum* process are playing roles of master, pigs and chickens. The ScrumMaster is not the leader of the team, but just the team meetings director like a game instructor. Sometimes, this role is played by an outside expert as a third party, that encourages honesty and trust. The customer has the "pig" role that can be assigned also to some other leading system stakeholders. The "chicken" roles are played by the secondary stakeholders (people for whom the software is being built: vendors, the people who enable the project and for whom the project will produce benefits). Yet the size of the team is still restricted to five to nine members.

The first applications of this type of simulation came from the automotive, photo machine, computer, and printer industries. The *Scrum-ban* is a software production model based on *Scrum* and *Kanban*. The essence of the *Scrum-ban* is in the visualization of the work stages that is borrowed from the classic *Kanban* model.

The *Scrum* processes consist of the periodic team meetings. They are scheduled as daily and weekly sprints and bi-weekly or monthly project status meetings. The first ones are called a "daily scrum", or "the weekly standup". The daily meeting has specific guidelines:

- The meeting starts precisely on time.
- All are welcome, but only "pigs" may speak
- The meeting is timeboxed to 15 minutes
- The meeting should happen at the same location and same time every day

During the meeting, each team member answers three questions:

- What have you done since yesterday?
- What are you planning to do today?
- Do you have any problems preventing you from accomplishing your goal? It is the role of the ScrumMaster to facilitate resolution of these impediments.

[Schwaber, 2004]

The *Scrum* processes are close to the same **ViVaT** principles of **Vi**sualization, **Vi**rtualization and **Va**riation in **T**ime found in business games. During the meeting participants plot their remarks on post-its on wall posters or on whiteboards that represent the virtual models of system. The timing of the meetings and of job completion is compressed as much as possible.

The third cycle of a metagame starts with the approval of the development plan by the customer. The customer works out tests to examine the compliance of design to the system requirements. The customer approves what components of the system may be filled with COTS (commercial-off-the-shelf) and GOTS (government-off-the-shelf) products and what components need to be of custom design. It forms the vision of the second prototype of the system and allows the playing of the third session of the *NewProDev* game. During this game the team simulates system development and finalizes software requirements. Testing of the second prototype of the system may finish the metagame or indicate the necessity of an additional cycle of the design process.

System documentation must contain business game hardware (game board or sandbox presenting the structure of the system), software (models and modules of game) and wetware (rules and regulations). Teams of designers fill in the spiral metagame board inside-out, in the opposite way then in the game-simulating existing system of the same structure. This metagame is the tool of creating the wetware as system knowledge from a live experience stage (repetition — analysis — creation) specified in Chapter 1. System wetware development belongs to the planning sector of the spiral model as coordination of design schedules and requirements between customer and designers. Unlike hardware and software which might be designed by professionals in solitude of their workstations, the wetware can be developed only during the process of interaction between designers and customers.

The contents of subsystems are the matter of design prototypes that correspond to the nature of their components. Their simulation can be organized in separate *NewProDev* games as production of components by subcontractors. It allows inclusion of design components and software modules that were used before. Various COTS and GOTS components of hardware and modules of software are available on the market. The development of the engineering requirements involves both the hardware architects and software engineers. The mission of the metagame is in finding compromises between designers and customers to meet constraints in costs, requirements and schedules. The contemporary trend of a universal approach to system design is presented by Fred Brooks in the book "Design of Design" [Brooks, 2010].

10.2. SYSTEM DESIGN ORGANIZATION

A business game for system design provides the integration of the three parts of game contents: model, cases and exercises:

(1) The model of the system starts with the structuring of the system. It must be based on the INCOSE classification of systems and components.
(2) The main source of cases is from the customer's experience of "What Went Wrong?" cases such as accidents, collisions, attacks, strikes, spills, etc.
(3) The exercises in hardware and software design are provided by the professional toolbox of system architecture design and software design practices.

The team of designers should play the game in several groups. There are two possible ways of splitting an aggregate team into diversified groups. One option is structuring teams according to the architecture of a system.

The other is functional specialization (architecture, hardware, software, integration, implementation). The first approach is the best for the relatively small and less dynamic systems. The second approach is preferable for the large, complex integrated systems. The software (SW) design for these systems is complicated and should be performed in the following steps:

- **SW Architecture Development:** Produce the high-level software architecture and update existing architecture documentation for subsequent releases or sub-releases;
- **SW Analysis:** To produce specification work products and to provide a detailed description of SW modules;
- **SW Package Development:** To produce the documentation of the software design, source code & unit test this code;
- **Pre-Integration:** To integrate and test the software packages together;
- **Integration:** To deliver fully tested portions of software for conducting further testing and also to generate modification requests for any detected defects.

During the consecutive sessions of the *NewProDev* game the prototypes of subsystems become more coordinated. The teams representing the design of subsystems may reach agreements on acquiring COTS, GOTS and of services subcontracting. The division of teams in hardware and software which mirrors the system architecture has many strength and weaknesses. For example, if elements in an architecture are tightly coupled, representing them by teams needs intense communication. Loosely coupled architectural elements can expect implementation teams with less coordination between them. A grouping of tasks for the best team formation will be presented next as an optimization on the DSM model.

The additional stage of the metagame may be necessary after testing of system software. Teams representing subsystems are ready for the clarification of risk analysis and for the planning of the third prototype design. The metagame ends after the risk assessment of the prototype of the system is accepted by the customer. The customer tests the system and compares the operational model with the parameters of the system and with the benchmarks. The time for benchmarking can be substantially reduced through utilizing Internet resources that are recommended for the business games of new product development. Teams may find benchmarks and best practices through Internet search engines from the websites of organizations, businesses and professional publications to make the benchmarking process much quicker and cheaper.

The last session of system design business metagame should simulate implementation of systems as interaction between designers, manufacturers, users and service providers. Implementation planning is a key element in ensuring the successful functioning of the system. The purpose of this step is to describe measurable parameters of the system, to demonstrate that intended system requirements will be satisfied. The Benefits Statement should provide a clear description of the intended beneficiaries and expected benefits of the system.

The structuring of a system into subsystems and then into tasks can be done top-down or bottom-up. A first step in business game organization needs a listing of tasks. A top-down defining of subsystems is preferable for a game with a design of a new system based on a theoretical model. It can be done on different scales and with different levels of aggregation. Both ways of structuring are supposed to give approximately equal sizes and complexity of subsystems. INCOSE provides us with a detailed classification of system structural levels: component, subassembly, assembly, subsystem, system [INCOSE, 2010]. It may be presented for the concrete system with all its specifics. We may show a dynamic, more aggregated universal classification of tasks of system design. The initial list of design tasks for the *System Design Metagame* is presented in Table 10.2.

Most of these tasks are interrelated and constantly refined during the system design stages by clarifying consecutive versions of the design. This requires the optimization of their sequence to minimize the necessity of redesigning. The most convenient tool for organizing design process as a system is the Design Structure Matrix (DSM) [Eppinger, 2001]. It represents informational connections between the structure of the game and the formation of the groups of designers. The initial list of tasks may be organized according to the architecture of the system (static DSM) or according to the design process (dynamic DSM). An initial aggregation of tasks in a dynamic DSM may be not optimal for the design sequence.

The DSM is a square matrix. The cells of the matrix represent tasks that are labeled in the rows to the left of the matrix and in the columns above the matrix in the same order. The diagonal cells marked by black dots represent

Table 10.2. Classification of tasks for *System Design Metagame*.

Stages of business game design	Stages of system life cycle		
	Design	**Deployment**	**Maintenance**
Concept	Concept of the game		
Preliminary design	Business requirements	System requirements	
Hardware design	Technical specifications	Engineering design	
Software design	Operations engineering	Billing implementation	Network plan
Wetware development		Launch and training	Customer service

internal tasks independent of the other elements. The off-diagonal cells indicate the relationships between different elements. The cells marked (**X**) indicate which task in a row needs information from the task naming that column. The matrix should be rearranged by reducing the number of non-zero cells above the main diagonal marked by gray dots. Those tasks above the diagonal will require a rework after clarifying the results of the preceding tasks. A dynamic DSM matrix with the initial sequence of tasks classified in Table 10.2 is presented in Fig. 10.2.

		A	B	C	D	E	F	G	H	I	J
Concept	A	●									
Business Requirements	B	X	●					●	●	●	
System Requirements	C	X	X	●			●	●			
Network Plan	D	X		X	●	X	●	●			
Technical Specifications	E	X		X	X	●	●		●		
Engineering Design	F				X	X	●				
Billing Implementation	G		X	X	X			●		X	
Operations Engineering	H		X	X	X	X			●	X	
Customer Service	I		X	X				X	X	●	
Launch	J						X	X	X	X	●

Fig. 10.2. Initial structure of a system design matrix for the *System Design Metagame*.

The initial DSM matrix contains many tasks that are in a unanimously irreversible order, for example, "Business Requirements" may be formulated only after the "Concept". Yet some of them are interrelated, for example, "Business Requirements" and "Billing Implementation". It means that the first one will definitely need to be reviewed after the second is finished. It may happen much later when the second task is clarified. Such reversals are unavoidable, but can be minimized by restructuring the initial matrix. Shadowed blocks of tasks along the diagonal represent an aggregation of interconnected tasks to be assigned to one team.

In order to minimize task redesigns and to avoid the problems of coordinating between groups of designers we need to increase the concentration of matrix elements along and below the main diagonal. It can be achieved when the sequence of tasks is rearranged for the triangulation of the initial matrix. For that purpose, the DSM is analyzed with a clustering algorithm. The rows and columns of a DSM matrix should be rearranged simultaneously. A clustering algorithm requires a decision about the number of subsystems we will need to organize. The aim of the algorithm is the concentration of the majority of elements below and closer to the main diagonal of the matrix. It improves the design process sequence. The required algorithm is the method of cluster analysis that seeks to build a hierarchy of clusters. The strategies for hierarchical clustering generally fall into two types:

- **Agglomerative:** This is a "bottom up" approach, each task starts in its own cluster, and pairs of clusters are merged as one moves up the hierarchy.
- **Divisive:** This is a "top down" approach, all tasks start in one cluster and splits are performed recursively as one moves down the hierarchy.

The result of partial agglomerative clustering of the initial matrix is illustrated in Fig. 10.3.

This matrix still contains several elements above the diagonal, but they are now closer to the main diagonal than before. It means that a redesign will concern only neighboring groups of tasks instead of long recursive iterations. The improved tasks aggregation justifies the corresponding rearrangement of teams of players that represent subsystems. Some designers may belong to two or more teams permanently for the coupled tasks or on

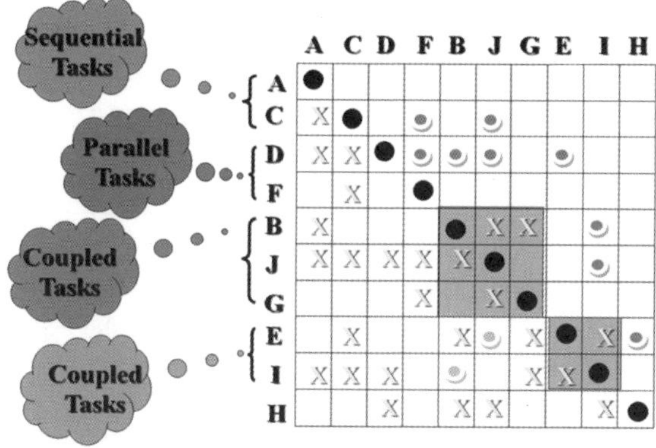

Fig. 10.3. Improved structure of design tasks groups.

the specified time on out-of-order tasks. The roles within a team might also need revision, especially if a designer participates in more than one project teams that develop business games in parallel.

The *NewProDev* and *HELLO* games provide organizational support for integrating neighboring groups of tasks. It is done by including in every team a role of liaison player responsible for the coordination with interconnected tasks. This role must be performed by the person who demonstrated abilities of a gatekeeper or game champion during the Forming stage of team development (Table 7.1). In a game with a small number of players this function can be performed by the leader of the group.

There are different types of customers of business game design. A systems approach is focused on the system as a whole, but treats the separate parts of the system differently before integrating them into the total model. This is reflected in the representation of different participants of design in *Scrum* teams as shown in Table 10.3.

A variety of electronic tools exist to provide feedback, but a simple task board represents simple technology and visual control of lean principles. The value of such a simple method of workflow management is that it is easy to manage and more importantly, it is easy to change. Huddling around a computer monitor, even at a large interactive screen, is not a substitute for the tactile and social interactivity that accompanies manipulating a large task board. A kanban in a business game for systems design, integrated with Scrum, represents agile thinking or Scrum-ban. A scrum-ban hybrid can be

Table 10.3.   Representation of different participants in the business systems design teams.

Type of customer	Scale of development		
	Product, assembly	System	System of Systems
Individual user	Customer, designers	Customer, designers, subcontractors	
Closed market	Stakeholders, designers	Stakeholders, designers, subcontractors	Customers, experts, designers, subcontractors
Open market	Government, designers	Stakeholders, expert, designers	Government, experts, designers

described as a statement in the systems language to describe system design control. This is useful for Scrum teams who are looking to improve their work scheduling. It will also be useful for customers and users of a game as a method of forecasting the progress of design.

10.3. NETWORK-CENTRIC MODEL OF ECONOMIC SYSTEM

An economic system is a special example of a system that is connected by the material more than by technical or organizational links. Such systems develop from linear supply chains into complex networks of interconnected businesses. Every business is a supplier of products and services to external markets as well as a customer inside the system. Such systems are integrated as regional or corporate conglomerates of businesses. Those businesses are connected by cooperation in technology transfer, by mutual internal supply, and by a competition for resources. The internal supplies must be balanced by transfer prices ensuring satisficing criteria for every business. The system behavior is represented by the global optimization on the network of cooperation.

Economic systems represent the integration of two basic network-centric structures, hierarchy and network into a holarchy. The hierarchy connects vertically subordinate or organizationally inclusive elements within a separate business. The network connects interdependent autonomous businesses of the same horizontal level. The holarchy integrates systems of different types of all organizational levels. The structure of a network was presented by the Design Structure Matrix (DSM). The hierarchy was presented in Sec. 1.4 by the $[\alpha - \gamma]$ matrices. Holarchy combines advantages of hierarchy and networks for the system design. Ideal hierarchical system provides effective operations control and technology management. A purely horizontal network ensures faster dissemination of information and a higher viability of the system.

Most businesses are providers of goods and services to the external market and intermediate components to other businesses of the system. In performing both roles they follow the duality principle of local optimization of decisions by every business based on its own criteria. The duality model was introduced in Chapter 2 for an individual business that plays the roles of supplier and consumer at the same time.

Economic system is modeled as the interaction of its elements (businesses) converging to a dynamic equilibrium. The duality model for every business is industry specific. The model may have a linear programming shape or represent nonlinear relationships, be deterministic or stochastic. Linear deterministic models are usually adequate for describing business activities in the narrow range of practically possible solutions.

The optimization problem for business j depends on its position in the current cooperation with other businesses. When j plays the supplier's role, it solves the primal optimization problem; when it plays role of a customer, it solves a dual problem. Negotiations with other businesses are necessary to formulate solutions that satisfy both participants. The mathematical model of an economic network-centered system of business optimization is formulated as the following.

Primal Problem		**Dual Problem**
Maximization of revenue:		Minimization of distribution costs:

$$x_j * p_j + \sum_{\Gamma j} x_{jk} * p_{jk} \quad = \quad b_j * u_j + \sum_{\Gamma j} b_{ij} * u_{ij}$$

| With constrained resources: | | Providing efficiency of production: |

$$(x_j + \sum_{\Gamma j} x_{jk}) * [A_j] \leq b_j + \sum_{\Gamma j} b_{ij}$$

$$A_j * u_j \geq p_j$$
$$A_j * u_j \geq p_{ij}$$

The criteria of local optimization for individual business is the equalizing of total revenue to total costs (including the profit margin). The nodes i, j, k belong to the same graph Γj of the businesses network, where i denotes suppliers to business; j and k denotes i's customers. Vector p_j represents prices and vector b_j defines the quantities of resources consumed by j from the external market; p_{ij} are the prices of supplies offered to business j by the other businesses of the system, denoted by i. Vector p_{jk} are prices that business k is ready to pay for these supplies to businesses j. Vector x_j is the volume of products and services that business j offers to the external market and u_j are the transfer prices (transaction costs) for the external market resources; vectors x_{jk} and u_{ij} are the corresponding decision variables for the internal supplies.

$[A_j]$ is the technological matrix of the business j showing the average usage of external resources b_j and internal cooperation b_{ij} per unit of product or service. The production plan includes the external output x_j and internal supply x_{jk} for other business k.

The optimal plan for business j is in maximizing revenue $x_j * p_j$ by selling quantities x_j at the external market prices p_j; plus maximizing revenues $\sum x_{jk} * p_{jk}$ from its supply to the other businesses k of the system in quantities x_{jk} of intermediate products. This plan for each participant of this system is possible only when demand and supply are balanced. It is achieved when the transfer prices p_{jk} for intermediate products offered to businesses by suppliers will be equal to the dual shadow prices (opportunity costs) u_{jk} of supplies from other businesses as customers of the network. Then a business game is the best mechanism of balancing prices and quantities of supplies inside the open economic system. Similar equalization is desirable for p_j and u_j for an open economic system, but it is less dependent on this economic system governance.

The convergence of economic systems to a dynamic equilibrium is theoretically proven for the closed decentralized economic system [Arrow & Debreu, 1954]. For an open business network this problem cannot be resolved just analytically because of uncertainty in the behavior of individual businesses. In the real life convergence of their decisions to satisfy everyone usually agrees through multilateral negotiations. Its results depend on trust between participants:

> "Nobel Prize Laureate Kenneth Arrow famously remarked that "virtually every commercial transaction has within itself an element of trust". Societies with high levels of trust are fertile ground for developing large corporations and innovative enterprises. Low-trust societies feature people who don't like to do business with folks outside their family or community; smaller, family-run companies are the norm."
>
> [BusinessWeek, June 2010]

Business games are the best tool for establishing the trust between partners in the economic system. This result might be achieved for a closed system by business games like *STRAT-PLAN* [Hinton & Smith, 1985] and the *ReActOr* [Bazilevich, 1979]. The supply chain simulation games *BML* (*Business Management Laboratory*) [Jensen & Cherrington, 1984] and *HELLO* [Bazilevich, 1992] facilitate the establishment of trust between business partners in an open economic systems or System of Systems (SoS). These games are also useful for teaching economics, management and systems engineering. Inclusion of governmental, technological and environmental systems and enterprises as subsystems of business system makes it actually SoS.

The developers of economic systems are focusing on a system that ensures reliable results within the constrained resources. The SoS cannot be designed, it develops itself by the actions of comprising systems. In the best case this development might just be forecasted and regulated by a proper governance. SoS includes participants of different sizes, complexities, dynamics and specializations. A separate system may be designed or redesigned to fit into SoS, but the combined result of the interaction between systems is hardly predictable. These relationships extend the duality model of business with technical, technological, environmental and social problems. The relations between designers and customers also include negotiations for converging local optimal solutions for reaching global satisficing decisions. Besides the prices and quantities of supplies, decisions include scheduling of supply, quality requirements and risk evaluations. Software application modules should ensure that the optimization plug-ins can be used, with the host application and a protocol for the exchange of data.

Plug-ins depend on the services provided by the host application and do not usually work by themselves. Conversely, the host application operates independently of the plug-ins, making it possible for end-users to add and update plug-ins dynamically without needing to make changes to the host application.

10.4.   FROM SYSTEM DESIGN TO SoS SIMULATION

The *Holarchy* platform allows development of business games for the SoS simulation. It integrates the vertical hierarchy of elements in a system with horizontal processes between these systems. David Spandler offers an organizational definition of a holarchy. He writes:

> "In a hierarchy, participants can be compared and evaluated on the basis of position, rank, relative power, seniority and the like. But in a *holarchy* each person's value comes from his or her individuality and uniqueness and the capacity to engage and interact with others to make the fruits of that uniqueness available."
>
> [Spandler, 2008]

The purpose of a *Holarchy* platform for business games is the visualization of SoS development under the conditions of uncertainty. Statistical uncertainty is generated from a distribution of component cards representing resources between players. Strategic uncertainty is generated by the trump cards that represent decisions. This distribution is random for games simulating existing SoS and regulated for SoS development simulation. The medium of a board for card games provides the "playing field" on the table, on a wall, or on the computer screen. It displays organizational structure, roles and their resources, and decision processes. The board is supported by material, energy and information flowcharts, system dynamics diagrams, decision trees. The holarchy is a visual model of several systems of different types at several organizational levels. Holarchy integrates hierarchy within systems with networks of these systems.

A holarchy board for the visualization of SoS development can be used as a structure for detalization of the *System Design Metagame* procedure presented in Fig. 10.1. Then four sectors of process model become pyramids

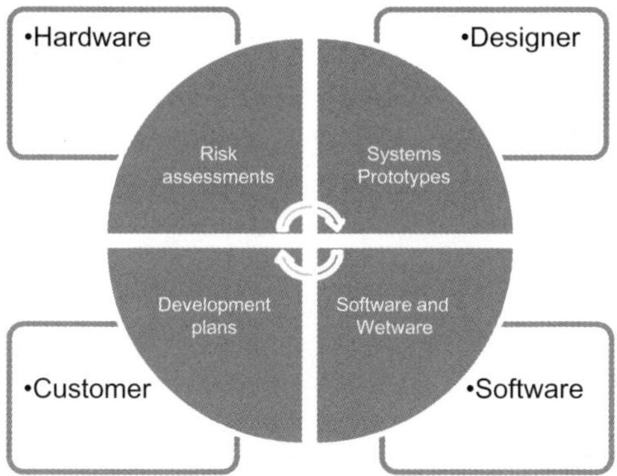

Fig. 10.4. The *SimSoS* platform for business metagame.

representing Customer, Designer, Hardware and Software on the board. The quantity of levels within pyramids depends on the number of required system prototypes. For practical reasons it does not exceed four levels for an average SoS. We named this simulation platform **SimSoS**. It has an aggregated structure presented in Fig. 10.4.

The integration of vertical and horizontal scales of an SoS is designed as a combination of several pyramidal structures into a playing field. These are 2D or 3D multi-sided one-layer or multi-layer boards or screens. Number of basic components (N) on the first level vary from three to eight. Technically, it may be even more, but it makes the structure too large and the game runs too long. The number of levels (L) increases from L = 2 for N = 3 and 4, to L = 3 for N = 5 and 6, then to L = 4 for N = 7 and 8. The pyramids may represent the interdependence of components on the base level, subsystems on the next level, etc. The board organizes the structure of the game by the assignment of roles for individuals or areas of responsibility for teams.

The detailed design of a game board for four 3-level systems as a rectangular 5 × 5 *Holarchy* structure is illustrated by Fig. 10.5.

The movement of cards or tokens on this field symbolizes SoS operations of existing systems by filling it up from components to resolution. For development of an emerging SoS board, it is filled in beginning with resolution cards spirally inside-out. The simultaneous presentation of systems structures and design processes transforms a holarchial model into the structure of a *SimSoS* platform. An integration of technological, environmental,

Trump card	Component card	Component card	Component card	Component card	Trump card
Component card	Trump card	Assembly Card	Assembly Card	Trump card	Component card
Component card	Assembly Card	Resolution card	Resolution card	Assembly card	Component card
Component card	Assembly Card	Resolution card	Resolution card	Assembly card	Component card
Component card	Trump card	Assembly card	Assembly card	Trump card	Component card
Trump card	Component card	Component card	Component card	Component card	Trump card

Fig. 10.5.   6 × 6 *Holarchy* structure of a game board.

economic and social systems on the holarchy platform is also possible, but complicated. This is a 3D structural graph which is defined by a set of multidimensional or space matrices. An economic system as a supply chain network after adding cooperation of businesses in R&D, in environmental and information strategies becomes an SoS. Several different regional transportation systems were introduced in Chapter 1 as a Metropolitan SoS (Fig. 1.6). An integration of local transportation, security and consumption systems becomes a Maritime SoS.

The SoS metagame architecture may be either functional or organizational. In the functional option of the game, teams represent aggregated functions of SoS **governance**. These may be macro functions of infrastructure development, environmental protection, economic growth, social policy. The other option of a macro architecture is isomorphic to the industrial structure of SoS. In this case, duality models are solved analytically for relatively stable industries (construction, energy, heavy machinery). SoS containing dynamic businesses such as transportation and electronics are balancing supply and demand during the game. This architecture was used in the *HELLO* business game representing teams of manufacturers, distributors and customers. The more complicated logistics problems require a different approach based on multifunctional teams.

The second option is an explicit micro architecture representing each business and enterprise by a separate team. Balancing the SoS is provided by direct negotiations between teams playing the roles of cooperating businesses. They are using a duality model for the optimization of their proposals before negotiations. During negotiations, they work out *satisficing* for all partners' volumes and prices of supply and demand.

The Maritime Transportation System of Systems (MTSoS) can be structured as containing five systems: Ports, Ships, Waterways, Intermodal Connects and Users [Gorod *et al.*, 2010]. The board aggregated structure for two levels of SoS is presented in Fig. 10.6.

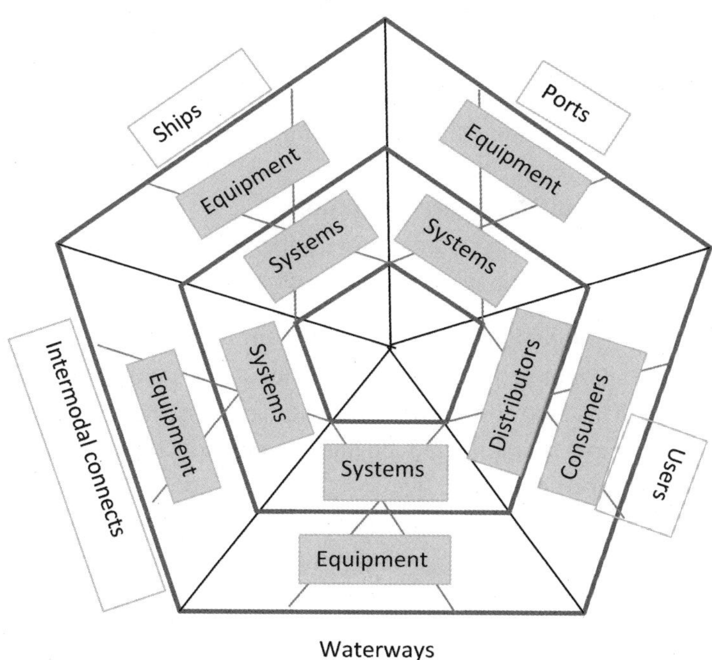

Fig. 10.6.   Structure of Maritime Transportation SoS (MTSoS).

System engineering design and business game simulations are applicable to separate technological, environmental and economic systems. Integrated SoSs require different approaches to be presented to their government. The *SimSoS* game platform is an application of a holarchy platform for the design of new systems and for the testing of new procedures. The *SimSoS* platform integrates systems projects by including the testing of separate systems as a spiral process (Fig. 10.1).

The basic structure of each system is clear from its technology and may be detailed for several levels. The critical part of the MTSoS model is the definition of trump cards representing possible hazards to certain levels of different systems. Trump cards reflect hazards from terrorist attacks to natural hazards such as hurricanes and floods. Entering the port, huge vessels are vulnerable to accidents like collisions and disruption of port operations. Operations disruptions may also be ignited by worker strikes and corporate bankruptcies [Mansouri *et al.*, 2010]. The extent of disruptions may be measured in lost time, material resources or in universal monetary losses. Our proposal for the *Maritime SoS Game* assumes the following structure of game architecture.

- 5 teams representing the systems listed above;
- 4 levels of each system: 8 or more components, 6 assemblies, 4 subsystems;
- 5 game runs simulating yearly operations;
- 2 organizational models to simulate: cooperation and competition;
- 2 modes of information exchanges to test: closed and open.

The global interests of SoS might be simulated either by the team representing regional or industrial authorities or by instructors and jurors of the game. This may be built as an extension of the *Capstone* game. SoS requires more complicated business metagames simulating *governance* in System of Systems. These metagames are more dependent on the arts and behavior wetware than on the game hardware and software design. The system engineering component of the metagame then stays behind the screen. These games are the concern of great responsibility for designers and participants. There are few published examples of these games applied to business. Most of them are applied to military and political areas such as the *CyberShockWave* game. They are usually organized as virtual field games that allows them to simulate a dynamic interaction between different systems. We will illustrate their design by a few civilian applications.

10.5. SYSTEM OF SYSTEMS BUSINESS AND ENTERPRISES GAMES

Examples of System of Systems are logistics networks, transport and energy infrastructures and environmental SoS. They combine production, transportation, communication and security systems in different proportions as was illustrated for transportation SoSs. We illustrated the design of SoS business game *HELLO* on the supply network example [Bazil, 1992]. This game is based on a network-centric model that we used before for transfer prices optimization on the duality system model [Bazilevich, 1969]. Contemporary SoS designers implement elements of a game for the self-managing of multifunctional teams. The main mission of SoS games is simulation of delivery and payment times, resolving disputes between designers and customers, between principal designer and subcontractors. Most SoS projects are dominated by software issues that designers may handle with role-playing approaches. The designers of systems are relying upon games:

> "The danger of signing off requirements at the end of the project is that resources will be focused on the end-game to have requirements clearly verified and not upon opportunities for capability enhancement. Much of the discipline is focused on the end-game not on the progressive building of SoS."
>
> [Ireland *et al.*, 2010]

We concentrate all procedures of the game around the game board as a basic model of an SoS architecture. The SoS development process is represented by the placement of cards in the appropriate areas of the SoS model. It visualizes the current situation and does not allow players to be distracted by the peripheral questions before principal problems are resolved. During a game players place cards into the appropriate cells of a board. Filling the board starts from the conceptual center as shown in Fig. 10.1. After all system concept resolution cards are placed in the center of the board, the subsystem and assembly cards may be placed on the next level. The trump card may be placed at any time during the game opening, destroying appropriate levels of systems. Customer's trump cards have a meaning of acceptance or rejection of a design. Designer's trump cards representing requirement of a system rework at the Scam meeting will be placed in a diagonal cell. When placed, the design of the corresponding level of the pyramid is either allowed to start or stop. These cards may be positive as a permission; negative as a destruction; or reflect some other kind of influence on the elements of the appropriate level. The filling of all cells of the board with cards signals the end of the game.

The meaning of cards for the simulation of an existing SoS can be adjusted for different games. For technological and economic systems, component cards represent material or informational resources of a system (equipment, raw materials, energy, human resources, schedules, etc.). For an ecological systems model, it is the natural biological or agricultural food chain. The basic level of the pyramid will be fertile soil for farming, plankton for fish. Trump cards may be floods and fires, fishing and hunting, pollution and industrialization, etc. In an economic system, the board represents organizational, regional or professional resources. For social systems the basic level consists of living conditions for different demographic groups of population.

Every next, upper level of a pyramid may be formed when all components of a lower level are in place. Trump cards indicated by the arrows are presenting positive or negative interferences in the corresponding level of a pyramid. Horizontal levels of interactive systems should be of the same order of significance. In system design games they are mainly positive, presenting approval of construction for the corresponding level of the system as the conditions for building of the technological and economic system. There trump cards represent decisions of professional or executive boards allowing starting of constructive activities on the corresponding level of a system.

In a simulation game the players may rise on the next level after all requirements of the previous level are satisfied. The trump card for existing systems usually have negative meaning representing some obstructions for the effective functioning of the corresponding level of a system. After a trump card is placed, players must take back cards representing this level and from upper levels depending on this level. The team then should start building destroyed levels again. Trump card acts only once, staying on the board up to the end of the game. For technological and economic systems, a trump card requires returning all components of a level back to the initial state. All assembly cards are also returned to the players and may return back to the board after completion of the components level again.

Games based on the *Holarchy* platform may have different missions and corresponding rules and criteria of an winning. Simulation of an existing system may be organized as competitions of individuals within a team. The game is finished when a resolution card is placed by the winner of the round of the game. The rest of players then count sums of values of the cards left on their hands. The criterion of winning is minimization of resources left on hand in the simulation of personal competition in existing systems. The game of new system design simulates cooperation between teams. It has no individual winner of the whole game. The criterion is minimization of time for completion of the project of system building. The scores for players are defined later by their input to the system development.

There are many possible variations of the rules and scoring related to the contents of the *Holarchy* structure and procedures. In economic applications of this model cards left on hands represent unused resources, in ecological applications unused trump cards represent lack of experience in prevention of disastrous interferences in natural processes. Allocation of cards between players or between teams might be different according to the process of the system design or its purpose. Predetermined distribution is preferable for technological and economic system, and a random allocation for ecological and social systems. Simulation results are especially sensitive to the allocation of trump cards that may ignite drastic consequences.

Game boards may represent a third dimension of a system structure by placing stacks of cards in a cells or by using 3D tokens or Lego bricks in place of flat cards. This 3D model reflects more complicated subsystems like subassemblies in technological games, cooperatives in economic applications and alliances in social systems. The provision of placing cards into proper places can be made by using color-coded cards or jigsaw puzzle pieces as shown in Fig. 10.7.

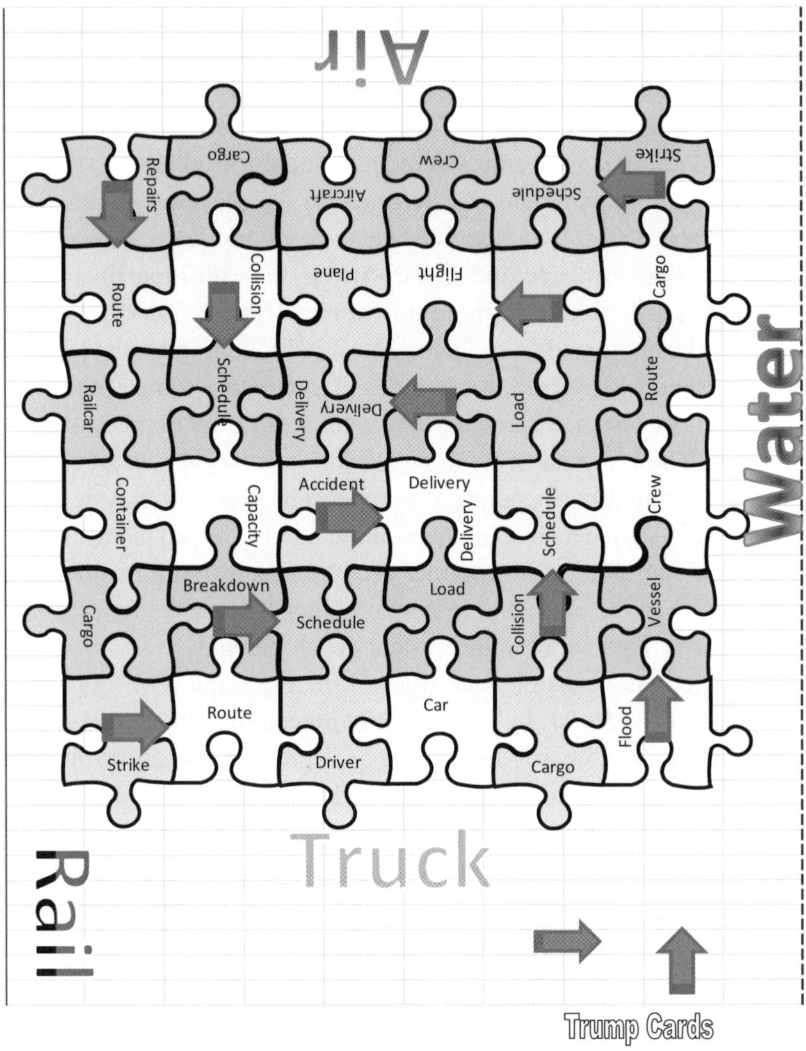

Fig. 10.7.   Jigsaw puzzle organization of *TranSport* game board.

The latest versions of virtual models for business games *TranSport* and *FinanceSoS* represent *Holarchies* of four systems each. In the transportation SoS they are: Rail, Truck, Air and Water (Fig. 10.8).

The game board has color-coded sectors for four types of transportation: Green for Rail, Yellow for Trucks, Light Blue for Air, Dark Blue for

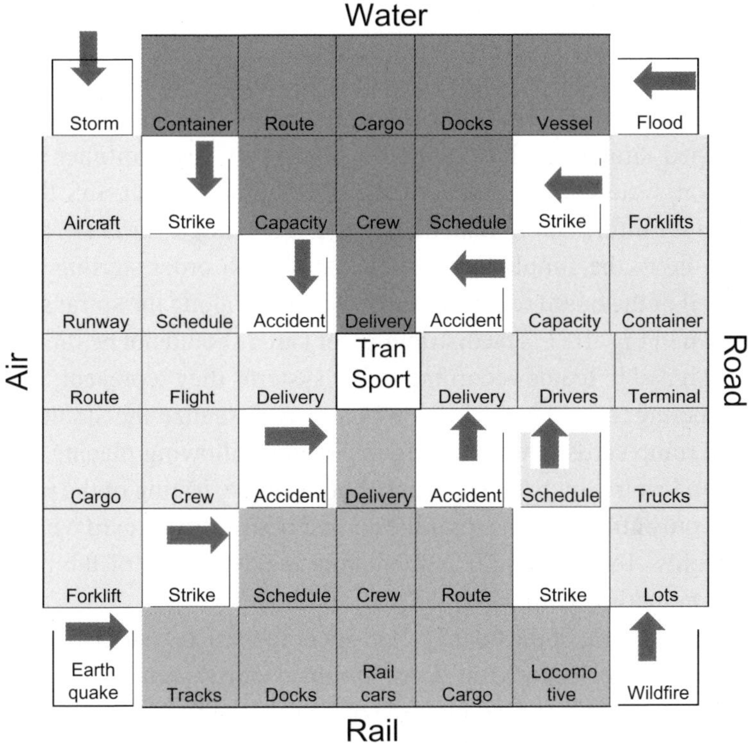

Fig. 10.8. *TranSport* game board as a virtual model of Transportation SoS.

Water. Players should fill in the pyramid with appropriate cards starting from bottom level. Players place one card at their turn or miss a turn if they have no relevant card.

In this version of the game, the printed board contains 48 cells for placing 20 cards of components, 12 of assemblies, 4 resolution cards and 12 trump cards. All cards are dealt between the players randomly and placed on the board in circular order. This 7×7 size of the model is convenient to accommodate four to eight individual players. These players have the same goal to get rid of all cards. When the number of players is six or more, they may form teams responsible for building up certain systems. In the digital version, players move virtual cards on the computer screen which shows the situation to all players. A multiuser option allows synchronized playing when change on the board is shown after all players have made their decisions.

The game should be organized in a multimedia situation room with several displays to accommodate the game model. The situation room may be equipped similar to those used for control of large military or space exploration systems. In a game of the development of an SoS the board has a mainly information-visualizing purpose. Design cards are placed in the opposite to the simulation of the existing SoS order starting from the central cell of the board representing SoS concept along the spiral arrows as was shown in Fig. 10.1. The distribution of cards should not be random, but rather assigned to teams according to the systems they represent. During a scrum meeting, teams nail cards on boards to visualize the status of their system. Trump cards have the positive power of allowing placing cards on the system levels which they approve. For example, testing of the prototype may start only after customer puts the corresponding trump card with system requirements. Technical staff immediately makes copies of the board for every participating team.

The appearance of the board is SoS specific to each system architecture. The filling of the cells goes top-down to subsystems, assemblies, subassemblies and components (or modules of software). The SoS requires a creative approach to business games.

CONCLUSION

We traced business games from the simulation of repetitive operations through a critical analysis of systems growth to a creative synthesis of SoS. Business games are the next logical step in the historical development of tools to system value adding as illustrated in Table C1.

Economic Value Added (EVA) is a result of product quality, Information Value Added (IVA) reflects customer satisfaction, and Joy Value Added (JVA) provides designer's self-actualization. The progress goes from SixSigma in manufacturing to focus groups of customers in services and to business games between designers and customers of systems. A business game is supposed to provide educational, scientific, social and emotional results in different proportions and at different stages of the game. From the satisfaction of getting familiar results we go to the analysis of unexpected

Table C1.   Evolution of tools for the areas of value adding.

Value	Definition	Area of implementation	Tools	Results
EVA	Economic value added	Product manufacturing	SixSigma, TQM	Repetition
IVA	Information value added	Services providing	Focus groups	Analysis
JVA	Joy value added	Systems design and SoS development	Business games	Creation

situations and finally to the joy of new system creation. A system integrates customer expectations with industry resources. The SixC capabilities of business games are the result of the synthesis of wetware on the base of system's hardware and software.

During the game we accumulate information about all events in order to make the evaluation of an individual player's participation, efficiency of teamwork and overall results. The analysis of results is expected to be presented to the class or executive board. The game report may include multimedia presentations by players and by an instructor and in the jury final analytical summary. Some games are keeping protocol, recording video or audio for follow-up or for advertizing purposes.

The evaluation of game players consists of two parts: current activity and conclusive analysis of results. Activity in a game might best of all be evaluated mutually by the players themselves. Conclusive analysis is the instructor's obligation or might be made by the external experts. Many business games include some "jury panel" consisting either of instructors or industry representatives. A jury is responsible for the observation of the game and sometimes for the analysis of results. The more unexpected results a game provides, the better. As one of the leading contemporary software designers expressed: **"You can learn more from failure than success. In failure you're forced to find out what part did not work."** [Brooks, 2010].

Appendix

Fantasy Island

Bertha Suwidji
MGT 503 Fall 2001
Team 2

 RING! RING! RING! My alarm came on to try to wake me up for work. It is another day added to my countdown. I'm counting down until the day I can retire. I have only 6 years, 3 months, and 5 days or 2287 days more to go.

I have been working in this company for 13 years and it has been 13 years of struggle in the corporate ladder. I started out as an Administrative Assistant to one of the middle managers in the IS department of J&J in NJ, a pharmaceutical company. From there I was able to move up to a system specialist in one of my manager's IS groups. I learned so much as an Admin that I was able to perform the functions equal to a support specialist. So after that I started to climb my way up to my current position. I am currently holding the middle manager's position in the same IS group and now I have my own admin. It has taken me thirteen years to get to this position and I worked my butt off to get this far. I never imagined that by starting off as the Admin of the IS manger, I could become that very same IS manger. 

Now I've been stuck in this position for 5 years and I don't think they are going to let me move any higher. I guess they feel threatened about my initial status as an admin. I could never shake that reputation off. Everyone will always see me as the Admin. I know they didn't like it when I was able to move up, but I'm the most qualified for this manager's position. I worked my way up and learned everything the hard way. I didn't have a degree in IS or anything in the computer field but I learned all that I needed to learn to get to this position. So now I'm stuck doing the same job for the last 5 years and I have 6 more years to go before I can retire. I really don't want to retire. I wouldn't know what to do with myself. I would be bored in a week, let alone to do nothing for the rest of my retired years. If my job were more exciting and challenging, I would work until my dying day. But such as life, no company wants an old woman working for them. I know my time is short and I can see how some higher managers have hindered my climb to higher positions, I get the hint. What bothers me the most is that I train younger people to become my future bosses. I see how fast they can climb the corporate ladder. They are still young and can still be molded to whatever the company wants them to be. At my age, the company doesn't want to waste their time and money with little old me. So now I have to wake up and start another dreary day.

As I arrive at work, something was in the air. I saw my staff buzz a lot more than normal. There have been lots of rumors flying around about layoffs due to the recent tragedy across the water in NYC. I don't have time to concern myself with all that gossip; I have work to do. So I walked passed everyone and went straight to my office. My Admin followed me in and said that my boss was here waiting for me in the conference room. I thought that was strange, I didn't receive a meeting notice from him and he's never here this early. I didn't know what to think. So I marched into the conference room to meet with him.

When I came out, my admin was waiting for me and asked what happened. She told me to sit down because my face was all white and I didn't look well. I took a few minutes to recover and I told her to start packing my stuff from my office. Then she looked as bad as I did a few minutes ago. I explained to her that I'm being forced to take early retirement. The company was hurting due to the slow economy and I am being let go early. I also asked her to get the rest of the staff together for a meeting so that my boss can announce this news to them. So she scrambled to do what I requested.

I was still in shock as I walked back to my office. I could feel the eyes of my staff as I walked past them. I couldn't face them yet so I closed my office door to gather myself. I picked up the phone and called my best friend, Amy, to tell her the news. I know she would be happy when she heard the news. Amy was already retired and she always tries

to get me to go with her on her long vacations. So when I called her, she was trilled and started to plan trips that we can go together. I was feeling better after speaking to Amy. But now I have to face the music as I announce my early retirement. When I finally get home, Amy had left me an urgent message on my answering machine. Before I could call her back, she was knocking on my front door. She told me it's time to move on and celebrate retirement. How can I celebrate when I'm not ready to retire? So to cheer me up she told me about a vacation spot on a remote island far, far away called Fantasy Island.

2001 — Retired

I was on my way to Fantasy Island with Amy. I'm on my way to begin my new retired lifestyle. I was ready to try the relaxing life. I don't know how good I will be at relaxing but Amy was here to help me

get there. When we got off the island, the first thing I noticed was the amount of people that occupied this little island. I asked the host if all these people were vacationing too. My host, Jay, explained that a lot of these people worked here on the island and others are vacationers. He also mentioned that a lot of retirees end up working here because they love the Island so much.

I said to myself, that might not be such a bad idea, I'll have to see how my vacation here turns out.

Jay took us on a tour of the Island and showed us the two major businesses that dominated the Island, Tropicana Inc and National Travel Services. He also showed us the palace where King Dave lived. I was surprised to see that the island had a monarchy instead of a government. Jay explained that King Dave's family ruled here for generations but it was only under King Dave that the island was opened up as a vacation spot. No outsiders were allowed on the island without permission from the king. But King Dave saw that a lot of his people wanted to go to the mainland (U.S). So he allowed them to leave the island and by doing so he was losing money and his workers. King Dave decided to open the island up to get more revenue into the island and to get workers to replace those that had left.

After the tour Jay took us to our hotel suite and left us to relax. Of course I tried to relax for a week and that didn't go well. I was anxious to do something else. I just happened to bum in to Jay again and I was telling him how much I wish I could relax but I can't, my mind won't shut down. He told me to meet him and he would take me to a few places.

So the next day, I met up with him and he drove me to Tropicana Inc. He was giving me a tour of the warehouse, the production plant and the manufacturing plant. At the end he took me into an office and asked me if I wanted to work part time. He knew how bored I was so he offered to hire me. He said that I could make my own hours and would get paid $10/hr. I was shocked but thrilled at the same time. This was the solution to my bored. He said I could stay as long as I wanted and quit anytime. I would also be able to move around until I found a job function I enjoyed. I asked him whom I would have to talk to, in order to get the job, he said, "no one, just me". My jaw dropped to the floor. He told me he owned this company so he hired me that day and I start tomorrow.

I went back to my hotel room to tell Amy the great news but she didn't see it the same way as I did. She couldn't believe I got a job again. I was supposed to be retired now she said. So after two more weeks, Amy would go back home without me. I liked this island and I was going to say a little longer. So the next day I started my new part time job.

I enjoyed the freedom to move from function to function. I learned a lot and I got to know Jay very well. We have been dating for 6 months now and wouldn't you know it, a whole year went by already. 2002 was coming around the corner and I was thinking of going back home. I couldn't just stay here forever, so I told Jay that I might want to go home for a while.

The next day, Jay took me into his office and we had a long, long talk about our future, if there was going to be a future. He showed me

2001	Services Winnie Yau		Industry Milan Mitra		Retired Bertha Suwidji		Working Javier Moreno	
	Plan	Actual	Plan	Actual	Plan	Actual	Plan	Actual
Products (Offered)								
Commodities (lbs)	12,000	11,000	48,000	46,000	8,000	9,000	45,000	48,000
Price ($/lb)	1.00	0.91	1.00	0.91	1.00	0.91	1.00	0.91
Luxuries (days)	48	43	12	10	42	46	5	7
Price ($days)	1,000	800	1,000	800	1,000	800	1,000	800
Factors (Requested)								
Labor (hours)	3,000	2,700	3,000	2,740	1,000	1,000	4,000	4,000
Wages ($/hours)	10	10	10	10	10	10	10	10
Capital ($'000)	500	500	500	500	800	800	200	200
Interest Rate (%)	5	5	5	5	5	5	5	5
Taxes (17%)								
Efficiency								
Total Revenue ($)	60,000	44,410	60,000	49,860	50,000	50,000	50,000	50,000
Surplus from last year ($)	0	0	0	0	0	0	0	0
Total Costs ($)	55,000	52,000	55,000	52,400	50,000	44,990	50,000	49,280
	5,000	-7,590	5,000	-2,540	0	5,010	0	720
Gross Profit ($)	5,000	-7,590	5,000	-2,540	0	5,010	0	720

2001 Totals	Businesses Milan and Winnie		Households Bertha and Javier	
	Plan	Actual	Plan	Actual
Products (Offered)				
Commodities (lbs)	60,000	57,000	53,000	57,000
Price ($/lb)	1.00	0.91	1.00	0.91
Luxuries (days)	60	53	47	53
Price ($days)	1,000	800	1,000	800
Factors (Requested)				
Labor (hours)	6,000	5,440	5,000	5,000
Wages ($/hours)	10	10	10	10
Capital ($'000)	1,000	1,000	1,000	1,000
Interest Rate (%)	5	5	5	5
Taxes (17%)				
Efficiency				
Total Revenue ($)	120,000	94,270	100,000	100,000
Surplus from last year ($)	0	0	0	0
Total Costs ($)	110,000	104,400	100,000	94,270
	10,000	-10,130	0	5,730
Gross Profit ($)	10,000	-10,130	0	5,730

the figures for the island for 2001. He went slow and broke down the numbers for the individual households and business and their totals. He used me as the example for the retired household to show how the island made out this year. From these charts, he explained that both businesses didn't make any profit this year. The number of tourist that came to the island had reduced after the incident in NYC. Therefore both businesses were losing a total of $10,130 this year alone. He next started to explain how much the demand for both luxuries (vacation days) and commodities (food) had decrease as compared to 2000, all due to the reduced amount

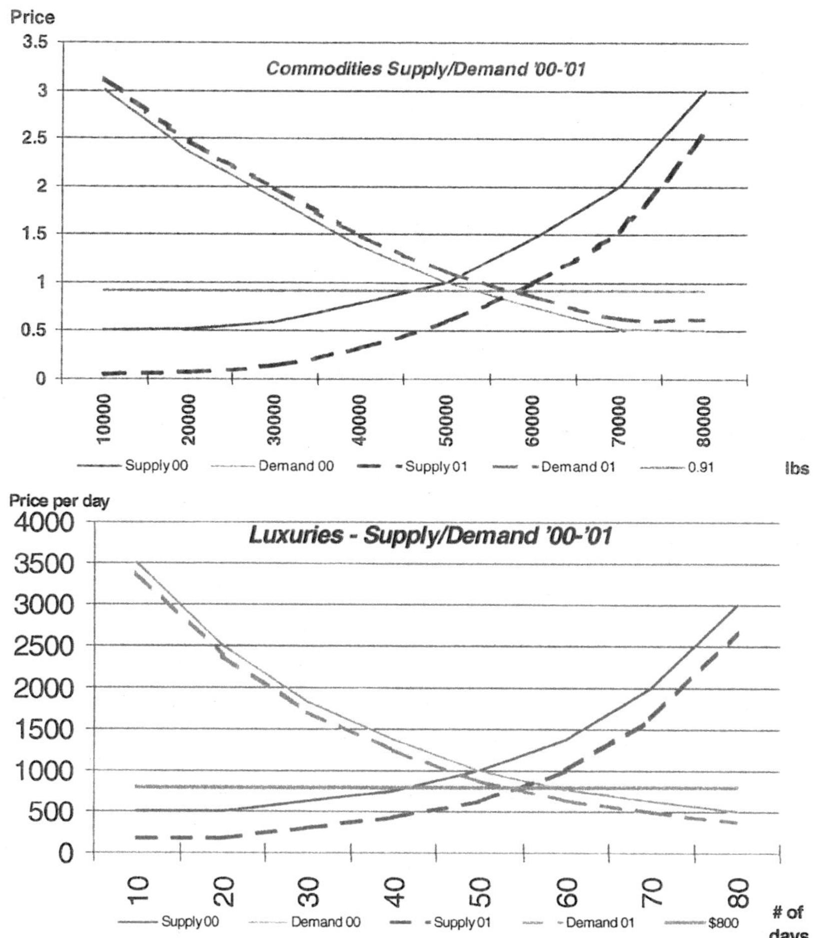

of tourists. As you can see from the supply and demand charts below, the price for both products were reduced as compared to 2000. The equilibrium price had dropped 9% to \$0.91 for commodities and 20% to \$800 for luxuries.

I couldn't believe that the island was going down hill. I was very saddened by this. I decided not to go back home so that I can help and support Jay in any way that I could. Next he showed me the utility curve (next page) for the retired household. He used me as an example and used the amount of money I had made this year. Jay said that with my budget of \$50,000, ideally, I could have 14,000 lbs. of commodities instead of my 9,000 lbs. and taken 48 days of luxuries instead of only 46 days. Even though the budget was the same as year 2000, due to the price dropped of 2001, I was able to buy more than I would have in year 2000. This was

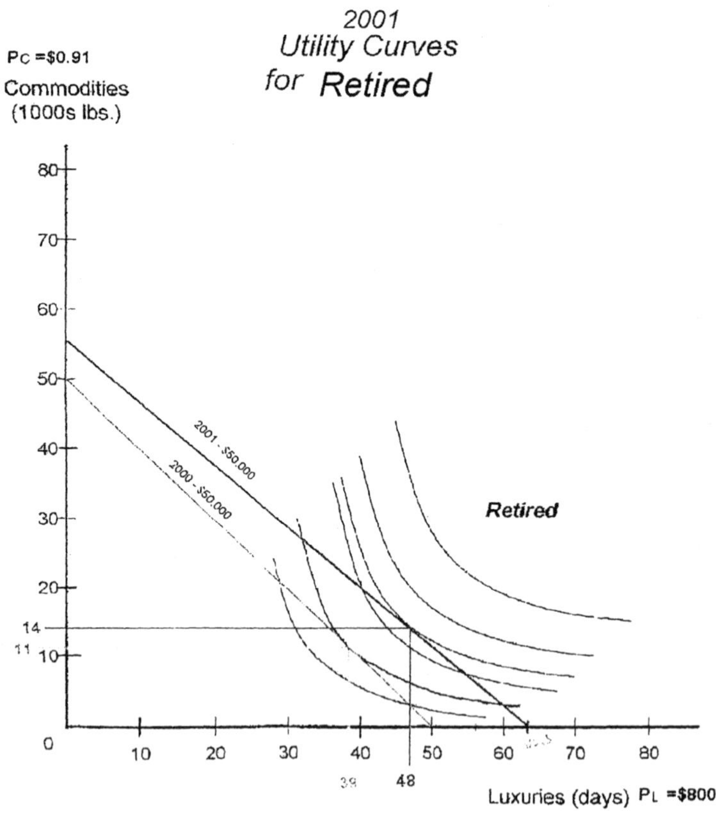

good news for the households on of the island but it was bad for all the business. This meant that the goods produced would have to be sold at a lower price because the supply was much higher than the demand. Jay hopes that next year the island would attract more people and get more revenue.

After Jay was done explaining all of this to me, I didn't understand why he was showing me all of this to begin with. So I got to the point and ask why. He told me that he hoped it would convince me to say here longer and not go home. I already made the decision to stay and help. He then asked how I would feel about running this company. WHAT!!! Was all I could say. Why would you want me to do that. He explained that he just bought off the other major company on this island, National Travel Services (NTS). I couldn't believe what he was telling me. I now understood why he let me hoop all around this company for the last year. He said he was going to manage the other company and he would like me to take over for this company.

2002 — Industry

Well here goes nothing. As Jay gets busy managing and reorganizing NTS, I have to get busy with Tropicana too. I started to look at the numbers that Jay showed from last year. And I wanted see if I could find a way to make more money for Tropicana so that Jay would be proud of me. I saw that productions were overly projected so they had surplus at the end. King Dave saw how terribly the prices went down last year, so he put a price floor to help ensure profits for the businesses. I knew that the price couldn't go any lower than $0.95/lbs, for commodities and $900/day for luxuries. I decided to try to make a profit by producing 42,000 lbs but at an increased price $1.15/lbs. I thought that if I sold more, I would get more money with higher price.

 Business Games

2002	Services — Javier Moreno		Industry — Bertha Suwidji		Retired — Winnie Yau		Working — Milan Mitra	
	Plan	Actual	Plan	Actual	Plan	Actual	Plan	Actual
Products (Offered)								
Commodities (lbs)	13,000	13,000	42,000	40,000	8,500	8,920	42,000	44,080
Price ($/lb)	0.95	0.90	1.15	0.90	0.95	0.90	0.95	0.90
Luxuries (days)	45	43	10	10	44	45	8	8
Price ($days)	1,000	900	900	900	900	900	900	900
Factors (Requested)								
Labor (hours)	2,200	2,254	2,583	2,646	950	940	4,000	3,960
Wages ($/hours)	11	10	11	10	11	10	11	10
Capital ($'000)	500	500	500	500	800	800	200	200
Interest Rate (%)	5	5	5	5	5	5	5	5
Taxes (17%)								
Efficiency								
Total Revenue ($)	57,350	50,400	57,300	45,000	49,975	49,635	52,000	50,590
Surplus from last year ($)	-7,590	-7,590	-2,540	-2,540	5,010	5,010	720	720
Total Costs ($)	48,100	48,104	52,122	52,122	47,675	48,528	47,100	46,872
	9,250	2,297	3,172	-7,122	2,300	1,107	4,900	3,718
Gross Profit ($)	1,660	-5,294	2,638	-9,662	7,310	6,117	5,620	4,438

2002 Totals	Businesses — Bertha and Javier		Households — Milan and Winnie	
	Plan	Actual	Plan	Actual
Products (Offered)				
Commodities (lbs)	55,000	53,000	50,500	53,000
Price ($/lb)	0.95	0.90	0.95	0.90
Luxuries (days)	55	53	52	53
Price ($days)	980	900	900	900
Factors (Requested)				
Labor (hours)	4,783	4,900	4,950	4,900
Wages ($/hours)	11	10	11	10
Capital ($'000)	1,000	1,000	1,000	1,000
Interest Rate (%)	5	5	5	5
Taxes (17%)				
Efficiency				
Total Revenue ($)	106,150	95,400	101,975	100,225
Surplus from last year ($)	-10,130	-10,130	-14,955	-14,955
Total Costs ($)	100,222	100,225	94,775	95,400
	929	-4,825	7,200	4,825
Gross Profit ($)	-4,202	-14,955	-7,755	-10,130

But that plan didn't work too well. Jay and I still produced more than was demanded. Tourism didn't pick up too much this year either. So we both lost more money.

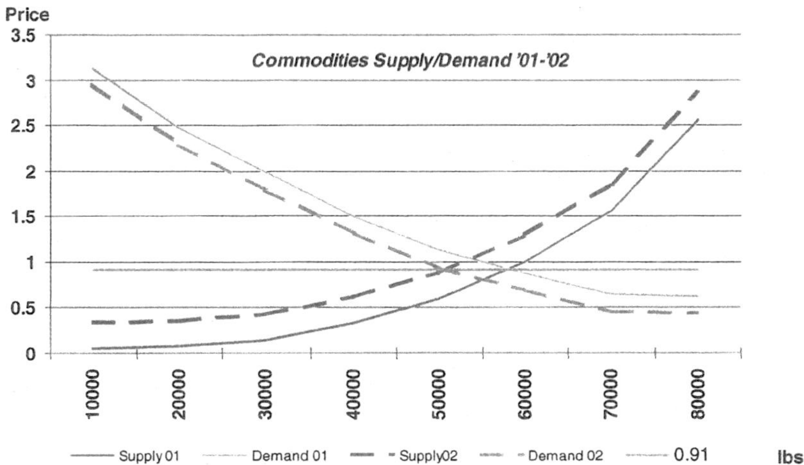

Ultimately I had to face Jay to give him my yearly reports and also to explain to him why I lost more money. So I got all the numbers together and created some charts to show him how I turned out this past year as compared to last year.

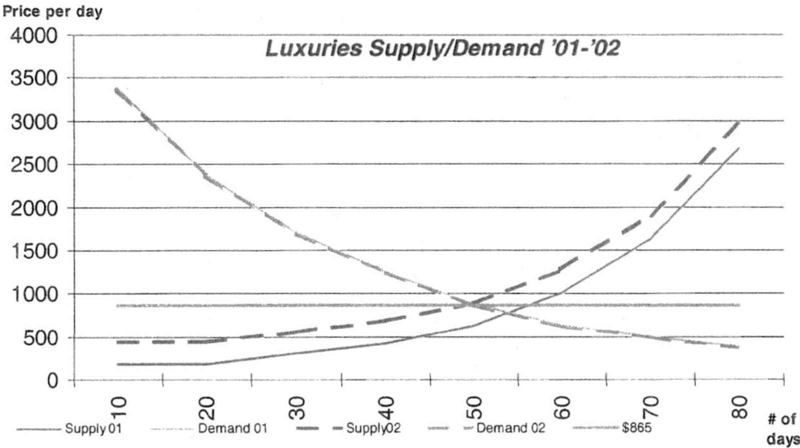

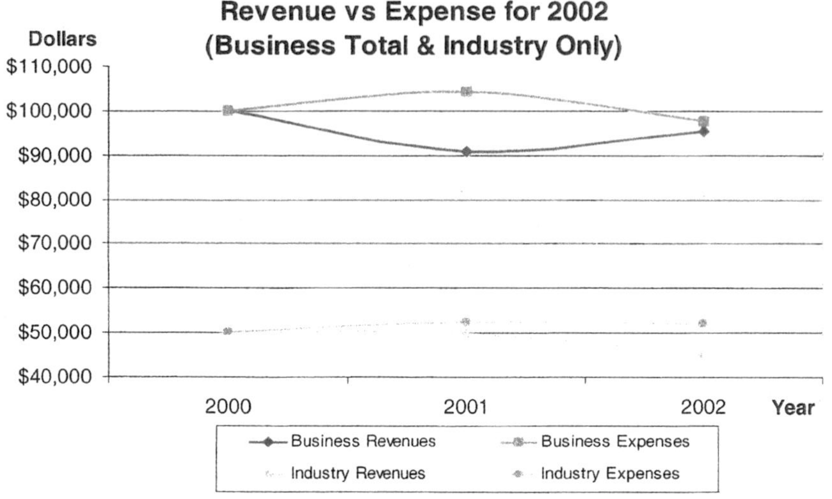

Jay came over to discuss this year's outcome. He wasn't upset too much because he did badly too in NTS. I started to talk about the lack of tourism and lack of demand. Both businesses rely on the tourist/retired and the working households to make profit. People were still not flowing into the island as we had anticipated. So overall, both of our expenses were higher than out revenues for this year.

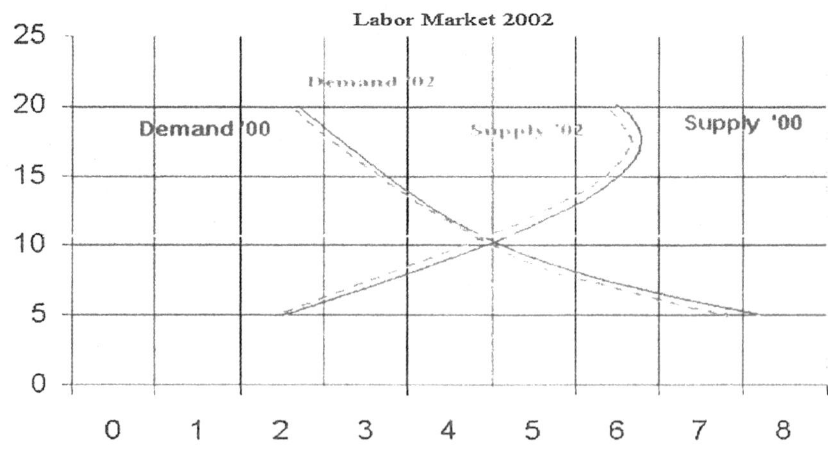

The labor supplied by the households was slightly higher than what we demanded so the price dropped from \$11 to \$10. The households were not too thrilled about that price change.

So overall, in 2002 Tropicana suffered more losses. I showed Jay that in commodities, I broke even but in luxuries, I suffered some losses. Even with the price floor King Dave had set, the price of commodities went back down to \$0.90/lbs and luxuries stayed at \$900/day.

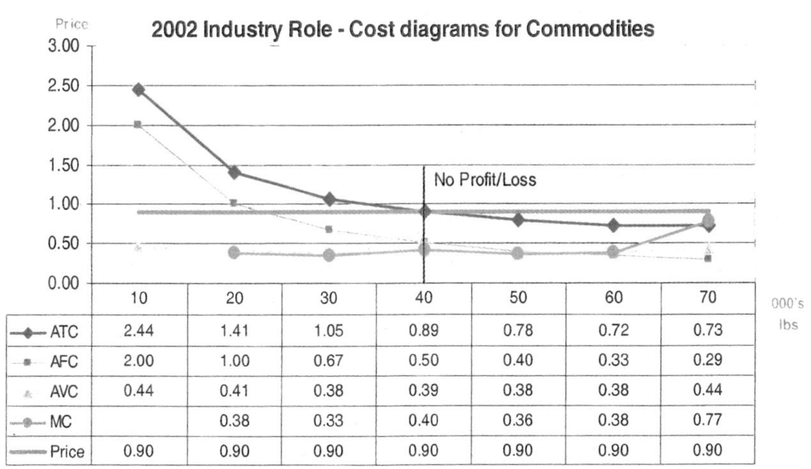

	10	20	30	40	50	60	70
ATC	2.44	1.41	1.05	0.89	0.78	0.72	0.73
AFC	2.00	1.00	0.67	0.50	0.40	0.33	0.29
AVC	0.44	0.41	0.38	0.39	0.38	0.38	0.44
MC		0.38	0.33	0.40	0.36	0.38	0.77
Price	0.90	0.90	0.90	0.90	0.90	0.90	0.90

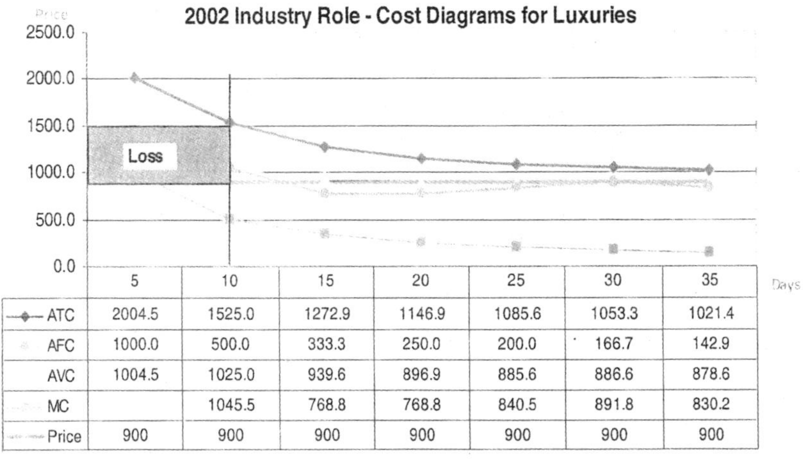

	5	10	15	20	25	30	35
ATC	2004.5	1525.0	1272.9	1146.9	1085.6	1053.3	1021.4
AFC	1000.0	500.0	333.3	250.0	200.0	166.7	142.9
AVC	1004.5	1025.0	939.6	896.9	885.6	886.6	878.6
MC		1045.5	768.8	768.8	840.5	891.8	830.2
Price	900	900	900	900	900	900	900

This year we both didn't do well, so we decided that next year we would discuss a new strategy to make a profit for 2003.

2003 — Industry

Jay and I had discussed about the both of the products we produced. I suggested that we try to concentrate on our primary product. This would cause a monopoly for that product. I figured that if we worked as a team we could end up with a profit. So after that was agreed, I went to work to decide on the amount I would produce if this monopoly strategy worked correctly. So this year, I will only be producing commodities of the island. All food demand will have to come to only me, or so I thought ….

It turns out that Jay did not stick to the plan. He still produced both of his products. I was so upset at him for not telling me that he had changed his mind. Jay just reduced his production of commodities to half of what

2003	Services		Industry		Retired		Working	
	Javier Moreno		Bertha Suwidji		Winnie Yau		Milan Mitra	
	Plan	Actual	Plan	Actual	Plan	Actual	Plan	Actual
Products (Offered)								
Commodities (lbs)	5,000	4,950	50,000	49,550	9,000	9,083	45,000	45,417
Price ($/lb)	0.90	0.90	0.90	0.90	0.90	0.90	0.90	0.90
Luxuries (days)	45	52	0	0	50	44	9	8
Price ($days)	900	1,125	900	1,125	900	1,125	900	1,125
Factors (Requested)								
Labor (hours)	2,000	2,368	1,583	1,874	900	779	4,000	3,463
Wages ($/hours)	10	9	10	9	10	9	10	9
Capital ($'000)	500	500	500	500	800	800	200	200
Interest Rate (%)	5	5	5	5	5	5	5	5
Taxes (17%)								
Efficiency								
Total Revenue ($)	45,000	62,955	45,000	44,595	49,225	46,622	51,000	39,436
Surplus from last year ($)	-5,294	-5,294	-9,662	-9,662	6,117	6,117	4,438	4,438
Total Costs ($)	45,900	45,128	41,226	40,929	33,100	57,675	42,600	49,875
	900	17,827	3,774	3,666	3,835	-11,053	2,400	-10,440
Gross Profit ($)	-5,794	12,534	-5,887	-5,996	2,242	-4,936	6,838	-6,002

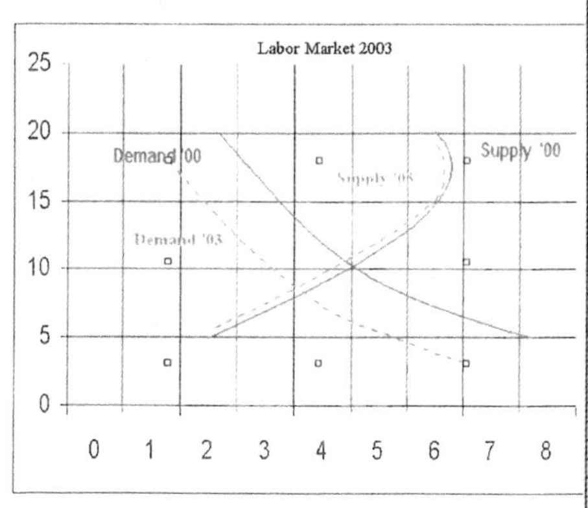

2003 Totals	Businesses		Households	
	Bertha and Javier		Milan and Winnie	
	Plan	Actual	Plan	Actual
Products (Offered)				
Commodities (lbs)	55,000	54,500	54,000	54,500
Price ($/lb)	0.90	0.90	0.90	0.90
Luxuries (days)	45	52	59	52
Price ($days)	900	1,125	900	1,125
Factors (Requested)				
Labor (hours)	3,583	4,242	4,900	4,242
Wages ($/hours)	10	9	10	9
Capital ($'000)	1,000	1,000	1,000	1,000
Interest Rate (%)	5	5	5	5
Taxes (17%)				
Efficiency				
Total Revenue ($)	90,000	107,550	100,225	86,057
Surplus from last year ($)	-14,955	-14,955	10,555	10,555
Total Costs ($)	86,726	86,057	101,700	107,550
	1,274	21,493	-1,475	-21,493
Gross Profit ($)	-11,681	6,538	9,080	-10,938

Price per day

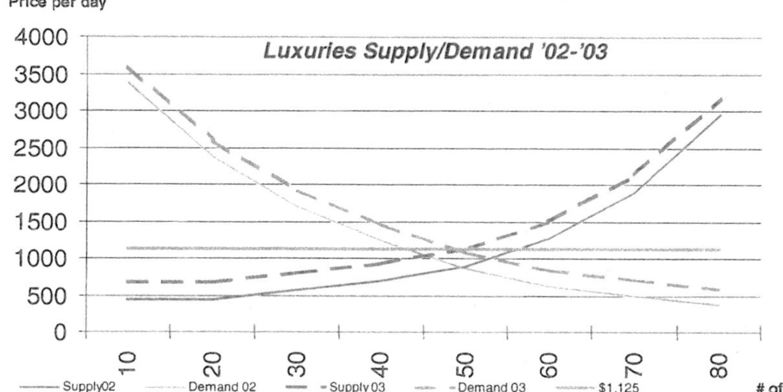

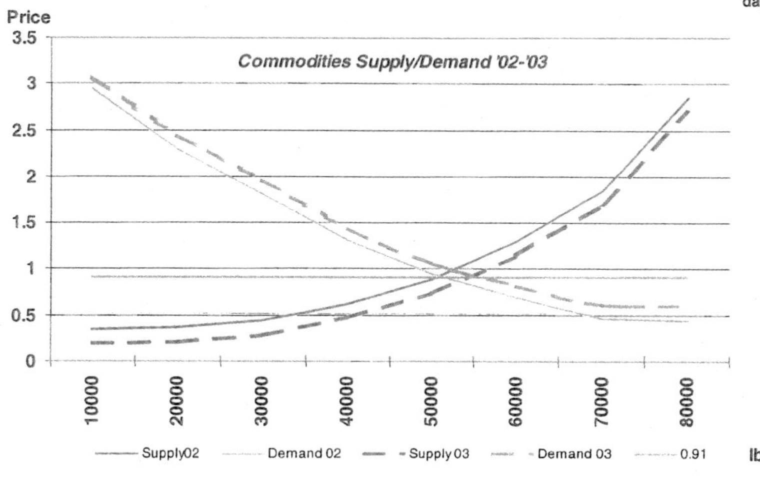

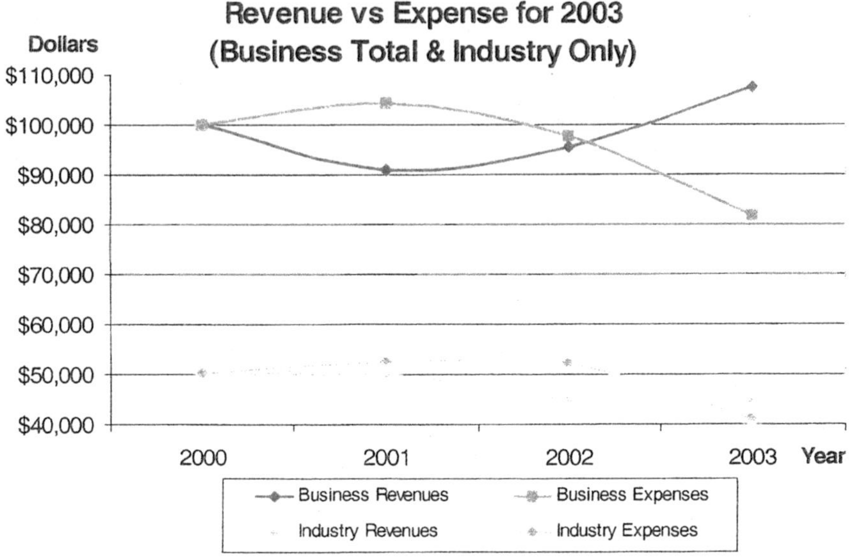

he would have normally produced. So price for commodities stayed at $0.90/lbs and luxuries skyrocketed to $1,125/day.

Plus, on top of that, tourism picked up this year, out of all years. So I did not reap the benefits of the increased tourism revenue. The demand for luxury days was much more than what was produced because I did NOT produce any. The demand for luxuries was so high that the price jumped up too. Jay was making a huge profit from that alone. I could not believe he would leave me out of the loop like that. He was able to make $17,827 in profit while I only made $3,666. I didn't even break even with that amount.

So now it's time to give my yearly report to Jay. I was *steaming mad* all week when I was trying to prepare for this meeting. And I was starting to like Jay a lot, maybe even fall in love with him. Well after this stunt that he pulled, I don't even know if I could look him in the eye. I was planning to walk out right after the meeting. So I came in to my office to wait for him and instead of finding Jay there, I found a bouquet of flowers with a note and directions. It said to meet him at this location for out meeting. He also said he would apologize and make it up to me. So I figured what the heck, it can't get any worse.

So when I arrived at my destination, I walked in to this beautiful garden. I never seen this place, it was like a hidden magic garden in the middle of nowhere. I saw a trail of rose petals so I followed it until I saw Jay. He was waiting for me by the water fountain. Next to him was a romantic table set up for two. I was a little leery about this whole thing, but I guess he must know how upset I was at him. So I shut my mouth and waited to see what he was up to.

Jay sat me down and said that he knows that he should have told about changing his plans but he was pressed for time and didn't get the chance to. He also told me that his business advisors didn't like the idea of not producing both products so he compromised and reduced half the secondary production. He would have told me right away but he had to sign legal documents to not leak this out until the end of the year. Now was the end of the year, so he was finally able to tell me the whole story. I was still upset about the whole thing but we had to get some business done before I can walk out on all of this. So I ate the lunch with him as we discussed this past year's outcome.

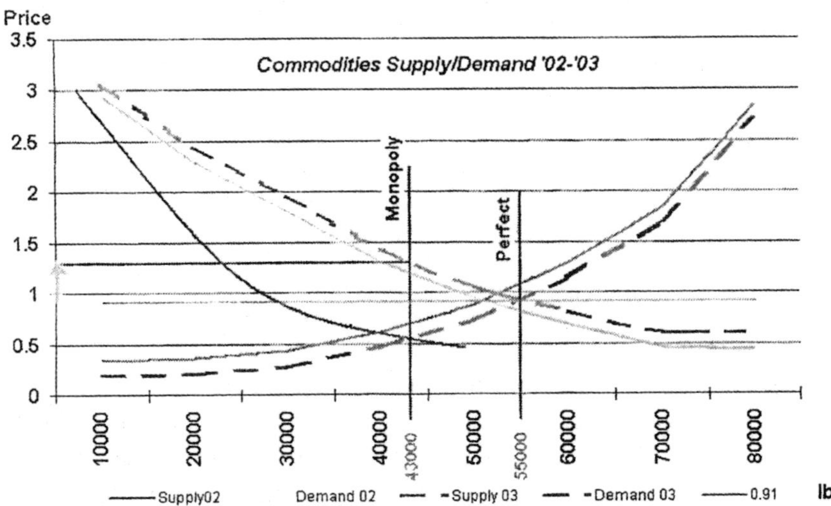

I started talking about the monopoly that was supposed to happen for the both of us; instead it only worked for him. I showed him the price that I would have would have sold my commodities if I was the only one who produced them. The price could have gone as high as $1.30/lbs at monopoly price but it stayed at $0.90.

Then I showed him the cost diagrams with the same monopolistic projections that should have occurred if it worked out correctly. I showed how much profit I did make from last year. I still didn't break even from all my debt and it was not way near the mount of profit he made. Using the same chart, if the monopoly occurred for commodities with the monopolistic price of $1.30, my profits would have been as much as Jay's profits. But as you can see from this chart, my profits were minimal.

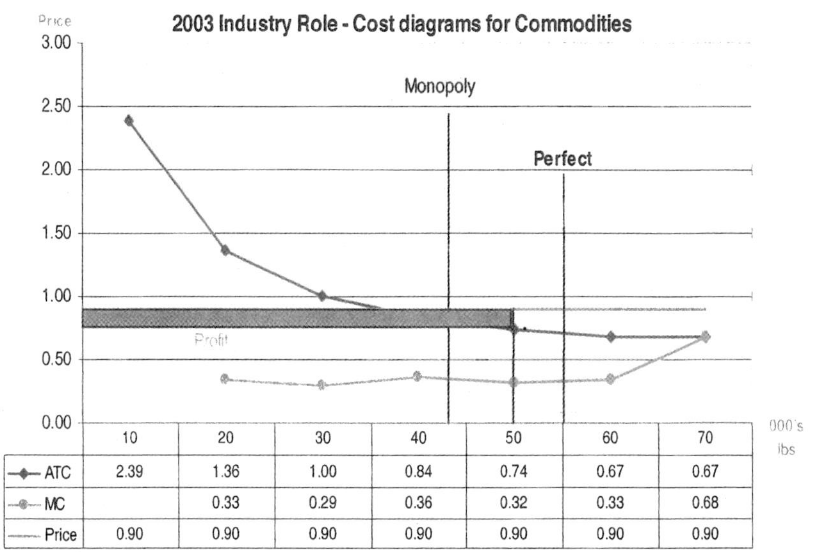

	10	20	30	40	50	60	70
ATC	2.39	1.36	1.00	0.84	0.74	0.67	0.67
MC		0.33	0.29	0.36	0.32	0.33	0.68
Price	0.90	0.90	0.90	0.90	0.90	0.90	0.90

I also showed him how much I could have produced if I used all my $500,000 capital to produce only commodities. According to the production function chart, I could have been producing at 72,000 lbs of commodities if I had $600,000. But my budget would only allow a maximum of 70,000 lbs at $500,000. But what's done is done. So I wrapped up our meeting and was ready to leave for good. But Jay stopped me by saying that he had two proposals and he would only take yes for both. One was that he would

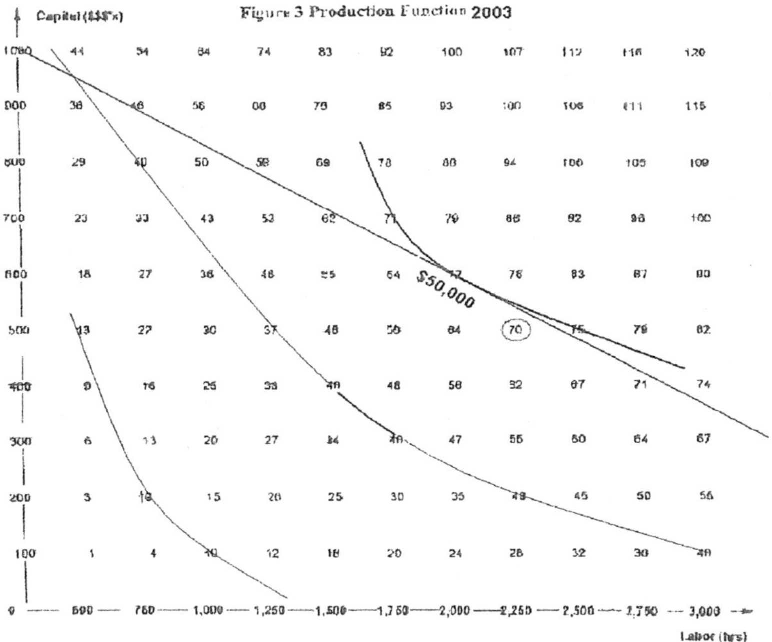

like me to swap management of the companies, and two he asked me to marry him.

2004 — Services

Of course he got a "Yes" for both, how could I resist. So now I have to figure out what to do for this company, NTS. Jay made lots of money last year so I don't have to worry too much about making more profits. Nothing could top of the outcome of last year's profits. So this year I decided to reduce production slightly; I figure the workers could use the break. So I reduced production of both products and thus reduced labor hours.

2004	Services Bertha Suwidji Plan	Actual	Industry Javier Moreno Plan	Actual	Retired Milan Mitra Plan	Actual	Working Winnie Yau Plan	Actual
Products (Offered)								
Commodities (lbs)	3,000	3,349	40,000	44,651	9,000	8,150	44,000	39,850
Price ($/lb)	0.90	1.06	0.90	1.06	0.90	1.06	0.90	1.06
Luxuries (days)	33	35	5	5	35	34	6	6
Price ($days)	1,125	1,225	1,125	1,225	1,125	1,225	1,125	1,225
Factors (Requested)								
Labor (hours)	1,725	1,725	2,000	2,000	1,000	1,000	4,000	4,000
Wages ($/hours)	9	9	9	9	9	9	9	9
Capital ($'000)	500	500	500	500	800	800	200	200
Interest Rate (%)	5	5	5	5	5	5	5	5
Taxes (17%)								
Efficiency								
Total Revenue ($)	39,525	46,425	41,625	53,455	49,000	51,363	46,000	46,417
Surplus from last year ($)	12,534	12,534	-5,996	-5,996	-4,936	-4,936	-6,002	-6,002
Total Costs ($)	40,525	40,525	43,000	43,000	47,475	50,289	46,350	49,591
	700	5,900	1,375	10,455	1,525	1,074	350	-3,174
Gross Profit ($)	11,834	18,433	-7,137	2,682	-3,411	-3,862	-6,352	-9,176

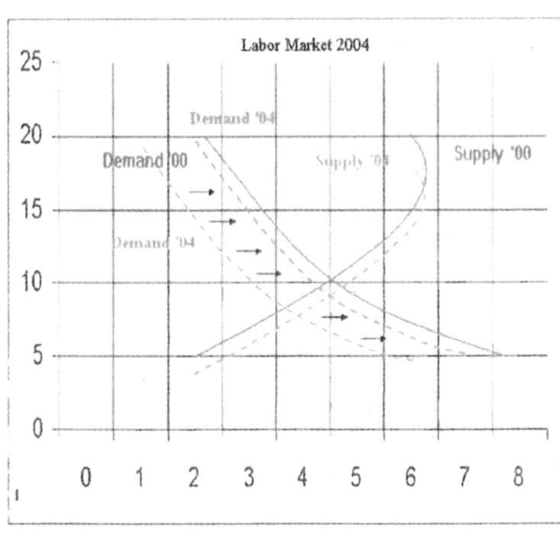

2004 Totals	Businesses Bertha and Javier Plan	Actual	Households Milan and Winnie Plan	Actual
Products (Offered)				
Commodities (lbs)	43,000	48,000	53,000	48,000
Price ($/lb)	1	1	1	1
Luxuries (days)	38	40	41	40
Price ($days)	1,125	1,225	1,125	1,225
Factors (Requested)				
Labor (hours)	3,725	3,725	5,000	5,000
Wages ($/hours)	9	9	9	9
Capital ($'000)	1,000	1,000	1,000	1,000
Interest Rate (%)	5	5	5	5
Taxes (17%)				
Efficiency				
Total Revenue ($)	81,450	99,880	94,647	97,780
Surplus from last year ($)	6,538	6,538	-10,938	-10,938
Total Costs ($)	83,525	83,525	93,625	99,880
	2,075	16,355	822	-2,100
Gross Profit ($)	4,816	20,113	-10,116	-13,038

As the year few by, I was ready to leave the business life completely. It's too stressful for me. I was ready to get married and settle down. I don't think I'll be ready for retirement yet but at least any job after this should be a breeze. So I looked forward to giving my fiancee my last end of the

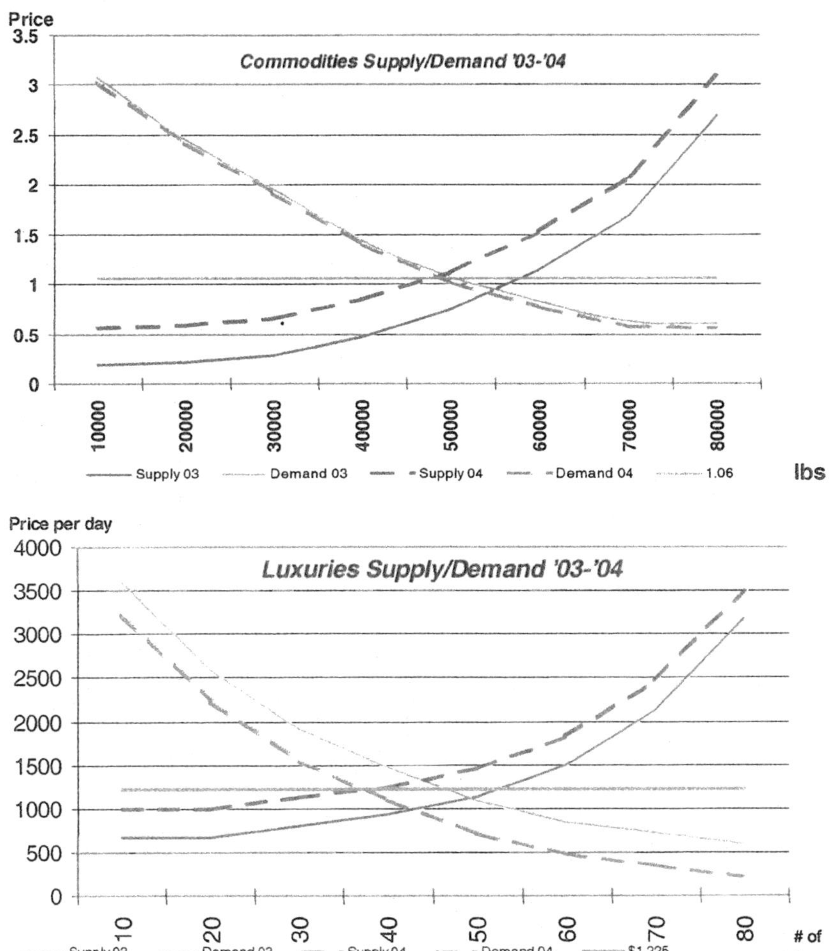

year report. Jay doesn't know it yet, but I'm really going to quit this job. So finally the time drew near and I prepared my charts for our meeting.

So as we discussed this year's numbers, we also talked about the increase of unemployment due to both of us reducing our productions. King Dave was nice enough to help out the households by creating new jobs to help beautify the island. This helped to even out the labor hours that was demanded and supplied.

The demand for commodities was higher than the supply, thus the price of commodities reached $1.06/lbs this year.

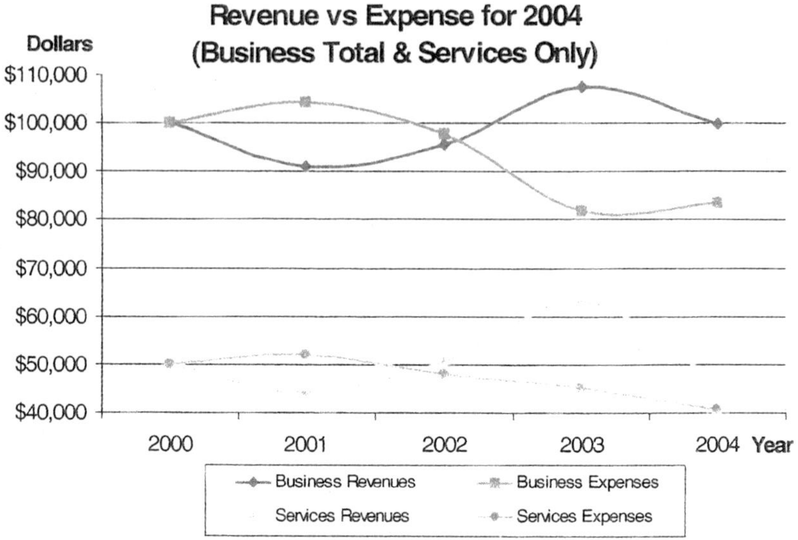

Jay made more profit for Tropicana this year. I don't know how he does it. I too had some profits but of course not as much as Jay. Jay made $10,445 and I made only $3,900. I'm just glad I made some money this year.

I sawed Jay my cost diagrams for the year. I was able to make some money from the 33 days of luxuries I produced but I lost money in luxuries even thought I only produced 4,000 lbs.

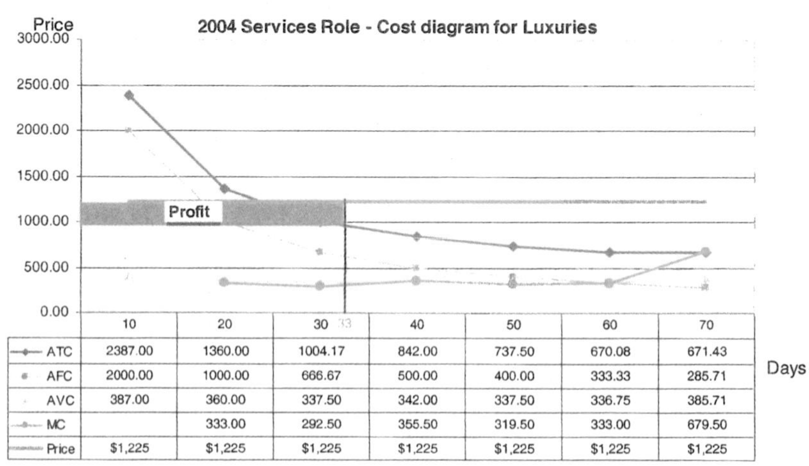

	10	20	30 33	40	50	60	70
ATC	2387.00	1360.00	1004.17	842.00	737.50	670.08	671.43
AFC	2000.00	1000.00	666.67	500.00	400.00	333.33	285.71
AVC	387.00	360.00	337.50	342.00	337.50	336.75	385.71
MC		333.00	292.50	355.50	319.50	333.00	679.50
Price	$1,225	$1,225	$1,225	$1,225	$1,225	$1,225	$1,225

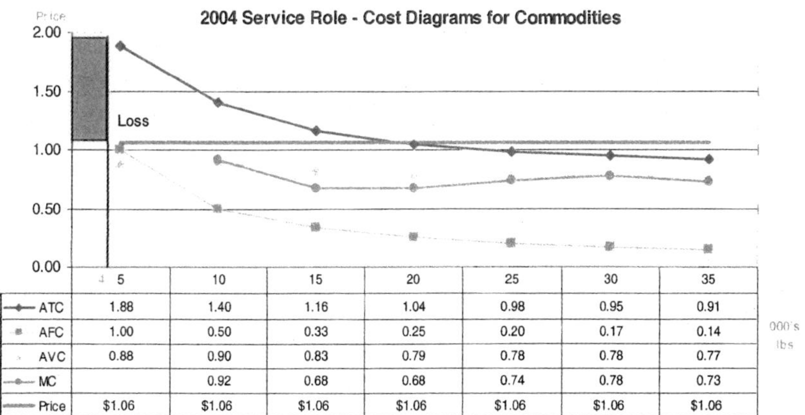

	5	10	15	20	25	30	35
ATC	1.88	1.40	1.16	1.04	0.98	0.95	0.91
AFC	1.00	0.50	0.33	0.25	0.20	0.17	0.14
AVC	0.88	0.90	0.83	0.79	0.78	0.78	0.77
MC		0.92	0.68	0.68	0.74	0.78	0.73
Price	$1.06	$1.06	$1.06	$1.06	$1.06	$1.06	$1.06

I also calculated the marginal rate of product transformation to show if I had only produced at $300,000 instead of $400,000 for luxuries for this year.

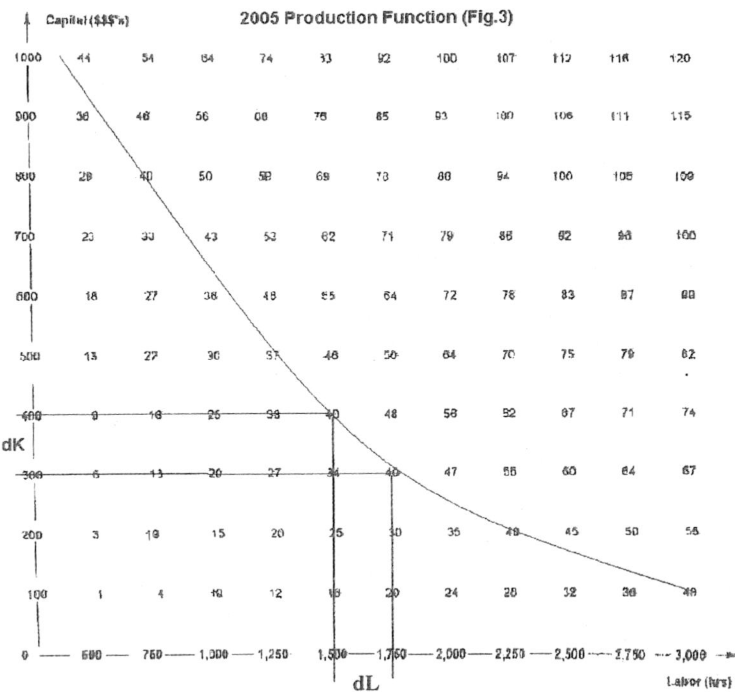

$$\text{Marginal rate of product transformation} = dK/dL$$
$$\text{"dK"} = 400{,}000 - 300{,}000 = 100{,}000$$
$$\text{"dL"} = 1{,}750 - 1{,}500 = 250$$
$$= 400$$

So if the company produced with this scenario, the company would sacrifice $100,000 to gain 250 hrs of labor.

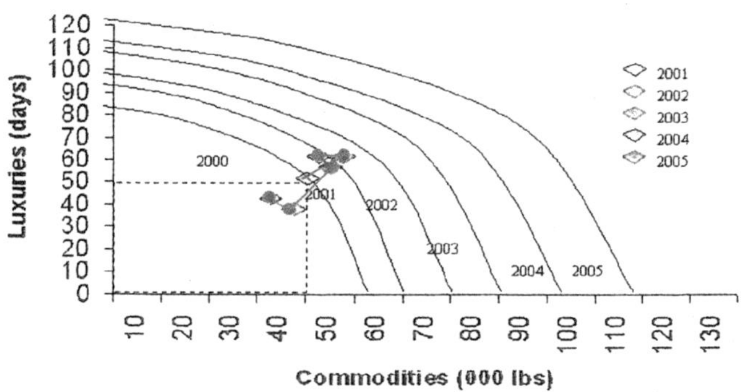

Lastly, I showed him the PPF for both businesses for the last 5 years. He noticed that production was neither steady nor constantly increasing. But he knew it was due to the reduced tourism on the island. So after all of this, I told him I'm ready to quit. Surprisingly he agreed as well.

2005 — Working

Ahhhh… Finally, I have a job that I can relax in. I decided to take a job as tour guide. I still love the island but I just couldn't retire yet, maybe next year. Jay decided to retire this year because he wanted to concentrate on building out life together. So he is now seeking for a piece of land on the island to where we will build out retirement home. We both decided it was time to retire. So while he does that, I too this tour guide job until the house is ready. Once we are ready

2005	Services Milan Mitra		Industry Winnie Yau		Retired Javier Moreno		Working Bertha Suwidji	
	Plan	Actual	Plan	Actual	Plan	Actual	Plan	Actual
Products (Offered)								
Commodities (lbs)	4,000	3,837	45,000	43,163	7,000	7,311	38,000	39,689
Price ($/lb)	1.06	1.02	1.06	1.02	1.06	1.02	1.06	1.02
Luxuries (days)	40	40	5	5	30	30	5	5
Price ($days)	1,175	1,175	1,175	1,175	1,175	1,175	1,175	1,175
Factors (Requested)								
Labor (hours)	1,930	1,930	2,200	2,200	1,000	1,000	4,100	4,100
Wages ($/hours)	9	9	9	9	9	9	9	9
Capital ($'000)	500	500	500	500	800	800	200	200
Interest Rate (%)	5	5	5	5	5	5	5	5
Taxes (17%)								
Working Rebate:								
Efficiency								
Total Revenue ($)	51,240	50,914	53,573	49,901	49,406	49,314	50,553	49,725
Surplus from last year ($)	18,433	18,433	2,682	2,682	-3,862	-3,862	-9,176	-9,176
Total Costs ($)	42,370	42,370	44,800	44,800	42,670	42,707	46,155	46,358
	8,970	8,544	5,101	5,101	6,607	6,607	4,492	3,367
Gross Profit ($)	27,303	26,977	9,439	6,610	2,834	5,788	-4,773	6,668

2005 Totals	Businesses Milan and Winnie		Households Bertha and Javier	
	Plan	Actual	Plan	Actual
Products (Offered)				
Commodities (lbs)	49,000	47,000	45,000	47,000
Price ($/lb)	1.06	1.02	1.06	1.02
Luxuries (days)	45	45	35	35
Price ($days)	1,175	1,175	1,175	1,175
Factors (Requested)				
Labor (hours)	4,130	4,130	5,100	5,100
Wages ($/hours)	9	9	9	9
Capital ($'000)	1,000	1,000	1,000	1,000
Interest Rate (%)	5	5	5	5
Taxes (17%)				
Efficiency				
Total Revenue ($)	104,315	100,215	99,038	99,038
Surplus from last year ($)	20,113	20,113	-13,038	-13,038
Total Costs ($)	87,170	87,170	89,065	89,065
	13,645	13,645	11,133	9,973
Gross Profit ($)	13,699	30,619	-1,904	12,456

with the house, then we will finally get married. So I'm working more to save up for the house and the wedding. Jay was able to save a good nest egg fund from the last few years of his success. So we don't have to worry too much with money.

This year households didn't demand as much for both products but they did want to work more to get more money. The business did not need as much labor so King Dave supplied work around the island again to relieve unemployment. The commodity price did drop slightly due to surplus but luxuries remained the same.

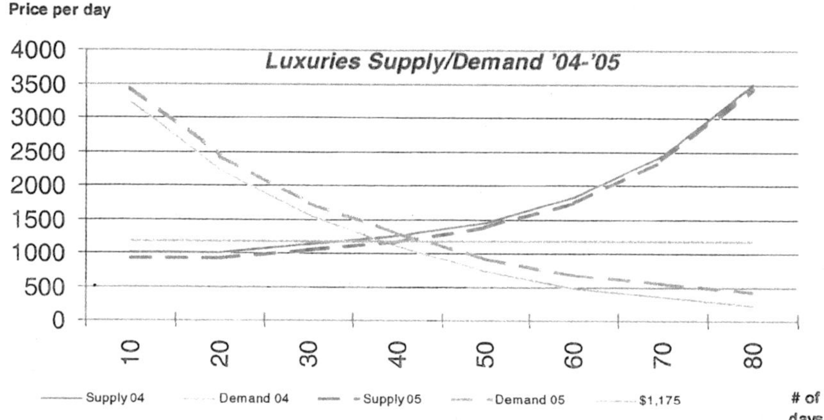

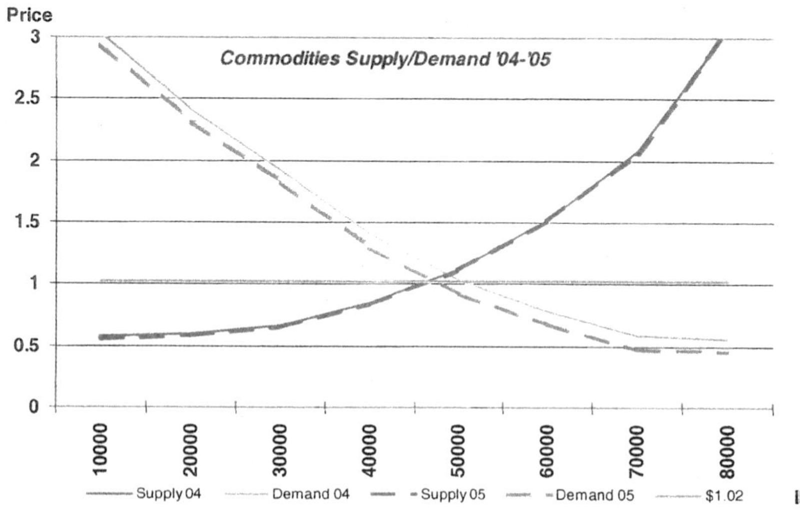

So before I fully retire, I couldn't resist in doing another chart. I had no one to show it to but I was able to calculate the marginal rate of satisfaction for myself.

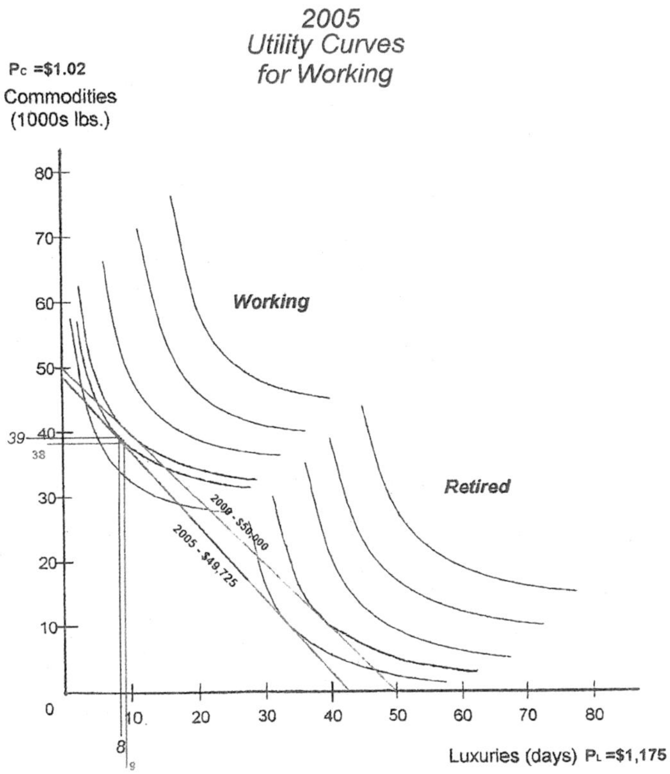

Marginal rate of substitution $=$ dCom/dLux

"dCom" $= 40,000 - 39,000 = 1,000$ lbs

"dLux" $= 9 - 8 = 1$ day

$= 1,000$ lbs/day

So according to the utility curve, I would still have the same level of satisfaction, if I give up 1,000 lbs of commodities and gain 1 day of luxuries.

We got married and lived happily ever after.
The End.

References

Altov, H. (pen name of Altshuller, G.S.), *"And Suddenly the Inventor Appeared. TRIZ, the Theory of Inventive Problem Solving"*, Technical Innovation Center Inc., Worchester MA, 1994.

Altshuller, G., *"Creativity as an Exact Science"*, Gordon & Breach, New York, 1988.

Arnold, R., Valdiviourivich, E., Sarkar, V., *"Glo-Bus Business Strategy Game Demystified"*, 12th January, Lulu Publishing, 2011.

Arrow, K. J. and Debreu, G. "The Existence of an Equilibrium for a Competitive Economy" *Econometrica*, vol. XXII, pp. 265–290, 1954.

Ashby, W., *"An Introduction to Cybernetics"*, Chapman & Hall, 1956.

Bakken, B., Sterman, J., International Oil Tanker Management Flight Simulator. Cambridge, MA 02142, MIT Sloan School of Management, 1993.

Bakken, B., Sterman, J., Commercial Real Estate Management Flight Simulator. Cambridge, MA 02142, MIT Sloan School of Management, 1993.

Ballou, R., *"Business Logistics/Supply Chain Management"*, Pearson Education, 1992.

Bates, B., *"Game Design: The Art and Business of Creating Games"*, Prima Tech Publishing, 2001.

Bazil(evich), L., *"Composition Models of Organizational Systems"*, Ph.D Dissertation, Moscow State University, 1969, (in Russian).

Bazil(evich), L., *"Models of Organization Structures"*, Leningrad University Press, 1979, (in Russian).

Bazil(evich), L., *"Computer-Aided Organizational Design"*, Leningrad University Press, 1984, (in Russian).

Bazil(evich), L., *"HELLO Business Game"*, University of Maryland, CIBER occasional paper # 44, 1992.

Bazil(evich), L., "Transition from Command to a Market Economy: Creation of a Valid Management Information System", *The Journal of Information Systems,* Vol. 6, #1, pp. 14–31, 1993.

Bazil, L., "CyberMarket Business Game", *Annual ASEM Conference Proceedings*, Huntsville, AL, 2003.

Bazil, L., For Whom Bell Curve Tolls?, *Annual ASEM Conference Proceedings, Annual ASEM Conference Proceedings*, Virginia Beach, 2005.

Bazil, L., "Pyramids of Nature Games", 25th *Annual System Dynamics Society Conference Proceedings*, Boston, MA, 2007.

Bazil, L., "Production and Supply Network Optimization", 5th *Annual Conference on Systems Engineering Research*, Stevens Institute of Technology, Hoboken, NJ, 2007.

Bazil, L., "Business Games and System Management Simulations", 8th *Annual Conference on Systems Engineering Research*, Stevens Institute of Technology, Hoboken, NJ, 2010.

Beatles, 1968, from Brown, T., Kutner, J., Warwick, N.; *The Complete Book of The British Charts: Singles and Albums* (3rd ed.). London: Omnibus Press, 2004.

Bednar, Joseph: "Fun and Games", *Business West: The Business Journal of Western Massachusetts*, May 1, 2006.

Bennett, N., Miles, S., *"Your Career Game"*, 2010, Stanford Business Books.

Benoit, W., McDougall, D., "Cellulose Aircraft, Inc.", *Games and Exercises for Operations Management*, Prentice Hall, 1995.

Beer, S., Cybernetics and Management, Science books, 1966.

BigFishGames, *"Top 100 PC Game Downloads"*, Customer Favorite Awards, 2010.

Blanchard, B. S., "Systems Engineering Management", 3rd ed., John Wiley & Sons, 2004.

Bloomberg Businessweek, *EXECUTIVE PROFILE: Mark A. Zurack*, March 2011.

Boardman, J., Sauser, B., "Systems Thinking", *CRP Press* , 2009.

Borschev, A., "XJ Technologies: AnyLogic 6-New IDE & Engine for the Most Powerful Simulator", 2006 *Winter Simulation Conference Abstracts*, Lappentantta, Finland, 2006.

Bowden, M., Moore's Law and the Technology S-Curve, in *Current Issues in Technology Management*, Issue 1, vol. 8, Winter, 2004.

Bray, J., "Microsoft Flight Simulator X — Flights of Fancy", TechnoFile.com, 2006.

Brooks, F., *"Gesign nof Design: Essays from a Computer Scientist"*, New York: Addison-Wesley, 2010.

Buede, D., *"Engineering Design of Systems"*, John Wiley & Sons, 2009.

Department of Defense (DOD), "Defense Acquisition Guidebook", Version 1.5, Washington, DC, 2004.

Burnett, M., *"Dare to Succeed: How to Survive and Thrive in the Game of Life"*, Hyperion, 2004.

Burns, A., Gentry, J., Wolfe, J., "A Cornucopia of Considerations in Evaluating the Effectiveness of Experiential Pedagogies" in Guide to Business Gaming and Experiential Learning", 1990, Nichols/GP Publishing.

Business Week, June 2010.

Caillois, R., *"Les Jeux Et les Hommes (Games and Men)"*, Gallimard, 1938.

Cadotte, E., Bruce, H., *"Management of Strategy in the Marketplace"* Innovative Learning Solutions, Incorporated, 2007.

Capelli, P., Hamori, M., "The New Road to the Top". *Harvard Business Review*, January 2005.

Capstone Business Simulation, Team Member Guide. *Management Simulations Inc.*, 2003.

Chikofski, E., Cross, J., "Reverse Engineering and Design Recovery: A Taxonomy", *IEEE Software*, vol. 7, no. 1, pp. 13–17, Jan. 1990.

Claypool, K., Glaypool M., "Teaching Software Engineering Through Game Design", *Proceedings of the 10th Annual SIGCSE Conference on Innovation and Technology in Computer Science Education*, Monte De Caparica, Portugal, 2005.

Cloud Computing: Clash of the Clouds, *The Economist*, October 2009.

CNN, *"CyberShockWave Simulation"*, February 10, 2010.

Cobb Douglas Production Function Calculator: *Boise State University*, www.boisestate.edu/econ/lreynol/web/Excel/Cobb_Calculator.xls.

Corbett, S., "Learning by Playing: Video Games in the Classroom", *New York Times*, September 15, 2010.

Cotroneo, T., "Algorithms in Behavioral Systems Theory", *University of Groningen*, 1972.

Crawford, C., *Chris Crawford on Game Design*, New Riders, 2003.

Darrow, C., *Monopoly Game*, U.S. Patent 2,026,082, 1935.

DeBono, E., *"The Use of Lateral Thinking"*, Penguin, 1967.

DeBono, E., *"Teaching Thinking"*, Penguin, 1976.

DeBono, E., *"Opportunities: A Handbook of Business Opportunity Search"*, Penguin, 1978.

DeBono, E., *"De Bono's Thinking Course"*, Facts on File, New York, 1982.

Dickinson, J., "A Random Strategy Criterion for Validity of Simulation Game Participation", *Simulation Gaming*, vol. 28, no. 3, pp. 263–275, September 1997.

Department of Defense (DOD), "Defense Acquisition Guidebook", Version 1.5. Washington DC, 2004.

Economist, The, "Game not Over", August 7th, 2010.

Edery, D., Mollick, E., "Changing the Game. How Video Games are Transforming the Future of Business", Pearson Education Inc., 218 p. 2009.

Education Clearinghouse, NEWS, January 2003.

Edwards, G. P., Winter, P. K., & Bailey, J. P. 2002. *Leadership in Management*. Ross-on-Wye: The Leadership Trust Foundation.

Eisner, H., "Essentials of Project and Systems Engineering Management", (2nd ed.), J. Wiley & Sons Inc., New York, 2002.

Elizandro, D., Taha, H., "Simulation of Industrial Systems", *Auerbach Publications*, 2008.

Eppinger, S., Innovation at the Speed of Information, *Harvard Business Review*, pp. 149–158, January 2001.

Evans, R., Camm, J. *"Management Science and Decision Technology"*, South-Western College Publishing, 2003.

Evans, R., *"Introduction to Simulation and Risk Analysis"*, South-Western College Publishing, 2004.

Fisher, D., *"Lessons in Mathematics: A Dynamic Approach with Applications Across the Sciences: Teacher's Guide"*, ISEE Systems, 2010.

Forrester, J., *Industrial Dynamics*, Cambridge, MIT Press, 1961.

Fullerton, T., Swain, C., Hoffman, S., *"Game Design Workshop: Designing, Prototyping and Playtesting Games"* (Gama Network Series, CMP books, Kindle Edition, 2010.

Gagnon, J., "Mary M. Birshtein: Mother of Soviet Simulation Gaming", *Simulation & Games*, 18, 3–12, 1986.

Gagnon, J., Greenblat, C., "Life Designs: Individuals, Marriages, and Families", 1978.

Gardner, R., *"Games for Business and Economics"*, New York, NY: John Wiley & Sons, 2003.

Gentry, J. (ed.), *"Guide to Business Gaming and Experiential Learning"*, Nichols/GP Publishing, 1990.

Gerber, B., "Saturn's Grand Experiment", *Training*, June 1992, vol. 29, #6, p. 27.

Goetemiller, C., *"Method of Playing a Travel Board Game"*, US patent #2,128,608, 1938.

Gorod, A., Mansouri, M., Wakerman, T., Sauser, B., "Maritime Transportation System of Systems Management Framework: A System of Systems Engineering Approach", 8th *Conference on Systems Engineering Research*, Hoboken, NJ, March 2010.

Greenblat, C., "A Building Block Approach to Simulation", *Simulation & Gaming*, vol. 20, 1988.

Greenlaw, P., Frey, M., Vernon, I., "FINANSIM: A Financial Management Simulation", St. Paul, MN: West, 1979.

Guilick, L., Urwick, L., *Papers on the Science of Administration*, New York, 1037.

Hanson, S.&J, *All about Mancala. It's History and How to Play,* Happy Viking Crafts, Mahomet IL, 2003.

Hill, J., 2010, Industry Masters Game on, *"In The Black"*, CPA Australia October, 2008.

Harrigan, K., "Numbers and Positions of Women Elected to Corporate Boards", *Academy Journal*, vol. 24, #3, 1977.

Harrington, A., "Business Acumen Training for Managers, Sales Professionals and Employees", *Zodiak®: The Game of Business Finance and Strategy*, Paradigm, 2002.

Harvard Business Review, "Business Case Development: Harvard Manage Mentor", Online Tools, June 30, 2010 .

Haushalter, D., Klasa, S., Maxwell, W., "The Influence of Product Market Dynamics on the Firm's Cash Holdings and Hedging Behavior", *Journal of Financial Economics*, Penn State, 2007.

Heineke, J., Meile, L., *"Games and Exercises for Operations Management"*, Prentice Hall, 1995.

Hinton, R., Smith, D., *"STRATPLAN: Participant's guide"*, Prentice-Hall (Englewood Cliffs, N.J.), 1985.

Holmes, T., Rahe, R., *"Introduction to Stress Management"*, Mind Tools Ltd, 1967.

Huizinga, J., *HOMO LUDENS: A Study of the Play Element in Culture* (Boston: Beacon Press, 1955).

Holmes, T., Rahe, R., Stress Rating Scale, *Journal of Psychosomatic Research*, 1967, vol. 2, p. 216.

Howard, R., Snyder, M., *"Emerging Non-governmental Organizations and Transitional Economies"*, Ford/Knight Projects, 06-07, 1986.

http://www.iseesystems.com/softwares/Education/StellaSoftware.aspx.

Huizinga, J., *"HOMO LUDENS, A Study of the Play Element in Culture"*, Beacon Press, Boston, 1955.

INCOSE, *Systems Engineering Handbook. Version 3.2*, 2010.

Ireland, V., Croser, P., Croser, S., Moving organizations from a systems engineering approach to a System of Systems approach, 8th *Conference on Systems Engineering Research*, Hoboken, NJ, March 2010.

Ivanenko, L., Simulation Games as Mass Population Experiment, *Cybernetics* vol. 4, 1982 , Kiev (in Russian), 1982.

Jackson, J., "Learning from Experience in Business Decision Games", *California Management Review,* 1 (No. 2), 1959.

Jackson, P., *Getting Design Right: A Systems Approach*, New York: CRC Press, 2009.

Jarvis, G., *Transportation Game*, US Patent # 5,380,011, 1995.

Jensen, J., "Teaching Success Through Play: American Board and Table Games, 1840–1900". *Magazine Antiques*, December 2001.

Jensen, R., Cherrington, D., *"Business Management Laboratory: A Computer Simulation"*, Gloriabooks, 1984.

Jeruchim, M. C., Balaban, P., Shanmugan, K. S., "Simulation of Communication Systems: Modeling, Methodology, and Techniques", 2nd ed., Kluwr Academic/Plenum Publishers, 2000.

Kavtaradze, D., "Green Backpack" Toolkit: Simulation and Games for Education for Sustainable Development", *The Nature of Success: Success for Nature*, 2006.

Keys, B., "Organizations Advancing Business Simulation and Experiential Learning", *Guide to Business Gaming and Experiential Learning"*, Nichols/GP Publishing, 1990.

Karoly, L., Bigelow, J., *The Economics of Investing in Universal Preschool Education in California*, RAND Corporation, 2005.

Kirby, N., *"Introduction to Game AI"*, Delmar Cengage Learning, 2010.

Kiyosaki, R., "Rich Dad, Poor Dad", Warned books, 1990.

Kiyosaki, R., Lechter, S., "Rich Dad's Cashflow Quadrant", Warned books, 2000.

Kiyosaki, R., Cashflow board game, US patent # 5,826,878, 2002.

KNAPP ELECTRIC, INC. *"The Fascinating Game of Finance"*. INDIANAPOLIS, IND. Copyright, 1932.

Koopmans, T., Representations of Preference Orderings with Independent Components of Consumption, and Representations of Preference Orderings Over Time. In C. B. McGuire & Roy Radner (Eds.), *Decision and Organization*: vol. 57_100. Amsterdam: North-Holland.1971.

Kosnik, T., Capitalism game, Enlight-Timeline, 1996.

Kossiakoff, A., Sweet, W. S., "Systems Engineering: Principles and Practice", John Wiley & Sons, 2003.

Lemov, D., *Teach Like a Champion*, Jossey-Bass, 2010.

Levitt, S., Dubner, S., Superfreakonomics, HarperCollins Publishers, 2009.

Li, M., Simchi-Levi, D., The Web Based Beer Game, *MIT Forum for Supply Chain Innovation*, Cambridge, MA, 2002.

Lang, M., Duggan, J., "Tool to Support Collaborative Software Requirements Management", *Requirements Engineering*, vol. 6, pp. 161–172, 2001.

Laguna, M., Markland, J., *"Business Process Modeling, Simulation and Design"*, Pearson Prentice Hall, 2005.

Levitt, S., Dubner, S., *"Freaconomics"*, HarperCollins Publishers, New York, 2007.

Levitt, S., Dubner, S., *"Superfreaconomics"*, HarperCollins Publishers, New York, 2009.

Looney, A., "Regarding Icehouse Patents (and Lawsuits)", http://www.wunderland.com, May 31st , 2002.

Madison, J., "A Brief Treatise Upon Constitutional and Party Questions, and the History of Political Parties, as I Received It Orally from the Late Senator Stephe" (1787), Nabu Press Publication, 2010.

Magie, L., *"The Landlord's Game"*, US Pat. #748,626, 1904.

Maier, M., "Teaching About Stocks for Fun and Propaganda", Dollars & Sense, 2001.

Maier, M., Nelson, J., "Does the national economics assessment test high school students for economic literacy — or economic ideology?", Dollars & Sense, 2010.

Marshall, A., *"Principles of Economics"*, London: Macmillan; reprinted by Prometheus Books. 1920.

Martin, J. N., "Systems Engineering Guidebook: A Process for Developing Systems and Products", *CRC Press*, 1997.

McGonigal, J., *"Reality is Broken"*, Penguin, 2011.

Merillian Games, <www.merillian.com/press.html>, 2008.

Meadows, D., Meadows, D., Randers, J., Behrens III, W., *"The Limits to Grow"*, New York: Universe Books, 1972.

Meadows, D., Toth, F., "Stratagem-1: A Microcomputer-based Management Training Game on the Dynamics of Energy/Environment Interaction." *Simulation and Games*, No. 2,1985.

Michel, B., *Trucking Simulation Game*, US Patent # 4,426,084, 1984.

MicroBusPub.com, "Office Home and Student", 2010.

Miller, J., *"Game Theory at Work, How To Use Game Theory To Outthink and. Outmaneuver Your Competition"*, Mc Graw-Hill, New York, 2003.

Moore, A., *"Invention, Discovery, and Creativity"*, Anchor Books, 1969.

Morabito, J., Sack, I., Bhate, A., *"Organizational Modeling: Innovative Architecture for the 21st Century"*, Prentice Hall, 1999.

Nakamura, S., "Blue LED Inventor Shuji Nakamura on Rewarding Innovators in Japan", *In Shifting Contexts, Japan Society*, New York, October 21, 2004.

Nasar, S., *"A Beautiful Mind"*, Touchstone, 1998.

Nash, J., Equilibrium Points in n-person Games. *Proceedings National Academy of Sciences* 36: 48–49, 1950.

Nature, vol. 466 , pp. 756–60, August, 2010.

Newstorm, J., Scannell, E., *"The Big Book of Team Building Games: Trust-Building Activities, Team Spirit Exercises, and Other Fun Things to Do"*, McGraw-Hill, 1998.

Nilsen wire, "Video Games Score 5% of U.S. Household Entertainment Budget", 2010.

Nobelprize.org, *"Educational Games"*, 2010.

Northwestern, *"NetLogo Models Library"*, 2006.

Novak, L., *"Game Development Essentials"*, (2nd edition), Cengage Learning, 2008.

Orbanes, P., "Everything I Know *About Business I Learned from Monopoly"*, Harward Business Review, March 2002, pp. 51–57.

Osterwalder, A., Pigneur, Y. *"Business Model Generation"*, John Wiley & Sons Inc., Hoboken, NJ, 2010.

Patent US #4,643,430, *"Trucking Business Simulation Game"*, 1985.

Perry, D., DeMaria, R., *"David Perry on Game Design"*, Cengage Learning, 2009.

Pflieger, P., *"American Children's Periodicals, 1841–1860"*, The Child's Friend and Family Magazine, 2008.

Porter, T., Shueller, K., *MarketSim Student Manual*, Thomson Learning, 2005.

Rahmandad, H., Repenning, N., Sterman, J., Effects of Feedback Delay on Learning, *System Dynamics Review*, vol. 25, no. 4, 2009.

Rapisarda, P., Willems, J., Recent Developments in Behavioral System Theory, July 24–28, 2006, MTNS, Kyoto, Japan, 2006.

Reich, Robert., *"The Work of Nations"*, Random House Inc., New York, 1998.

Reiley, C., Sandor., D., Simpkin, P., "Using CORE Model-Based Systems Engineering Software to Support Program Management in the U.S. Department of Energy Office of the Biomass Program", *The 17th International Symposium of the International Council on Systems Engineering (INCOSE 2007)*, San Diego, CA, 2007.

Rescorla, E., *"SSL and TLS: Designing and Building Secure Systems"*, Addison-Wesley, 2001.

Ribault, A., Children Who Represented the Student Body — Those from the Advanced Placement classes, *Topography of Y.N. Erlich*, St. Petersburg, 1912.

Roller Coaster Tycoon Games <http://www.rollercoastertycoon.com/>.

Rowe, G., Wright, G., Expert Opinions in Forecasting. Role of the Delphi Technique. In: Armstrong (ed.), *Principles of Forecasting: A Handbook of Researchers and Practitioners*, Boston: Kluwer Academic Publishers, 2001.

Ruffer, R., Usip, E., *MarketSim, Student Manual*, Thomson-South-Western, 2005.

Russ, L., *The Complete Mancala Games Book: How to Play the World's Oldest Board Games*, Da Capo Press, 1999.

Ryschkewitsch, M., The Art and Science of Systems Engineering, in *Systems Research Forum*, vol. 3, no. 2, World Scientific Publishing, Singapore, 2009.

Sage, A., *"The Systems Thinking Approach"*, Research Bibliography, Haines Center for Strategic Management, Beverly Hills, CA: 1994.

Salen, K., Zimmerman, E., *"Rules of Play. Game Design Fundamentals"*, MIT Press, 688 pp, 225 illus, 2003.

Salen, K., "Teleragging Monster Movies", in *Game on: The History and Culture of Video Games*, London, Ling Publishing Ltd., pp. 98–111, 2004.

Samuelson, R., *Economics*, McGraw-Hill, New York, 1973.

Scannell, E., Newstrom, J., *"Even More Games Trainers Play"*, McGrawHill Education, 2007.

Sandhu, I., "Appropriate Age Range to Identify Gifted Children" *National Child Education Conference and Exhibition*, Pinnacle Media Group, 2006.

Scott, L., *About Jenga*, Greenleaf Book Group Press, 2010.

Schell, J., *"The Art of Game Design. A Book of Lenses"*, Morgan Kaufman, 2008.

Schwaber, K., *"Agile Software Development with Scrum"*: Microsoft Press, 2004.

Scott, L., *"About Jenga: The Remarkable Business of Creating a Game that Became a Household Name"*, Greenleaf Book Group Press, 1995.

Senge, P., Kleiner, A., Roberts, C., Ross, R., Smith, B., *"The Fifth Discipline Fieldbook. Strategies and Tools for Building a Learning Organization"*, Random House, Inc., 1994.

Shannon, C., "Prediction and Entropy of Printed English" in *Bell System Technical Journal*, vol. 30, 1951.

Shenhar, A., Dvir, D., *Reinventing Project Management*, Harvard Business School Press, 2007.

Shorrock, T., "Spies for Hire", Simon & Schuster, 2008.

Schwaber, K., *"Jeff Sutherland's SCRUM log"*, Agile Apache, ASP.NET Blog Books, 2004.

Siegfried, T., "A Beautiful Math", 2006, Joseph Henry Press.

Siegler, R., *How Children Develop, Exploring Child Development Student Media Tool Kit & Scientific American Reader to Accompany How Children Develop*. New York: Worth Publishers, 2006.

Simon, F., "Creating a Learning Lab — and Making it Work" in *The Fifth Discipline Fieldbook. Strategies and Tools for Building a Learning Organization* ", Random House, Inc., p. 557, 1995.

Simon, H., Behavioral Model of Rational Choice. *Quarterly Journal of Economics*, p. 99–118.

Skalak, S., "Implementing Concurrent Engineering in Small Companies", Marcel Dekker, Inc, 2002.

Smith, R., "Game Design Principles and the Way We Work", *Innovation-exchange*, November 14, 2010.

Spandler, D., "Vision of Holarchy", *"Seven Pillars: House of Wisdom"*, New Lebanon, New York, 2008.

Sterman, J., Meadows, D., STRATEGEM-2: A Microcomputer Simulation Game of the Kondratiev Cycle. *Simulation and Games*, 16(2), pp. 174–202, 1985.

Sterman, J., "Teaching Takes Off: Flight Simulator for Management Education", *OR/MS Today*, October 1992, pp. 40–43, 1992.

Sterman, J., *"Modeling for Learning Organizations"*. Edited with John D. W. Morecroft, 1994.

Sterman, J., Paich, M., Simons, K., Beinhocker, E., *"B&B Enterprises Management Flight Simulator"*, available from Sloan School of Management, MIT, 2000.

Sterman, J., *"Business Dynamics: Systems Thinking and Modeling for a Complex World"*, Irwin, McGrawHill, 2000.

Sterman, J., *"Instructor's Manual for Business Dynamics: Systems Thinking and Modeling for a Complex World,"* New York, Irwin/McGraw-Hill, 2001.

Stokes, J., Classic Ars: Understanding Moore's Law, *Ars Technica*, 2003.

Stoll, J., *"The Trucking Game"*, US patent #1329812, 1920.

Swarm, *"Tenth Annual Swarm Agent-Based Simulation Meeting"*, University of Notre Dame, June 23–24, 2006.simulation software, 2006.

Tamblyn, D.,Weiss, S., *"The Big Book of Humorous Training Games"*, McGrawHill, 2000.

Tannenbaum, A., "Modern Operating Systems", 2nd ed., Prentice Hall, 2001.

Taylor, F., *"Scientific Management* (comprising *Shop Management, The Principles of Scientific Management* and *Testimony Before the special House Committee* (New York: 1911), 1947.

Taylor, J., Walford, R., *"Simulation in the Classroom"*, London: Penguin Books, 1975.

Teach, R., "Designing Business Simulations" in Guide to Business Gaming and Experiential Learning", Nichols/GP Publishing, 1990.

Terninko, J., Zusman, A., Zlotin, B., *"Systemic Innovation: An Introduction to TRIZ (Theory of Inventive Problem Solving)*, CRC Press, 1998.

The Guardian, *"'Climategate' was 'a game-changer' in science reporting, say climatologists"*, 4 July 2010.

Thompson, A., *"Glo-Bus Business Game"*, HBS Essays and Term Papers, Coca-Cola 1987.

US Patent #4,426,084, *"Trucking Simulation Game"*, 1984.

USA Today, "Merck CEO sets sight on change", February 27, p. B1, 2006.

Vajda, S., *Theory of Games and Linear Programming*, John Wiley & Sons, New York, 1956.

Vajda, S., *Mathematical Games and How to Play Them*, Dover Publications, Inc., 1992.

VIRTONOMICA , "Economic online game "Virtonomics" was Named Best Play of 2007 (RU)". Internet.ru. http://www.internet.ru/news/2008-01-182232010.

Von Neumann, J., Morgenstern, O., *Theory of Games and Economic Behavior*, Princeton University Press, 1944.

Walker, T., "The Sims Overtakes Myst". *GameSpot*. CNET Networks. http://www.gamespot.com/pc/strategy/simslivinlarge / news_2857556.html. Retrieved 2008-03-17.2002.

Ward, J., Schwarz, L., Shell game, *Games and Exercises for Operations Management*, Prentice Hall, 1995.

West, E., "201 Icebreakers: Group MIxers, Warm-Ups, Energizers, and Playful Activities", McGraw-Hill, 1996.

Whitney, L., "Highway Construction Board Game Apparatus and Method", US patent #5,456,473, October. 10, 1995.

Wilson, J., "What Do The "Sim"ple Folk Do?", *Computer Gaming World*: 16–17, May 1989.

Wired, "Kevin Kelly and Steven Johnson on Where Ideas Come From", October 2010.

Wittgenstein, L., *"Philosophical Investigations*, Blackwell Publishing, 1953.

Wright, W., Podcast interview, *The Times*, November 19, 2007.

Wright, W., *"Will Wright Chat Transcript"*, http://simcity.ea.com/ community/ events/will_wright, 2008.

Wright, W., *"Designing User Interfaces to Simulation Games"*, A summary of Will Wright's talk, Wired, 2010.

www.cyber.org, 2010.

www.XJTechnologies.com, 2006.

Index